Edward Everett Hale

The Christian Examiner, Volume LXXXII.

Edward Everett Hale

The Christian Examiner, Volume LXXXII.

ISBN/EAN: 9783337163631

Printed in Europe, USA, Canada, Australia, Japan

Cover: Foto ©Lupo / pixelio.de

More available books at **www.hansebooks.com**

THE CHRISTIAN EXAMINER.

VOLUME LXXXII.

NEW SERIES, VOLUME III.

January, March, May, 1867.

"Porro si sapientia Deus est, . . . verus philosophus est amator Dei." — St. Augustine.

NEW YORK:
JAMES MILLER, PUBLISHER,
522, Broadway.
1867.

Entered according to Act of Congress, in the year 1867, by

JAMES MILLER,

In the Clerk's Office of the District Court of the United States for the Southern District of New York.

CAMBRIDGE:
PRESS OF JOHN WILSON AND SON.

NOTE.

THE CHRISTIAN EXAMINER, in commencing the second year of its new series, has no change to announce in its policy. Its conductors are entirely satisfied with the wisdom and justice of the principle that has guided them for the last year. Aiming to be a vehicle of the best thought and scholarship of the Unitarian Body, and of all minds in sympathy with the Liberal Christian movement, whether connected with the Unitarian Denomination or not, they recognize the duty of keeping its pages open to serious students and earnest thinkers, who desire to use them for the reverent and thoughtful discussion of questions still in controversy in our own ranks. Pretending no indifference to the two main tendencies of theological thought in our Body, the EXAMINER will strive to exercise strict impartiality in its treatment of those who write for its pages, allowing a fair proportion of space to what are known as the "conservative" and "radical" tendencies in our Denomination. The names of the writers being uniformly given, the EXAMINER holds itself responsible only for the sentiments that appear under the Editor's own hand.

To those who have desired to see the EXAMINER open only to such as agree with the Preamble adopted in the Constitution of the National Conference, we have only to say, respectfully, that an earnest sense of the importance of holding the Unitarian Body together compels us to differ from their wishes. We do not believe that the authority of Christianity will be weakened, or the Unitarian Denomination injured, by free discussion, in the established and honored organ of our body, of those questions which no considerable portion of the Denomination ever meet together without debating. Abundant proof exists, that great good has come from this free discussion; and it is our full faith, that it will result, not only in a better mutual appreciation and in a religious philosophy more large and generous, but in the ultimate triumph of positive, historic Christianity.

HENRY W. BELLOWS, *Editor.*

CONTENTS.

No. CCLIX.

ART.		PAGE
I.	THE DESTINIES OF ECCLESIASTICAL RELIGION. — *Frederic H. Hedge, D.D.*	1
II.	RECENT GERMAN LITERATURE: AUERBACH. — *H. J. Warner*	15
III.	WHAT IS THE VITAL TRUTH UNDERLYING THE TRINITY? — *J. C. Kimball*	36
IV.	ON SOME CONDITIONS OF THE MODERN MINISTRY. — *J. H. Allen*	51
V.	BANCROFT'S HISTORY OF THE UNITED STATES, Vol. IX. — *E. E. Hale*	63
VI.	THE ATLANTIC TELEGRAPH	78
VII.	ALLEGED NARROWNESS OF CHRISTIAN FAITH	92
VIII.	REVIEW OF CURRENT LITERATURE	105

Theology. Schenkel's Character of Jesus Portrayed, 105; Coquerel's First Historical Transformations of Christianity, 107; Coquerel's Forçats pour la Foi, 108; Gastineau's Monsieur et Madame Satan, 109. — *History and Politics.* International Policy, 110; Howells' Venetian Life, 114; Maurice's Workman and the Franchise, 115; Boissier's Cicero and his Friends, 117. — *Antiquities.* Hartung's Die Religion und Mythologie der Griechen, 118; Marquardt's Handbuch der Römischen Alterthümer, 120. — *Art and Travel.* Schack's Poesie und Kunst der Araber in Spanien und Sicilien, 122; Porter's Bashan, 125; Lin-le's Ti-ping Tien-Kwoh, 127; Boner's Transylvania, 128; Smyth's Great Pyramid, 130; Ward's Life of Percival, 131.

NEW PUBLICATIONS RECEIVED 132

No. CCLX.

Art.		Page
I.	CHRISTIANITY AND PSEUDO-CHRISTIANITY. — *E. C. Towne*	133
II.	LESSING. — *F. Tiffany*	151
III.	SCHENKEL'S CHARACTER OF JESUS. — *J. W. Chadwick*	186
IV.	HERBERT SPENCER AND HIS REVIEWERS. — *E. L. Youmans*	200
V.	CRETE AND THE CRETANS. — *H. J. Warner*	224
VI.	REVIEW OF CURRENT LITERATURE	246

Theology and Philosophy. Mansel's Philosophy of the Conditioned, 247; McCosh's Examination of Mill's Philosophy, 249; Miss Carpenter's "Last Days in England of the Rajah Rammohun Roy," 250. — *Miscellaneous.* Woodbury's Ninth Army Corps, 252; Channing's Prize Essays, 254; Napoleon's Julius Cæsar, 254; Staunton's Great Schools of England, 256; Meyer's Vergleichende Grammatik, 260; Magill's French Grammar, 261.

NEW PUBLICATIONS RECEIVED 263

No. CCLXI.

I.	WESTERN CHARACTER AND WESTERN LIFE. — *A. D. Mayo*	266
II.	GEOGRAPHY OF PALESTINE. — *C. H. Brigham*	282
III.	MADAME RÉCAMIER AND HER FRIENDS. — *W. R. Alger*	299
IV.	MAURICE DE GUÉRIN. — *J. H. Senter*	328
V.	SOCIAL EMULATION AS A FEATURE OF AMERICAN LIFE	335
VI.	EARLY TRANSFORMATIONS OF CHRISTIANITY. — *E. E. Du Bois*	342
VII.	THE INCARNATION	355
VIII.	REVIEW OF CURRENT LITERATURE	371

Theology. Castelli on Ecclesiastes, 371; Galletti's Rationalism, 372; Brugsch, *Aus dem Orient*, 373. — *Geography and Travels.* Turks, Greeks, and Slavons, 378; New America, 380. — *Poetry and Art.* The Tent on the Beach, 382; Samson's Art Criticism, 384; Palgrave's Essays on Art, 385. — *Miscellaneous.* Alger's Genius of Solitude, 389; Report on the Cornell University, 391; Hertz's King René's Daughter, 392; Weeks' Poems, 393.

NEW PUBLICATIONS RECEIVED 393

THE
CHRISTIAN EXAMINER

JANUARY, 1867.

CONTENTS.

ART.		PAGE
I.	THE DESTINIES OF ECCLESIASTICAL RELIGION. — *Frederic H. Hedge, D.D.*	1
II.	RECENT GERMAN LITERATURE: AUERBACH. — *H. J. Warner*	15
III.	WHAT IS THE VITAL TRUTH UNDERLYING THE TRINITY? *J. C. Kimball*	30
IV.	ON SOME CONDITIONS OF THE MODERN MINISTRY. — *J. H. Allen*	51
V.	BANCROFT'S HISTORY OF THE UNITED STATES, VOL. IX. — *E. E. Hale*	63
VI.	THE ATLANTIC TELEGRAPH	78
VII.	ALLEGED NARROWNESS OF CHRISTIAN FAITH	92
VIII.	REVIEW OF CURRENT LITERATURE	105

Theology. Schenkel's Character of Jesus Portrayed, 105; Coquerel's First Historical Transformations of Christianity, 107; Coquerel's Forçats pour la Foi, 108; Gastineau's Monsieur et Madame Satan, 109. — *History and Politics.* International Policy, 110; Howells' Venetian Life, 114; Maurice's Workman and the Franchise, 115; Bolster's Cicero and his Friends, 117. — *Antiquities.* Hartung's Die Religion und Mythologie der Griechen, 118; Marquardt's Handbuch der Römischen Alterthümer, 120. — *Art and Travel.* Schack's Poesie und Kunst der Araber in Spanien und Sicilien, 122; Porter's Damascus, 125; Lin le's Ti-ping Tien-Kwoh, 127; Boner's Transylvania, 128; Smyth's Great Pyramid, 130; Ward's Life of Percival, 131.

NEW PUBLICATIONS RECEIVED . . . 133

NEW YORK:
JAMES MILLER, PUBLISHER,
522, BROADWAY.

BOSTON: WALKER, FULLER, & CO.

Cambridge: Printed by John Wilson and Son.

JOSEPH GILLOTT'S STEEL PENS,

OF THE OLD STANDARD QUALITY.

GILLOTT'S PENS.

THE POPULAR 303 EXTRA FINE. Suitable for light, fluent styles of writing.

GILLOTT'S PENS.

DOUBLE (604) ELASTIC. Fine and Extra Fine points, 1-4 gross boxes.

GILLOTT'S PENS.

PUBLIC (404) PEN. Very popular in Schools, and for Commercial use.

GILLOTT'S PENS.

SCHOOL (351) PEN. Fine points, suitable for medium style of writing.

GILLOTT'S PENS.

LADIES (170) PEN. A delicate and beautiful pen.

GILLOTT'S PENS.

BLACK SWAN (808) QUILL PEN. The best for a large, bold style of hand.

GILLOTT'S Pens, in such variety of style as to suit every kind of handwriting.

THE CHRISTIAN EXAMINER.

JANUARY, 1867.

Art. I.— THE DESTINIES OF ECCLESIASTICAL RELIGION.

A CONCIO AD CLERUM.

BY FREDERIC H. HEDGE, D.D.

There has been much lamenting of late about the want of recruits for the gospel ministry. The body of the Clerus is not re-enforced from year to year by men who can fill with acceptance the vacancies caused by retirement and death, or meet the demands of the new congregations which are yearly springing up, and which, however they may differ in other respects, are strikingly unanimous in asking that the preacher sent them be one of commanding ability. One would say that never was harvest so plenteous, and never surely were laborers so few. The youth of the universities are slow to enter a profession which ought to attract the best spirits and the richest talents to its service. The vigor and talent of this generation seek other channels, and leave the pulpit to be served hereafter with inferior ministrations, if served at all.

Various causes have been assigned in explanation of this deficiency, and various methods proposed for replenishing the ranks, which are growing thinner in numbers, and, as some will have it, poorer in quality, from year to year. A portion opine that the difficulty lies in the meagre temporalities with which parishes second the spiritual service: others ascribe it to the ever-increasing opportunity and solicitation of industrial adventure; others still, to the fickleness of popular, parochial favor, on which the ease and stability of clerical fortunes so largely depend. I cannot think that either or all of these causes suffice to account for the evil in question. I impute it to moral and intellectual, rather than prudential, reasons. I impute it to certain prevailing influences, partly scientific and partly social, which have alienated the youthful mind from the old sanctities and ecclesiastical uses with which religion has been associated in time past. The fact is, the spirit of the age, or the speculative mind of the age, as in the decline of republican Rome, has broken with ecclesiasticism. I believe the rupture to be merely temporary. Society requires a Church, requires ecclesiastical organization for the use and maintenance of public worship, and, with varying method and symbol, will have them, until the New Jerusalem, descending from the heavens and organizing itself in human practice, shall realize the word of the seer, "I saw no temple therein." A Church there will be, ecclesiastical organizations there will be: science may modify, but cannot abolish them. The speculative mind of the age must accept them, and adjust itself with them, or else go down before them as one of the false prophets and spirits of antichrist, which from time to time, as we read, "have gone out into the world."

Meanwhile, I respect the scruple which detains a young man from this ministry, who is conscious in himself of no internal vocation for the office. Without that vocation, the minister's function is the hardest and dreariest of all pursuits. Without that vocation, there will either be mechanical routine, oppressing and quenching the life of the spirit; or, with greater intellectual activity, there will be a retarding friction between thought and function, between the private conscience and the old traditional requirements; speculation will put the brake on devotion; there will be an insincerity in the sacraments, fatal to the spiritual health of preacher and hearer; or, if sacraments be abandoned as indigestible formalities, too tough for the feeble stomach of "Naturalism," the mere statedness of worship will become at last an intolerable burden.

To make the ministry profitable, or even tolerable, — I mean the ministry in existing communions, I do not mean those exceptional associations which are formed on the simple basis of prophetism, — there must be a decided preponderance of religious sensibility, and even of ecclesiastical consciousness, over speculative and critical tendencies of mind, a preponderance which shall make the positive truths and traditional requirements of the Church seem more important, in the preacher's estimation, than his private speculations or his critical doubts. There is a place for criticism, for thorough, unsparing criticism, and frank negation of all that criticism finds untenable. I certainly have no quarrel with criticism: I am only speaking of the function of the pulpit in existing ecclesiastical relations. Not critical demolition, but practical edification, it seems to me, is the pulpit's true function. I would not have the preacher ignorant of the negative results of criticism; but they should not stick out in his preaching. He should know how to merge and absorb them in the positive doctrine of his broad and reconciling word. He should not, regardless of time and place, say all he knows, or thinks he knows, much less all that he fancies or suspects.

What! shun to declare the whole counsel of God? Not if you surely know what that counsel is. Who has that certainty? You deny that the whole counsel of God is contained in the Bible. You deny, in the words of another, "that the whole mind of God, as made known to man, has been put in print, and consigned to the bookbinder." Very true! but let this truth be impartially implied. Beware of supposing that the whole mind of God is contained in the text-books of science; that recorded observation embodies all that is, or can be. The dogmatism of theology is bad, but the dogmatism of unbelief is no better.

There is a wisdom, not of concealment (for that implies trickery), but of reticence. So far, I think, the distinction of esoteric and exoteric is perfectly consistent with Christian simplicity and rectitude of purpose. "I have many things to say unto you, but ye cannot bear them now." It takes two to make truth. The object presented is one of the factors; the mind to which it is presented is the other. Truth is a right relation between the two. Change the condition, the point of view of the mind that receives, and you change that relation. The proposition which is true to one mind, with its given conditions, may not be true to another with very different conditions. The truths of science present the same aspect, and therefore are equally true to every mind that is capable of comprehending the literal import of the propositions which contain them. No difference of mental condition can make the statement that an equilateral triangle has equal angles more or less true. But outside of the realm of exact science, and especially in the region of theology, you can hardly lay down a proposition which shall be absolutely true to all minds and times. Hence the separation which philosophy has sought to establish between the field of science proper and the supersensuous world of metaphysic and religion. In that separation consists the essence of what is called the "Positive Philosophy." It has recently been proposed to apply the principle of positivism to theology, and religion has been declared to be in danger of dissolution unless that application is made. The proposition mistakes, I think, the essential nature of the subject. The truths of theology are not topics of scientific knowledge, but of faith. We cannot know them as we know the facts of science, although the *assurance* of them may be as great or greater than that which science gives. In religion

> "We have but faith, we cannot know;
> For knowledge is of things we see."

We may systematize those facts of psychology on which the truths of theology rest, and may formulate inferences from them; but the gulf which divides the facts experienced from the facts inferred, the beliefs from the objects of those beliefs, is one which no science can bridge. Respect " the deep irony of God," which baffles every attempt to fix his idea by scientific demonstration.

But, waiving all this, the proper element of religion, the only element in which religion can thrive and be a power in society, is an element of mystery and faith, the very opposite of positivism. Explode that element, and you have a *caput mortuum*, intelligible enough, but soulless and powerless, a mummy instead of a living organism. For here especially it is true that —

> " Our meddling intellect
> Misshapes the beauteous forms of things
> We murder to dissect."

The world of knowledge and the world of faith are principially distinct. They are not even concentric circles. The world of science is a little epicycle which rides the deferent of an unknown orb.

It is a great mistake to suppose that religion is the offspring of theology. On the contrary, theology is the offspring of religion. Science would never give it: scarcely will science recognize it. Even now, in some of its prominent representatives, science prefers an *atheology* instead. You may substitute science for religion; but you cannot identify them, you cannot square them. It is like squaring the circle, — an insoluble problem. Therefore I say, " The Bible or the Mathematics," — the spirit or the flesh, — as the basis of preaching.

" Theism and atheism," it is said, " are in the scales, and Science holds the balance." The saying reminds me of many things. " To-morrow, gentlemen, I shall make you a God," said Science, speaking through the lips of a German professor. And certainly Fichte was as well qualified for this species of manufacture as any Positive philosopher of our time. Carlyle once told me of a man who came to him with a cherished project. The age had lost its God, he said; thence all the woes of this evil time. Something must be done, and that straightway. He had hit upon a plan for remedying the difficulty, — a cheap magazine, to be called the " Elah." Would

Mr. Carlyle be a contributor, and so aid the good work of restoring God to the people of Great Britain?

Heinrich Heine, whose sarcasms had not always so legitimate an object, has satirized the application of science to theology, alike in its negative and positive results. He likens Kant to Robespierre, and thinks the former the greater terrorist of the two.

"The 'Critique of Pure Reason' was the sword with which Theism was beheaded in Germany." — "You French are tame people compared with us Germans. The most you could do was to behead a king, and he had lost his head already before you cut it off. And, in doing that, you made a drumming and a screaming and a trampling with the feet that shook the whole earth. Really, it is doing Maximilien Robespierre too much honor to compare him with Immanuel Kant." — "Kant far exceeded Robespierre in terrorism; but they had much in common. . . . In both there was a spice of cockneyism. Nature had designed them to weigh coffee and sugar; but Fate willed that they should weigh quite other things, and placed for one a King, for the other a God, in the scales." — "Since Kant's polemic, theism has been extinct in the realm of speculative reason. It will take some centuries to disseminate the doleful tidings; but we philosophers have put on mourning long ago. You think you can go home now. Wait a bit. There is another piece to be performed. After the tragedy comes the farce. Hitherto Kant has shown himself the inexorable philosopher. He has stormed heaven and earth, and made the whole celestial concern walk the plank. The Sovereign of the universe lies weltering in his blood, unproved. There is no infinite mercy, no fatherly goodness, no reward beyond the grave for continence here. The immortality of the soul lies at the last gasp. Everywhere death-rattle and death-moans; and old Lampe [Kant's servant] stands by, a mournful spectator, with tears in his eyes. But now Immanuel Kant has compassion, and shows that he is not only a great philosopher, but a good man. And he says to himself, half good-naturedly, half ironically, 'Old Lampe must have a God, he can't be happy without; and man was made to be happy. So says practical reason. Well, then, let practical reason vouch for the being of God.'"

Alas for mankind if Science holds the balance between theism and atheism! I have a notion that He who "hath comprehended the dust of the earth in a measure, and weighed the mountains in scales," himself holds the balance, where Science, with her shallow theisms and atheisms, the one as shallow as the other, are in one scale, and the everlasting Mystery in the other; and I rather think that wise men at present, after the example of Lessing, will cast their votes into the latter scale.

The first attempt to apply positivism to theology, according to an ancient myth, was made by a youth at Sais, who sought certainty behind a forbidden veil, and found death. The meaning of the myth is fitly expressed in the phrase "dead certainty." A very significant phrase! We say a calculation is reduced to a dead certainty. Observe the fatal propriety of the word "dead" in this connection. Absolute certainty belongs to the past, — *fait accompli*. And the past is dead. Dead certainty, — the death of inquiry, the death of expectation, the death of hope.

Do you want absolute certainty in religion, the understanding's ultimate? You want death. Will you look into the sepulchre for the Lord of life? He is not there, "he is risen." Behold, he re-appears! Will you pin him now with your inquiries? A cloud receives him out of your sight. Will you peer into the blue for the vanishing assurance? "Why stand ye gazing up into heaven?" Go to work; and the Comforter, Truth, will come down out of the heavens, and work by your side.

The scientific mind of the age has fallen out with its ecclesiasticism. Whose is the fault? No blame to either party. It is a mutual misunderstanding, such as will sometimes arise in well-regulated families. For both belong to one family after all, — Christian society. A temporary misunderstanding. Mutual jealousy of each other's rights. Ecclesiasticism, good mother, refuses to perceive that her full-grown daughter, Science, having now arrived to years of discretion, can no longer be kept in leading-strings, and fed on pap, but must be allowed to judge for herself, and to regulate her own diet. And when the fond dame pursues the strapping lass with bib and porringer, "Here, my love, is the sincere milk of the word, better for you than those hard rocks and all your *ologies*," no wonder the daughter becomes impatient, and conceives an unconquerable disgust for the proffered harmless diet. On the other hand, the daughter forgets that the mother is still, by divine right, mistress of the house which she holds by hereditary title, and held before Science was born, and will hold, with whatever modification of structure and name, for indefinite time. Society may outgrow this or that particular form of Church life; but society can never outgrow the idea of the Church, and will not, in our day, outgrow the tutelage of religion.

Mr. Wasson, in his eloquent inaugural discourse, "The Radical Creed," has expressed a contempt for the idea of "ecclesiastical continuity," as having its source in the notion of "an inspired institution, which, by its mechanical working, shall grind out divine truth and law." I can by no means adopt this view of the matter. Ecclesiastical continuity is not the perpetuation of an institution which acts mechanically, nor indeed of any institution at all, or any human device, but the recognition and visible representation of a fact. That fact is the progressive, divine education of human society, considered as one organic and continuous whole. The *ecclesia* is society conscious of its unity and calling in God,—society in its Godward relation; and ecclesiastical continuity is the continuity of human growth and divine education. It is the main current of humanity flowing down from an unknown past, distinguished in different periods by different dispensations, but the same in all; sometimes moving, with fleet foot, beneath the impulse of fresh revelation; sometimes caught in the doldrums of a stagnant sacerdotalism, but never immovably fixed; receiving into itself contributions, affluents, from all religions and civilizations, identical with none, though identified with one or another in each stage of its course, as at present with the Christian,—that being the chief minister of human progress for this millennium. Ecclesiastical continuity is therefore the method of history. Not to recognize it is not to recognize the divine significance of history: it is to want the key to the right understanding of the problem of history. It is to sever, to one's own apprehension, the spinal cord of humanity: it is to make the religious convictions of each period the accidental product instead of the mating of the time. Ecclesiastical continuity means that mankind do not consciously and wilfully foreshape their own future; that history is not the product of human foresight, but divine ordination, education; that we are under tutelage, one schoolmaster after another having charge of the race for a season, and, in fulness of time, delivering up his charge to the next. That schoolmaster for the time being is not an institution, but an idea, or system of ideas, to which the institutions of the time owe their birth. We are under this tutelage of ecclesiastical continuity: we cannot escape it. The individual may think he is rid of it: but his fancied emancipation is only the flight of the aëronaut, who seems to detach himself from the earth when he cuts the rope which held his balloon; but all the while an invisible rope — we call it gravitation — has fast hold of him. The length of his tether is the quantity of gas there is in him. The gas escapes, the tether shortens; the gas all gone, ecclesiastical continuity resumes its sway.

There goes, I fancy, a conceit among that class of secularists whose secularism rationalizes its dissent, that the Church as a power is about to retire from public life, though Christianity as a principle may survive; that Christianity, as an administration of more than a thousand years' standing, must soon deliver up its portfolio, its sacred books, and, if recognized at all, exist as a pensioner of the new regime. It may be so, and it may be that periodical hibernation is mistaken for decrepitude and demise. All along the course of history there have been periods of religious indifference, when forward wits would suppose that the Church of the time was moribund, supernaturalism effete, and philosophy or naturalism about to assume the stewardship of such sanctities as might still command the faith of mankind. In the latter half of the century preceding the Christian era, and the first of the century following, intelligent and cultivated Romans had lost their faith in the popular religion, although the conservative among them refrained from open contempt of the established rites. Yet Cicero, the gravest of conservatives, in his work, *De Divinatione*, argues with Quintus, his brother, against the possibility of any such knowledge of the future as superstition ascribed to the haruspices. He would have the function maintained as a part of the established religion for religion's and the republic's sake; but " between ourselves," he says, " I don't believe in it."—" *Quam ego reipublicæ causa, communisque religionis, colendam censeo, sed, soli sumus; licet verum exquirere sine invidia, mihi præsertim de plerisque dubitanti.*" Yet, though he denied for himself the validity of their vaticinations, he condemned the consuls, P. Claudius and L. Junius, for disregarding them: "*Parendum enim fuit religioni, nec patrius mos tam contumaciter repudiandus.*" Yet this cautious conservative could say, in the Senate, that only in poetry and on the stage did the gods intermeddle in human affairs. Other writers of the time concurred with Cicero in relegating traditional religion to the region of popular superstition, reserving for philosophy the natural interpretation or critical elimination of the ancient beliefs. Livy coolly speaks of Numa's religious institutions as excellent devices for influencing, in those days, the ignorant multitude. Quintus Curtius thought nothing so efficacious for the governance of the rude rabble as superstition. Fill their minds with religious nonsense, he says, and they will mind the priest, if they do not obey their secular leaders: "*Melius vatibus quam ducibus suis paret.*" Varro distinguished three kinds of religion, — the mythological, for poets and the stage; the natural (naturalism), for philosophers and wise men; and the ceremonial, for the people. The learned could not accept the crude religion of the stage and the State: they must have a religion of their own. Whereupon St. Augustine exclaims in the " City of God," " O Marcus Varro! thou most acute of men, and without doubt the most learned, thou art still but a man and no god, and hast not been led by the spirit of God to the seeing and proclaiming of things divine, to the furtherance of truth and of freedom. Thou seest that things divine should be separated from human folly and lies, but thou fearest to offend popular opinion and custom in the matter of public superstitions. Thou desirest to worship the God of Nature, but art forced to worship the God of the State."

Already Lucretius had made atheism popular,— had commended it by the charm of his immortal verse. Enlightened Rome no longer believed in the gods. Even the unlearned, according to the testimony of Juvenal, had outgrown the traditional faith in a future retributory state. Cicero himself says that no old woman could be found so inept as to tremble at what was once universally received. A philosophic observer, from the time of Sulla to the time of Vespasian, would have said that the old religion was utterly effete; that the Flamens must presently doff their fillets, and grave haruspices, for very shame, confess and renounce the solemn joke. But religions die hard: altars that once have burned with the sacrifices of faith do not go out until new altars are ready to receive the flame. Although, fifty years before the Christian era, Epicurus was praised at Rome for delivering mankind from the fear of the gods, and Cicero and Varro and others had promulgated naturalism; though theism and naturalism divided intelligent minds, a half-century before Christ,— four centuries after, the Roman Senate, through the lips of her ablest representative, pleaded for liberty to worship those gods whose empire was now invaded by a far more formidable enemy than theism or atheism, the only foe that could ever dispossess them,— a new revelation, a new ecclesiasticism.

To take an example from Christian ages. The revival of letters in Europe was followed by a similar divorce of the intellectual and spiritual life of the age from the ecclesiastical. A courtier of Leo X., or a reader of the *Epistolæ Obscurorum Virorum*, might have fancied, not merely that the Church as a polity was tumbling, but that Christianity as a form of faith had sunk into hopeless decline. And again, toward the close of the eighteenth century in France, the encyclopædists and the men of letters deemed Christianity outgrown, and made enlightenment synonymous with unbelief. Voltaire was tired of the name of Christ; but Voltaire patronized theism, commending the Almighty in sounding verse. Robespierre undertook, with a *coup de théâtre*, to place it on the throne of a desecrated, disevangelized world. You know the result,—with what refluent zeal, with what fierce regurgitation, the repulsed and insulted faiths came trooping in the wake of the allied armies; with what re-assured consciousness they presided at the treaty of Vienna; and how in France of the Restoration ecclesiastical continuity resumed its sway.

Some thirty years ago, a club was formed of young men, mostly preachers of the Unitarian connection, with a sprinkling of elect ladies,—all fired with the hope of a new era in philosophy and religion, which seemed to them about to dawn upon the world. There was something in the air,—a boding of some great revolution,—some new avatar of the Spirit, at whose birth these expectants were called to assist.

> "Of old things, all are over old;
> Of good things, none are good enough:
> We'll show that we can help to frame
> A world of other stuff."

For myself, though I hugely enjoyed the sessions, and shared many of the ideas which ruled the conclave, and the ferment they engendered, I had no belief in ecclesiastical revolutions to be accomplished with set purpose; and I seemed to discern a power and meaning in the old, which the more impassioned would not allow. I had even then made up my mind, that the method of revolution in theology is not discession, but development. My historical conscience, then as since, balanced my neology, and kept me ecclesiastically conservative, though intellectually radical. There haunted me that verse in Goethe's bright song, "The General Confession," as applicable to ecclesiastical incendiarism as it is to political:—

> "Came a man would fain renew me,
> Made a botch and missed his shot,
> Shoulder shrugging, prospects gloomy:
> He was called a patriot.

> And I cursed the senseless drizzle,
> Kept my proper goal in view;
> Blockhead! when it burns, let sizzle;
> When all's burned, then build anew."

Others judged differently: they saw in every case of dissent, and in every new dissentient, the harbinger of the New Jerusalem. "The present Church rattles ominously," they said: "it must vanish presently, and we shall have a real one." There have been some vanishings since then. Ah me! how much has vanished! Of that goodly company what heroes and heroines have vanished from the earth! Thrones have toppled, dynasties have crumbled, institutions that seemed fast rooted in the everlasting hills have withered away. But the Church that was present then, and was judged moribund by transcendental zeal, and rattled so ominously in transcendental ears, is present still.

It was finally resolved to start a journal that should represent the ideas which had mainly influenced the association already tending to dissolution. How to procure the requisite funds was a question of some difficulty, seeing how hardly philosophic and commercial speculation conspire. An appeal was made. Would Mammon have the goodness to aid an enterprise whose spirit rebuked his methods and imperilled his assets? The prudent God disclaimed the imputed verdure; and the organ of American Transcendentalism, with no pecuniary basis, committed to the chance and gratuitous efforts and editing of friends, if intellectually and spiritually prosperous, had no statistical success. It struggled, through four years, with all the difficulties of eleemosynary journalism; and then, significantly enough, with a word concerning the "Millennial Church," sighed its last breath, and gave up the ghost. I prize the four volumes among the choicest treasures of my library. They contain some of Emerson's, of Theodore Parker's, of Margaret Fuller's, of Thoreau's best things; not to speak of writers less absolute and less famous.

Meanwhile, the association, if so it could be termed, had gradually dissolved. Some of the members turned papists,— I should say sought refuge in the bosom of the Catholic

Church. A few of the preachers pursued their calling, and perhaps have contributed somewhat to liberalize and enlarge the theology of their day. Some have slipped their moorings on this bank and shoal of time. One sank beneath the wave, whose queenly soul had no peer among the women of this land. Of one

> "A strange and distant mould
> Wraps the mortal relics cold."

Finally, a fragment of this strangely compounded body lodged in a neighboring town, and became the nucleus of an agricultural enterprise in which the harvest truly was *not* plenteous, and the competent laborers few; and of which, the root being rottenness, the blossom soon went up as dust.

What is the lesson of history and private experience concerning revolutions in religion? Ecclesiastical continuity,— that we are under tutelage. The Church does not exist by the will of man, but by his constitution. It cannot be abolished by the will of man; it cannot perish by disaffection. Only a new Church can supplant the old. And the new Church will not be an association of thinkers and critics, with correct and rational theories of God, discarding supernaturalism, and planting themselves on abstract theism. Such associations exist under all dispensations; but they have never succeeded in planting a Church, or supplanting one. In India, at this moment, in the midst of the popular polytheism, there exists a flourishing association of this description,— the sect of "Brahmas," pure theists. I received, not long since, a clever discourse from one of this body, entitled "Man the Son of God," in which Jesus Christ and Theodore Parker are coupled together as the two great lights of human kind. Theism is a theory of the universe which may or may not be true, but will never constitute a Church, and will never supplant one. A Church is the embodiment of a spiritual force, which, sallying from the heart of God, creates a vortex in human society that compels the kingdoms, compels the æons, in its conquering wake, and tracks its way through the world with a shining pyschopomp of saintly souls.

It seems to me somewhat important to understand this difference between a Church, and a school of religious philosophy. I care not whether a man be conservative or radical in his theology, provided he has sight of this fact; provided also he possesses the faculty of self-criticism, which shall teach him his own limitations, and the limits of his theme. Conservatism is wise, so it be the conservatism of intelligent homage to the past, and not the conservatism of worldliness and self-interest, or fear. But radicalism is wiser: I mean the radicalism of disciplined thought, not of impatience, of pugnacity and self-conceit. Wiser yet, wisest of all, is that historic sense which acknowledges the good in both these tendencies, but is too wide-eyed and self-possessed to be entangled with either; which sees that both are polarizations of a truth that neither quite comprehends; which recognizes the fact of tutelage, and knows that mankind must have spiritual leaders; and that, of spiritual leadership, the qualification and main constituent is not learning or philosophy or eloquence or any kind of intellectual eminence, but spiritual overweight, attained and attested by entire humiliation; that only to him who, being in the form of God, can take upon himself the form of a servant will every knee bow.

Art. II.—RECENT GERMAN LITERATURE: AUERBACH.

Berthold Auerbach's gesammelte Schriften. Erste, neu durchgesehene Gesammtausgabe. Stuttgart und Augsburg. J. G. Cotta'scher Verlag. 1857. Vol. I.-VIII. *Schwarzwälder Dorfgeschichten.* IX. *Barfüssele.* X.-XI. *Spinoza,* ein Denkerleben. XII.-XIII. *Dichter und Kaufmann,* ein Lebensgemälde aus der Zeit Moses Mendelssohns. XIV. *Neues Leben,* eine Lehrgeschichte, in fünf Büchern. XV. *Deutsche Abende.* XVI. *Schrift und Volk.* Grundzüge der volksthümlichen Literatur angeschlossen an eine Charakteristik J. P. Hebel's. XVII.-XVIII. *Schatzkästlein des Gevattersmanns.*

Village Tales from the Black Forest. Translated by J. E. TAYLOR. London: Bogue, 1846.

Christian Gellert and other Sketches. London: Low, 1858. Post 8vo.

Ivo: a Village Tale from the Black Forest. Translated from the German by META TAYLOR, with four illustrations by JOHN ABSALON. 16mo.

The Professor's Wife. A Tale, translated by M. HOWITT. London: Parker & Son, 1850. 12mo.

The Barefooted Maiden. A Tale. London: Low, 1857. 12mo.

Tagebuch aus Wien. Von Latour bis auf Windischgratz. September bis November, 1848. Breslau: Schletter, 1849.

Narrative of Events in Vienna. Translated by J. E. TAYLOR. 12mo. London: Bogue, 1849.

Andree Hofer. Geschichtliches Trauerspiel, in fünf Aufzügen. Leipzig: G. Wigand, 1850.

Deutscher Familienkalender auf das Jahr 1858. Mit Bildern (Holzschn.) nach Original-zeichn. Von W. v. KAULBACH, L. RICHTER und ARTHUR v. RAMBERG, u.s.w. Stuttgart: Cotta. 8vo.

Deutscher Volks-Kalender auf das Jahr 1859, u.s.w.

Der Wahlspruch. Schauspiel in fünf Acten. Leipzig: Weber, 1859.

Joseph in Schnee. Eine Erzählung von B. AUERBACH. Stuttgart: Cotta, 1860.

Joseph in the Snow. Translated by Lady WALLACE. London: Saunders & Oakley. 3 vols. Post 8vo. 1861.

Edelweiss. Eine Erzählung von B. AUERBACH. Stuttgart: Cotta, 1861.

Auf der Höhe. Roman in acht Büchern, von BERTHOLD AUERBACH. Dritte Auflage. Stuttgart: Verlag der J. G. Cotta'schen Buchhandlung, 1866.

IN the Black Forest, in Wurtemberg, in the charming valley of the Neckar, is a village called Nordstetten, inhabited by a mixed population of Catholics and Jews, who live together quite in harmony. Berthold Auerbach was born in this village, in 1812, of Jewish parents. And it is to this circumstance of his Jewish birth, and the Christian influences that were about him from childhood, that many of the characteristics of his writings are to be traced. After receiving the rudiments of his education in the Talmud, in the dilapidated little old town of Hechingen, twenty or thirty miles distant, once the capital of the infinitesimal principality of that name, and which the traveller remembers because he drove out from it once to see the castle of the Hohenzollerns, the original nest of that black eagle that now flaps its wings over Germany, — he went to complete his Jewish training at

Carlsruhe; but the obscure life of a Rabbi suited neither his tastes nor his ambition. And after having been for a time at the Gymnasium in Stuttgart, he entered the University at Tübingen. But, as he had been faithless to rabbinism, he soon deserted the study of jurisprudence, to which he had at first applied himself, and, under the guidance of the celebrated Strauss, he devoted himself to philosophy. His philosophical studies were continued at Munich, under Schelling; and, at Heidelberg, he studied history under Schlosser. Early involved in the political discussions of the day, in which he took the side of the people, he soon came into collision with the Government, which was as resolute in suppressing all free inquiry in the direction of politics as it was anxious to encourage it in every other. He was arrested at Munich, but was nevertheless soon released from durance; and, even while investigations were going on into the acts of the authors of the troubles in which he had taken part, he was permitted to continue his attendance upon the lectures at the University.

In Wurtemberg, however, he did not get off so easily; but was sentenced, in 1835, to expiate his political views in the dungeons of Hohenasperg, where the lives of so many noble patriots and thinkers had wasted away in solitude and misery; and where, but for that precipitate flight of which the story has been but rather recently told, the great genius of Schiller might have been extinguished in the madness of despair. The shadows which lay so dark, however, over the frowning Swabian height, do not seem to have affected the activity of Auerbach's mind; for he wrote in his prison a pamphlet entitled *Das Judenthum und die neueste Literatur* ("Judaism, and the Latest Literature"), — a pamphlet now long forgotten, if indeed it ever had any success. After being released from imprisonment, he set about writing a series of books under the collective title of *The Ghetto* (the term by which the Jewish quarter is designated in European cities); his purpose being to give a faithful picture of Jewish life in its poetical and historical aspects, before the levelling tendencies in modern manners and thought had wholly swept away its peculiarities, and buried in oblivion that treasure of oral traditions and tales of marvels which the Judaism of the Middle Age had accumulated.

He completed, however, but two of these books,—the first, which appeared in 1837, being entitled *Spinoza, ein Denkerleben* ("Spinoza, the Life of a Thinker"); and the second, which appeared in 1839, *Dichter und Kaufmann, ein Lebensgemälde aus der Zeit Moses Mendelssohns* ("Poet and Merchant, a Drawing from Life in the time of Moses Mendelssohn"). The former was a psychological and historical representation—founded upon a careful study of Spinoza's writings --of the course of that philosopher's evolution, so to speak, out of the Jewish life and tradition into the broad fields of universal thought; while the latter, in the life of Moses Ephraim Kuh, the Jewish epigrammatist of Silesia, illustrated with a wealth of fancy the social condition of the Jews in the second half of the last century.

The Jews had as yet furnished no illustration of their own manners and mode of thought, unless it be in the expression of that feeling of servitude which makes the undertone of their writing, as of their life. Auerbach undertook to exhibit the real significance of Judaism, its habits and opinions, in a philosophical, but at the same time artistic, form. "Philosophy, science, civilization," says a French writer, "have all had their legends of heroes and martyrs." Has not Israel had its heroes and its martyrs too? Among the Jews of the Middle Age and the Renaissance and the later centuries, have there not been men who have fought and suffered for the human race? To paint these combats and these trials was to exhibit the Jews as zealously co-operating in the liberal movement of modern society, and so to do something to explode the restrictions which still hamper them. For this purpose, no better subject than Spinoza, and perhaps no better writer than Auerbach, could have been chosen.

Spinoza was one of those self-contained natures that either fascinate or repel us. Neither Goethe, who favored his philosophy, nor Jacobi, who hated it, ever attempted to penetrate the character of the man. They merely took his philosophy, and made what they could of it. The influence, however, of Hegel had awakened a spirit of analysis which did not shrink even from the task of getting at the elements of such a character as Spinoza. The difficulty was, in doing so, to avoid adopting the ideas of Christianity as a standpoint, — a difficulty which, of all writers, Auerbach was best fitted to surmount; for, like Spinoza himself, he had been bred up in the Talmud, and had afterwards worked his way out of the limitations of rabbinism into the freedom of philosophical thought. Rabbinism and Catholicism were to him but diverse forms of the same inspiration. The Talmud was to the Bible what the scholastic philosophy was to the gospel; and, in his view, Spinoza, like Luther, was one of the liberators of religious thought. There is, indeed, in Spinoza's system much that is intelligible, and much that is salutary to one whose soul is open to the influences of nature; but it is also characterized, as Schmidt well says, by a certain severity of reflection, and a certain dryness of form, while in the hopelessness of its general tone it seems to trample coldly upon all individual life. But, trained by his own experience to enter into the mood and to appreciate the struggles of a thinker like Spinoza, Auerbach felt that there must have been many a sad vicissitude and conflict in the experience of such a mind before it arrived at conclusions apparently so gloomy.

The psychological explication of this problem, in an artistic form, is what Auerbach has aimed at; and, on the whole, it seems to us that he has succeeded very well in attaining his object. Saint-René Taillandier may complain that the separate pictures are but fragments, and Schmidt may think he breaks down when he touches upon the philosophy of Descartes: doubtless there are errors in its form, and defects in its substance; Auerbach was but twenty-five years old when he wrote it; and, although he has subsequently revised it carefully twice, it will hardly be expected to withstand very severe criticism. Of course, even in a philosophical romance, there must be something more than philosophy: for it is, after all, a work of art; and a work of art demands primarily the individual human element. You cannot portray pantheism in a picture, but you can represent in an imaginative form the sufferings and the struggles by which a devout mind works its way out of a narrow creed into a faith that comprehends the universe. You can depict the character of a man so mastered by his intellectual conscience as to turn away from all the prizes that the world has to offer, in order calmly to fathom the divine word that possesses his soul, and to pronounce it at last pure and majestic as he finds it. Auerbach's task, therefore, was not to unfold Spinoza's system; but to show, with all the clearness that the facts of history and well-grounded conjecture will enable him to attain, what sort of a man Spinoza was,—and this in a vivid, dramatic way, so that the reader should be charmed in spite of himself, and be led to recognize the beauty and grandeur of a life which the ignorance and bigotry of men had so long blackened with calumny that his very name had become but another term for the gloomy despair of atheism.

We have only to regret, that, when the author made the final revision of his romance for the collected edition of his writings, he did not think it worth while to preserve, if not the citations and proofs of the first edition, at least the list — contained in the preface to the second — of the passages which were taken word for word from Spinoza's works, so that the reader who desired to assure himself of the accuracy of the philosophical statements, as well as to scrutinize the grounds on which many of its biographical conjectures were made, could do so easily. The translation, however, which he afterwards published, of the whole of Spinoza's works, from Latin into German, rendered this perhaps unnecessary to the German reader, who could readily refer also to the sketch of Spinoza's life, which Auerbach had prefixed to his translation; and which, besides being the first philosophical and critical sketch that had been made, possessed the advantage of having been based upon a thorough examination of both the sources of information as to his life,— viz., the Christian and the Jewish.

At this moment, therefore, when general attention has been called afresh to Spinoza as one of the illustrious thinkers of the race, this representation of his inward experience — which to all the truth of a biography, so far as biography in this instance can go, adds all the fascination of a romance, so far as romance is allowed within the limits of probability — will not fail to be of service in dissipating many prejudices, and in opening the way to a wider recognition of the truth he taught, as also of the errors with which that truth may have been accompanied. For, as one of the ablest of living English writers has recently said,[*] "Spinoza shocks those who regard him from an antagonistic standing-point. No sooner is the mind disengaged from the trammels of old prejudice than we learn to look on his arguments as on those of Parmenides or Algazel: we ask whether they are true or false; whether they can be taken up into our philosophy, or rejected from it. This is the attitude of Germany. To some extent it is the attitude of France. It will become the attitude of England. For myself, I cannot accept Spinoza's system; but I see how it was perfectly compatible with his own pure morality, and do not fear lest it should disturb the morality of any one who could conscientiously adopt it."

Auerbach's second Jewish romance dealt with the same general subject of the struggles of a thoughtful mind against the limitations of an inherited faith. This contradiction of the Jewish traditions with modern life was no greater, indeed, than that of some of the creeds of Christian sects with the intellectual and scientific development of the age; but the interest of *Spinoza* was due in great part to the subject: the ascent of this great thinker from the low level of Jewish life, or any other life, was a striking spectacle to all men. But the wrestling of an humbler mind with the problems it could not master, and with the currents of thought that swept it away from its ancient faith, required greater skill in the handling, to give it a universal interest. The sketches of Rousseau and Lessing and Mendelssohn and the rest impart, indeed, a certain vivacity to its otherwise somewhat ponderous didacticism, and the various portraits of the Jewish fam-

---

[*] Mr. Lewes: Fortnightly Review, No. XXII., for April 1, 1866, p. 399.

ilies with whom it is concerned are well done: but it is more fragmentary than *Spinoza*, and suffers more from the want of that absorbing unity which carries the reader on fresh to the end. Kuh was a liberal thinker, the friend of Mendelssohn, and acquainted with Lessing and Gleim and Nicolai and Lavater; and it was doubtless for the reason that he thus obtained an opportunity for a series of clever studies, that Auerbach selected him. Taken by themselves, these studies are all interesting; that entitled " An Evening at Moses Mendelssohn's " is an excellent picture, quite in the tone of the last century,— the work of an artist and a thinker. But to unite these separate sketches in that harmonious whole which the rules of art require in a romance, either a greater personage was needed for the subject, or a more dramatic plot for the evolution of his character.

His subsequent brilliant career carried Auerbach away from the higher regions of metaphysical discussion, and from all the dust and din of the schools, back to the sweet fields and the silent forests, and the hamlets, so peaceful and so simple, that he had loved and lived in when a boy. But, true to his democratic convictions, he endeavored at various periods to diffuse among the people, by portraits of the distinguished men of his faith, by illustrations of the principles that should control a nation's literature, and by those *Volkskalenders*, peculiar to Germany, which, after the manner of Franklin's " Poor Richard's Almanac," treated the events of the day in a colloquial way, attractive to all capacities,— he endeavored to diffuse, we say, clearer notions of the tendency in the thought of the age to greater freedom; and, at the same time, to awaken a more general perception of the fundamental unity of all human relations, in Jew and Gentile alike, in those bound in the spirit as in those who, like Spinoza, had attained a final emancipation from earthly limitations.

In a couple of stories, which he afterwards inserted in his *Deutsche Abende* (" German Evenings "), he attempted to blend philosophy with poetry, after the manner of the Dialogues of Plato; and it was from the same general desire to make the highest truths in philosophy intelligible to common minds, that he wrote *Der gebildete Bürger, Buch für den denkenden Mittelstand* (" The Educated Citizen, a Book for the Thinking Middle Classes "). His *Volkskalender*, entitled the *Gevattersmann* (" Godfather "), had a circulation in its very first year of eighty thousand copies, and maintained itself for four years in the public favor, until the crisis of 1848 put an end to it. It was revived again, however, in 1858 and 1859.

In *Spinoza*, and in *Dichter und Kaufmann*, Auerbach had addressed himself more directly to persons of a certain refinement and learning; to those who were attracted to the delicacy and subtilty of truth, rather than to the representation of the coarser passions and the grosser life, so common in the literature of the day. But his *Schwarzwälder Dorfgeschichten* (" Peasant Tales of the Black Forest "), first published in 1843, lifted him at once into the front rank of popular European writers, and made for him a more than European reputation.

Peasant tales of a similar character were not, indeed, new in German literature. In the last century, Stilling's autobiography, so familiar to us in the English translation, was but a picture, simple and graceful, of rural life and its quiet joys. It differs, however, from the representations of the same life that are made to-day, in that it was wholly an unconscious creation, springing, not from a disgust at civilization, but from an unaffected love of the changing beauties and the mystic repose of nature. Again: the idyls of the Palatinate, by Maler Müller, and Voss's touching pictures, had done something to take the German mind out of the dark byways of feverish and busy cities into the sunlight of green hillsides and the soft air of fruitful valleys. The immediate predecessor of Auerbach, however, but in a narrow way, was Zimmermann, in the episode of the *Hofschulze* in his brilliant and ingenious romance of *Münchhausen*. In contrast with the world (so full of falsehood and corruption) about him, Zimmermann felt the need of a character, limited to be sure in its sphere, but grounded in that moral principle, the want of which made those about him the mocking phantoms they were. And, for the creation of this character, so rare, yet so true, he had many advantages. He had passed some of his earlier years among the peasants of Lower Saxony, the most original perhaps in all that diversity of peasant life in Germany; and, in the discharge of his official duties, he had become familiar with them in their daily pursuits. He was thus preserved from that false sentimentalism which tends to exaggerate one side of this sort of life, and so not merely to put the whole in a false light, but, if one may say so, in an impossible light. But Zimmermann died before he could follow up the vein he had so successfully opened. For the finer perceptions and the ideal purity of Goethe's *Hermann und Dorothea* and Voss's *Luise* had given place to a more direct study and an exacter appreciation of this peasant life, so naïve in its ignorance, and so gloomy withal in its simplicity.

There was also another writer, to a certain extent Auerbach's predecessor, but in great part his contemporary, and with whom he can only be compared in entire misapprehension of the fundamental diversity in the structure of the minds of the two men,— we mean, of course, Jeremias Gotthelf, or, as his real name was, Albert Bitzius, for many years the busy, faithful pastor of the little village of Lützelflüh, in the valley of the Emme, amidst the Bernese landscapes, where he died in 1857. His writings were little known, till Auerbach had developed the taste for this sort of literature; and, though one cannot but admire his wonderful vigor and frequent humor, there is such a lack of artistic finish in his pictures, that for this reason, if for no other, they would always rank below Auerbach's, who, in this respect, is without a master in this kind of fiction. Gotthelf was an earnest worker among an humble class of people afflicted with a good many ills of their own producing, and a good many for which the State alone was responsible. To expose these evils to the people themselves on the one hand, and to the Government on the other, was the object he had in view when he took up his pen; and he did not lay down his pen, till, restless philanthropist that he was, he had written twenty-four solid volumes, many of them indeed quite open to the charge of being but literary manufacture, if one does not bear in mind that, like the sermons he spoke in public, and the incessant sermons he extemporized in private, they all had an immediate purpose and a definite audience in view. The Bernese peasants pass before us in painful reality, with all their virtues and vices in their faces, and with their torn and muddy garb, rank with the smell of the farmyard,—just as they passed before Gotthelf's eyes daily to be catechized and reproved, to be taught a new way of preparing fodder for the cattle or cheese for the market, and to be indoctrinated with a proper abhorrence of radicalism; not less fatal, in his opinion, to religious belief than to all dutiful subordination to civil authority.

Gotthelf had a healthy, vigorous faith: life to him was positive,—a sphere for work, not for speculation. Auerbach began his career in an anxious seeking after the unknowable: from being a Jew he had become a Pantheist, and, as a Pantheist, it was upon him to explain life to himself and to others; and the mighty unrest of that task is visible in all his writings. As a Jew, indeed, by birth he was well fitted to lead the way in the endeavor, apparent in a good deal of the literature of the day, to show how the conscience of man can recognize sin, and how his will may be trained, and must in the necessity of things be trained, to wrestle with it upon grounds independent of those presented by Christian doctrine. But, as a mere thinker, Auerbach is not original: the philosophy which he has adopted as the explanation and the rule of life is not of his own discovery. He follows substantially in the footsteps of Spinoza, and shows the practical working of that thinker's doctrine in life, helping us to judge for ourselves of its worth by the success with which he unfolds it in action; as is especially the case with his last quite remarkable romance, entitled *Auf der Höhe*, of which we shall speak in a moment. We have merely to remark now, that it was this very philosophical freedom which helped him more than any thing, perhaps, to the peculiar success he obtained in his peasant tales; for there he not only had full scope for his faculty of acute observation, but a basis of human nature, so to speak, unoppressed by the burden of dogmas, free from the disturbing elements of speculative thought.

For this modern civilization we fancy so permeating is found after all in many countries, when carefully scrutinized, to be but a sort of superficial polish: it goes down really but a little way into the masses of the people, and the bottom stratum is very likely to be wholly untouched by it. The Christianity these peasants of Auerbach had been taught might as well have been any other code of decent behavior, accompanied by sufficient superstitions to sanctify it. The men and women he had known from boyhood, along these bubbling mountain-streams, in these crowded hamlets, in these lonely wastes of forest, were men and women as near the state of nature as you could get for Auerbach's purpose. And so he described them just as they were, but made his description poetic; and the world was charmed with the beauty and veracity of it, and overjoyed to find in these unaccustomed ways, where no flower of sentiment, no fragrant poetic blossom, was ever gathered before, such a freshness of life in the midst of what was thought such a pestilent miasma. But the world had perhaps little insight into the conditions of that success. In Gotthelf, there was a solemn repose of faith like that of the Hebrew prophets. But along every page of Auerbach's runs an undertone of that *Welt-schmerz*, which his philosophy cannot banish, and which he has no religion to help him master. Yet let it not be supposed, that Auerbach is wanting in faith. To him, as Taillandier says, the world is beautiful, and life is sweet: it is the mystics, the false idealists, who, under pretence of embellishing, disdain it; it is the *blasés* who mock at it; it is the materialists who disfigure it. Let us, on the contrary, find out life, — what it contains. There is more poetry in reality than in the inventions of fancy; for the study of reality is the basis of science, and science is the noblest poetry. Let us study reality, then, not merely physical, but moral reality; for that alone is true and durable reality, and, in the end, explanatory of the other: that is, let the artist be a moralist.

The reading world in Germany had grown weary of the

triflers, who, by concealing their want of creative power under a forced frivolity of manner, had succeeded in keeping it in the heated air of the saloons, amidst gorgeous upholsteries and resplendent mirrors; and it was weary, on the other hand, of the sensuous mysticism of the illuminati. The boudoirs of the Countess Hahn-Hahn, and the aristocratic saloons of Sternberg, were even more oppressive than the schools where young Germany preached, it was thought, the rehabilitation of matter. It was, therefore, like a fragrant breath of the blossoming springtime, like a breeze redolent of farmyards and freshly-ploughed furrows and long reaches of oaks and beaches that came up now from the Black Forest, and braced the unstrung nerves, and gave a tone to the jaded mind. For these characters, so simple and true, were not the representatives of a system: they were neither demagogues nor preachers; they were soldiers and wood-cutters and schoolmasters and schoolboys and emigrants, painted with a loving hand, with all their caustic *bonhommie* and all their vulgar vices. Living pictures, as it were, on the canvas, they answered the general craving for greater reality and a more earnest purpose. Political lyrics were stirring the people again, the national drama was reviving, the whole poetic tendency of Germany was taking a more vigorous and a more reflective turn.

And what these peasant-tales were to literature in general as the re-action from an over-refinement of culture, they were to Auerbach himself as the re-action from merely speculative, unfruitful thought. He had been knocked about for years amongst all the doctrines of the schools; he had sat at the feet of Rabbies, and been overborne with the scholasticism of the Talmud; he had listened to the lectures of famous professors, and tasted of the ripest fruits of philosophy and science: but in all these labyrinths of speculation, amidst these dust-heaps of dead learning, he had sought in vain for the lost peace of his soul. After all this intellectual exile, this spiritual vagabondage, he returned like the prodigal son to his old home among the forests and the hills, and, writing his peasant tales, began a new epoch in the history of German fiction.

But the very qualities for which these tales were at first most prized are perhaps the very ones which they most lack, — originality and naïveté: they are, above all things, the products of reflection and experience. It is not the consciousness of the peasant that speaks out of these sturdy figures; but the poet of fine æsthetic culture, reflective, and never losing sight of the questions that so vex the mind of the age. "The fundamental law of all poetic creation," says a German critic, "is the free elevation of a given subject into the sphere of the universal." Judged by that law, Auerbach has not succeeded in attaining the highest excellence in art; for, instead of creating idyllic scenes, he makes real events and characters pass before us: he goes down almost among the proletaires, and brings them up, brutal and filthy as they are, and makes a psychological study, so minute often as to be painful. Deficient in the deepest poetic feeling, his speculative tendencies have overborne a good deal the freedom of his fancy. He is too thoughtful to idealize, and, moreover, too earnest in his purpose to do so.

And the immediate and universal success which he attained is due to the very fact, that in this seriousness he was true to the literary traditions of Germany; that his pictures were not open to the reproach under which so much of the current literature lay, of an excessive idealism or a dangerous indifference: for Germany had been drifting slowly into a denial of its own peculiar genius. It had taken up with a Voltairean turn, very ill adapted to it; and this perversion had gone so far, that schools were at one time founded in which irony and raillery were recommended as a salutary remedy for the intoxicating seductions of mysticism. And, side by side with this abnormal tendency, the old sin also of Germany had re-appeared: it began to dream, not, as of old, the golden dreams that floated it into the luminous heaven of spiritualism, but the turbid dreams of socialism. The new spirit, therefore, which Auerbach now breathed into literature, was of an assuring kind. He was a clever story-teller; but he was also a serious artist: he had an end in view, and his readers had come to have one. His morality and theirs, however, was no longer a string of commonplaces, which might be addressed as well to everybody and to all relations. Inspired by a certain philosophical optimism, he had conceived the profoundest reverence for the dignity of human nature; and this reverence he expressed, not in decorous phrases, but in the keenest analysis of individual and real characters. For true poetry was to him the study of details, and every literary work which pretended to exert a moral influence must justify itself by its realism. One feels, in reading him, that his mind was set upon the elevation of Germany, and set upon it with passion; and that, faithful to the German traditions, in observing the precept so well expressed by Boileau, that the merit of the man is not to be separated from that of the writer,— a principle, however, apt to be looked upon in France and elsewhere as a ridiculous notion of olden times by those, and they are many, who can find the indication of genius nowhere but in disorder, — faithful to these traditions, Auerbach may have lost something of the artist in the moralist; and to many of us, therefore, unaccustomed to look in fiction for any thing more than amusement, he may seem dull. But it must be remembered that he is a true type of the German character, and of the literary society in Germany in general, which knows nothing of adventurers and Bohemians, but recognizes in every man, poet, romancer, historian, or what not, a grave and special mission; and which insists, that all the more as the people give themselves over to industrial activity and to trade, the men who represent the interests of thought shall be held to respect themselves, in order that so their work may be respected. Hence that fragrance, as it were, of sincerity that refreshes us, even in works of a second or third rate sort; and hence that general subordination of the imagination to the law of duty, and that universal protest against an enervating or demoralizing literature.

In Auerbach's tales, therefore, it was not merely the subject, of a genuine character, limited as it was, that attracted attention, but the way in which it was treated,— terse, realistic, with a severe avoidance of empty phrases and swollen metaphors, and an earnest effort to explain the significance of a certain kind of life in its permanent forms. The style, indeed, was so far removed from the usual *belletristic* flow, and yet so precise and graceful, that, in working out their great dictionary of the German language, the brothers Grimm paid special attention to Auerbach among contemporary writers. He had not that fulness of vocabulary so fatal to many; but his effort to express his thought exactly, his struggle for reality in words as well as in things, made him in many respects an authority. Critics may complain, that he made his peasants talk sometimes as no peasants ever did talk or could talk; but it was not for want of a thorough understanding of their dialect: it was from his tendency to analyze rather than create. As a psychological study, there is perhaps nothing of the kind in any literature like his *Geschichte des Diethelm von Buchenberg*, in the fifth volume of the *Dorfgeschichten*. And though he fails in following out logically or sustaining a passion to the end; though his story progresses, not organically, but by separate leaps, as it were, — there is nevertheless in the various *motives* and situations such a wealth of fancy, and such a wonderful reality in the various moods of mind he pictures, that the interest seldom flags; and one leaves him instructed by an inward vision of human experience he never had before.

Der Tolpatsch, Die Kriegspfeife, Befehlerles, and *Ivo der Hajrle,* in the first volume of the *Dorfgeschichten,* afford charming specimens of his *genre* style; while, in the second volume, *Die Frau Professorin* is looked upon as one of his best creations in general, and it is indeed a veritable pearl in German literature: but we cannot discover its special superiority to some of his other efforts, nor should we be inclined to rank it with the ballads of Uhland, as the chief illustration of the Swabian genius. *Florian und Crescenz* and *Der Lautenbacher,* in the same volume, may also be taken as delightful instances of his general merit. In *Lucifer,* in the fourth volume, he endeavors to show how rural manners and modes of thought are assailed by every forward movement of civilization, and that, although many of the charms of rural life are thus destroyed, mankind on the whole gains in the process; and in this instance, again, he shows how far removed he is from that romanticism which, properly translated, means a preference for ignorance over culture: for he has never for a moment been faithless to the obligations his earlier training imposed upon him; his very fidelity to them, indeed, has led him into artistic errors which he would otherwise have avoided. For the unsparing severity of his representation of the internal conflicts and confusion in these stolid peasant hearts leaves on the whole a somewhat gloomy impression. The tragedies he exhibits playing about us under the surface of a life apparently so unruffled startle us by their violence; and the keener his psychological analysis, the more vividly do these passions take form, and the more unwholesome is the atmosphere we breathe, — we feel as if everywhere about us were the phantoms of a disordered and darkened world, waiting to repeat their wild, degraded play of discord and of vice. Moreover, in order to be still truer to the reality, Auerbach, like Balzac, has made some of his characters re-appear in almost all his stories, while the scene of all of them is the same, — namely, his birth-place of Nordstetten. His aim has been to depict a whole hamlet, just as it is, from the first house to the last; but, if these pictures are to be taken together as illustration of the morals of a single place, has he not painted a second Gomorrah?

The question, therefore, cannot but arise as to the import of such representations. Have these peasants, with all their stupidities and ignorance and *naiveté*, a claim to this careful study from a poetic point of view? Other novelists have introduced peasant characters; Walter Scott has many of them: but no other novelist has made them a speciality with such wonderful microscopic power as Auerbach. And therefore, if the subject, which in some aspects of it he has exhausted, yields fruits no greater than we find in these tales, may we not assume that the limits of it have been reached? As a German critic says, "There is no dialectic of passion or feeling among peasants." Like the unbroken monotony of their features, which show no trace of intellectual processes, their feelings have none of that variety and complexity which you find in more cultivated classes; for they lack that sensitive nervous organization which is the product of culture, and is as natural to the better educated as the typical rigidity of the peasant's face is to him. Hans may be very fond of his Grethe; but his feelings at sight of her will hardly resemble those of Dante contemplating Beatrice, or of Goethe at the feet of Frau von Stein, or of Alfieri by the side of the Countess of Albany. In love, as in every other emotion of the soul and in every intellectual activity, there is a certain gradation of culture. The most highly developed minds and the best nurtured hearts are alone capable of the profoundest thought and emotion. Peasant tales, therefore, taken by themselves, are subordinate and limited in their character; for they are the picture of a dreary, poverty-stricken world, in which it is scarcely possible in an æsthetic point of view to interest the cultivated mind, which aspires ever to something beyond itself and still further developed. The moral and scientific importance of the subject, of course, we are not considering: how great that is, appears directly in every line that Auerbach has written, although he does not profess to make it his aim to indicate it.

Nevertheless, in thus leading the way back to realism, which must always be the basis of all true art, Auerbach has certainly rendered a great service to literature. Yet we fear in the end it will be, as Schmidt says, that we have tasted so much of the sweet poison of civilization that we can no more go back to the simplicity of a peasant hut in the Black Forest than we can live in a kraal on the banks of the Orange River; for, though we have taken down fairy tales from old women's lips as they sat spinning, and caught up curious sayings of journeymen artisans as they jogged along the highway, it has been with a view to make use of them in the saloon or opera-house or learned academies; and it will probably be the same with peasant tales: they will live on in poetry, but die out in reality.

Of Auerbach's later novels, *Barfüssele*, — which was translated for us several years ago by Mrs. Lee, — *Joseph im Schnee*, and *Edelweiss*, we have only to say, that, although deficient in some of the qualities which made his "Peasant Tales" so famous, they are nevertheless somewhat livelier in tone, and more cheerful in coloring. But if Auerbach's genius slumbered a little for a time, it revived again in all its vigor and freshness and exquisite charm in the romance which he published this last year, entitled *Auf der Höhe*. We count it as next to the *Dorfgeschichten*, his leading work; and, moreover, as one of the few good novels that have, as yet, been written in Germany. The right of translation is advertised as reserved to Dr. Max Schlesinger in London, and to Bayard Taylor in America; and we hope that either the one or the other will see to it, that it is soon put into an English dress. The plot of it is simple, yet the interest of the reader, although not kept at a feverish heat as in the popular fiction of the day, never flags; for there is less of what an English reviewer calls "that fatal skill of Auerbach's in throwing a charm around separate incidents, to the detriment of the unity of the subject." In its general conception, it aims to illustrate the wrestlings of a noble mind with sin, from a pantheistic point of view; the passing out of the purified soul from the limitations of its turbid individuality into the grandeur of the universal life. Irma, the heroine — and moreover the chorus, as it were, of the drama, revealing its significance — is a high-spirited, gifted daughter of the nobility, maid of honor to the queen, and beloved of the king. She repents of her fault, and withdraws to the solitude of a peasant's hut to work out her repentance; and, at last, when she has ascended up out of the discords of earth, to die at one with the peace of nature and the laws of her moral being. In contrast with these higher scenes are pictures of a lowlier life, in which Walpurga, the shrewd, guileless, faithful peasant-woman, who has been brought to court as a wet-nurse, is the chief character. The realism with which she is depicted is sometimes coarse, and often tedious; but, on the whole, she is one of Auerbach's best creations, wonderful for its originality and veracity, and all the more true to the reality of things in that the sphere in which she moves is represented as subordinate to a higher one. Upon the other characters — the lackey Baum, and the lonely Eberhard, and the wise, thoughtful Gunther, to say nothing of Zenza, and the black Esther, and the brutish Thomas, and the pitiable Bruno, and the rest — we need not dwell. Irma's diary, as she wrote it out in the agony of her self-imposed expiation, marked as it is by great delicacy of thought, may be said to be the burden of Auerbach's philosophy of life. The restless reader, of course, will skip it; but one who seeks in art the profoundest revelation of life will linger over it as the mournfullest exhibition of a human soul struggling to right itself by its own unaided powers that has ever been presented to him. This Magdalene, without a religion; this contrite heart, with only the vast spaces of nature to take note of its repentant throbbing; these weary eyes, red with weeping, and no face to look upon but the great sweep of nature's processes; this haunting consciousness of evil, and no bosom to lay the burden of it in but the swelling sea of the universe, — what a picture is that of philosophy striving to allay this burning fever of sin!

With his early political tendencies, Auerbach could not fail to sympathize with the Revolution of 1848; but he had been recently married, and the illness of his wife, soon followed by her death, prevented him from taking part in it other than in opposing the Polish agitators at Breslau, who claimed all Silesia as far as watered by the Oder for their future republic. In the autumn of that year, however, he made a journey into Austria, and was a witness of the Revolution in Vienna, of which he wrote an account that was translated into English. He married again afterwards, and lived for a good while at Dresden, which, with Munich, has become one of the brilliant centres of the German imagination; the home of Ludwig Richter, so popular even in this country for his humorous illustrations; and, for a good while, of the sculptor Rietschel, now dead. He lives now in Berlin, and is described as "a person of fine appearance and singular sweetness of disposition, with uncommon social and conversational powers."

The Revolution, however, of 1848 suggested to him a tragedy, the political violence of which he lived to outgrow. The character of the Tyrolese chief, Andree Hofer, celebrated for the short-lived part he played in the resistance of the Tyrol to the French in 1809, has been the subject of a good deal of discussion: on the one hand, he has been represented as vacillating and of feeble ability; and, on the other, as the incarnation of heroism. When Zimmermann published his tragedy of Hofer in 1828, the Tyrolese veterans who had aided him could not recognize the features of his naïve and hardy character in the transformation he had undergone into a Judas Maccabæus; and perhaps, in the midst of Auerbach's violent declamation against the sovereigns of Germany, they could recognize him as little in the latter's representation of him, as the victim of the cowardice and treachery of the Emperor of Austria.

But Auerbach has grown wiser as he has grown older: he has given over political for moral revolution; for, individual and interior reforms once made, legitimate revolutions follow of themselves. His motto, as has been well suggested, might have been borrowed from Angelus Silesius, *Le bien ne fait pas de bruit: le bruit ne fait pas de bien.* The patience which he recommends is the patience of the man who will reform himself: the courage which he illustrates is the courage of the man who can see his illusions melt away, and yet not become indifferent. "In the midst of his rustic stories, he inserts a discourse," says a French writer, "grave, solemn, evangelical, a sort of sermon on the mount; and this sermon is the glorification of human activity. 'There is a pulpit, who knows where it is? There is a congregation, who can tell its name? In this pulpit, before this congregation, a preacher without office or title might say, I have come to speak to you of the majestic crown of man,—and the name of it is TOIL.'"

This idea of individual regeneration appears in his long and unsuccessful romance entitled *Neues Leben.* It was under this title that Dante related the mystic ecstacies of his youth; but Auerbach applies it to the present situation of Germany, to the doubts which have obtained possession of many minds, to the disenchantments which have afflicted many hearts. His doctrine is, "You believe in God, and do not lose your confidence, though his every way may seem dark and mysterious. I believe in humanity, and believe that it is destined to attain absolute sanctity and absolute beauty." Yet this new life, is it the religion of Strauss? or the humanism of Bruno Bauer? or the atheism of Feuerbach?

Art. III.— WHAT IS THE VITAL TRUTH UNDERLYING THE TRINITY?

It has come to be a recognized principle among the most advanced students of theology, that every great and widespread belief, every doctrine which has been clung to and lived in through a long series of years, no matter how false its form may be, must have its core in some precious and substantial elements of truth. The human mind was never made, even in its lowest and grossest state, to be satisfied with error alone. A lie — which is a lie and nothing more, the same as a body which is all disease, or a soul which has sinned till it is utterly without goodness — must die inevitably of its own nature. It is the truth inside of falsehood which gives it life and beauty, which makes it loved and clung to, which enables it, like a fortress full of men, as compared with one which is only dead matter, to resist attacks and repair the ravages, which from time to time are made in its walls. The pertinacity with which the world clings to many things which we regard as superstition and poison, is evidence not of its love for error, but of that craving for what is true which will take it even in its worse forms, rather than not have it at all. There is no false system of doctrine which has not had a providential mission, either as a poison neutralizing some other poison, or a bitter shell holding within it the germ of a precious fruit. God is to be found in the history of error, not less clearly than in the progress of truth and the course of events. It is better for our moral, the same as for our physical health, to have all the elements of food, even though mixed up with some things which are inert or hurtful, rather than to have none at all, or to have one separated entirely from the others. And when we find a doctrinal statement, which we feel sure is wrong, resisting all our attacks, and held not only in the minds of scholars but by the great common heart, it is absolute proof that the world needs it, is better off with it, errors and all, than with our pure half truth, and that it is something we need conquer to possess, not to destroy.

Recognizing this principle, it is an interesting and most important question, what is the vital truth which underlies the Church doctrine of the Trinity? We have no doubt, that every statement of this doctrine, which was ever made, and which ever can be made, is false. It is contradictory in itself. It is opposed by the most explicit terms of Scripture. There is no analogy for it in nature. Again and again its defences have been battered down, and the doctrine itself logically demolished. Yet somehow it has survived all its destructions. It is one of the oldest doctrines of the Church. Nine-tenths of the strongest and best Christians that have ever lived have believed it. It is connected with all the great revivals of religion; is as prominent in all light of modern science, as in the darkest night of the middle ages; and is held to-day, by the whole Christian world, Protestant as well as Roman Catholic, except a mere handful of liberals, as a most vital part of its religious faith. What is the secret of its strength? How are we to reconcile our position as Unitarians with these undeniable facts of Trinitarianism?

Rev. J. F. Clarke, in his recent most valuable book, "The Truths and Errors of Orthodoxy," has stated, in its best form, one of the ways by which a reconciliation has been attempted. He supposes the essential truth, which underlies the doctrine of the Trinity, to be, that "the Deity has made, and is evermore making, three distinct and independent revelations of himself; each revelation giving a different view of the Divine Being, each revelation showing God to man under a different aspect." "The Father would seem to be the Source of all things, the Creator, the Fountain of being and of life. The Son is spoken of as the manifestation of that Being in Jesus Christ; and the Holy Spirit is spoken of as a spiritual influence, proceeding from the Father and Son, dwelling in the hearts of believers, as the source of their life,— the idea of God seen in causation, in reason, and in conscience, as making the very life of the soul itself." "There are these three revelations of God, and we know of no others. They are distinct from each other in form, but the same in essence. They are not merely three names for the same thing; but they are real personal manifestations of God, real subsistences, since he is personally present in all of them." "It is the same God who speaks in each, but he says something new each time. He reveals a new form of his being. He shows us not the same order and aspect of truth in each manifestation, but wholly different aspects." "It teaches that God is immanent in nature, in Christ, and in the soul." "So that, when we study the mysteries and laws of nature, we are drawing near to God himself and looking into his face. When we see Christ, we see God who is in Christ; and when we look into the solemn intuitions of the soul, the monitions of conscience, and the influences which draw our hearts to goodness, we are meeting and communing with God."

There seems to be some confusion in the language here used, as to whether Dr. Clarke makes the Trinity consist in the three aspects of God which are spoken of, or in the three modes by which he is manifested; also whether the Father is to be considered one of the manifestations of Deity, or as the entire Being who is manifested. The meaning, however, that we get from his words, as a whole, is not that there is any real distinction in the Divine nature otherwise than of its attributes, but that the one eternal person of the godhead is revealed to us in the three ways of nature, Christ, and the soul; and that, through each of these ways, we get a view of something in him which is different from what we get in the others.

Now, there can be no question as to the general facts on

which this reconciliation is based. God is manifested in nature, in Christ, and in the soul; and it is the same Person who is manifested in all these different ways. But is this really the vital truth which underlies the Church doctrine of the Trinity? Is it the source from which it grew, and the reason for which it is held? Or is it an after-thought, made to explain away its logical difficulties, and make it more acceptable to the thinking mind?

The objection starts up at once, that, whatever truth the view itself may have, it is not, in the proper sense of the words, a truth of Orthodoxy. It is not the kind of trinity in which the Orthodox churches believe, and which they have clung to for so many ages. The doctrine, as generally held, is that God is revealed in Scripture as three persons,— Father, Son, and Spirit,— having special points of difference; and that these three together are one God. Even Sabellianism, which comes nearest the view of Dr. Clarke, makes the distinction consist in the relations of God to the world as Creator, Redeemer, and Sanctifier, rather than in the modes by which he is revealed. There is no prevailing statement or conception of the Trinity which lays any stress on his being manifested in any separate modes. Hence, as an explanation of the vitality there is in the Church doctrine, it entirely fails.

Then, in regard to the view itself, it does not do full justice to the words of Scripture. Christ says, "He that hath seen me hath seen the Father." The Father, however, is a term which denotes not an attribute or manifestation or aspect of God, but the Eternal Being himself. It is the name of all he is; the word which expresses the highest conception of him the human mind has ever reached. And it is hardly possible that Christ meant to say otherwise than that he was a revelation of the entire Deity. So with the words of Paul in Colossians, "For in him dwelleth all the fulness of the godhead bodily." What other meaning can they have, than that Christ was a manifestation, not merely of one part of God, different from what we have in nature and in the soul, but of the whole God, of his wisdom and power, and justice and quickening influence, as well as of his love and mercy and redeeming grace? And, in general, the idea of a Trinity of manifestations through nature, Christ, and the soul is as foreign to the phraseology of the Bible as that of a Trinity of persons.

It is not a view which is corroborated by any thing which is seen in the world around us. The difference there is in the manifestations of God through nature, Christ, and the soul is not so much of kind as degree. It is not so much a different, but a larger, view of him that we get in Christ, over what we find in nature and the soul. Is it in Christ only that he is seen as Father and Friend? Have the sparrows and the lilies nothing to say of his care and tenderness? Has the Spring no lesson of his life-giving power? The golden sheaves and the bending fruit of Autumn, do they show us nothing of his friendship and paternal love? There is no real ground for the words, "He shows us not the same order and aspect of the truth in each manifestation, but wholly different aspects." Christ only speaks in clear, articulate words what the soul whispers faint and low, and what nature is striving, with its poor dumb lips but its speaking face, evermore to tell.

But the gravest objection to this view, as containing in any way the vital truth of the Trinity, is that the division of the ways in which God manifests himself into the three of nature, Christ, and the soul, is entirely arbitrary. What ground is there for saying, "There are these three revelations of him, and we know of no others"? Are not the revelations of himself in history, in society, in the moral order of the universe, as distinct from those of nature, Christ, and the soul, as these are from each other? Is he not revealed as Providence, Legislator, Judge, and Ruler with the same distinctness that he is as Creator, Redeemer, and Spiritual Quickener? And are not the embodiments of his truth and justice, in principles and laws, ways in which we know him, as truly as those of his power and life in nature and the soul? Yea, what ground is there for calling any of these manifestations *one?* Are not the modes of revealing himself in the beauty

of the flower and the sweep of the hurricane, as much two
as those in Christ and in the common soul? And, in the
creation of our intellectual and moral and emotional life, do
we not see him in forms which are quite as different as in
those of our natural and spiritual being? There are a thousand, nay, there are countless things of which it may be said,
"he speaks in each, but says something new each time,"
"reveals a new form of his being," "shows us not the same
order and aspect of truth, but wholly different aspects," just
as truly as it is said of these which are now taken to make
up the Trinity. The selection of these merely is like the old
notion, that there must be four elements and only seven
planets, or like dividing the stars into any fixed number of
constellations. The truth is, the whole universe is a manifestation of God; and there are as many modes of this
manifestation as there are objects in it, rising in clearness,
one above another, and culminating at last, not in three
orders, but in the one Christ, "the brightness of his glory
and the express image of his person."

No: we believe the vital truth of the Trinity lies at once
nearer the surface, and is wider reaching, than this idea of
three manifestations. There is one principle, one great law,
which extends throughout all religions, just as there is through
all the complicity of the natural heavens, explaining alike their
motions and forms. It is the same truth which underlies
fetichism, polytheism, gnosticism, dualism, Mariolatry, and
pantheism,—a key which unlocks not only the mystery of three
persons in the Godhead, but all the multiplied forms in which
the Deity has ever been conceived of. It consists in this.
The human soul is made, in its very nature, to want in its
worship the whole circle of Divine perfections, the almighty, gracious, good, and fair,—to want it both as an object
of contemplation and as one with which to commune. This
want, indeed, is very far from being one of which it is permanently conscious; but it is always in it as a controlling
force, at once leading it to worship, and shaping its conceptions of what is worshipped. The spirit, even in its lowest
and most grovelling state, will not be satisfied with a limited

divine nature, with that which embodies only one or two or three of the attributes of Deity. It craves them all in some form or other. And if they are not presented to it in the knowledge of one being or one person, then inevitably it is led to seek after and adore them in others.

It has been a question with theologians, whether the earliest form of natural religion was that of monotheism or polytheism. It would seem, however, both from history and on the general grounds of what the condition of human nature was in the earliest ages, that man had a countless number of deities, and deities not far away but resident with him on the earth. Brute animals, plants, the elements, things most obvious to the senses, were the ones in which he first saw the divine element. No one of these, however, could present him with all the attributes of God. The bull was a manifestation only of strength; the owl, of wisdom; the serpent, of eternity; the sun, of life-giving energy. Hence, in order to get all which the heart craved for in its worship, it was necessary to have, not one or two, but a vast number of deities. Fetichism, in some of its aspects, is false and degrading enough; and yet to the larger view there was a grand reason in it. It testifies to the aspirations of our nature for a divinity, such as could be found in no one object of earth, — not the greatest. Its truth was, that God is not far away, but manifest in the most familiar objects around us; its falsehood, the very same that we find now in the Orthodox conception of Christ, — that that which manifests God is God himself.

But men cannot be satisfied always with the worship of animals and things. These are seen to be limited and imperfect expressions of what they want. Many different things present themselves as the types of wisdom, strength, beauty, and goodness. The tendency is to idealize, to combine, to get at something better and fairer than any visible object, the unseen attribute of divinity which lies behind them, and give that a local habitation and a name. Men are deified. The various powers, first of the material then of the spiritual world, are supposed to have a personal head;

and the different departments of nature and life, the ocean, heavens and under-world, commerce, art, learning, and agriculture, are regarded as having special divinities, who preside over them, and take their interests in direct control. This multiplication of gods, especially as we find it in the mythologies of Greece and Rome and Northern Europe, is apt at first glance to seem absurd, the mere vagaries of the imagination, a useless burden placed on the religious nature. But, as we look deeper, there is seen to be a method about it. It results inevitably from the desire within us for the full circle of divine perfections. The human mind has not yet arrived at the sublime conception, that one Being is able to unite all excellencies, and to be present everywhere at once. Minerva has only wisdom; but a man wishes to adore something else than wisdom. Diana has purity; but purity alone cannot satisfy the soul. Venus has beauty and love; Apollo, grace and strength; Mars, force: but with each of these there is wanting all the rest. And so, by the very necessity of our nature, when man once starts with the idea that one person can have only a part of the divine attributes, there must be persons enough to supply them all. The same principle holds in regard to the multiplication of local divinities. Jupiter can be only in one place at once, Neptune in another, Pluto in another. But man wants to find Deity in every place, wants his care and help in every interest of life. And so, when one was localized, it became necessary to have enough for all possible localities. A pantheon, which united all the parts, was the logical result of a partition which separated the divine nature among different persons. And the truth which lies at the centre of all polytheism, is that the Divine somehow must embrace every possible perfection, and be present everywhere.

The step from polytheism to the belief in one God, perfect and omnipresent, was too long to be taken all at once. It had to be made by various stages. The work began with the Hebrews, whose great teachers, far back, spirit-taught, proclaimed the simple unity of the Divine nature, "Hear, O Israel! the Lord our God is one Lord." But the mere doc trine of God's unity was not enough, could not satisfy all the spirit's wants. The Hebrew conception of him was narrow. He was self-existence, power, purity, justice; but the God only of one people, and without those sweeter and gentler attributes which are revealed to us in the Christian Father. Hence, inevitably, the Israelites, seeking after more of God, fell into the worship of the heathen divinities around them, Bell, Dagon, Astarte, Moloch, some of whom represented those very qualities which they had failed to get in their idea of Jehovah. It was an idolatry, paradoxical as it may seem, that in one sense was divine,—a going away from the true God only to seek more of him. There was no kind of punishment—earthquake, pestilence, famine, subjugation—that was ever able to cure them of it. And it is a notable fact, that only when the sweet singers and the later prophets of Israel had enlarged the conception of Jehovah, representing him as grace and mercy and tenderness, do we find the people settling down quietly into the permanent condition of monotheism.

But with the process of combining the divine attributes into one Person, not only among the Jews but among all nations, there was another and backward movement almost inevitable, going on at the same time. The original conception of their deities, with all religions, seems to have been that of their immediate presence. Jehovah went with the Hebrews in all their wanderings, a cloud by day and pillar of fire by night: he abode in their ark, led them to battle, and governed their state. Olympus and Asgard, the dwelling-places of Jupiter and Odin, were parts of the earth. And the hosts of divinities which gathered around them—Apollo, Mercury, Venus and Minerva, Thor, Freir, Balder—were conceived of as mingling daily in the affairs of mankind. But with the doctrine of God's unity, with the conception of him as one mighty Being, embracing all the attributes which had been divided among countless divinities, the tendency was to remove him away from earth and earthly things. It was a more terrible thing to hold communion with such a Being. He could be gone to only on great occasions. A set order of men was necessary to deal with him, and his favor could be gained only by costly offerings and sacrifices. And this process of exaltation continued in the East, until he was considered not only to have no present connection with the world, but to be too great and holy even to have made it with his own hands.

But a deity like this could not long satisfy the human heart. It wanted a being, not only perfect and infinite as an object of adoration, but near and genial, to hold communion with. And out of this want we have the æons — Mind, Reason, Wisdom, Truth, Power, Life — of Gnosticism, the innumerable Buddhas of Buddhism, and the trinity of Brahma, Vishnu, and Siva, that we find in the religion of the Brahmans. They are the media by which the Deity, far removed from earth, was supposed to make it and control its affairs, — not separate persons from Deity, nor yet God himself, but emanations from him, as light from the sun, the stream from its fountain, the branches from the tree. They were incarnated in earthly forms; and it was only through them that men could know anything of the divine nature. These religions are vast heaps of superstitions, philosophic subtilties, and the wildest speculation. It is not possible for any human mind, in the present age of the world, to comprehend their full meaning, or enter into their spirit. And yet, beneath all their crudity and extravagance, the one great truth is recognized, that, however great and far away God may be, he is present likewise somehow in human affairs, and to be communed with by the human soul.

With the exaltation of the Divine attributes into one perfect Being, there came also another doctrine which has had a vast influence in the world, — that of dualism. The deities of polytheism had a mixed character, had human passions, desires, and weakness, side by side with their divine powers; and it was easy, with such aid, to explain the origin of evil. But when the Deity was conceived of as one infinite Being, the centre of all goodness, wisdom, power, the questions at once arose, What is the source of the wickedness, the imperfection, the pain, of which the world is so full? Would a good Being have created these? Could they have come into existence of themselves? Surely not. Whence, then, could they have been derived, but from another being, the embodiment of all evil qualities, and powerful enough to match God? Hence the belief in two principles, beginning far back among the sages of ancient Persia, taking, in the third century, the form of Manicheism, and descending to our own time in the popular doctrine of Satan, the prince of darkness, as opposed to God, the Father of Light. And with the common idea of evil, — as an essence and not an incident in the universe, a part of the final consummation of all things and not a stage of imperfection through which we are to pass on, with the idea that an evil place and some evil souls are to be eternal, — there is no escape from dualism. Its logic is unanswerable. An omnipotent and all-wise Deity, so good as to hate evil, would not create it to be an ultimate part of his universe. And it is this truth, too great and precious to be slurred over, that lies at the base of the dualistic philosophy.

And now we are prepared to see how these principles, running through so many other doctrines, are carried out in the origin and meaning of the Church doctrine of the Trinity. With the Hebrews themselves, the idea of God, which had come to them finished from the later prophets as one exalted Being, was enough, especially when combined with their anticipation of the Messiah and his reign on earth, to satisfy their wants. But not so with the Greeks and Romans, when Christianity, and with it, in spite of our Saviour's revelation of the Father, the old Hebrew idea of the Divine nature, went forth among them. They wanted him as a present Deity, and wanted somehow to incorporate in their worship those larger and grander conceptions of the Divine which had come to them through Christ, — justice and mercy, hatred of sin and love of the sinner. A Deity dwelling in the heaven of heavens, and yet present everywhere on earth, they had not yet learned to conceive of as possible in one person. They were qualities which, it seemed to them, could not dwell together, yet which were all divine, and all what they could not help adoring. And hence, what more natural than that, with the unity of God's being, they should strive to unite the conception of three persons, one in the heavens, just, wise, mighty, the eternal Father, whom no man had seen or could see; one in Christ, loving, merciful, tender, supplementing what they thought was impossible in the character of the first; and a third, the spirit of God descending on earth, operating directly on the souls of men, and with whom they held communion? It was not done all at once, not done consciously at first. The three persons seem to have been made divine separately to begin with, and then afterwards, from logical necessity, united in one; the process being helped by the subtilties of Greek philosophy, and the result apparently sanctioned by some things in the phraseology of Scripture. But, however this may be, the thing itself was no work of human ingenuity, no exceptional development, but a legitimate growth, the inevitable continuation, if not culmination, of a process which had been going on from the very dawn of religious thought. And from that time, yea, and all down through the ages, it has been the only form, under existing conditions, in which the highest truth about God could show itself.

We find, then, two vital elements of truth in the Church doctrine of the Trinity. The first is its placing before us all the attributes of divinity as objects of adoration, the gentler ones of mercy, love, sympathy, as well as the sterner ones of justice, power, wisdom, and holiness. It is all of these which the soul needs. It is better that we should have them in two persons, rather than to have only a part of them in one; the error of form being of slight moment as compared with that in substance. The real question is, how much of the Divine nature do we get before the soul, not in what ways do we get it. And the mere unity of God in that age of the world would have been a bald, unsatisfying faith. Then, too, with the richer, deeper aspirations which Christianity aroused in the human soul, it was inevitable, that, if Christ had not been deified, some other and lower being must have been. It is a curious fact, mentioned by Mrs. Jameson, that in the Middle Ages the conception of Christ as the embodiment of mercy and compassion was gradually obscured, the idea of him as a stern judge taking its place. And what was the result? Why, the human soul could not give up the worship of these divine qualities, and the Virgin Mary was endowed with them, and made the object of the people's adoration. She is represented in paintings of that period as the pure, tender, loving woman, interceding before her Son, just the same as Christ had been before the Father, for the welfare of our lost race. She is now adored in all Roman Catholic countries equally with the Father, Son, and Spirit; is really a fourth person of the Godhead. It is worship which arose in precisely the same way, and on the same grounds, as that of Christ. The only reason why it was not transferred to Protestantism, along with the doctrine of the Trinity, is, that the necessities of Protestant theology have restored Christ to his original place as the embodiment of grace and mercy. It shows how inevitably the soul must have these qualities somehow in its conception of Deity, and is a most striking confirmation that this is, indeed, a vital thing in the doctrine of the Trinity.

Another truth which underlies it is the immediate presence of God in the world and with the soul. It matters not how exalted and pure and immaterial we consider him to be, how far removed from men in the grandeur and holiness of his character, there is one part of his personality, the Holy Spirit, not a dim influence but God himself, that is taught as pervading the world, and dwelling most intimately in the human heart. It is a most glorious truth. There was never any thing in the polytheistic conception of religion, with all the earthly locality which it assigned its gods, no lares or penates presiding over the household, no idol in its shrine, no image carried on the breast, which brought the divine so near, so immediate to the world, as the Church doctrine of the Spirit. We ourselves are his temple. He warns, directs, convinces, comforts. His breath is our inspiration. Our joy is in his touch. And through him we mount up, ever and ever, to the higher life. It is impossible to estimate too highly what the value of this truth has been through all the

Christian ages. It has been the connecting link between the Father, removed far off in dim eternity, and his children here on earth; the only way in which the faith, if not the heart, of the Church could have had a present God. And the intellectual fiction of a divided personality, by which it has been accomplished, has been a slight matter in comparison with the greatness and worth of the truth which has been within it.

It is these facts about the Trinity which suggest the true method of doing our Unitarian work. Two tendencies, each of them towards the unity of God, are now in operation with the Christian Church. One is the concentrating of all the divine attributes in the person of Christ; the words of one of the most popular Orthodox teachers, that the Father is only a dim and shadowy effluence rising up far away behind the deity of the Son, being true very largely of the common heart. The other tendency is to the oneness of the entire godhead in the person of the Father. And it is between these two issues,—not between the authority of Christ and the intuitions of the soul, which is merely a preliminary skirmish,—that we believe is to be fought the great battle of the future. It is in the line of this faith, the conception of God the Father as all in all, that our work lies. And there is only a single way in which it can be done. All past experience shows, that to attack the Trinity,— or what is now becoming the chief point in the doctrine, the deity of Christ,— on its logical side, is utterly in vain. It is clung to in face of the clearest demonstrations of its untruth. It somehow feeds the soul, gives it the fulness of the Divine nature; and what avails it to prove by argument that food is dust and ashes when millions of beings are using it every day, and finding it give them grandest health and strength? The only way is to make sure, that all the truth which is in their doctrine is furnished likewise in ours. There is nothing in the logical form of the Trinity which its believers care for. There are thousands of them who cannot repeat its terms, and scarcely any two, even of its scholars, who define it the same way. It is the underlying truth which makes them hold it. We need to show, that all the divine attributes, all which the soul craves for of God, inhere and must inhere in the one person of the Father; and to insist that the whole of that one person is here on the earth, is ready to dwell in the humblest soul, as truly as in the heavens. We want to show, not by demonstration merely, but actually, experimentally, that our faith can afford as much of Deity and the Divine nature, and bring men as truly into communion with the Eternal Spirit, as that of the Trinity. It is only so far as we can do this, only so far as we can show that all which is vital in their system belongs just the same to ours, that they ought to take it, that the world will really be the better for their having it. And, when we have accomplished this work, we shall find without argument, without one thrust of logic, its intellectual form, like a body without life, will shrivel up and waste away. We might learn a most important lesson in this respect from our Universalist brethren. When they started as a denomination, instead of asserting directly the doctrine of the Divine Unity, the exigencies of their cause led them rather to insist on those attributes of the Father's character which had been obscured, or ascribed only to Christ, — his mercy, goodness, love, and grace. The result is, that not only is the whole denomination itself Unitarian in theology, but it has done a work in this way, with the world at large, which is more significant even than that of extending its own original doctrine.

We believe, then, that, as a whole, the Church dogma of the Trinity has had a most important and providential mission to perform in the religious education of our race. Its error was the partition, not the negation, of truth. There was no doctrine of the Divine Unity possible in that age of the world when it was first developed, which could ever have done its work. It is, perhaps, one of the finest examples in all history, not only of the soul of good in things evil, but of the way in which the Eternal Spirit makes one imperfection play into another, and from the shapeless blocks of falsehood builds up the mighty arch of truth. But, with all the service this doctrine has done in the past, we cannot regard it as a finality, cannot believe it is the absolute verity. The law of its development, like all the rest of God's laws, is running forward into the future not less than coming up from the past. The same forces, acting on the same principles which led to the world's growth out of fetichism and polytheism, are still at work. And the culmination of the process, the final doctrine in which the whole race is evermore to rest, is that of one Person, the Eternal Father, embracing all excellence, immanent in all things, and accessible, without rite or priest or intercessor, directly to all souls.

Art. IV. — ON SOME CONDITIONS OF THE MODERN MINISTRY.

Proceedings of the National Unitarian Conference, in Session at Syracuse. — Report on the Supply of Ministers. By S. H. WINCKLEY.

THE claims and prospects of the Christian ministry have generally been urged, as they are urged here, with a noble disregard to certain material conditions of its existence. It is to the honor of the profession, that this disregard is especially conspicuous in all its own appeals for encouragement, and the inducements it offers to its own recruits. It has left to the literature of romance, such as "The Minister's Wooing" and "Dr. Johns," the statement of its actual relations with the public that maintains it; and to secular journals, like "The Nation" or "The Round Table," the protest against the straitened terms by which it often lives. Among themselves, the members of that profession — whatever their private confessions of difficulty or hardship in their experience — have said little, we might almost say have been unconscious, of what to many has seemed its chief embarrassment, in comparison with that great spiritual want, that great Christian task, to which its services are pledged.

And yet there are reasons why the members of that profession should make their own voice heard on a point which has attracted so much public attention. It is well that it should be looked at from their position, and spoken of in counsel with one another, and with the community at large. Curious misunderstandings, and injustice in the zeal for justice, are sure to follow when it is looked at only from a distance. Thus a writer in "The Round Table," commenting indignantly on the scanty ministerial salaries in Connecticut, speaks of three thousand dollars as the *least* that ought to be paid, charging the prevalent scale of maintenance to a deliberate wrong on the part of the public. We say nothing of the very desirable standard of recompense proposed: would that it were possible! But, as to the charge, we extremely regret that it should have gained ground, and even been echoed from some professional channels. So far from doing wilful injustice to its religious institutions, we consider that, in the older parts of the country at least, they are the pet extravagance of the people, and that the community is taxed to a very unreasonable amount for their support. True, this extravagance consists generally in the multiplication of sects and accumulation of church debts; rarely, though sometimes, in paying salaries unreasonably large. But it ought to be more distinctly seen, that the public is not ungenerous, but unwise, in its expenditure for church purposes; and that the chief ecclesiastical want, financially speaking, is not a greater munificence, but a truer economy, in the appropriation of its means.

There is one fact, at the outset, which it appears to us important to state very explicitly. In plain terms, it is simply this: This profession, along with a cordial welcome, with many social privileges, with as sure and liberal and honorable support as any to the individual who enters it, does not, as things are, provide — *and the public does not care that it shall provide* — for the maintenance of his family, or the costs of a domestic establishment. We say nothing of the few instances to the contrary that might be pointed out, except to say that they are exceptional. In every case with which we are well enough acquainted to speak with confidence, a preacher who maintains his family respectably, and clear of debt, does it by means outside of his profession. We need not press the details. But we know that many a young man, on entering it, does not understand this cardinal financial fact; and for want of it we constantly see cases of what, in any other profession, would be a criminal and reckless haste in assuming the heavy responsibility of what is called a "settlement in life," together with a false and hurtful expectation on the part of one's parish or friends, that he shall do it. Hence, in more instances than we like to confess, the humiliating and painful spectacle of chronic insolvency and hopeless debt, in a man in full health, in full activity, in full course of professional success; or else a secret, dreary, painful struggle, aggravated perhaps by the dread of parochial change, and darkening with years into the sure prospect of poverty for one's self, dependence and suffering to those for whose welfare he has pledged his own.

We have alluded, in a single word, to those changes of parochial relation which make this point press so much more keenly. But we must stop to show how it affects this more than most other professions. In the first place, a change of this sort suspends — in many cases, definitely cuts off — the whole of one's customary resources. Few will have the courage or ability to wait for the loss to be made fully good. Many will be compelled, by stress of need, to accept such measure of compensation as presently offers. So, by sharp and sudden steps, a man may decline from comparative ease to real indigence, from the mere lack of ability to bide his time. Again, in almost any other profession, a faithful workman may reasonably hope that his legitimate income in it will be larger at fifty years than at thirty, corresponding with his increasing needs. In this, almost alone, the likelihood is that it will be less, — relatively, perhaps, much less. Pride, expectation, sympathy, popular gifts, are often mostly on the side of the young: the older must win what they win with less enthusiasm, and by a soberer esteem. The days of anxious dependence, or perhaps penury, come just when the harvest of life is gathered in other callings; as the ease of an ample present maintenance comes in this just in those early years when other callings bring their season of anxiety and struggle. So that, in a great measure, the pecuniary conditions on which the ordinary economies of human life rest, are in this case reversed.

Again, a compulsory change of residence — whether actual, impending, or only seen as probable in the distance — takes out the heart and the stability from whatever else a man may bethink him of for a resource. We wonder, sometimes, at those miracles of thrift by which country ministers of the older times, on salaries almost nominal, could afford a style of living and a hospitality unknown to their successors, and still provide college education for their boys, and a comfortable independence for their old age. But in truth it was a comparatively simple matter. The salary was a *life-annuity*. The parish was a life-long home. A modest estate of two or three acres — perhaps thirty ; a social position, definite and unchallenged ; an absolute deliverance from restless ambitions or apprehensions of change; a thrifty turning of the soil at need, or, frequently, the resource of family pupils or college exiles, — made conditions of material support such as most men might envy, and any wise man find sufficient. Besides, the salary was no measure of the real professional emolument. Was a parsonage to be built? the foundation-stones, a large part of the lumber, and half the days' labor would very likely be voluntary gifts ; did charities and hospitalities strain the narrow income? the housekeeping stores might be swelled from the larders of half the parish ; in "killing-time," the choicest side of bacon would find its way to the minister's ; in apple-harvest came, with brief emphasis, a message from the largest orchard in town, "Send your barrels."* All this, not in the way of "donation-parties," —

---

* In illustration, we copy from the record kept by a country minister's wife of her first month's housekeeping : —

Feb. 4, 1818. — Barrel of apples, barrel of sweet apples, loaf of wheat bread, and bowl of cream, Mr. and Mrs. Williams. Two loaves of brown bread, sausages, pork-steaks, salt, pickles, Mrs. Col. Whitney. Bottle of wine, Lewis Eager.

Load of walnut wood, Col. Eager. Bowl of soap, Mary Ann Whitney.
5. Cheese, sausages, Col. Eager. Roasting-piece of beef, Mr. Benj Munroe. Bottle of cream, Mrs. B. Munroe.
6. Pot of honey, Mrs. Williams

too often a shabby apology, in the guise of charity, for the neglect of justice, — but in the way of frank reciprocity and neighborly custom. We do not speak of it as a thing whose loss is on the whole to be regretted. It belonged to a state of things which has passed away, and is not likely to return. But it has left us two real embarrassments in dealing with this matter, — first, a state of general feeling or expectation, touching a minister's style of living, which ill fits the change in his relations to the public; and, second, a standard of pecuniary recompense which encourages the multiplying rather than the strengthening of parishes. If a seceding church can muster its six hundred dollars of revenue, — the amount of its old pastor's life-annuity, — it considers itself justified in offering it, as the uncertain income of an uncertain term, to the candidates for a position growing ever more and more precarious, — we need not say with what probable effect on the dignity and ability of the profession. In showing how the

---

Half-a-peck of Indian and 2 qts. of rye meal, Mrs. Col. Whitney.
Cruden's Concordance, 2 pairs of gloves, Madame Whitney.
7. Bottle of cream, 2 quarts milk, Mrs. B. Munroe.
Bottle of milk, Mrs. Williams.
Bottle of currant wine and figs, Madame Whitney.
Half a large squash, Col. Whitney.
8. 7 lbs. of flour and 1 pair of chickens, Dr. Ball.
A pot of soap, Mrs. Oliver Eager.
10. Beefsteaks, &c., Mrs. Benj. Munroe.
11. Piece of beef and bushel of rye, Winslow Brigham.
Piece of beef and a cheese, Jonas Ball.
Piece of beef and 4 lbs. butter, Abel Warren.
Shoulder of pork, Phin. Davis.
Loaf of bread and mince pie, Col. Eager.
Bottle of cream, Mrs. O. Eager.
Bottle of cream, Mrs. B. Munroe.
12. Bottle of cream, Mrs. Williams.
13. Load of wood, Abel Warren.
14. 8 pints of milk, Col. Whitney.
4 lbs. butter, lard, honey, sausages, Mrs. Joel Parmenter.
Load of wood, Silas Bailey.
16. Bushel of oats, Benj. Munroe.

17. Bbl. of cider, piece of beef, Col. Crawford.
A spare-rib, N. Brigham.
A chine of pork and sausages; loaf of bread.
19. Piece of beef.
Three pecks of Indian meal, one peck of rye meal.
20. 3 quarts of milk, Mrs. Williams.
21. Load of wood, Jonas Bartlett.
30 sausages, bowl of cream, Benj. Munroe.
Piece of beef, peck of apples, a cheese, a loaf of brown bread, ditto of white bread, and four quarts of soap, Silas Bailey.
23. Bottle of cream, Sol. Sherman.
26. 4 cords of wood, Asa Fay.
27. A large spare-rib, Jonas Ball.
Mar. 1. — A keg of pickled cucumbers, Col. Crawford.
2. A salmon-trout (5 lbs.) from Winnipiseogee, Sam. Seaver.
March-meeting cake, Mrs. Col. Whitney.
4. 8 quarts of milk, Mrs. B. Munroe.
8 quarts of milk, Mrs. Sherman.
5. Load of wood, Oliver Munroe.
Half a day's work (chopping wood), by Asa Maynard, Luke Howe, Taylor Brigham, John Carruth, Mr. Rice, and Nahum Eager.

economies of the earlier time were possible, we have shown, at the same time, how hard they are to practise now. Little encouragement to underdrain the glebe or plant the orchard, where five years is a long tenure, and most are less than three; nor of other avocations will many flourish in a migrating and itinerant life. And, such as they are, public opinion sets sharp limits. We remember the scandal in Hollis Street, when Mr. Pierpont sought to "turn an honest penny" with his lathe; a most estimable friend and excellent minister, of inventive genius in mechanics, was carped at as "that machinist" by some who heard him preach; scarce any measure of gospel grace would sustain a carpenter, a tentmaker, or a fisherman in the apostolical succession now; and, though a minister may put his spare revenues in public stocks, he may not, without cavil, give them openly to the exchangers, and so receive them back with usury. Wise or foolish, we do not complain of these restrictions; only refer to them to show, that the one economical condition of *permanence* in the elder ministry has not yet been made good.

Perhaps we shall be pardoned for a word, in this connection, touching the equivocal relations with parishes, which grow out of unsettled questions of professional duty. We refer to those cases where a man's honest conscience brings him into direct collision with the dominant feeling, or dominant interest, of his parish. The case of Mr. Pierpont was one heroic and memorable instance; but Mr. Pierpont was the winner in that long struggle of fourteen years, purely through the legal advantage of his life-tenure. It is only justice to younger men to say, that his very success has made any similar struggle far more difficult for them; since it did something to establish the now universal stipulation, for the termination of contract at a few months' notice. Morally regarded, such collisions as these we refer to have shown the very noblest side of the professional character, particularly among our younger men, who had every thing to risk, and little to hope, in a conflict of conscience and self-interest. Still, aside from class feeling or personal feeling, let us endeavor to look at the simple fact. It is not *being true to one's own conscience* that makes the sore point, but *doing it at others' expense*. A man of sensitive feeling is compelled to see, that, unless he stands frankly ready to forfeit his professional support, when he engages in such a controversy, he does one of two things: either he compels a part of his congregation to pay him money against their own wish, — a thing in the highest degree repulsive to one of honorable feeling; or else, by a division in the parish, he compels his friends to pay twice as much as they agreed, or would willingly consent, that his salary may be unimpaired. Either alternative is apt to appear equally discreditable to him and unjust to them. And the only solution that will probably seem to him at once dignified and honest, — a sorrowful solution at best, — is, in event of such a collision, frankly to submit the question of the continuance of his relation to the fresh, unbiassed, decision of the parish. He may sacrifice, for a time, his personal interest, and even his means of livelihood; but he has done his very best service to the real honor and independence of his calling, — a service of which his successor, if not himself, is sure to find the benefit. A man says he cannot afford it. Very well, then, he cannot afford to stay in that particular pulpit; at least, he cannot afford to press that particular point of conscience. An honest man, in such a case, is likely to consider that he has entered into a definite business contract, to fulfil a course of duty assumed to be well understood, and that he expects, quarterly or monthly, to draw his stipulated pay. What entitles him to that pay at all, excepting the free consent of the body corporate of his parish? This reciprocal obligation, official on one side and pecuniary on the other, very greatly embarrasses the simple case of conscience, which seems at first sight to be offered.* It is very much to be regretted,

---

* A friend of our own, minister of a Unitarian congregation in England, met a case of this nature in a way which seems to us manly and honorable. Learning that part of the revenue of his chapel was derived from the rent of beer-shops, — which, as a consistent temperance man, he earnestly opposed, — he first remonstrated with the trustees of his congregation; then, on their declining to withdraw the property from that use, he declined to receive so much of his salary as was derived from that source. The result naturally was his withdrawal at the end of the year, — with no hard thoughts on either side, — to useful and honored service in other fields.

that the problem, when it comes up, is not left to solve itself (as it often might) in a natural and right way: but a pressure is brought to bear from without; a cry of "political preaching" is raised on one side, and on the other there are never wanting those to goad a sensitive conscience into a position which there may be neither force of will nor capacity of intellect nor popular gifts to sustain. There are cases, again, where a wrong public spirit seems to offer a direct challenge to whatever of right conscience and Christian manliness there may be in the profession. And, whatever a scrupulous casuistry may decide in any given instance, this at least ought to be said, that the profession owes the rescue of its honor to those, many and nameless, who have proved their simple allegiance to duty; and, to their great cost, have accepted the challenge in the same obstinate and indomitable temper that offered it.

We look, for the solution of these embarrassments, to the truer relations between the profession and the public, which we are sure will grow from this long controversy,—truer, not in the sense of mechanical fixity, but of adjustment to altered conditions of thought and other habits of life. In particular, as we hold, there must be developed, in forms as yet unsettled and unfamiliar, a style of professional character and expectation, and a code of professional duty, the equivalent of that *loyalty to the welfare of the parish as such*, which prevailed when this profession was a more definite and precisely recognized order than it is now. And this must come mainly from the general recognition of a precise and definite sphere of duty in it,—one not quite commensurate, perhaps, with all the ranges of human thought, or all the applications of divine morality, yet broad enough and grand enough to enlist the enthusiasm and command the loyalty of competent men. In a period of "drift," of party passion and of restless change, it has been inevitable, that many of the noblest minds enlisted in this profession should believe in ideas, not institutions; should even expressly disclaim any loyalty to the Church, claiming to be only servants of the Truth. But the task of a liberal Christianity will be incomplete, until it shall have perfected an organization so divinely generous and noble, so humanly tender and dear, so entwined with the best traditions and affections of the past, as to be worthy, for its own sake, of the utmost devotion that a man can give.

To this, then, our argument and illustration tend, — to an organization of the Christian ministry among us, better adapted than any we have attained as yet, to the needs of the time, to the fitnesses and opportunities of its members. The conditions which appear to us most important to be observed are these two, — first, that it shall turn to account the spontaneous enthusiasm and exuberant vitality that belong to the first years of active manhood; and, second, that it shall interpose some check to those personal anxieties and embarrassments which often take from the later years of professional life full half their vigor. It is not too much to say, that every thing turns on the direction given to the first five years of service. Here let the Church take a lesson from the State. When the young, highly-educated officer enters the army of the nation, it is on a low grade, with hard service and poor pay. He does not grudge that he must spend weary years in a frontier garrison, or risk his life in a pitiful skirmish with half-naked savages, or reach the prime of manhood rarely knowing the charm of cultivated society, and never expecting the secure comforts of a home. And yet, in this service, with all its petty rivalries and jealousies, its few opportunities of a finer culture, its sullen and haughty pride, we find the very type, all the world over, of professional honor, fidelity unto death, and a self-respect that bides no stain. Shall that which some of us love to call the service of the Lord Jesus, the captain of our salvation, — what others of us prefer to call the service of truth, humanity, and the living God, — win less enthusiasm, fidelity, zeal, than the following the nation's flag? We are well assured, that a very large proportion of those who enter this profession at five-and-twenty, do it with hearts all ready to respond to the call for service just as arduous and as poorly paid as that, — service on the frontier, in weary circuits, or among the poor in the city streets, — if any man would show the way. And this service would educate and train them, as nothing else could, for the very highest work and the very noblest privileges of the Christian ministry in riper years.

In illustration of what we have urged, and by way of experiment, we add the following outline of a *working plan*, which has received the approval of some of our most intelligent and experienced men. Let us suppose, that the American Unitarian Association — or any similar body, holding sufficient funds — should offer to enlist for special service, under its own direction, a limited number of young candidates for the ministry.* We would suggest some such conditions as these: That the term of enlistment be for a definite time, say five years; that the immediate compensation in money be a sum strictly limited for personal expenses, — say two hundred dollars a year, — understanding that lodging and board will be found in the place of service, and that the necessary costs of travel will be defrayed; that an equal sum, say one thousand dollars in all, be paid at the end of five years' acceptable service, or a just proportion of it in case of disability or death; that any candidate who, by marriage or settlement or engaging in any other vocation, relinquishes the service, loses all further claim upon the Association; while the directing council or committee are held bound in honor to promote, in all fit ways, the professional advancement and welfare of its faithful servants. Such a plan would offer no interference, or even modification, to such professional relations or personal aspirations as now exist; but we are sure that it would open to a class of young men (however small), standing always ready, — those to whom the ministry is not a profession merely but a *vocation*, — an opportunity which

---

* Among the forms which this special service may take, we may indicate missionary service in prisons or hospitals, or among the poor; the gathering of churches and Sunday schools in cities; education of freedmen and refugees; the supply of old and dwindling parishes; experimental labors in new communities; together with auxiliary service in large and laborious city parishes. All these are tasks eminently fit to be done under responsible direction; essential to the complete work of the Church as an institution in society; and the very best training for the early years of professional life.

they would embrace with joy, and would be the beginning of a new and nobler future for the profession. The certainty of employment and support in his chosen work is the best privilege a young man can ask; the habit of personal economy, rigidly taught, is one of the first steps to a manly independence in it; a definite, modest capital in hand is one of the best guaranties of that independence; while that immense vitality, that vast fund of moral enthusiasm, in the educated young,—always existing, as much as when it flashed itself suddenly into notice all over the land, five years ago, at the nation's call,—would be used to noble account, instead of being wasted among mean anxieties, or lost in the weary, broken, unprofitable way.

Moreover, we hold that a council of wise and experienced men, such as our proposition supposes, might do a much-needed service of guardianship and direction for those to whom the work of the ministry is new and strange. It is needless to point out the many ways in which it might be exercised, to check serious mistakes of inexperience, to prevent fruitless and painful controversies, to adjust the special qualities of the men to the fittest line of service. What wastes of moral force, what sharp personal grievances, might be saved! Any jealousy lest young men should be unfairly dealt with, and kept injuriously in the shade, would of course be met by the fact, that the service proposed is purely voluntary, and is suggested not as a substitute, but as a supplement, to the actual methods of professional employ. Any broader and broadening control over the work of the ministry, as now constituted, it must win by the demonstration of its fitness. We assume, in suggesting it, that *the need really exists* which is set forth so earnestly in a class of documents we have referred to; and that the need must increase very greatly, in proportion to the large and magnificent scale of action contemplated in our more recent enterprises. If liberal Christianity is ever to do its perfect work, or any respectable share of it, in the great Christian regeneration which our civilization needs, it must be by agencies more extended, more harmonious, more wisely directed, controlled by a truer economy, and capable of enlisting a nobler enthusiasm, than any we have established in the past.

And, finally, it appears to us clear, that the first step towards such a consummation must be taken by a body actually existing, commanding public confidence, and having the disposal of revenues sufficient to make a fair experiment. We therefore urge it, with all respect, upon the directors of the Association we have named. To the suspicions that might be whispered as to ecclesiastical rule and spiritual control, we answer, that some confidence may well be yielded, and some discretion entrusted, to men of our own choice, responsible from year to year to the public that commits to them its voluntary gifts; while the experience of all the world, we think, shows the vastly greater enthusiasm and efficiency of any service under responsible, acknowledged leadership. It has often seemed to us the cruellest among the real hardships of this profession, that the young candidate for its services and honors is ushered at once from the seclusion of his preparatory years, from "the quiet and still air of delightful studies," upon the responsible duties and among the complicated social relations of the modern ministry. There are strong, able, and willing men — there are, occasionally, men of genius and power — to whom this prompt assumption of all manly responsibilities is easy, glad, and natural. For such, — men of strong convictions and matured energies, — the ordinary conditions of the Protestant ministry seem to have been specially created. For them, we are glad of all its liberties and all its trusts. But there are other men, — of less natural force perhaps, yet not less valuable in the diversities of administration which the Church requires, — to whom a season of preliminary service, a novitiate (as it were) in the duties and trials of their profession, under the guidance of wise counsellors, seems the one thing needful for the ripening of their powers. Who can tell the number of those, uncomplaining and unknown, who find themselves, at middle life, in a false position, out of which they see no way of escape, simply from the lack of an opportunity at the start to test their powers, or adapt them to a suitable field? Fine, venerable traditions, touching many of us personally and closely, have made this profession very dear and honorable to us; and we greatly desire to see the adoption of any course which shall endue it with fresh honors, by giving fresh nobleness and inspiration to its work.

Art. V. — BANCROFT'S HISTORY OF THE UNITED STATES, Vol. IX.

Six years ago, we welcomed the eighth volume of Mr. Bancroft's History. It was the first in the history of the Revolution. Since that time, the people of this country have carried through another war, for the complete determination of those eternal principles which led them to their first struggle. They have worked through it with unwavering resolution, worthy to be compared with that in which their independence was born. The second struggle has also resembled the first in its varying fortunes; failure and success alternating in the efforts of the true cause, as they only do in the very noblest of dramas. May we add, perhaps, that this second war of independence has resembled the first in its illustration of the worth and power of a people, whether that people have leaders or have none? Led or not led, even "a headless democracy drifts to victory." As, in the crucibles of history, the reputations of the Revolution are tested, straw and wood gave way long ago, paste and colored glass lasted a little longer, and now all the foils and pinchbecks are beginning to fuse, and there are left, all the more brilliant because the rest are gone, a few real diamonds set in pure gold. Of the time " that tried men's souls," there were many showy reputations, but, after all is over, so few real heroes. The last six years have tried men's souls as the seven years of the Revolution never did. And the verdict of history upon them, after a hundred years, will be of the determined resolution, the serene faith, and so of the unhesitating power of a free people. Will there be more than one or perhaps two names of men whom history will remember as of the very first, rising above the general crowd of those who have nobly dared and nobly suffered?

While the nation has, in these immense studies, reviewed all it knew of the histories of its fathers, Mr. Bancroft, forward among the foremost in the cause, speaking and acting his best wherever he seemed most needed, has been, at the same time, steadily working on in the history of the Revolution. We have now his second volume of that history, the ninth volume of the history of the country. Beginning with the morning after the Declaration of Independence, the volume ends, with a certain dramatic fitness, with "that broadest generalization of all" which follows the narrative of the presentation of Franklin to Louis Sixteenth, when France recognized the independence declared two years before. This volume of the old history is all full of the lessons of the new. The American people will read it in a different spirit from that in which they read the volumes before; just as the author has written with new power, and with purposes newly defined, under the light of present illustrations. It is not simply that we know the difference now between a haversack and a howitzer; it is not that we have general officers who had never seen a regiment together seven years ago, who have now had a wider experience than ever Greene had, or Washington. It is no mere matter of the surface which has been illustrated. We have seen the jealousy of competitors whose quarrels for rank seemed to them more important than victory over the enemy; we have seen the passionate favor of a moment of success changed into blame as passionate in a moment of failure; we have seen the cowardice by which barking curs can accuse, before the nation, public officers, whose duty to the nation compel them to make no reply. So we have had living before our eyes the miserable intrigues of the Continental Congress, of the Conway cabal, and of those poor ambitions in which Lee and Gates lost their short-lived reputations for ever. Most remarkable of all, the struggle in which the Union was preserved has taught us, in present life, the essential principles from which the Union was born. Mr. Bancroft could not have written his noble chapter on the Confederation before these years of analysis and victory, which have tested the worth and the strength of the Constitution.

The volume divides itself first into the effects of the Declaration of Independence at home and abroad. Next come the military operations of 1776, interrupted only by the chapters which describe the negotiations of the Howes and the course of opinion in England. Next, and before the history of 1777, is a valuable study of the American constitutions, as they were formed at various periods of the war. Burgoyne's campaign in the North and Howe's movement upon Philadelphia both come into the volume, which then closes by the very curious study of the Confederation to which we have alluded, by an analysis of the Conway and Gates intrigue, and by the narrative of the foreign negotiations which brings it to a close.

We were all of us bred to regard the revolutionary period as a golden age, so far as our fathers were concerned. Indeed, to the very youthful mind, there arose sometimes the anxious question, — How it could be, seeing the American armies seemed to be all made up of virtuous heroes, despising death, and led by paladins of superhuman valor, of whom Arnold was the exceptional traitor, that, in a war between them and the English and Hessian mercenaries, the struggle could have lingered so long. As our readers know, this fond delusion has been ruthlessly dissipated since we were children. Mr. Bancroft stands in the front rank of relentless analysts who dispel all such glamour, and, in doing so, show the real difficulties which the determination of the people and the gallantry of their best leaders had to encounter. In this volume, he bravely stands with his back to the wall, and strikes right and left at almost all comers. Schuyler, Lee, and Gates; Heath, Putnam, Greene, Sullivan, Wayne, and Reed; and, of the civilians, both Adamses, most of the members of Congress, Arthur Lee, Silas Dean, and Izard, with others, "too many for to name," — come in for a rap from relentless history. Even Robert Morris does not pass quite scathless. So much of justification is there for the charge made in conversation, that Mr. Bancroft wishes to make of the history an historical romance of which Washington and Franklin are the only heroes.

But this charge is by no means just. Mr. Bancroft bears steady testimony to the constancy of the people to its determination to carry the thing through; and to the wisdom which, on the whole, characterized the popular endeavor, whenever to the people a fair appeal could be made. It is idle to pretend, as a certain sentimentalism in France did pretend at the time, that the armies of the Revolution were armies of Arcadian shepherds, whose crooks were hardly developed into firelocks. It is the duty of the historian, writing at the end of a century, to expose what is left of such absurdities; and, if Mr. Bancroft has failed, it is a failure on the right side.

The truth is, that the first two or three years of the Revolution were spent, by officers as well as soldiers, in learning the art of war. We need only the illustration to which we have already referred, of what went on, both in the loyal and confederate armies, in 1861, 1862, and 1863, to show how impossible it is to acquire a working knowledge of that art excepting in the field. Washington himself says, in the autumn of 1776, that he had not a general officer who had ever seen more than two regiments together before the war began. It is no discredit to such men to say, that they made mistakes when they were first called upon to apply in practice such theoretical knowledge as they had gained. Nor do we believe that the military men whom they received from Europe rendered to them the help in this regard that they expected. It was twelve or thirteen years since the Continental wars had ended. And, although many men from Europe presented themselves wishing high command in the American armies, very few of them had held service in Europe requiring them to direct the movements of bodies of men. Lee, Montgomery, Conway, and Stirling were certainly of very little service in the lead of men. Steuben and Pulaski were probably the best of them. But Steuben had attained no higher rank in Frederic's active service than that of a captain who had acted as a brigade adjutant, and Pulaski is probably correctly described by Carlyle as "having a talent for impromptu soldiering." It may be added, that the experience of three centuries now, from the time of De Soto to this moment, has shown that the military science of Europe requires immense changes before it can be adapted to America. On the other hand, indeed, the light-infantry tactics of modern times were carried from America by Cornwallis and the other foreign officers, and introduced into the English and Continental services. Very fortunately for us, there was no more experienced skill in the conduct of the English armies than in that of our own. Where we should be to-day if Clive had lived to be placed at the head of them, instead of the incompetent illegitimate uncle of the king, is a question which the students of "ifs" are fond of asking. For ourselves, we believe we should be just where we are. The steady determination of the American people was something which no skill in leadership could break down. For all that, we are glad that we were left to the very tender mercies of Howe and Clinton, directed by the waywardness of Germaine and the pig-headed obstinacy of the king.

Let us grant, then, that all the American generals were learning their business in the first years of the war. That is no disgrace to them. Let us grant, that when Putnam, at Brooklyn, sent a brigade to repulse the whole English army, he acted under the impulse of fight, which makes men determine to do something, without much study how much will come of it. It is not a disgrace to Putnam's memory. It is simply the acknowledgment that he was a brave, impulsive man, used to wood-fighting, but without any experience in the broader movements of the field. We find it necessary to say all this, because it is evident that the publication of Mr. Bancroft's volume will call forth a multitude of side-discussions as to details in the great conflict, and that half the skirmishes and battles of the war will have to be fought over again — on paper.

In the limited space which we can command, we do not propose to go into any such discussions. Unless some of them assume more critical importance than we now think probable, we shall not enter into them. We have attempted, in what we have already said, to enter into the general principles which we think should govern the discussion. Certainly we do not think Mr. Bancroft is to blame in awakening it again.

Of the two commanders who led the English forces in 1777, it is hard to say whether the English people had most right to be indignant with Burgoyne or with Howe. It appears from a good-natured excursus of Mr. Carlyle, in his "Frederick," that Burgoyne won his laurels in an attack on Valencia d'Alcantara, in Spain, Aug. 27, 1762. The storm was very grand, according to the English newspapers of the time; and the troops behaved with great courage. As their loss was four killed and twenty-one wounded, the perils were not of that kind which now make reputations. Such as they were, however, Burgoyne made his. With the assistance of some good plays which he wrote for the theatre, and with the controlling advantage that he was the illegitimate son of one lord and the son-in-law of another, he was, at the end of fourteen years, put in charge of the best-equipped army which England could send out, to separate New England from the middle provinces, and to crush out the war. Burgoyne arrived in Quebec on the 6th of May; on the 6th of June, he had taken Ticonderoga; and the war minister then wrote to General Howe that he anticipated an early junction of the two armies. On the 19th of September, Burgoyne had advanced fifty miles as the bird flies, half of it by uninterrupted lake navigation,—not half a mile a day. On that day, he met the repulse at Saratoga; and, on October 17th, his army capitulated.

This seems a very miracle of inefficiency. But General Howe's performances at the same time, which have not been so vividly displayed in history, deserve the palm, as it seems to us, for superior lethargy; although we cannot but regard Howe as the superior officer of the two. The whole plan of the campaign being co-operation with Burgoyne, Howe, for his own reasons, was very languid about co-operating. He had the favor of the king and the support of Lord North, but was always at swords'-points with Lord George Germaine. But he was left free to conduct the campaign as he chose, and very remarkable choices he made.

What he chose was this. He made, in April, a raid on Connecticut, with a handful of troops, which lasted three days. In May he did nothing. In June he concentrated his forces in New Jersey. By the 12th of June, he had seventeen thousand at Brunswick, — the finest body of men in the world. But he gave up the idea of marching on Philadelphia, if he had ever had it, and, on the 5th of July, began to embark his troops to go to that city by water. The fleet was three hundred sail. The men lay in New-York harbor, in the stifling heat, till the 23d; then sailed; and on the 25th of August, after a voyage of thirty-three days, anchored in Elk River, fifty miles from Philadelphia. As Howe was but eighty miles from Philadelphia when he started, he gained twenty-six miles in the fifty-one days between the 5th of July and the 25th of August.

To compare this movement with Burgoyne's, not for rapidity but for slowness, is to measure snail against tortoise. Going more than half the way by water, Burgoyne advances at the rate of a little less than half a mile a day. Going all the way by water, Howe makes the same speed to a very small fraction, — half a mile a day.

In eight days more, the army is disembarked, and ready to march. On the 11th of September, Howe fought the battle of Brandywine successfully, — a well-planned battle, in which Cornwallis's spirit and good sense, as so often in the war, won their reward; and, on the 26th, he took possession of Philadelphia. But what he went there for, or why he stayed there, it is impossible to say. "You say Howe has taken Philadelphia," said Franklin: "I think Philadelphia has taken him."

Mr. Bancroft has made large use of a body of information, wholly new to the people of this country, which he has secured in Germany. It is made up of the official reports, and private letters and journals, of German officers who served here with the mercenaries bought by the English Government. They are popularly called "Hessians" in this country, though all of them were not furnished by the principality of Hesse. The account of the transaction by which the smallest of sovereigns furnished these troops to the least military of war departments is a chapter of history about as disgraceful as any that has ever been written down; and, if there is left one sentimentalist who has a tear for the disposition which, in the order of Providence, has been made of many of the small German princes, and, as we hope, may be made of all, his sorrow will be relieved, and his tears will be dried, as he reads this exposition of what such principalities and dukedoms come to. Why the English Government could not recruit any troops worth speaking of in England, does not very clearly appear. Fighting has, at other times, always been sufficiently popular in England for a sufficient number of sergeants, with a sufficient number of shillings, to get together a sufficient number of recruits for foreign service. But, on this occasion, home recruiting hardly seems to have been tried. The agents of England in Germany were even instructed to say that every thing would be overlooked in supplying mercenaries, if they were only promptly furnished. But the whole scheme, for practical purposes, broke down, under the opposition of Frederick the Great, who set himself firmly against it as soon as it was attempted in the second year.

The private journals and the despatches of the German officers, with the exception of some of Baron Riedesel's, to which his wife's journal called attention, have been hardly noticed by our historians. They furnish some very interesting details in addition to those we had before, which were but scanty at the best, from the pens of English officers. Some of these were printed at the time, and have been exhumed by Mr. Bancroft from forgotten journals. Many of them are quoted from the original manuscripts first brought to light by him.

The twenty-sixth chapter, which examines philosophically, and in some detail, the Articles of Confederation, discloses the foundation of our present institutions, with the notions or prepossessions in the minds of those who were then conferring together for the first time, from which the articles themselves took shape and color. Our recent trials give special interest to the examination thus made; and, of the thousand theories thrown out by different disciples of Mr. Calhoun in the last twenty years, half would have been spared us, had those who propounded them made any such study as is here, of their lamentable insufficiency for the purposes of government. The idea of the Confederation, according to Mr. Bancroft, was to substitute the power of the Confederacy for the right and prerogative of the King under the old state of things. He makes this out, even in some curious detail. Now, as all the Revolutionary statesmen had already, in the discussions of their separate colonies, gone to the very edge in abridging the prerogative of the king, it followed, in mere consistency, that in the new system they abridged the function of the Confederacy with the same severity. It is scarcely fair to suppose, that all the shackles which, by its own act, the Continental Congress imposed on all its successors, were due merely to mutual jealousy among States, which were, on the whole, working very cordially together. Something of such jealousy there was; there was also, very predominant, the fear on the part of the small States, that they should be swallowed up by the large, as the kingdom of Man might be devoured before breakfast by the King of Great Britain. Then there were all the warnings from history of the power which Austria gained in the German Confederation, and like examples all the way back in time. But beyond this, as Mr. Bancroft very fully shows, there was the habit, ingrained now in near twenty years of controversy, of abridging central power for the enlargement of that of the separate members of the State.

We have been so accustomed to kick and cuff the old Confederacy, whenever we dug it up from its half-forgotten grave, as to forget that there was in it any advance on the social order which preceded it, or that we inherited any thing of prime value from it when in that grave it was buried. But Mr. Bancroft calls attention to "four capital results, which Providence, in its love for the human race, could not let die," which were secured by this misshapen and loose-jointed instrument, — this child of revolution, whose birth was so long protracted, and at last effected in such agonies, that it began to die as soon as it was born, and that all men rejoiced when at last its sufferings were over.

First, that a republic was possible through a continent. This principle was first announced, and really first established, by the Confederation. The old republics were simply the governments of cities; the Continental Congress proclaimed that republicanism may equal the widest empire in its bounds. So triumphant has been the demonstration of this truth, that, in this generation, we forget that it was ever doubted. But, in truth, the leading political writers of the last century speak of republics, almost of course, as being the governments of small communities, precisely as the ecclesiastical authorities are fond of speaking of congregational order in the Church, — as an order belonging only to scattered communities or to the infancy of things.

Next, the Confederation recognized the rights of men, as men, and it gave reality to the Union by making the recognition. It permitted no distinction of sect, color, or race: free "inhabitants" were free citizens. This was an immense enlargement of the measure of acknowledged right and privilege. The necessities of slavery still compelled the distinction between "free" and "slave;" but, within that distinction, all other distinctions vanished, however sharply they might have been drawn in the local statutes or constitutions. "The United States, in Congress assembled, suffered the errors against humanity in one State to eliminate the errors against humanity in another."

A consequence almost necessary of this catholicity was the granting to the free inhabitants of each State "all privileges and immunities of free citizens in the several States." To this equalizing process, involved in the central bond, do we owe the gradual assimilation of the various State constitutions to each other,—the disappearance, one by one, of the tests by which at first they tried to screen Jews or Gentiles or Unitarians or Catholics out of their body politic. While the elective franchise in each State was regulated by its own decisions, all the "free inhabitants" of the United States were subjects or citizens of the nation. Mr. Bancroft well remarks, that, notwithstanding the anxiety with which the term "people of the United States" is avoided in the Articles of Confederation, the nation, as a unit, was really recognized, not to say organized, when the fealty or allegiance to it of each white inhabitant was thus proclaimed. Mr. Tayler Lewis has well shown that this nationality existed already,—before the colonies had confederated,—in the common relation of English subjects, in whatever colony, to the English crown. As Mr. Bancroft puts it, "America, though the best representative of the social and political genius of the eighteenth century, was not the parent of the idea in modern civilization, that man is a constituent member of the state of his birth, irrespective of his ancestry. It has become the public law of Christendom. Had America done less, she would have been, not the leader of nations, but a laggard." America did her utmost, in this matter, by proclaiming that the "state" of a man's birth was the whole continent in which he was born. No accident could limit his nationality to "the Hampshire Grants," or to one of the "Counties on the Delaware."

Lastly, the Confederation attempted the largest liberty to individual man. In the Greek republics, "the state existed before the individual, and absorbed the individual. . . . The Greek citizen never spoke of the rights of man. The individual was merged in the body politic." But, in the Articles of Confederation, the freedom of the individual could be recognized, because conscience had asserted its rights; and, in the assertion, the unity of despotic power was broken.

These four principles, now like household words with us,— the indefinite territorial extent of a republic, the relation of the United States to the natural rights of its inhabitants, the identity of privilege of each citizen in whatever State, and the freedom of the individual everywhere,— were completely asserted for us, so as never to be lost again in the much-abused Articles of Confederation.

Our limits do not permit us to go at present further into an abridgment even of the more remarkable results of this remarkable volume. The eight volumes — published successively in thirty-two years, almost a generation of men — have led up to the period of romance, of excitement, and of critical interest, which we wisely call "The Revolution," as if there were no other. Of "the Revolution," the critical years pass under review in this volume, and in the volume which is to follow. Mr. Bancroft is grateful, doubtless, that the concentrated white light of another revolution is brought to bear on the examination, so that no detail may be thought insignificant, and no secret of the circulation lost in some provoking shadow. He seems to us to rise worthily to his theme. We have been particularly pleased with the simplicity and consequent clearness of his descriptions of battles. Without a diagram on the page, he fixes for us the position of regiments, squadrons, and batteries, so that each reader can prepare his own diagram. Again, he does not come to an event till he has fairly shown its cause. If we are surprised, it is because history itself is surprised. And, indeed, often we find, that, a hundred years after the fact, we understand it better than those who were standing by. Once more, the narrative is relieved by the philosophy which inquires into principles and into consequences, but never so overwhelmed by a cloud of speculation, that we forget the substratum that is below.

The narrative is always brilliant, and the reader follows from page to page with interest, and wishes there was more. On the whole, there is little to be asked for, in the way of improvement of Mr. Bancroft's historical style. It seems to us sometimes marked by the defect of a supposition that the reader is already well acquainted with the history, even in details, as if that this new volume were rather a discussion of facts which are widely known, than an original statement of them. Now, the truth is, that four readers out of five, who take this volume in hand, will have read no other full history of the war; and for such readers in truth, as for all readers of history in theory, the narrative should be written for the first time. For instance, the following sentence, loosely constructed as some of Mr. Bancroft's sentences are, does not tell the new-born reader, who here first drinks in his American history, any thing that he needs to know: —

"The unfitness of the highest officer in the naval service, as displayed in his management of a squadron which had gone to sea in the spring, had just been exposed by an inquiry; and, in spite of the support of the Eastern States, he had been censured by a vote of Congress: yet from tenderness to his brother, who was a member of Congress, a motion for his dismissal was obstructed, and a majority ordered the aged and incompetent man to resume the command which he was sure to disgrace."

There is nothing in this sentence to show that the aged and incompetent man was Hopkins; and, on the other hand, all that has been said before leads the reader to suppose that it was Nicholas Biddle. It is only afterwards that an allusion made to Hopkins leads to a guess that it is he.

The boys who write most of the literary criticisms, so called, for the newspapers, are in the habit of complaining that Mr. Bancroft uses archaisms of language. Indeed, we remember one constitutionally ill-tempered person, who said of the eighth volume, that one needed an archæological dictionary to understand it. In regard to this volume, this charge is founded on three expressions: —

"Dearly did the Cherokees *aby* their rising."
"The Landgrave of Hesse, though a Roman *Convertite.*"
"*Laveering* against the southerly winds."

All that is to be said of these three words is, that, if people do not know what the words mean, it is time they did. They are words used by the best English writers of the best period of English literature. The fault which we should find with Mr. Bancroft's style is, not that he indulges too much in the use of words carefully chosen for precision of meaning, but that, in the occasional pursuit of those phantoms which lead men into the bogs and jungles of "fine writing," he sometimes uses words for their sound, without caring much for their meaning. Take the following sentence: "The uneven upland . . . is bounded, for more than two miles, by walls of primitive rock, or declivities steep as an escarpment." Now, in truth, there are no walls there: whether the rock is primitive or fossiliferous is a geological matter of no interest to the reader, and to say "steep as an escarpment" is as if one said "steep as a garden bank," or "steep as an inclined plane." The fact to be communicated is, that, on the Haerlem-River side, the shore is bold, so as to be easily held against invading troops. "Walls of primitive rock" and "declivities steep as an escarpment" come into the statement of the fact, not because they illustrate it, but because they sound well. Such details, however, are of little or no importance. We have been betrayed into them because other people have been. What is important is, that the style of the book is attractive and intelligible, and floats the reader easily and quickly on from the beginning to the end.

The "largest generalization of all" is that which closes the volume.

"We are arrived at the largest generalization thus far in the history of America.

"The spirit of free inquiry penetrated the Catholic world as it penetrated the Protestant world. Each of their methods of reform recognized that every man shares in the eternal reason, and in each the renovation proceeded from within the soul. Luther opened a new world, in which every man was his own priest, his own intercessor: Descartes opened a new world, in which every man was his own philosopher, his own judge of truth.

"A practical difference marked the kindred systems: the one was the method of continuity and gradual reform; the other, of an instantaneous, complete, and thoroughly radical revolution. The principle of Luther waked up a superstitious world, 'asleep in lap of legends old,' but did not renounce all external authority. It used drags and anchors to check too rapid a progress, and to secure its moorings. So it escaped premature conflicts. By the principle of Descartes, the individual man at once and altogether stood aloof from king, church, universities, public opinion, traditional science, all external authority and all other beings, and, turning every intruder out of the inner temple of the mind, kept guard at its portal to bar the entry to every belief that had not first obtained a passport from himself. No one ever applied the theory of Descartes with rigid inflexibility; a man can as little move without the weight of the superincumbent atmosphere, as escape altogether the opinions of the age in which he sees the light: but the theory was there, and it rescued philosophy from bondage to monkish theology, forbade to the Church all inquisition into private opinion, and gave to reason, and not to civil magistrates, the maintenance of truth. The nations that learned their lessons of liberty from Luther and Calvin went forward in their natural development, and suffered their institutions to grow, and to shape themselves according to the increasing public intelligence. The nations that learned their lessons of liberty from Descartes were led to question every thing, and by creative power renew society through the destruction of the past. The spirit of liberty in all Protestant countries was marked by moderation. The German Lessing, the antitype of Luther, said to his countrymen, 'Don't put out the candles till day breaks.' Out of Calvinistic Protestantism rose in that day four teachers of four great nationalities, — America, Great Britain, Germany, and France. Edwards, Reid, Kant, and Rousseau were all imbued with religiosity; and all except the last, who spoiled his doctrine by dreamy indolence, were expositors of the active powers of man. All these in political science, Kant most exactly of all, were the counterpart of America, which was conducting a revolution on the highest principles of freedom with such circumspection that it seemed to be only a war against innovation. On the other hand, free thought in France, as pure in its source as free thought in America, became speculative and sceptical and impassioned. This modern Prometheus, as it broke its chains, started up with a sentiment of revenge against the ecclesiastical terrorism which for centuries had sequestered the rights of mind. Inquiry took up with zeal every question in science, politics, and morals."

Art. VI.—THE ATLANTIC TELEGRAPH.

Report of the Proceedings at a Banquet given to Mr. Cyrus W. Field by the Chamber of Commerce of New York, Nov. 15, 1866. pp. 94.

THE city of New York has done itself honor, in so conspicuous a reception of one of its greatest benefactors. On both sides of the water, Mr. Field is recognized as the man without whom the Atlantic Cable would not have been laid in our generation. He has, therefore, a rightful claim to the foremost place in the gratitude and honor of the world, specially of his fellow-citizens. No one can read his speech at the Banquet without feeling its truthfulness and magnanimity, nor without plainly recognizing the personal qualities which enabled him to achieve his grand success.

The city of New York has twice emphasized its sense of the world-wide significance of the Atlantic Cable,—once, and most magnificently, when, in 1858, it welcomed Mr. Field, after the temporary success of that year; and now again, when permanent success may be deemed secure, with two cables in daily improving action between the Continents.

Great cities are the centres and sources of civilization, and their condition affords the best indications of the present state and prospects of humanity.

To return to cities, from the sparse settlements of a new country, is to return to multitudes. Here it is that the masses are seen in their density, and felt in their power for good and for evil. Our great common humanity, in its average quality and condition, in bodies too large to allow individual tastes and opinions much influence, in a current too strong to suffer much restraint from the feeble resistance of any superior class, there passes before us. A great city is a majestic spectacle at any time, for it is the house of an enormous family; but far beyond any vision of vastness or splendor or beauty in the municipal house itself is the sight of those who built, who occupy, who own it. No one can long be content to look at the marble walls that embank the Broadway of our American metropolis, while the captivating stream of human faces is running through it. The ordinary tide of humanity that ebbs and flows in that channel is, of all the constant curiosities the world affords, the most astonishing, the most untiring. Niagara has no rapids so dazzling, no roar so deafening, no rainbow so gay, no current so solemn, no significance so sublime. But when this daily phenomenon of the densest and busiest multitude in the world is raised to its highest possibility by some extraordinary summons of the people; when the country is poured into the town, the suburbs into the centre; when labor, released from its dispersing duties, is crowded into the public thoroughfares, and the population of States is compressed within the area of a capital, — then the constellations of the clearest night are not so beautiful, the waves of the wildest ocean not so sublime, nor all else that heaven and earth can congregate so exciting and tremendous, as the prospect. There is no spectacle equal to that of a countless multitude of human beings. What splendor of military trappings, what marshalling of significant chariots of industry, what gay, curious, meaningful procession, winding its mottled way, like a vast iris-hued serpent, through enamelled streets, — such as we have seen in public processions on days of high festival, — vies in interest for every eye with that motionless mass, — the magnificent, the overpowering crowd, that forms the ground of its display and the field of its progress? What can the torch-lights of ten thousand men, blazing with scarlet and with fire, illumine, which is like in beauty and splendor to their own faces, and the eyes of the myriads of lookers-on? We have seen the upturned countenances of a hundred thousand people, crowded on a hill-side, lighted up, and condensed into one awful and glorious picture, by the attractive art of the pyrotechnist; and not all the resources of his magical skill, in its most dazzling crises of splendor, could win our eyes away from the spectators to the spectacle. Man is ever God's greatest work, and the multitude ever the sublimest sight for human eyes.

In all ages, the *multitudes* have been objects of peculiar and mysterious interest to men, and strictly so in proportion to the capacity and insight of those who have contemplated them. But this interest has been of very different and widely contrasted kinds. Always intense, it has commonly been painful and alarming. For ages, men in general were regarded hardly as more than finer animals, capable of a superior mischief; creatures that were either to be intimidated or tamed, as their rulers chanced to be better supplied with force or with guile. The only expedient of governors was to turn the passions of one multitude against the passions of another, or one passion of the same multitude against another passion of its own. Thus natural ferocity was converted into the art of war; jealousy and envy, into pride of country and hatred of rival powers; sloth and apathy, to the account of those willing to substitute their own thinking and their own energy for that of the masses, and make them the tools of their ambition.

Thus multitudes have awed, crushed, and restrained each other, for the benefit of the few, who made themselves exceptional to the mass. Any self-directing power, any intelligent sense of community, any essential worth and goodness in men as men, any right of the race as a race to possess, enjoy, and govern the world, did not enter into the head of antiquity, if we except a few theoretical philosophers. Accordingly, the very name of the people was a reproach and an alarm. Οἱ πόλλοι, the many, was a monster, — either a stupid and loathsome, or a ferocious and fearful one, as climate and age affected him. Our most opprobrious appellation — the *mob* — is altogether too dignified a word for the ideas associated with the mass of human creatures before our Saviour's day ; and, indeed, out of the narrow circle of his true disciples long after. *Hordes, hvies, herds*, the spawn of the teeming swamps, the litter of the rank fens, — these terms expressed the prevailing sense of the commonness, the miserable origin, the hopeless character, the alarming increase, of their own kind. "Mob" is a word of much less contemptible import. It suggests the existence of some slight concert and design, hides a struggling sense of political aspirations, and hints the possibility of good neighborhood and peaceful relations between an existing civil order and itself. From "scum" and "herd" and "horde" to "mob," from "mob" to "mass," from "the masses" to "the people," from "the people" to "the race," from "race" to "brotherhood," we have a regular ascending series of terms, recording the historic progress of the multitudes as plainly as the geological strata do the history of the earth's advance to a habitable condition. And it is easy to gauge the social and Christian status of any community, by observing the ordinary and spontaneous use of the terms in which the multitude is spoken of, and in which it speaks of itself.

The great peculiarity of ante-Christian days was this: the multitudes were despaired of, and therefore both feared and despised. They were, it is true, courted by the ambitious, flattered by the cunning, but still feared and despised at once by the upper classes. All that we recognize in these days as philanthropy, — a feeling and principle based upon a conviction that the condition of the masses is the fruit of unhappy and discouraging circumstances, which may be removed or relieved, with a certainty of improving their condition and character, — this was unknown. It was not that the intelligent and superior classes in those days were less well-disposed, more selfish or cruel, than we are. But the *relative proportion* of the civilized and the uncivilized, the educated and the uneducated, the rich and the poor, was so much less favorable to hope, that the problems then offered to the wise and good were totally different from ours, and utterly appalling. It was inconceivable then that men everywhere could become educated, civilized, and sensible of the advantages of morality. The very fact of the unknown geography, the imperfect navigation, the slow and difficult intercourse, of ancient times fostered continual fears of possible eruptions of barbarians, — first realized, indeed, in the destruction of the Roman empire, but always operating to prevent any generous hope of the common elevation of the race. The absence of any general commerce, with a total ignorance of the very name of political economy, rendered precarious supplies of food a proper ground of jealousy and dread,—a fear which is one of the most active and steady causes of hostility and division among men. Nations could not afford to be at peace with their rivals in the corn markets; it was a matter of life and death who had possession of the fertile fields: and so war, jealousy, and hatred seemed a necessary, and even a justifiable and statesmanlike, policy in the conduct of public affairs, and the relation of states with each other.

When our Saviour appeared, his most affecting and characteristic quality was the new feeling with which he regarded the *multitude*. Objects of lively interest were the multitude, indeed, to the princes and rulers of those days. Herod did not dare, until lust and wine had driven him beyond reason, to behead John; for he feared the people. The chief priests and scribes did not dare to lay hands on Jesus till they were backed by the Roman governor, for the same reason, that they *feared* the people, who had instinctively felt that they had found a friend in our Saviour. But it was not FEAR, but *compassion*, an entirely different kind of interest, that Christ was to manifest towards them. For, in the language of St. Matthew, "when he saw the multitudes, he was moved with compassion on them, because they fainted, and were scattered abroad, as sheep having no shepherd."

The grounds of our Saviour's compassion are, it is worthy of notice, the very grounds of the fear entertained towards the people by his predecessors and contemporaries. Because they *fainted* with hunger, were maddened with unsatisfied appetite, and driven to reckless and ferocious ways,—this, which moved the dread of them, and an ever-watchful and armed resistance to their gatherings and their demands, was the first spring of our Saviour's compassion for them. True, he who could multiply the loaves and fishes miraculously for its relief had less to fear from the rage of hunger than the commissaries of mere human princes. But Christ distinctly recognized *want* as the first cause of compassion for the people. This was their first, great misfortune, overshadowing all others, causing their degradation, and making them dangerous to themselves and others. He had to feed even before he could instruct them; to become the maker of their bread before he could be the Saviour of their souls. A solemn and most tardily recognized truth was here divinely affirmed. The physical and material degradation of the world has been the first and the chief cause of its moral and spiritual destitution. The science of supporting great bodies of people upon this planet in any other than a predatory, uncertain, and clashing way, has been one of very slow and difficult progress. But distinctly to recognize *destitution*, not as the curse of God upon those on whom it fell, but as the providential stimulus to effort, and the divine incentive to compassion; to regard it as a problem capable of solution, or worth the profoundest intellectual and moral sacrifices to fathom it,— was left to our Saviour. It was the mightiest step in human progress when the *faintness* of the people gained the compassion, in place of the dread and fear, of the great leader of the civilization of Christendom. To see and allow that men were made wicked, dangerous, and hopeless mainly by their *wants;* that thus they were shut up to criminality, kept base and fierce by the necessity of their condition; to pity them for this calamity; still more, to look upon it as one which it was the duty and privilege of the fortunate, the instructed, and the rich to relieve or remove,— this was the longest stride on, the highest step up, which the gospel made, politically considered.

But this is not all: the second ground of our Saviour's compassion for the multitudes is like unto the first. First, *hunger*, which stands for all other degrees, and implies all other forms, of destitution, moved his pity. Next, their unsocialized and neglected condition; or, to use his own words, because they " were scattered abroad, as sheep having no shepherd." In that grazing country, infested with wild beasts, where the flocks of the opulent were never sent to pasture without a strong force of protectors, our Lord could not have used a more striking illustration than this. It was not exclusively, or even primarily, the want of spiritual instruction that he compassionated in the multitudes; but their lack of *all* social and civilizing guidance and protection. They were not considered as within the fold of society, but kept outside with the beasts,—from a general conviction, that they must prey upon society if society did not leave them outside its pale to devour each other, or be devoured by want and exposure.

The greatest misfortune the human race can experience grows out of, and is connected with, its greatest necessity and blessing. It cannot obey the first condition of its perpetuity,—Increase and multiply, and possess the earth,—without *general dispersion:* it cannot have general dispersion without driving far the largest portions of the race outside the spheres of social culture and civil polity. The world, if the Scriptures are credible, did not commence in savagery or barbarism, but upon true civilized principles, in family life, and with rules of social subordination and order. But it necessarily fell, as a whole, into barbarism, through the inevitable disproportion which the rapid growth of its population bore to the slow increase in its machinery of intercourse and commerce. The people multiplied and dispersed faster, vastly faster, than law and order, traditionary truth and wisdom, could follow them. Civilization, young and delicate, was compelled to shelter itself within the most circumscribed limits; and, beyond its self-protecting walls, the masses of humanity were scattered abroad, without the means and materials of self-elevation. For many generations, the disproportion between the civilized and. the savage world must have been constantly increasing in favor of barbarism. Indeed, the ratio must have continued to become ever more and more frightful, as the geometrical increase of the earth's population faster and faster outstripped the arithmetical increase of its socialized and civil portions. In the absolute ignorance of the physical geography of the world,—which was not then even called a *globe*,— no bounds could be placed to the probable growth of this despairing disproportion of the savage to the civilized, of the predatory and outcast to the orderly and moralized, portion of the human race. So long as the earth held out, there was room for a boundless increase in the ratio of ignorance, brute force, and animal necessity to cultivated and socialized humanity; and, had the world been a limitless plain, as it was deemed, there was even greater reason than was duly recognized, to fear the absolute extinction of civilization beneath the inroads of a myriad-mouthed barbarism. The South-African natives, living far in the interior of their continent, when the great missionary of modern times, Dr. Livingstone, brought them to the coast at Loanda (the place where the wretched cargo of the " Echo," captured by one of our national vessels, was basely gathered), and they beheld, for the first time, the ocean, in describing to him afterwards their feelings, said: "We marched along with our father, believing that what the ancients had always told us was true, — that the world *had no end;* but all at once the world said to us, ' *I am finished: there is no more of me.*'" If the circumambient ocean had not thus *finished* the world; if it had not been, in short, a moderate-sized globe, with an easily exhaustible area; if the extension of its population had not been thus positively limited (particularly as to its power to support, by spontaneous fertility, a population) to a number which was happily attained before the disproportion of the civilized to the uncivilized became so great as to be hopeless, there is no rashness in saying, that utter deterioration and absolute brutality must have been the final fate of our race. Doubtless, by the original plan of the Almighty, the limit of population was reached before this ratio was totally desperate; for the size of the globe may be considered as having been accurately adapted to the fortunes of the race for whom it was made. The moment the ratio became fixed, not increasing, there was hope; but a long pause was made on that line. The instant it began to diminish was the signal of Christ's coming, and the birth-hour of human redemption had arrived. The preponderance — not in numbers, but in power, courage, confidence — of the social and civil forces of society over the instincts and appetites of the uncivilized and barbarous masses of the race, is the only adequate cause, under God (who has had his own now obvious and glorious plan in human history), of the progress of humanity as a whole, or of the safety of society. When, therefore, our Saviour compassionated the multitudes, because they were scattered abroad, he bestowed on them the pity they most needed. Next to absolute hunger, exclusion from social and civil privileges, by a wandering, dispersed, and uncalculated life, is man's greatest misfortune, and the chief source of his moral and spiritual degradation. We may talk of spontaneous genius, of self-correcting powers and attributes in humanity, of necessary, self-evolved improvement as the true hope for the masses; we may reason about the natural and inevitable tendencies of man to civilization and progress: if we leave out of this calculation the providence of God,— which has chosen centres of light and life, kindled altars of piety, written tables of law, and erected models and standards of domestic, social, and civil life, which are the primal and chief means for the education and rescue of the race at large,— we shall lose the only key to the history of the world, and the only clue to the substantial progress of the race. Probably there is *no* tendency in savage or barbarous tribes and races to self-elevation,— only a capacity for improvement, under the guidance and inspiration of higher branches of the one great family, specially prepared by God for this work. Specially, God has committed to modern civilization, which is the child of Christianity, the salvation of the world. Civilization has, by approximate steps, reached the conviction, that there is no way of civilizing but by intercourse; and that intercourse is worth little or nothing except it be easy, constant, and general. It has perceived that the "scattering abroad"— Christ's own ground of compassion — was still the great obstacle to progress; and, therefore, the grand instinct of modern efforts at improvement has been road-making,— the construction of the highways of civilization,— ways on land, ways over water, ways through air, ways under ocean; ways between civilized and civilized, the more to strengthen each other by exchange of wisdom, experience, and products; ways between civilized and uncivilized, to extend knowledge and commerce and industrial arts; ways into Africa and New Holland; ways to the neighborhoods of the Northern and the Southern Poles; ways to the Pacific and across the Atlantic; ways for the products of subdued fields, conquered streams, and powers of nature enslaved to man's will; for the products of the loom, the forge, and the plough; ways for the traveller, be he the missionary of commerce, of science, or of religion — each equally valuable and all co-operative; ways for thought, the greatest of all products, the most urgent and enterprising of all travellers, the grandest of missionaries. To throw the net of roads, — its woof of iron and stone, its warp of wire and water, — that great net, of which every track that civilized man pursues, whether with his foot, his beast, his wheel, his sail, his iron-rail, his electric flash, is a mesh that catches and holds in some estray and outcast interest, some scattered and otherwise lost member of humanity, — this is the providential passion and sacred instinct of modern civilization. It is the perpetuity of Christ's compassion that inspires and vivifies this grand movement. That the multitudes may not *faint*, may not be scattered *abroad*, Christian civilization must seek them, must hem them in, bind them to its girdle, make swift ways to the scenes of their ignorance and their despair, pierce their rivers and jungles, cross their deserts with the rail, abolish oceans and seas, and declare every part and portion of the earth explored, open, safe, related, in connection with all other parts, and so united to the race, to Christ, and to God.

And now, finally, within the bounds of Christendom — at any rate, within the bounds of that happiest and most blessed portion of it which we occupy — a new and higher sentiment than even that of compassion, through the grace of God and his Son, animates our hearts when we look on the multitudes, — the sentiment of confidence and hope. Fear gave way, in our Saviour's courageous and loving mind, to compassion, when he saw the multitude. Have not the reasons for that compassion — at least within our immediate sphere of life and influence — most sensibly lessened, and almost totally disappeared, under the influence of the Saviour's own ever-advancing work? He himself, new as compassion then was, did not fail to add exultation to it in the triumph which humanity, under his guidance, was finally to accomplish over all its degrading conditions. He "saw Satan as lightning fall from heaven," when the Greeks came to inquire into his gospel. How literally pierced with lightning is the enemy of souls, when DISTANCE, that scatters men abroad and makes them faint on the long way, transfixed on the darting thought of the lightning, dies in mid-heaven and falls headlong into the sea! How long is superstition to make it irreligious to recognize the fulfilment of any of our Lord's promises, the answers to any of his prayers? Is the world's progress never to be confessed; and is a mock humility to drape the very mid-day of hope, and cheer with curtains of despondency, lest it outshine the Christian dawn? The stones would cry out if we were silent, when the very key-stone has so evidently been put into the arch of Christ's triumph over the barbarism and want and dispersion of his scattered flock of humanity. Be it said, then, to his eternal honor and to God's everlasting glory, that the day has come when we can look upon the multitude with something better than compassion,—even with confidence and joy. And this, if we mistake not, is the great distinction, as it is the glorious conquest of the times and the day, to which the recent triumph of enterprise and art, the Atlantic Cable, so naturally and properly sung, feted and illumined, is but a tongue and voice. That slender thread of fire explodes a mine of emotion, conviction, and experience that had been slowly but long accumulating in the bosom of our age. That delicate cord moors nations together that were drifting to each other in spite of seas and icebergs. That swift messenger, dark and silent as night, but keener and subtler than light, carries words of brotherhood, long waiting for their vehicle; that syphon, so slender and so patient, empties hearts into each other whose blood had for ages yearned to mingle. God in his providence, by making us the last-born of the great nations and powers of the earth, and giving us half the world for our home; by emptying the blood of all nations into our national veins; by diversifying us with all climates, without colonial separation, and by the vastness of all the circumstances and conditions of our territory, our origin, our growth and history, as well as by the happy fortune of the splendid age of commerce, liberty, and inventive genius in which our lines have fallen — has prepared us, as no people is prepared, to demand, to expect, to understand, and to enjoy *universal ideas*, — feelings that embrace the world, schemes that include the race, hopes that outrun place and time, destinies that are perfect and complete.

We look upon the multitude — blessed be God's providence and Christ's gospel for our power to do so! — no longer with fear, and not even characteristically, in this land, with compassion, but with sympathy and hope, and almost with reverence. For we see them no longer faint, and no longer scattered abroad; and every day we are, by economic science and motive art, eliminating the unknown or suspended elements in the great equation of human progress. That vast problem is no more a bottomless mystery and a baffling speculation. The obstacles which oppose the advance of the race, immense as they are, are measurable; dense as they are, are penetrable. There is nothing hopeless or desperate in human affairs. Progress is possible, is real, is certain, is inevitable. The relative forces of good and evil, of peace and war, of truth and error, of civilization and barbarity, of brotherly love and selfish antagonism, are weighed, and the balance is favorable *for once*, and *therefore for ever*, to the kingdom of God in the salvation of our race. The multitude is accordingly to be trusted and respected. We thank God that we are able, and are compelled by the highest convictions of the heart, to trust and respect them. Nay, in this country, we trust and respect them far more than we do those who make them objects of secret suspicion, and who would gladly reproduce the repressive systems of aristocratic governments. The cultivated and refined classes in America understand less of the true spirit of our institutions, and do far less to maintain them, we fear, than the body of the people at large. Sensitive to defects, fastidious in tastes, overborne by memories of the past, they overlook the enormous advantages, the broad magnificence, the grand general effect of institutions where human nature, for the first time, is trusted with liberty, education, and plenty, and cultivate the poor satisfactions of a superiority based on criticism, doubt, and evil prophecies. A distinguished and most acute English visitor to this country told us, just before the war, that he had scarcely talked with an educated and thoughtful man in America who had not expressed doubts and fears of the success of our institutions. Thank God, the *people* have no doubts and no fears. Thank God, those who make and uphold our liberty, love it, trust it, and estimate it at its value, believe in its durableness. They have no misgivings of God's clear intention; no backward looks, no cautious apprehensions. And they are right; wiser, because simpler and more childlike, in their patriotism. They are animated by the fresh instincts, the original convictions, the startling realities, of a new era. And thus, while learned science, and thoughtful philosophy, and even grave experience, shake their heads and mutter, "Impossible," the mighty hope of the people, sure of God's willingness and help, attempts the *impossible*, and changes it into the *accomplished*. "I thank thee, O Father! that thou hast hid these things from the wise and prudent, and hast revealed them unto babes."

The great popular instincts of a new era in the life of man are the vast powers, the mighty discoveries, the wonder-workers, of the age. The multitude is doing for Christ the miracles he did for them. They, too, say "Peace" to the sea in his name; they, too, are in and out, where all doors are shut; they, too, repeat the Pentecostal marvel, and bring all tongues together, and make them alike intelligible to all. Like Joshua, they stop the sun, not to fight their battles, but to paint their pictures and perpetuate their friends. "Canst thou send lightnings that they may go and say unto thee, Here we are?" asked the scornful Job; and the multitude now first is able to answer, "We can." — " Hast thou entered into the springs of the sea, or hast thou walked in the search of the depth?" and the multitude now first replies, "We have." — " Who hath laid the measures of the earth, or who hath stretched the line upon it?" and the multitude again answers, "Glory be to God who has first given *such* power to men, in our own days."

The great and all-emboldening confidence of our time is, that the multitude — historically and naturally incapable of estimating human nature as it is, or suspecting their own latent powers, and therefore absolutely dependent on the delivering mercy and energy of the providentially awakened and inspired portion of the race — has now got beyond this syncope and self-oblivion, beyond its dependence on any powers but God's direct inspirations through that same human nature, aided by all recorded revelations, which, to this time, he has kept in pupilage to indirect human instrumentalities. The multitude now elects its own teachers, judges of its own wants, chooses its own creed, rejects and accepts, on its own judgment, the propositions of the learned, the philosophical, and the exalted. Of course, it makes great mistakes, does very rash and injurious things, and gives skepticism and aristocracy abundant superficial arguments for their despairing creed. But what are all the mistakes it makes, compared with the astounding fact of an *attempted self-government, an attempted self-education, an attempted self-reliance,* on the part of the people? When, in 1858, we heard that a single sign had flashed across the Atlantic, what cared we for the stuttering and stammering of the instruments? The great thing was done; the miracle was wrought: and, had the cable parted the next moment instead of a month later, the hemispheres would not have moved an inch from the close moorings effected by that single fact. And so no wretched local rulers, no inefficient police, no insecurity of life and limb, no mistaken outbreaks of self-protection, no exceptional blots and blotches in the fabric of our prosperous, safe, and successful life of freedom, shall introduce one ray of despondency or doubt into the patriotic conviction, that — measured by positive, not by negative standards; measured by the sum of intellectual, moral, and physical activity; by the amount of happiness, intelligence, and virtue; by openness to improvement, by tendencies to truth, by humane sympathies, by religious aspirations — the multitudes were never, in human history, so little an object of compassion, so much an object of hope, confidence, and joy, as here and now.

If our hearts swell with pride and gratitude at the contemplation of this truth, let us not conceal, let us not fail to blazon the fact, that it is God's power manifested in man that has brought about this result; let us not forget how entirely it is the Divine wisdom that has planned the great drama of human history, and which is now permitting us to see the beauty and benevolence of the plot, and the bliss of the consummation. Let us not forget that, because it is God who is working in us to will and to do of his good pleasure, it is all the more our bounden and grateful duty to work with him, — to work indeed with a new kind of fear and trembling because of the greatness of the inspiration and the enormous importance of the task; to work, in short, as the high-hearted projector, the original supporters, the scientific operators, the officers and sailors, of the Atlantic Telegraph Company worked, when, after repeated failures and terrible difficulties, they at last laid in silence and amid prayers, but with herculean toil and almost deadly anxieties, God's bond between the nations, God's bow under the sea; not dissolving and inconstant like the first which was over it, but a steadfast sign from heaven to our generation, that no deluge of ignorance, barbarism, and despair shall ever again cover the hopes, the interests, and the destiny of a United Globe and an inseparable Human Family.

Art. VII. — ALLEGED NARROWNESS OF CHRISTIAN FAITH.

It is important to understand, and frankly meet, a modern frame of mind which makes the gospel of Christ, and all distinct profession of it, distasteful to some enlightened and religiously inclined persons. This frame of mind utters itself in a complaint of *narrowness* against the whole idea of revelation, miracles, personal authority, and binding example,—against rites and forms of any kind, however simply administered or interpreted. Christianity, it is now asserted, has too strait a gate and too narrow a way for the breadth of modern intelligence and the width of recent spiritual and scientific discoveries.

In short, it is complained of Christianity that it is not as broad as Natural Religion, in that it mingles historical facts, personal experiences, local geography, external authority, miraculous evidences, and outward forms with those general principles, absolute ideas, and universal experiences which natural theology gives us in her own great abstract and sublime way, and so narrows and particularizes religion. Of what importance is it, it is asked in this spirit of superior breadth, where truth comes from, if it only be truth; or goodness, if it is only real goodness? Why are virtue, justice, charity, piety, any better for being Christian than for being Buddhish or Mahometan or Judaic or wholly Natural? Is the golden rule any more binding, or any more beautiful, for being taught by Christ than if it had been (as indeed it is claimed that it was) taught by Confucius and Menu? And what advantage is there, the objector continues, in going to God by the way of Christ, if we can, more conveniently to ourselves, get to Him by any other way? People that never heard of Christ must find God by some *other* road, if they find him at all; and surely it is very narrow to affirm, or even to think, that none have attained the knowledge of God without the knowledge of a Saviour who came from heaven only eighteen hundred and sixty-six years ago, and the world is now at least six thousand years old. Besides, some of the Jews did know God without Christ; and we ourselves improve even our *Christian* faith by reading David's psalms and Isaiah's holy prophecies. If the knowledge of God, and the love, adoration, and obedience which the study of his character nourishes in man, be the sole object of religious quest, then certainly the help of Jesus Christ may gratefully be accepted in making this search; and the

most unqualified naturalist in religion would not deny the
value and importance of Christ's life and teachings as a *means*
of knowing God. But what they would complain of is that
any insistence should be put upon the use of this special
means as in any way indispensable, imperative, or authoritative. They would have Christianity put into the market with
other religions, and with other means of religious growth and
culture. If it is a better article, it will command a better
sale. If it is more serviceable, people will find it out and use
it. But, if anybody prefers Judaism to it, or Mahometanism
or Buddhism or Platonism or pure theism, why should Christians take offence or make any stir about it? All things
do not suit all people. Some most readily find religious and
worshipful thoughts, they tell us, in looking at the works of
nature. The stars, the forest, the ocean, speak for them a
language more divine than any book. Others discover in
theories of intuitive morals, or in Mr. Emerson's essays or
Mr. Carlyle's hero-worship, a finer moral and religious inspiration than the New Testament affords. Still another set find,
in the study of color and form, their completest revelations of
a divine beauty, and choose to let their worship flow on the
Sunday from the point of a pencil or a paint-brush, rather
than from a hymn-book or in acts of common prayer. Still
another variety find the microscope and the scalpel more
religious than the font and the communion table. They see
God in the infinitely small, and discover the hidings of his
power by untwisting the fibres of the plant or the tissues of
the human body. Another class declare that they find a ram-
ble in the fields, a play with their children, and a pleasant
time with their comrades quite as religious as a seat in a
Christian church, or the prayers and praises of a demure and
unsmiling congregation. Beyond all these, a growing class
of minds and hearts, claiming still more breadth and intelligence, are now beginning to doubt whether religion in *any*
form is not a narrowing thing, — whether what is called natural religion is not merely a little less narrow and superstitious
than what is called revealed religion. Some not immoral
people of our day, and not ignorant and uneducated persons

either, think that the Christian Church and so-called religious folk have squandered the attention that should have been given to improving the world and their own condition in it, upon the cultivation of an artificial relationship to an imaginary Providence called the Christian God, or, what is almost as bad, the God of the theists. Their notion is that if there *be* any such person, we shall find it out quite time enough when we come naturally to it; that if there be any future or immortal state we shall find that out too when we arrive at it : but that here and now there is pressing business to be done, and urgent happiness to be enjoyed,—happiness and business wholly peculiar to this time and place,—and that we misdirect our energies when we allow any thing else, no matter how sacred its name and pretensions, to divert our thoughts and efforts from this present world and its natural immediate work.

But this is not the most illuminated class yet. There is in Germany and France still another set of philosophers,—not without disciples in this country,—who go much further than this, and insist, not only that religious speculations and interests, whether called natural or revealed, narrow the mind and heart and impoverish the life, but that *moral* questions have a similar narrowing tendency; that the world is ridden to death by an artificial conscience; and that all this solicitude about right and wrong is a waste of precious energy and time and feelings. Wrong, they insist, has just as good rights as any thing else. What we call *moral evil* is quite as necessary, and in accordance with our nature, as moral good. The bad is the counterpart of the good, and as necessary to it as the night to the day. Criminals are such by a necessity of their constitutions; and crime is merely a conventional offence against a conventional code which the majority of social beings have set up for their own protection. The self-complacency, or feeling of moral superiority, which the righteous and pious indulge in the presence of the vicious and impious, is as unreasonable as a dove's complacency in her freedom from the serpent's sting, or a lamb's in his exemption from wearing the tiger's claws and teeth.

We have had a plain purpose in leading our readers through the logical career of that protest against the narrowness of a positive and historical faith, which induces some of the finest and freest minds among us to object to the Lordship of Jesus Christ, and the exceptional authority of the Christian religion. We have endeavored to show that, if narrowness, meaning definiteness, and an authority not purely self-justified and impersonal, is a fatal objection to a religion, we shall be obliged to give up natural religion and all religion. Philosophy is far wider than any religion can be; and life is still wider than philosophy. Fatalism is, in one sense, even more widely religious than any system which recognizes free agency and human accountableness; because it makes God the sole agent in the universe, and gives his sovereignty absolute sway. All the odious ideas of personal affinities and pre-ordained relationships, which have from time to time disparaged and set aside marriage vows and the Christian conceptions of wedlock, have come in under the claim of a higher spirituality and a broader understanding of moral and religious laws.

We are well aware that the argument from consequences is one which superstition and fanaticism have abused, and are always likely to abuse. We remember, too, that it is not fair to hold *people* accountable even for the logical consequences of their opinions. But you may properly hold the *opinions* themselves accountable for their own logical consequences; and this is a distinction which it is very important to appreciate.

For we do not hesitate to say, that the pure and lofty lives of many persons, holding what we consider to be very non-Christian opinions, is helping to delude many with the idea that there can be no *danger* in opinions which such excellent persons entertain. But this proceeds wholly on the assumption that they gained their excellence by the aid of these opinions, and not rather in spite of them. Ideas never produce their consequences in the generation that gives birth to them, but rather in the next. Opinions dwell inoperatively in the intellect of their producers, but passionately and actively in the blood of their inheritors. Each generation lives mainly on the ideas of its precursor; for it is only what has passed out of the understanding into the prejudices, or rather instinctive thoughts and feelings, that shapes a man's conduct, and characterizes his temper and spirit; and the same is true of an age. Communism did the early apostles no harm; but all know what its wretched fruits were in some of their successors. The French Revolution was started by pure and philanthropic men, whose worst thoughts were uttered under solemn convictions of truth and duty; but how soon its mischievous but honest notions slipped into horrid, bloody filth and cruelty we all recall. Principles and ideas, not triable by abstract methods, *must* be judged by their consequences; but these consequences must be sought in a large, generous, average way. It will not do to judge the law of primogeniture by three or four generations; but when it ends in putting half the lands in all England into the hands of less than one hundred and fifty proprietors, and threatens, first, the outbreak of Chartism, and next, Fenianism; and, finally, a general rising of the disfranchised and landless millions, before which the solid powers of a throne and an aristocracy more than a thousand years old tremble and totter, — we are justified in characterizing it as an unjust, impolitic, and un-Christian institution. So it will not do to judge democracy by an occasional mob in a city, or the disgraceful municipal legislation in a metropolis that receives and admits to suffrage the scum of all Europe. But when we behold it producing, in less than one century, a nation like our own, having the largest number of independent homes, and the greatest relative proportion of educated and virtuous people, to be found in any country in the world; when we see it sustaining itself, its order, its laws, and its finances, under the vastest civil war ever known to history, — we are entitled to say, "Democratic principles have proved themselves, by their consequences, to be the true principles on which to found stable governments."

It will not do to judge polygamy by Utah, — a sink of all violence, corruption, and filth; but the history of all the nations in which it has been allowed has determined its absolute incompatibility with social progress, political freedom, or moral dignity.

Thus nobody could venture to say in advance what would be the final consequences of setting up a purely natural religion, into which all moral and spiritual truth of Christianity, pressed out and separated from its mere historic and personal concomitants or circumstances, had been drained off. Prior to experience, it certainly looks as if such a religion of sound principles,—absolute in its self-proving and self-recommending authority, in which God was deemed and taken to be the synonym for absolute goodness and wisdom and holiness, but without the limiting notion of personality; and retribution wholly the operation of self-acting laws; heaven a frame of mind, and hell its opposite; sin an offence wholly against one's own soul; immortality exclusively a state of feeling,—it looks as if such a religion ought to produce very worthy and commendable disciples.

But we are not left to speculation and surmise in regard to the success of such a religion. The plan has been fully tried. In fact out of Judea, so far as thoughtful, philosophic and lofty minds had any religion at all prior to Christ's coming, it was precisely this absolute and universal religion. It had its very distinguished and lofty teachers. Confucius, Zoroaster, Zeno, Plato, and Socrates, among the wisest of men, taught this absolute religion. It was the very flower and fruit of their philosophical studies; but, whatever influence it may have had in the academy, the porch, or the haunts and groves of philosophy, who ever yet heard of its producing any moral or saving influence upon *the people at large*,—who, indeed, under that system, were deemed not worth attention? The moment the ideas of mere philosophers reached any shape which brought them within the people's range, the essential truths of natural religion were blent in with the coarsest and most puerile superstitions. We may see what the lofty piety of Confucius became by studying the idolatrous and disgusting religion of the Chinese at this late day. We have ourselves been in their josh-houses or religious temples in California, and seen them cutting off the feet and heads of chickens as offerings to those wooden and tapestried idols, taking care to carry home the only edible portion of the offering for their own consumption. Natural religion, even in the form which Socrates and Cicero gave it, — the purest and highest form it has attained out of Christian bounds, — had no influence upon the personal character of any persons excepting a certain select few, who themselves cultivated it more as a theme for literary ambition than for personal growth and guidance. There never was a worse era than that of Socrates, if it were not Cicero's, — the two greatest moralists of Greece and Rome.

We are firmly convinced that what is called natural religion, — that is, the last result of unassisted human thinking on the theme of man's relations to God, — is a thing which never had, as an operative system of thought, any clear statement, except out of Christian mouths; or any considerable influence except over those born and bred under Christian influences. Take away from it the support of Christian institutions, founded on a revealed gospel, and we are entirely convinced it would fall to the ground in half a century, and leave the world the prey of atheism, idolatry and universal worldliness and folly. General ideas, however pure, demonstrable on absolute principles, and self-recommending, have no force until embodied in institutions, and made a part of the methodical training of society. Nations, like individuals, are finally shaped by their habits more even than by their ideas, — by their usages and customs, more than by their abstract opinions. You may have ever so much vague and unorganized Protestant thinking going on in Italy; but it is the organized Catholic Church that shapes the Italian mind. You may have ever so much red republicanism floating in the minds and fancies of Frenchmen; but it is the Emperor, the Court, the bayonet, and the *octroi* that settle the features of French society. You may have ever so much Liberal Christianity suspended in the literature, the air, the thought or tastes and tendencies of the American people; but it is Orthodoxy, holding the churches and keeping the schools, that really shapes the American mind, and decides its creed. We put good things and bad together, the more impartially to illustrate a common principle. Government, society, religion, must all be incarnate in positive forms, to exert any general influence, or maintain any permanent life. It is so now. It has always been so. It will always continue so. Thoughts and feelings, principles and ideas, are clouds drifting across the sky; they must condense into practical acts and get body, like the rain, before they can touch the earth, fertilize its surface, shape the courses of things, and give configuration to the globe.

Thus Judaism, from its embodying the first principles of natural religion in a positive and authoritative shape, made a whole nation feel the power and influence of thoughts elsewhere confined wholly to sages and a few natural saints. It united these ideas with a positive worship; brought each and every Jew into close and awful contact with them; won his daily attention, and drilled and disciplined him, by a tedious but most effective process, which had something of the irresistible force of a military routine, to feel at every point of his intellectual and moral surface, at every pore of his skin, and in every throb of his heart, the significance, sanctity and importance of certain cardinal religious ideas. We need not say what this Mosaic religion did for its people and for the world. Scoff at its puerile customs, its cumbrous rites and ceremonies, as we may, it made a literature which will outlast all Greek, all Roman fame; it created a people that has shaped the civilization of nineteen centuries, by giving birth to Jesus Christ, a Jew. It fashioned a race whose mental and moral vigor has penetrated the world with a genius which all the arts and all the business of modern civilization feels thrilling its very marrow. Who ever knew a stupid Jew? Who ever has calculated the influence to resist, to persist, to insist, which has come from that institutional people, whose genius and inspiration seem only to prove that human nature must be shut up to vigorous laws and fixed usages, and definite and authoritative ideas, before it ever becomes concentrated enough to boil with thought, or crystallize in art and action?

It is of the nature of roads and gates to be narrow or strait, relatively to the countries through which they pass, and the fields into which they lead. Anybody who has had an open prairie or a broad ocean for his only path — without bounds or track, without obstruction too, but also without reason for going in one direction rather than another, — must know what is the significance of this language which says, "Strait is the gate and narrow is the way which leadeth unto life;" and how necessary and blessed it is, that revealed religion presents us not absolute and general principles, universal precepts and abstract truths merely, but specific facts and concrete and personal ties, — presents us, in Jesus Christ, a door and a way, a definite track and guidance; and, in place of absolute statements touching the importance of duty and truth and charity, gives us a schoolmaster and pattern and guide to lead us, by patient obedience and by the influence of sacred usages and customs, to the final goal of a spiritual life and character. Christ insisted upon personal discipleship; his chief disciples magnified the part that the Master himself had in his own religion. They seemed bent on fastening attention on the personal history and events in the life of Jesus. Christ uses the word "*I*," with a frequency and significance that no other moral and religious teacher ever practised; and it is the chief distinction between all other systems of religion and Christianity, that its founder dares to speak, and claims the authority to speak, from his own personality, as from the throne of absolute truth. There is no more egotism in his use of the word *I*, than there is in the sun's eternal claim to be the light of the world. Christ does not distinguish between *himself* and the precepts and doctrines and commandments he imposes. He says distinctly, "I am the way, the truth, and the life." "I am the resurrection and the life." "I am the light of the world." "He that hath seen me hath seen the Father." He announces himself as the Son of God, as Immanuel. He asserts powers and authority which are either enough to convict him of the greatest arrogance and presumption known in all history, or else to place him in a position of rightful spiritual pre-eminence such as the Church and human nature for nineteen centuries have accorded him. And it is precisely this priceless fact of the appearance of a Being made in our own likeness, and yet claiming to be the Son of God, and to speak with divine and final authority, and sealing that authority with miracles, which has made the gospel of Christ the religion and the inspiration of the nineteenth, as of all preceding Christian centuries. God, speaking by the man Christ Jesus, endowed with plenipotentiary powers, has *made* the Christian Church, sustains the Christian Church, and is the eternal rock against which the gates of hell will never prevail.

And, after all that humanity owes to the gospel, it is this blessed narrowness of the road, and straitness of the gate,— that is, the definiteness, certainty, concreteness, and personal characteristics of a revealed religion, in contrast with the abstractness, vagueness, and coldness of natural religion,— that is a special source of disquietude, alienation, and disgust to some of our modern *illuminati*. They seem to forget that revealed religion is not a *substitute* for natural religion or a supersession of it, but an addition to it, or superstructure upon it; that it is not substituting spectacles for eyes, but adding telescopes to vision. And as to the narrowing influences of it, who ever heard that the surveyor, the mapmaker, the road-builder, narrowed the geography of a tract of country, by making it accessible and fixing its points of compass? It is from an everlasting confusion of mind,— in which the ends and aims of Christianity are confounded with the ways and means,— that this modern prejudice against the narrowness of a revealed faith has derived its support. Christianity is not distinguished in its ends and aims from most other religions, the best of which propose union with God and goodness as their final purpose and result. It is wholly peculiar only in its method; and it is its method, and not its aim, which is really deserving our fixed attention. It proposes to bring people to God and goodness, to heaven and eternal life, by uniting them to Jesus Christ, through the study of his life and character; and the keeping of his precepts, learned diligently and systematically in that special school which he opened and called the Christian Church.

When we complain of our common-school system, that it only teaches arithmetic, and spelling, and grammar, and therefore, being very narrow in its scope as compared with the teaching of nature and life, ought to be abandoned,—then, and then only, may we reasonably talk of abandoning Christianity, because it is the common-school of babes and children in the knowledge of God, adapted to human nature and mortal circumstances.

Christianity recognizes natural religion fully, and without the least jealousy. Nay, if the image gives any comfort to its exclusive friends, she stands upon it as a dwarf on a giant's shoulders. But natural religionists are proud enough to think they can do without revelation. They think the giant is tall enough without the dwarf. But where would natural religion be but for the whispers this dwarf has dropped into the giant's ears? All that natural religion now knows, and in the pride of which she abjures revealed religion,—all that is definite, satisfactory or binding, she has really learned from the Church of Christ. And, when told this, her answer is, "Be it so; but, having learned it, why should we still keep our Teacher?" Why should the climber of Mont Blanc not dismiss his guides, and fling down his ladders, at the top of the first precipice? Because there are other precipices before him. And those who think they have learned Christianity out, and got to the very top of the eminence occupied by the Master and Saviour, will in due time discover their mortifying mistake. We verily believe that, to desert the Divine Guide whom God has sent to lead us safely through this new and unexplored country, is to invoke the loss of our way, to plunge into darkness and cold, and probably ruin. Christ is the way, and he will continue such to the most advanced disciples, who will only feel his moral and spiritual superiority more the closer they come to him, the more nearly they imitate him. The greater our spiritual sensibility, the finer for us the revelations of his character, and the fuller for us the measure of his inspiration. We should believe that *branch* of the Church destined to wither, that severed its connection with the true vine; and the sooner it withered the better, for its fruit could be only ashes, and its seed barrenness.

Let us not think meanly of the revelation with which God has lighted up the once gloomy and unattractive halls of natural faith. Look reverently upon that grandest monument of time and history, the Christian Church, founded on the living corner-stone. Honor, support, and uphold those venerable and significant forms, which only the precipitate and prosaic could long undervalue,— the Lord's Supper and Baptism, which have been the very wings by which the Holy Dove has made its difficult way down the centuries,— rites which are to the gospel what marriage and legitimacy are to society,— true sacraments, to maintain which every Christian should lend his enlightened and grateful support. Let those who despise the forms that hold civil society together, the legal instrument, the proper official signature, the prescribed seal,— forms by which we hold our property,— deride the conventional character, the temporary importance, the superstitious value, put on the sacred rites of the Christian Church. They have a significance, a value, and a providential destiny which scoffers and scorners will finally learn to respect; and nothing claiming to be a Church of Christ will, we predict, long continue to bear that name, or even to desire it, which has outgrown faith in these symbols. Let us not neglect or misunderstand the relation which the simple forms have to the holy spirit of our religion, nor think ourselves wiser than he who built the Church on his own broken body.

Art. VIII.—REVIEW OF CURRENT LITERATURE.

THEOLOGY.

Dr. Furness has added to his series of original and striking studies of the Gospels, by a translation of remarkable felicity and skill from a writer of kindred spirit, but of views often quite different from his own.[*] The work of Dr. Schenkel, which has received this high testimony to its excellence and value, represents a style of moderate and pious liberalism, more familiar, we apprehend, to the German mind than to ours. It is also distinguished by a limitation and precision of aim, implying a certain modesty of judgment, and helping to keep the subject itself free of dogmatic assumptions and false expectations. It states frankly, at the outset, that we have not the materials for a Life of Jesus, — only for a Portrait. Renan has failed in his representation of the character, in aiming at too great completeness in the history. Of that character we have a "clearer image" in Mark than in either of the other Gospels, and along with it a more fresh and almost a first-hand narrative: the writer refers, with much confidence, to the *Urmarcus*, or original Gospel, differing considerably from the present form, as the real first authority for the portrait he seeks. Matthew and Luke represent successive stages of a "literary reconstruction" of the narrative, in which the primitive outline is already somewhat disguised; while there is an "insurmountable difficulty" in accepting the fourth Gospel in any sense at all that makes it of much value as an historical authority. In fact, the most prominent critical feature in the work is the extremely positive, clear, and decisive argument — decisive, we mean, as to the writer's own conviction — against the genuineness of that Gospel; together with his protest against the "bigoted sophistry" which attempts to foreclose the argument by an appeal to religious prejudice.

These points indicate the writer's general position, which is maintained with good ability and the best of temper; also with an easy, ample, and familiar scholarship, too rare in popular works of this

---

[*] The Character of Jesus Portrayed; a Biblical Essay. With an Appendix. By Dr. Daniel Schenkel, Professor of Theology, Heidelberg. Translated from the German edition. With Introduction and Notes, by W. H. Furness, D.D. Boston: Little, Brown, & Co. 2 vols. pp. 279, 369.

nature among us, which Dr. Furness has done a great service by placing within our easy reach. The undogmatic character of the book will prevent its being acceptable to either extreme wing of the religious public; while the evident check of a devout — not to say ecclesiastical — spirit and motive upon the freedom of its criticism lays it open, here and there, to the charge of feebleness and indecision. In its treatment of the cardinal question of miracles, it is, perhaps, better adapted to German habits of thought than ours. With an evident purpose not to deal in denials, and to accept the record for precisely as much as it can be fairly interpreted to mean, it shows as evident a reluctance (as Dr. Furness has remarked) to admit, fairly and squarely, any thing which is strictly a miracle proper, and can be explained into nothing else. Thus it accepts, without scruple and with but slight reserve, the works of healing, vindicating them by a very interesting discussion of the physiological truths or doctrines they imply; stories of control over the elements of nature, and the like, it treats undisguisedly as "legend" and "myth," holding them to belong to a later period of belief, as they are found mainly in later portions of the narrative; accounts of the raising of the dead are unauthentic, or a mistake; the resurrection of Jesus himself, it holds, existed only in the pious imagination of his disciples. In all these points he is met with distinct and steady protest by his translator, who rejoices, in each instance, to accept the narrative as it stands, — the more marvellous, the better illustration of that "nature" whose highest type he sees in the life of Jesus. We wish he were more explicit in conveying and vindicating his conception of this phrase, which, to his own mind, is so large, living, and glorious as to include with ease what most of us are obliged to remand to the vaster domain of the "supernatural." As examples of the difference we have mentioned, in the case of the daughter of Jairus, Dr. Schenkel takes for literal fact the words of Jesus, "The maid is not dead, but sleepeth;" and the raising of Lazarus is barely alluded to, as if obviously unauthentic, and out of place in the narrative: while, in each of these instances, Dr. Furness finds an illustration, particularly vivid and dear to him, of his conception both of the character of Jesus and of the nature of his works. So frequent, indeed, is this difference and protest, that the book itself is a singular illustration of that harmony of spirit and motive, which, on a higher plane of thought, brings together minds that must be ranked, we think, plainly on opposite sides of the line of division in sharpest prominence now.

Considering the book as a systematic recast of the gospel narrative, it has overmuch the air of a paraphrase, with comments for edification. This was perhaps inevitable, if it would avoid the opposite qualities of Strauss and of Renan, — of being a mere criticism upon the text, or else a free, imaginative construction. For the student, — who seeks positive results as stepping-stones, and is content to make absolutely sure of a little ground, hoping that the rest will be firmer by and by, — the more valuable portions will be those discussions which deal with definite points of criticism. But the main motive of the book is a practical and pious one : indeed, the definiteness of its theological view is in marked contrast with its vagueness of scientific handling. The reality of the Christian faith, and of the redeeming work of Christ, make the central thought, to be illustrated by a generous exposition of these earliest documents of that faith. In this, as well as in its style of speculation and its wealth of erudition, it is again in curious contrast with the limited range, the set ethical purpose, the official temper, the secular and assertatory style, of " Ecce Homo." We take these two books, thus discriminated, as studies of high value. Perhaps the value we attach to the first we take partly on the credit of the translator, who has given it an immensely added value of his own, both in the literary form under which he has presented it, and by blending with it the ripest results of his own long-continued, congenial, and devoted study.   J. H. A.

ATHANASE COQUEREL, the younger, deprived of his parochial charge in Paris by the bigotry and terror of re-actionary Calvinism, is doing good service in giving to the world the views of the Liberal faith, in a form that the people can understand and enjoy. His new work " On the First Historical Transformations of Christianity " * expresses the substance of a great deal of reading and thought. In successive chapters, it sets forth the Christianity before Christ ; the actual teaching of Jesus; the Jewish interpretation of the gospel ; the Hellenist interpretation of the gospel ; how it was modified by Paul ; how it was modified by Peter ; how it was modified by John ; the changes made in it by the Roman spirit ; the Christianity of the early Fathers, Greek and Latin, Catholic and heretic ; the Christianity of Constantine : and the conclusion of all is, that these modifi-

---

* Des Premières Transformations Historiques du Christianisme. Par ATHA-
NASE COQUEREL, Fils. Paris. 18mo. pp. 198.

cations of the original gospel were natural, necessary, honest; and that they help us to know it better, and value it more highly. He finds the Johannic type of faith perpetuated in the Greek Orthodox Church; the Petrine Jewish type, in the Roman Church; the Pauline type, in the Protestant Church. His little book is written in a clear, simple, serious style; and is invaluable to those who would find a summary of the opinion of the early Christian time. There is a deep reverence for the character of the Saviour, while there is a full recognition of the influence that both Pagan and Jewish thought had upon his utterances of truth. There is an intimation, at the close of the volume, that the plan may be farther followed, and that a sequel will give the larger history of the " Variations" of later ages. Such a history may be the antidote to the partial and harsh work of Bossuet.

ANOTHER recent contribution of the indefatigable Coquerel the younger to the ecclesiastical history of the French Protestant Church is an account of the "Forçats," or galley-slaves,* who were imprisoned and tortured in the reigns of the later Bourbons for no offence but their sturdy Protestantism. It is a very curious chapter of religious bigotry and oppression. The particular story of two of these victims, Marteilhe de Bergerac, noble by descent, and Jean Fabre, is told at length; and in an appendix is given the touching and simple autobiography of this Jean Fabre, who gave himself voluntarily to the slavery of the galleys as the substitute for his old father. There is nothing in all the annals of martyrdom more beautiful than this relation. This martyrdom for the sake of affection and conscience is the more remarkable, that we find in the story of Fabre no trace of pietism or fanaticism. He was more a philosopher than a religionist.

At the close of the volume, M. Coquerel gives a most carefully arranged list, in alphabetical order, for each year, of the names, ages, residences, and, in some cases, occupations and conditions, of the fifteen hundred who were arrested and condemned in that interval of ninety years, for the sole crime of an unlawful belief. Among these are found the names of many of noble birth; and rich and poor, high and low, meet as brethren in suffering on this roll of honor. Much as English heretics were called to endure, the sufferings of

---

* Les Forçats pour la Foi. Étude Historique (1684–1775). Par ATHANASE COQUEREL, Fils.

French heretics were far keener. The only fair parallel to these is in the sufferings of the prisoners at Salisbury and Andersonville, in the hands of the Southern chivalry. C. H. B.

Some five years ago, we had occasion to notice the "History of Satan," by the Abbé Lécanu, written in the spirit of most pious belief in the Devil and his doings. The more recent work of Gastineau* on the same theme, while it repeats some of Lécanu's facts, and goes over his ground, does this in the spirit of entire scepticism, in the interest of science, and not of religion. M. Gastineau hates the Devil, finds him a nuisance in the world, the plague of all ages, the hinderance to all knowledge, a chimera of superstition and priestly cunning. He has collected a vast mass of curious facts to prove the iniquities and absurdities into which this belief in the Devil entices men. He has ransacked history, ancient and modern, for tales of demoniac possession; and has certainly made the Satan of the Church, and the Satan of the popular fear, a very uncomfortable personage to believe in. He has done in a different way the work which Balthazar Bekker, a Protestant minister of Amsterdam, did, two hundred years ago, who, in order to kill the Devil, was thought to have spoiled the principal dogmas of saving faith, and to have annihilated the Christian religion.

There is too much repetition in Gastineau's work, and some of the facts are so gross as to make it unfit for translation. We are reminded of the novels of the late Mr. Ingraham in the theory here stated and discussed,— that Mary Magdalen was not only a harlot, but that she undertook to win Jesus to an impure love for her. The book, indeed, has overmuch to say of "Madame Satan," that is, the work of Satan through the female sex; yet we are promised another special work on "Madame Satan."

A good history in the English tongue of the idea and influence of the Devil in the world is a thing yet to be desired.

HISTORY AND POLITICS.

That certainly cannot be a bad philosophy which affirms that the fundamental doctrine of social life is the subordination of politics to morals; and it is in the light of that philosophy that the clever essays

---

* Monsieur et Madame Satan. Par Benjamin Gastineau. Paris. 12mo. pp. 552.

upon "International Policy" have been written.* Beyond that general statement, however, which may be considered as their starting-point, it is impossible to see what they have to do with the philosophy of Comte. For the positions on which the writers are agreed: first, that the international relations of mankind are a fit subject for a systematic policy; secondly, that such systematic policy is to be based on the acceptance of duties, not on the assertion of rights; and, thirdly, that the arguments advanced are, in all cases, to be drawn from considerations of a purely human character, as alone susceptible of legitimate and profitable discussion, — these positions are accepted by every liberal thinker as the necessary basis of progress; while the discussions themselves throw no light upon many of the topics which most interest us, and are most vital to England. To be sure, the immediate cession of Gibraltar is advocated as indispensable to satisfy the long-offended pride of Spain, and the Indian policy of England is to be shaped so as to prepare its Eastern possessions to govern themselves; but, upon the harassing questions which now vex the Continent, upon the adjustment of those international relations which a short but bloody war has so terribly disturbed, there are no practical suggestions made. Nor indeed was it the real scope of the philosophy which the book presents, however much it may profess to have them in mind, to deal with immediate political issues; for these issues are, in all cases, the result of causes long existing. But as the exponent of purer principles, as leading the way to a gradual revolution in the mode of thinking upon international relations, the book has a higher value than the advocacy of merely temporary measures could impart to it.

Yet though in the subjects discussed — The West, England and France, England and the Sea, England and India, England and China, England and Japan, England and the uncivilized communities, seven essays in all — there is nothing that is really new except the spirit in which they are written, that in itself, so far as our recollection of similar discussions goes, marks something like a step in English political writing; for, when Englishmen buy a thick octavo book of nearly six hundred pages, which aims to show in vigorous language how the whole course of England, in its advance to wealth and power,

---

* International Policy. Essays on the Foreign Relations of England. "The fundamental doctrine of modern social life is the subordination of Politics to Morals." — *Auguste Comte*. London: Chapman & Hall, 1866.

has been selfish and brutal, — much is to be hoped from the light thus let in upon the English mind. Of the English usurpation in India, there could be no fairer illustration than that which Mr. Pember gives in this volume; while the infamy of the Chinese opium war becomes even blacker, if possible, under the unsparing criticism of Mr. Bridges. But, apart from the genuine tone of the work, which is its chief value, the sketch of Chinese civilization and history by the latter writer, though necessarily brief, will be found valuable for its clearness and thoroughness; while the account by Professor Beesly of the manner in which England acquired its dominion on the sea will furnish some good suggestions in the philosophy of history; for it shows how the maritime supremacy of England cannot be traced back further than the battle of La Hogue (1692), and was not established beyond dispute till the battle of Trafalgar; and that, so far from being bound up with the national life, the very idea of it did not dawn on the nation till after the Revolution of 1688, — not an allusion to it can be found in Shakespeare, or so far as he is aware in Milton, yet the one was the contemporary of Raleigh and Drake, the other of Blake and Montague. It shows, moreover, how the idea of building up a maritime and colonial empire with a view to commerce, leaving France to have its own way on the Continent, first conceived by Cromwell, was never deliberately resumed till the policy of England was permanently shaped by the master-mind of the elder Pitt; and, again, how the real cause of the long war of England with France was the refusal, on the part of the latter, to close the navigation of the Scheldt, which was demanded by the commercial interests of England; and finally, how, instead of seeking war with England, Napoleon wanted nothing so much as peace, which England, obstinate in her greed, would never grant till she had overthrown her adversary, and in spite of the enormous expense of the struggle had come out of it ever so many times richer than she went in, — with the reputation, moreover, of having been fighting all the time for the liberties of Europe.

That nothing, however, absolutely new is contributed by these writers to political science is perhaps their best recommendation; for politics, like morals, do not progress by a special but by a general movement; nations do not advance in the line indicated by any one mind, but through the irresistible control of forces as multiform as their life. In the first essay, nevertheless, Mr. Richard Congreve has made an attempt to be original, — to show what the English mind is capable of in the way of political theory, to be striking without being *bizarre*, to be profound without being obscure. And his theory is, at first hearing, plausible: it is only as we subject it to a strict criticism that we discover the basis of it to be as impossible now as it ever was, since, in point of fact, that basis never existed, as Mr. Congreve claims.

Looking broadly at the history of the world, we find, ever since the absolute rejection of the Eastern element by the Greeks, a certain progressive civilization in the West, interrupted, indeed, for a time by the fall of Rome, but, nevertheless, steadily existing. Of this civilization the main elements have been the Greek intellectual culture, the Roman law, and the Catholic feudalism. The nations, therefore, that have shared most, or shared obviously, in these elements may claim to represent, or rather to be, the West, which of course in this discussion is assumed to be superior to the East, — an assumption which, so far as the beginnings of the West are concerned, is getting a good deal undermined by a wider and more dispassionate investigation of Oriental political systems and intellectual habits. These nations are the French, Italian, Spanish, English, and German; the various dependencies and offshoots of each nation being included in these general designations. Thus, France stands for the French in Canada and Algeria, and England for the Anglo-Saxons, wherever found, — in the United States or Australia; and, as adjuncts of these nations, Mr. Congreve is good enough to include, under the appellation of the West, Greece, the mother of all our *humanities*, though she had the misfortune to miss the benefits of Catholicism, and could never make up her mind to accept those of Mohammedanism; and also Poland, because the Poles were once our support against barbarism, though somewhat unsteady indeed, if we have read the histories rightly.

Now, side by side with the development of the conception of the unity of race, it has been seen more and more clearly how necessary was a hierarchical co-ordination of its several parts. Of this hierarchy, the West is manifestly at the head; and of this West, — if you exclude Russia, as you must, because Russia has never shared either in the Greek intellectual culture (Mr. Congreve forgets that the basis of the very alphabet of Russia is the Greek) or the Roman law or the Catholic feudalism, — you find that the centre, geographically as well as historically, is France. Thus, then, the new order of things is to be, not England and France at war with each other in India and Egypt, for the extension of their commerce and the opportunity of plunder; not Spain, drinking the life-blood of its colonies, and slowly rotting with the poison it imbibes; not Germany, split into a thousand fragments, and each fragment at sword's point with the others; but England and France and Spain and Italy and Germany are to combine in one grand brotherhood, for the regulation of the affairs of the rest of the world, and the harmonious adjustment of their own.

And this union, Mr. Congreve argues, is not altogether visionary. It was in this sense of a hierarchical co-ordination that feudal Europe had a unity wholly different from that which prevailed under the Roman administration. Supreme over many races and over all governments, the Church was the common bond of nationalities, the object of universal respect. And it was not till the Protestantism of the fifteenth century had broken up Europe into hostile parties, with ever-increasing animosities, that the feeling of unity was lost, and with it the commanding position of the West as a governing body.

It is difficult to deal with generalizations of this sort without a degree of fulness impossible in these limits; for there is such a mixture of truth and error, so many deductions that are false blended with so many facts that are true, that one can neither admit nor deny them absolutely. We shall only remark, therefore, that while the whole current of modern history is against such a position as Mr. Congreve seeks to establish for the West, it may very well be doubted, as a matter of science, whether this superiority of a portion of the white race (for it practically comes to that), really rests upon fact. Yet, perhaps, the American critic, far removed from the sulphurous atmosphere of European politics, may not go much out of the way if he finds in Mr. Congreve's theory an attempt at reconciling two of the most distressing difficulties which, to the English mind, are ever looming up in the future of England, — the vast aggression of Russia, not to be disputed, in the East, and the general military and social superiority of France, now clearly recognized at home.

For this readiness to stand by the fact, and to let go for ever an empty pride, we cannot do too much honor to these liberal English thinkers, so much in advance of their nation, in appreciating the tendencies of modern political life. When their generous spirit pervades the English mind, England will have little to fear from Russian aggrandizement or French ambition: and it may then come, perhaps, to admit that America must weigh in the scale of nations by something more than its mass, even by its ideas, which are the true leaders of the civilization of the West; for without their support all coalitions are in vain, ever ready to be overthrown by the first rocking of restless empires. For it is not, after all, any political system, however elaborately contrived which can govern the world, but the spirit of justice, and the love of law, and the general recognition of other than material ends; and these things do not come of political expedients, but of universal, intellectual, and spiritual illumination.

H. J. W.

THE attractive volume of Mr. Howells * contains by far the most interesting, most accurate, and most complete account to be found in our language of the environment and daily life of the inhabitants of modern Venice. Occupying the post of American Consul, richly endowed with the sensibilities of a poet, and with the keen insight and practised tact of a critical observer, Mr. Howells is well entitled to say, "I could not dwell three years in the place without learning to know it differently from those writers who have described it in romances, poems, and hurried books of travel; nor help seeing, from my point of observation, the sham and cheapness with which Venice is usually brought out (if I may so speak) in literature. At the same time, it has never lost to me its claim upon constant surprise and regard, nor the fascination of its excellent beauty, its peerless picturesqueness, its sole and wondrous grandeur." The singular enchantments of the situation, scenery, and art of Venice; the unequalled glory, tragedy, and romance of her history; the dismal squalor, monotony, and mournfulness of her decay; the varied characteristics of the different classes of her population, as illustrated in all the phases of their life, in all the seasons of the year, — are depicted by our author with remarkable, force, fidelity, and beauty. The substance of what he says is marked by sound judgment and conscientious impartiality. His manner of saying it is distinguished by a charm of airy grace, and by a deep fund of poetic feeling, relieved by the almost constant presence of quiet humor. We heartily recommend Mr. Howells's "Venetian Life" to the two large classes of readers, — those who have themselves visited Venice, and those who have not. The former will be delighted to have their reminiscences enlarged: the latter will be glad to have their deprivation lessened. We close with a single paragraph, as a specimen of our author's quality. He is writing of St. Mark's Place in a snow-storm: "Looked at across the Square,

---

* Venetian Life. By William D. Howells. New York: Hurd & Houghton.

the beautiful outline of the Church was perfectly pencilled in the air; and the shifting threads of the snow-fall were woven into a spell of novel enchantment around a structure that always seemed to me too exquisite in its fantastic loveliness to be any thing but the creation of magic. The tender snow had compassionated the beautiful edifice for all the wrongs of time, and so hid the stains and ugliness of decay that it looked as if just from the brain of the architect. The snow lay lightly on the golden globes that tremble, like peacock-crests, above the vast domes, and plumed them with softest white; it robed the saints in ermine; and it danced over all the work as if exulting in its beauty, — beauty which filled me with that subtle, selfish regret that yearns to keep such evanescent loveliness for the little-while-longer of one's whole life. The towers of the island churches loomed faintly and far away in the dimness; the sailors in the rigging of the ships that lay in the Basin wrought like phantoms among the shrouds; the gondolas stole in and out of the opaque distance, more noislessly and dreamily than ever; and a silence, almost palpable, lay upon the mutest city in the world."

MR. MAURICE'S very interesting lectures * on the political topics that just now occupy so much of the English mind and ours offer a text more suggestive than the commentary is satisfactory. He writes never in the clear, "dry light" of science, — always in the suffused and mellow light of imagination, sentiment, and conscience. He loves to melt away the edges of our sharp, dogmatic theories; and shows us the thought, as physiologists study the living organism, in solution and in germ. So he is more suggestive than instructive, and piques more curiosity than he satisfies. Always widening the horizon of our vision, he shows the object we view in the flickering, uncertain light, and in the strong refraction, that belong to the dividing-line of sky and earth, His style affects the soft, dim haze that seems to envelop his thought; and the hard, swift, positive habit of mind we are all fallen into is impatient at sentences and chapters written in a sort of unvarying potential mood. And yet his "may" and his "perhaps" and his "doubtful whether" seem in reality to be the veil of strong conviction, only the conviction is rather ethic than

---

* The Workman and the Franchise. Chapters from English History, on the Representation and Education of the People. By Frederick Denison Maurice. London & New York: Alexander Strahan.

scientific; and it is as if he sought to mark the *moral* quality of it by a form of speech as far at variance as possible from the dogmatic and scientific handling which we generally give to our political ideas.

These lectures are meant to be, in the strictest sense, practical. They are written in the interest of the "Workingmen's College," to which the copyright of them is presented. They deal with the precise points of representation and suffrage which have made and unmade Administrations within the year, and which now and then threaten to bring England to the very verge of a social revolution. Yet the mind of Mr. Maurice steadily refuses to see them in the light that illuminates them to other eyes. He does not deny the theories of reformers and propagandists. He only pleads with them to show how vain and insufficient those theories, or any thing that is rigid theory, must be. He will shed on them the wide, quiet light of history, which steadily rebukes all dogmatism; the pure sky-light of religion and morality, which dulls the passionate and artificial glare. So the reader is vexed to find no solution offered or attempted to the questions as they are apt to be practically put. Instead of it, he finds ethical meditation, historic example, and Christian exhortation.

And yet we doubt whether he will not carry away, at the end, as strong an impression, and as valuable instruction, as if he had found the answer to the thought that lay nearer the surface. That human society is not a mass or multitude of men, but an *organization* of them by their sentiments and their interests; that the PEOPLE is the community of freemen, giving each man a direct interest in the welfare of the whole; that a political community, like the Roman aristocracy, jealous of admitting to its privileges those standing outside, must perish of inanition and sure decay; that citizenship means, not so much right or privilege, as it does obligation and trust; that civil freedom is "the contrast rather than the counterpart" of a savage and unsocial independence, — these are truths, not precisely new, but very desirable to be stated with the force of conviction, and freshness of illustration, we find here; while the great lessons of history — traced from the germs of the Roman Republic to the time when the citizen's privilege was no longer jealously withheld, because it had lost all its glory and its worth; from the germs of English liberty to the dissensions and ambitions of to-day — are traced with that curious felicity of insight and intelligent sympathy so characteristic of the writer's mind. Of special illustrations, also, we have been greatly struck with the words said of our late republican President to the workingmen of England; with the exhibition of the first Christian communities as centres of living organism in a dissolving society, germs of the grander structures of the future; and with the review of the period of the "Holy Alliance," when a style of serious, noble, devout thought, respecting a true statesmanship and a Christian order of society, came into being, with Wordsworth for its chief apostle, relieved against the hard despotisms of the compulsory quiet of that era of peace and restoration. And we see and find in this volume, vague and defective as it may appear, one of the timeliest and finest expositions of the higher morality of a nation's life.   J. H. A.

AMONG the biographies or historical studies that have come to our knowledge, aiming to make the last days of the Roman Republic better known to us, we incline to rate highest the series of sketches included in Boissier's "Cicero and his Friends."* An admirable book, it seems to us, for translation, or perhaps for a recast. It is not a detailed biography; but presents the life of Cicero in a succession of views, each in a sense complete, and making together perhaps the most finished portrait yet attainable. The correspondence of Cicero is, of course, the main authority relied on; but this is supplemented, with curious skill, by the speeches and contemporary documents. One or two of the sketches stand out with peculiar vividness: for example, that of "Cœlius, or the Roman Youth;" in which the career of that fast young man, that prodigal son of the aristocracy, is traced through the dissipations and intrigues, the scandals and rivalries, of the life at Baiæ; through the wayward and petulant ambitions of politics, down to the disgraceful close in the miserable conspiracy against Cæsar's too firm and conservative rule. The temper of the sullen aristocracy that murdered Cæsar, the capricious and uncomfortable relations which Cicero maintained with the Dictator, the motives that stirred the men and parties of that evil time, are traced with very great skill and absolute seeming impartiality. In its mastery of facts, its clear historic sense, its wide sympathy, and its freedom from personal or party bias, this volume appears to us a fine example of that new French school of criticism, of which Taine is perhaps the foremost representative.

---

* Ciceron et ses Amis. Par Gaston Boissier. Paris.

ANTIQUITIES.

A WORK upon Grecian mythology, which departs from the prevailing custom of allegorizing, and treats of the *religion* of the Greeks, not merely of their *mythology*, is a welcome addition to philological literature.* Whether this is the correct point of view or not, it deserves more attention than it has received. From Forchhammer, whose key to all myths is *water*, and who makes out the Iliad to have been an *Ueberschwemmung*, — a truly Neptunian philosopher, — to Max Müller, who resolves them all into the *dawn*, it has seemed impossible for anybody to touch these creations of remote antiquity without unconsciously forcing them to take on the stamp of his own mind, or, at any rate, that of the century in which he lives. We believe that they have all begun at the wrong end. They treat religion, as Hartung says, "as a result of idle speculation and figurative philosophizing," rather than as something which has its origin in the nature and necessities of man. "Can any one believe," he asks, p. 131, "that the Romans would have consecrated altars and chapels to a Fides, Victoria, Concordia, or Honos, and offered them prayers and sacrifices, if they had held them for mere allegories?" — "It is moreover no symbolical representation by which the motion of the sun is called a course (*Fahren*), and chariot and horses, and, as a matter of course, a four-in-hand, attributed to it. The symbol is designed to bring something spiritual nearer to the senses; but here they had already before them something visible and corporeal, and one would suppose that every one could see that the sun has neither chariot nor horses. If, nevertheless, the religious man does not see this, it is clear that he holds the sun as a living god, not as a rolling ball. If, now, this god, like a madman, burns up every thing, he must either himself have become a cruel tyrant, like the Thracian Diomedes, or his horses must have become frantic and run away with him, as with Phaethon." (p. 132).

The author of the work before us begins, as we conceive, in the right way, by investigating, first of all, those modes of religious thought and forms of worship which belong to the Greeks as a people

---

* Die Religion und Mythologie der Griechen, von J. A. HARTUNG. Erster Theil. Naturgeschichte der heidnischen Religionen, besonders der Griechischen. Zweiter Theil. Die Urwesen oder das Reich des Kronos. Leipzig: Verlag von Wilhelm Engelmann, 1865. 8vo. pp. 218 and 250.

of primeval antiquity; when they were not the Greeks of history and literature, whom we know, but a rude race, just emerging from barbarism. His aim is, therefore, to trace out primitive ideas and ceremonies, not suffering himself to be drawn aside by the poets, who " were obliged to alter the myths for their own ends, without regard to their mystic meaning." For this reason, he adds, " Pausanias is of more importance, in my eyes, than Homer and Hesiod." (p. vii.).

He is thus led to give special prominence to the heroes and demigods, as being, originally, gods whose power is now passed away (*verkommen*) and obscured : " The interpretation of their myths gives a key to the interpretation of the traditions of the gods themselves; while these, on their part, are of service in the interpretation of those" (p. vii.). The characteristic of the fully developed mythology of the Greeks, as contrasted with the oriental nations especially, was anthropomorphism; but traces of the primitive worship of nature in the fetich, and animal or semi-human forms, still exist side by side with the fully humanized Olympus of the poets. " We find, contrasted with almost every one of the Olympic gods, one who represents the elements of nature (*Elementen-Geist*) ; the latter receiving little or no attention in the worship, because he belongs to an old, deposed régime, so to speak. Thus we have Okeanus by the side of Poseidon, Gê by the side of Demêter, Uranos by the side of Zeus, Rhea by the side of Hera, Helios by the side of Phœbos, Selene by the side of Hecate, Priapos by the side of Dionysos, Pan by the side of Hermes, and many more" (p. 188). The transition from the older to the newer system, the transformation of " the gods living in nature from shadows and phantoms to persons, with determinate human qualities of an ideal order," he attributes to the poets, and heads one section with the title, " How Homer and Hesiod created their gods for Greeks."

The two parts of the work already published are devoted to the primitive religion of nature which the Greeks held, — " the realm of Kronos" he calls it, — in which we meet with monsters, spirits of fire and water, —

"Gorgons, and hydras, and chimæras dire," —

dæmons, giants, nymphs, centaurs, and satyrs. All this, the natural outgrowth of the uncultivated Greek mind, is as it were the foundation upon which the poets and philosophers built the wonderful structure of mythology, by which they "overcame the horrors of Asiatic and Egyptian superstition [which had begun to invade Hellas], and developed a human, rational religion, whose greatest defect was that it was a national, and not a world-religion for all mankind, and must therefore necessarily die out with the other heathen religions when its time was past" (p. 67). We find less of "Comparative Mythology" in this volume than we anticipated; but what there is is very judicious, and generally by way of illustration rather than as part of the system.

ANOTHER instalment — the first half of the fifth volume* — has appeared of the great treatise on Roman Antiquities, begun by Becker, and continued, since his death, by Marquardt. The present volume is devoted to the family life of the Romans, a topic already exhaustively handled by Professor Becker, in his well-known work, "Gallus." A comparison of the two books, however, gives us no reason to regret that the completion of his task has fallen into Professor Marquardt's hands, whose treatment of the subject is clearer, more concise, and more judicious than his predecessor's, while the plan of the work is much better adapted to conveying instruction. To be sure, a man of genial imagination can convey a good deal of information in the guise of a simple fiction, as Böttiger did in his "Sabina," which is as superior (in its limited scope) to "Gallus" as a work of imagination is to one of dry detail. But after all, erudition is not to be *smuggled* into the mind by any appeal to the fancy, especially so dull and unskilful a one as "Gallus," which is a ponderous attempt to construct a romance out of antiquarian scraps, taken from Propertius, Petronius, Martial, and Juvenal.

The volume before us contains an exceedingly clear, concise, and well-digested statement of what is known upon the subjects discussed, illustrated by very copious references and citations. We cannot better illustrate its superiority to Becker's narrow and pedantic way of looking at a subject than by their respective treatment of, perhaps, the most important of the disputed points that come up in this volume, — the identity of the *atrium* and the *cavum ædium*. Pliny the younger, in the description of his Laurentine villa, speaks of both as *atrium* and

---

* Handbuch der Römischen Alterthümer. Fünfter Theil. Römische Privataltertümer von J. Marquardt. Erste Abtheilung. Leipsig: Verlag von S. Hirzel. 1864. 8vo. pp. 384.

a *cavædium*, clearly distinguishing the two. On the other hand, the inference naturally, and almost as certainly, drawn from the language of Varro and Vitruvius is, that the two were the same. How to reconcile these contradictions? Becker would disregard the difference in tone and circumstances, and follow Pliny as against the other authorities, forgetting that what might be true of a splendid villa in the second century after Christ, might not be true, as a rule, a hundred years earlier. A rich man, living in an age of unbounded luxury, might well enough have two drawing-rooms for distinct uses, but the question for us is, How was it with Dentatus, Marcellus, and Cicero?

The original Roman house was the *atrium*, — the square, single apartment, black (*ater*) from the smoke which escaped from a hole in the middle of the room. This one apartment served for the whole family, and for all purposes, just as in the case in our Western log-cabins. It was, at once, bed-room, kitchen, dining-room, and place of sacrifice. In time, as wealth increased, other rooms were added, — bed-rooms, kitchen, &c.; but still this original apartment remained the centre around which the others were grouped, — the gathering place for the family, of reception-room, "the open part of the house" (*cavum ædium*). The term *atrium* acquired now a more general signification, and was applied by the poets, for instance, like our word "hall," to any large single apartment for public use: size and splendor are its natural attributes. In ordinary houses, there was but one central room, called indifferently by both names, and used for all family purposes. In large establishments, however, the two sets of functions were naturally divided; and, besides the magnificent *atrium*, used for receptions, and open to the public, there was, after a smaller and more private family gathering-room, open to the air, like the *atrium*, the *cavum ædium* proper (called by Cicero *atriolum*). It is worthy of note, that, while Pliny mentions the two separately in his Laurentine villa, in the simpler Tuscan villa, he speaks only of an "atrium ex more veterum." The eight chapters of the part now published contain the whole of the in-door life of the Romans, the out-of-door life being left for the other part, which is to follow, we are told, "in not a long time." W. F. A.

ART AND TRAVEL.

THE works of the Provençal and Northern French poets, the remains of the Castilian and Middle High-German and Old-English and Scandinavian singers, have been collected and translated and analyzed, says Adolf von Schack, with singular zeal; but, in this choir of all nations, the voice of the very people who so long surpassed them all in culture has not yet been heard, — that of the Arab poets of Spain. And it is this want which he undertakes to supply in his somewhat discursive, but, on the whole, interesting and very useful book,* the fruit of several summers' residence in Andalusia and Granada. Hammer-Purgstall, indeed, has included a good deal of the Spanish-Arab poetry in his vast and chaotic storehouse of material for the history of the Arabian literature; yet Schack's work will be found to throw a good deal of light upon a period hitherto very obscurely known. The political history of the Arabs of Spain, indeed, may be said to have been worse than unknown, until the recent researches of the Dutch orientalist, Dozy, cleared away much of the confusion in which Conde, so long regarded as the chief authority upon the subject, had involved them; for, as Dozy shows conclusively, Conde has taken mutilated passages of Latin Chronicles for translations of Arabian historians; and, when he had the original text, has understood it so badly as to make two or more persons out of one, to take infinites for proper names, and to represent some men as dead before they were born, and others as playing imaginary parts who never existed at all. It is only lately that the publication of the Arabian historians in the original text, most of them edited by Dozy, has afforded a trustworthy basis for the examination of this brilliant period in mediæval history; while, of Dozy's recent critical history of the Mussulmans of Spain, from the eighth to the twelfth century, Schack says, that one must regard it, in connection with his researches upon the history and literature of Spain in the Middle Ages which it supplements, "as one of the greatest scientific achievements of our century; for it has rescued one of the most important periods in the history of the world from the darkness of falsehood and fable, and brought it into the light of historical truth."

The term "Moor," or "Moorish," as applied to the Arabs of Spain and their architecture, has perhaps withdrawn our attention a good deal from the fact, that this whole Mohammedan civilization of Spain was substantially Arabian. It was a term applied by the Christians

---

* Poesie und Kunst der Araber in Spanien und Sicilien. Von ADOLF FRIEDRICH VON SCHACK. Berlin: 1865. Verlag von Wilhelm Hertz, Bessersche Buchhandlung. 2 vols.

of Spain to their Mohammedan enemies, without distinction of the race to which they belonged; and, in this sense, it has passed into all European languages, and has led to the mistake of supposing that the Moorish architecture of Spain, as it was called, was something different from the Arabian, and originated among the Mauritanians or Berbers, who were so largely blended with the Arabs throughout the peninsula. The Mohammedan population of Spain was in truth very mixed, and there were, no doubt, among the many small rulers of Spain in the eleventh century, some of Berber origin; but, nevertheless, the Arabian civilization was everywhere predominant both in the country and in the cities. The Berber princes who made any pretence to culture were ashamed of their Berber origin, and assumed the manners and tone of the Arabs. Every thing that was done in either literature or art was Arabian. The Berbers were looked upon as *barbarians*, and really accomplished nothing; for they attempted nothing. And, if the Moors have any place in the history of art at all, it is, as Schack says, as the destroyers of Cordova and the plunderers of Az-Zahra.

The limitation of the Arabian genius to architecture, to the almost entire exclusion of pictures and statues, has commonly been ascribed to a prohibition, in the Koran, of the representation of the forms of living kings; but Schack maintains, that there is really no foundation for such an opinion. If there be any prohibition of the kind, it is contained in the passage of the fifth sura, where it is said, "O true believers! surely wine and lots [games of chance] and images and divining arrows are an abomination, of the work of Satan; therefore avoid them, that ye may prosper." But these words are understood by many commentators as applying only to idolatrous images, while others have looked upon them as applying only to the carved pieces or men with which the pagan Arabs played chess, and others to the representation of the forms of such bodies as cast a shadow. There are, indeed, many traditional expressions of the Prophet in disapproval of the representation of the forms of living kings; but there is no express law of his religion against it, as there is against the drinking of wine. And, even in this matter of wine, the prohibition was early disregarded. The poets of Damascus, at the court of the Ommiades, made the praises of wine the chief burden of their songs. · And, though music and dancing were also condemned in the Koran and the traditions, yet, before a century had elapsed after the Hegira, the palaces of the caliphs swarmed with guitar-players and female-dancers, and no feast among the people was complete without both. It is therefore not a law, but, at best, a strong prejudice among the Orthodox, which restrained the Mohammedan artists from representing the human form; and, in point of fact, we find numerous instances of such representation. The caliphs Moawia and Abd ul Melik, of the dynasty of the Ommiades, had their coins struck, bearing a full-length representation of themselves girded with a sword. Chomarujah adorned his palace at Cairo with statues of himself and his wives, made of wood highly carved, and painted in gorgeous colors, wearing crowns of purest gold on their heads, and turbans that glittered with precious stones. Carpets, moreover, the use of which is so common throughout the East, were often adorned with figures. The Fatimites had them inwoven with portraits of kings and celebrated men, while the tapestries with which the sides of their tents were hung were covered over with figures of men and animals, and porcelain dishes were found in their treasury supported upon figures of lions curiously wrought. And the workshops of Cairo were constantly turning out statuettes of gazelles and elephants and giraffes, which were used at banquets, except when the cadi or other Orthodox personages were present. The heretic dynasty of the Fatimites, indeed, affords the most numerous instances of painting and sculpture; but many others may be gathered from the history of the Mesopotamian kingdoms and other parts of the Mohammedan world. No external hinderance, therefore, stood in the way of the development of these arts among the Mohammedans. The cause must be sought elsewhere, — not, however, in the want of subjects; for a Mohammedan Titian would have found a congenial field in depicting the joys of the blessed among the black-eyed virgins of Paradise, and a Mohammedan Rembrandt would have found inspiration enough in the torments of the damned. The explanation, according to Schack, goes much deeper: it lies in the mental limitation of the Arab, in his want of clear perception of external things. His nature, as his poetry shows, is wholly subjective: the impressions which human life and the visible world make upon him are reflected in his mind, and understood; not the visible world itself, or human life in its manifold phases. The power of conceiving and reproducing the peculiar physiognomy of a subject is wholly wanting in him; and hence he has neither painting nor sculpture, standing in this respect, together with the rest of the Semitic races, in such striking contrast with the Greek, who was able to give a plastic, tangible form to his conception, — a form which expressed the thought in its clearness, as well as the internal subordination of each element of feeling to the pervading sentiment of the whole.

The Mosque of Cordova may not compare, in the perfection of its architecture, with the Parthenon or the Strasburg Minster; but it is surprising how, out of the discordant materials at their command, out of ancient pillars of various orders and Byzantine mosaics and African marbles, the Spanish Arabs contrived to erect a structure, which was not only one of the most wonderful works of human hands, but was so singularly adapted in its external form to the peculiar characteristics of the Arabian mind. For it typified to the Arab the Paradise that he imagined to himself as he thirsted in the burning wastes of the deserts after water and shade, — a spot cool and sheltered, where the murmuring of fountains lulled him to soft sleep and dreams of bliss. It was the concentration on earth of all the joys that the true believer was to possess on the other side of the grave. In its great court, under thickly-arching trees, played a bubbling fountain, like that by the side of which the blessed were one day to rest; and in the stillness of its vast spaces, dark as with the darkness of sacred groves, with the pillars thick as forest-trees, and the plinths and arches stretching from one to another and spreading themselves overhead, like branches of the tuba, the wondrous tree of Paradise, the pining soul of Islam revelled in solitary delight; for the Paradise it dreamed of was made real to the senses. But, marvellous as this creation of the Arabian architect was, it illustrates in its very conception this limited subjective character of the Arabian mind. For it was not an ideal type of beauty they aimed at, not even an imitation of nature, but simply a vast space sacred to silence and to rest. H. J. W.

THE author of "Five Years in Damascus" and of "Murray's Handbook for Syria" has not done so well in his account of the unvisited and almost unknown Bashan,* but that we wish he had done better. He has been too anxious to interlard his narrative with Scripture quotations, forgetting that all his readers have their Bibles at hand; but hardly any have any description of the Peræa which he was privileged to visit, which remained an unsuspected treasure-house

---

* The Giant Cities of Bashan and Syria's Holy Places. By the Rev. J. L. PORTER. New York: Nelson & Sons, 1866.

of magnificent ruins till a recent time, and even now is shut against almost every visitor of Palestine by ferocious hordes of Bedouins. One portion of this " desert land" is, however, an exception. Crossing the Bridge of the Daughters of Jacob, at the northern end of the Lake of Tiberias, we travelled three days through this Arab territory without molestation, and with only a single armed guard, — over the identical road which St. Paul took on his eventful journey to Damascus. But this is not the region of the grand remains, to which Mr. Porter devotes less than a hundred pages, unillustrated in the American edition by any map, tantalizing one by very brief details, rounded off with a passage from Ezekiel or Isaiah. But here is the wonderful fact: a country of exceeding beauty and rare fertility, a part of that Palestine now so easily and so frequently visited, exemplifying perfectly the patriarchal life among its tented tribes, containing numerous cities with perfectly habitable houses, yet less explored than the pestilential coasts of Africa, or the frozen solitudes of the North Pole. It seems stranger than fiction, that hundreds of cities in this once-crowded region contain numberless houses as habitable as when they were erected, not a roof shattered, not a wall rent, not a door removed, — stone cells we might term them, yet ornamented, comfortable, adapted to the sultry climate, giving unmistakable glimpses of domestic life two thousand years ago. From the battlements of the Castle of Saleals, Mr. Porter counted thirty towns and villages, dotting the fertile plain, whose nearly perfect houses had not boasted an occupant for more than five hundred years.

Suweideh, the largest of these deserted cities, being entered over a Roman bridge, through a Roman gateway, gave to view a straight, paved street, a mile long, lined with elegant remains, — now the ruins of a fountain, now a church, now a theatre, now an aqueduct, now a Corinthian peristyle, now what the author strangely styles an " opoea ; " but ruin heaped upon ruin, of various styles and different ages, — temples transformed into churches, churches into mosques, and all now abandoned to utter desolation, — in this city, however, relieved by a few hundred Druses, a fanatical sect, who till the soil rudely, and maintain a life-and-death struggle with the Arabs.

Bozrah, the ancient capital, contains two theatres, six temples, ten churches or mosques, besides palaces, baths, fountains, aqueducts, triumphal arches, and other structures, all in ruins, additional to a grand castle, the strongest in Syria. Just here, when we hope to pass hand in hand with the courageous missionary through these vast architectural monuments of a buried race, he mocks us with a Scripture passage, not written of Bozrah in particular: " Thus saith the Lord God of the land of Israel: They shall eat their bread with carefulness, and drink their water with astonishment, that their land may be desolate from all that is therein, because of the violence of all them that dwell therein. And the cities that are inhabited shall be laid waste, and the land shall be desolate" (Ezek. xii. 19, 20).

The principal part of the book is upon Jordan and the Dead Sea, Jerusalem and its environs, the land of the Philistines, Galilee and the Northern-Border Land, accounts of repeated visits through the length and breadth of the Holy Land, with continual references to prophecy, and the occasional discovery of lost localities; but not adding materially to the admirable collection of intelligence in his invaluable "Guidebook." Rev. Mr. Porter is a person of strict veracity, marked courage, and religious enthusiasm, but not a little mistakes as to the kind of intelligence even the Christian public, and far more the world of letters, desires at his hand.   F. W. H.

THE English commander of "the loyal and faithful auxiliary legion" in the Chinese Revolution, having lost his wife in battle, having seen his rebel friends driven back to a small territory near where they commenced the warfare, finding little more occasion for active service while the British Government turned its irresistible artillery against the almost unarmed Ti-pings, has yielded to the desire of the insurrectionary leaders, and become their historian in the beautifully illustrated work, "Ti-ping Tien-Kwoh."*

A personal interest is inwoven with the story: Lin-le marries a native lady; she is stolen; he rescues her at the peril of his life. By and by, after more than enough adventures for an ordinary novel, including one attempt at his life by the jealous lady, she falls at his side in battle. Of course, the hero of his own story is all that is heroic. But his judgment does not equal his courage. His censure of the rebels for not capturing Pekin, and for dividing their forces too much, by garrisoning various captured cities, may be just enough; but, whatever they did, while the English generals and admirals were abusing their pretended neutrality to fighting battles for the Imperialists, and winning victories where they had only known defeats, all

---

* Ti-ping Tien-Kwoh: the History of the Ti-ping Revolution. By Lin-le, Special Agent of the Ti-ping General-in-chief. London: Day & Son, 1866. 2 vols.

was certain to go wrong. The best opportunity Christianity ever had of working its way into the heart of these four hundred millions — under the patronage of men who swept away every vestige of idolatry, circulated the Scriptures, solicited missionaries, prohibited opium-smoking, torture in courts of law, prostitution, the slave trade, deformity of feet, and shaving of heads — was wantonly thrown away. Lin-le asserts that a single missionary's refusal to establish himself at the rebel capital ruined the rebel cause, and forfeited the greatest missionary opening of our time. This seems an extravagance. But it is hardly possible to keep calm, and read the capture of town after town, effected by English artillery, completed by the indiscriminate massacre of every man, woman, and child, with tortures too horrid to be told. And, even after Major Gordon was reproved by Sir F. Bruce for violating his promised protection by permitting the murder of thirty thousand at Soochow, in the capture of Wusee, Karangfoo, Hwhasoo, and Changchowfoo, like atrocities were perpetrated under the military superintendence of this same English officer. Nor were the battles such as civilized men should have engaged in a second time. The loss of the rebel natives in a single contest would amount to thousands, when not more than a single Englishman would be slain, because wooden stockades were assailed by sixty-two pounders, and defended by bamboo spears, gingalls, and brickbats. To rain destruction for twenty hours upon utterly helpless natives, who could not make any effectual reply, — in support of an effete tyranny which insulted its very defenders, paid no debts save upon compulsion, and arrayed itself against every step of civilization, — is not the warfare of which an Englishman should be proud. And all this defeat of new-born hopes, this conflagration of hundreds of towns, this starving of hundreds of thousands by the destruction of public granaries everywhere, to be wrought under the mask of civilized neutrality!

F. W. H.

TRANSYLVANIA is shown by Mr. Boner[*] to be one of the most backward countries in Europe, — rich in mines, of an exceedingly fertile soil, with baths of wonderful efficacy, and yet quite undeveloped. Partly because of its utter destitution of railroads, partly because of the superstitious attachment of its natives to the old ways, partly because of excessive taxation and governmental oppression, the people are

---

[*] Transylvania: its Products and its People. By CHARLES BONER. London: Longmans, 1865.

not happy, or progressive, or worthy of their position. Many of the Transylvanian customs have been kept hundreds of years unchanged: the same antiquated looms are employed as men admire to-day upon the monuments of Egypt; the same custom of storing the grain in the church-vaults as was caused by the invasions from Turkey; the ornaments of the women even are hundreds of years old; the very sayings of grandparents are repeated as unquestionable oracles;— every thing new is wrong, every thing antiquated is still the mode. To the best measures of the Austrian Government the Transylvanian answer is, "It is an innovation;" so that the wisdom of statesmen and the policy of cabinets seem to be kept at bay by this ignorant conservatism. Meanwhile, superb ruins all over the country are being destroyed for peasants' huts, public roads are left to perish for want of repairs, and only the Wallach and the Gypsy are increasing in numbers, wealth, and influence.

Disappointed of any information as to the Unitarian Church of Transylvania, we have to be satisfied with an anecdote or two about the Greek, agreeing as they do with what we have seen of that effete institution in adjoining lands. A friend of the author's, finding a party of natives dragging their priest along as prisoner on a Saturday, was informed that they were about to lock him up, so that he might not be too tipsy the next morning to read service. Another Greek priest begged of the Protestant minister some paper that was written upon, and was furnished with his daughter's old copy-books. Afterwards, strips of these books were given out by this illiterate priest as marriage certificates. Still another threatened his people, that, if they did not fast and pray more, God would send grasshoppers to desolate the land; and the same threat was found to have been circulated through the district.

Kossuth is spoken of very plainly as a consummate orator and an admirable writer, but neither a statesman nor a soldier; sincere and well-intentioned, but lax in discipline, irresolute, and insatiable. Boner's view, the view of the Hungarian nobility, is that Kossuth gathered around him a body of enthusiastic followers by the power of his eloquence, precipitated measures for which the better classes were not prepared, and hurried on reform faster than it was possible for the people to go. The failure of his measures injured the country exceedingly, though many of the enmities excited by the war are already forgotten, and no idea of another struggle seems to be entertained.

F. W. H.

PROFESSOR SMYTH has made a very beautiful and curious book in defence of a very fantastic and untenable theory. He solves the meaning of the Great Pyramid* in a strange way, which is more creditable to his ingenuity and piety than to his good sense. He separates the Great Pyramid by a broad line from all the other Egyptian pyramids. These may have been the tombs of kings; but the Great Pyramid is the divinely ordered and the divinely fixed standard of time, weight, and measure. It was set in its place by the special appointment of Jehovah, that all the world, henceforth and for ever, might know how to reckon days and weeks, feet and inches, pints and quarts, pecks and bushels. Such a standard was needed for the world, in the chaos of clashing opinions and customs; and, at last, after four thousand years, it has been revealed by Mr. John Taylor, whose interpreter and defender the Edinburgh astronomer is content to be. This monument was intended to outlast the ages; and, if the nations are wise, they will consult its symmetrical sides, its angles, its passages, its chinks in the wall, and especially the mysterious coffer in its central chamber, and adjust by this all their methods of time, space, and quantity. The riddle of the ages has at last been read, and England is summoned to pause from the sacrilege that would forsake the inspired pyramid-system for the profane decimals of unbelieving France.

Professor Smyth comes forth as a social and moral reformer in this key to the scientific marvel. It is to be feared, however, that he has damaged his scientific argument by his questionable exegesis of Scripture. His views of the Pentateuch are by no means in harmony with the views of Colenso; and he gives an earlier date and a more historic accuracy to the statements of the Book of Job than any careful critic will sustain. The scientific argument, too, has to be strained, in order to bring the tables of weight and measure which England uses into harmony with those lines of Egyptian stone. There are uncomfortable fractions which vex his calculations. All his enthusiasm for the new theory cannot blind his readers to the fact, that he leaves discrepancies unexplained, and that he twists resemblances into identities. We do not think that his fine drawings and photographs and diagrams dispel that mystery of the colossal monu-

---

* An Inheritance in the Great Pyramid. By PROFESSOR C. PIAZZI SMYTH, F.R.SS., L. & E., Astronomer Royal for Scotland. With Photograph, Map, and Plates. London: Alexander Strahan & Co., 1864. 12mo. pp. xvi. 400.

ment which has reigned in all the stories of the Pyramid since the day of Herodotus. And, after reading the work carefully, figures, fancies, digressions, pious protests, and all, we are prepared to say that it is unsatisfactory; that the theory is "not proven;" and that science still waits for the solution of the problem. We do not think that the British Association will be hindered in its favor for a uniform decimal system by this solemn warning from a mountain of stone and an empty sarcophagus. Some other must answer for us the question, "Who built the Pyramid, and for what was it built?"

C. H. B.

In the expectant period of American poetical literature, — thirty or forty years ago, — perhaps no name was more prominent, or associated with more confident anticipations, than that of Percival. It is pleasant to freshen the associations, which school-books and popular reputation have connected with it, by the interesting and beautiful biography lately published.* The fame of the poet has grown somewhat dim. He soon wearied of the task of keeping it bright by renewal; and there was not the live quality in it, or the patient artist workmanship, to make it classic and imperishable. So that we learn, with a sort of surprise, how high his rank was once thought to be among our native poets. And it is with still greater surprise that one comes to know how utterly that brief youthful fame was eclipsed by the solid achievements of his later life. One of the rarest heroisms, one of the painfullest tragedies, one of the noblest martyrdoms, in the history of letters, we find recorded here. A narrative direct, simple, full, unobtrusive, is filled out with letters of personal reminiscence of singular interest. Fighting with penury, disappointment, baffled ambition, and a temperament morbid to the very verge of insanity, here was a mind of almost unequalled wealth of positive attainments of restless activity, of scholarly and scientific faculty, bordering close on the highest genius. We do not know whether to call such a life unhappy, though, in almost all its outward aspects, it is very sad. The biography is very instructive, — if such a temper and mind could learn from precept or example. It is certainly one of the most interesting, curious, and valuable records that our literary annals have afforded.

---

* The Life and Letters of James Gates Percival. By Julius H. Ward. Boston: Ticknor & Fields.

NEW PUBLICATIONS RECEIVED.

The Works of the Right Honorable Edmund Burke. Revised edition. Vol. IX. Boston: Little, Brown, & Co. pp. 493. (Containing Articles of Charge against Warren Hastings, and Speeches in his Impeachment.)

The History of Christianity, from the Birth of Christ to the Abolition of Paganism in the Roman Empire. By Henry Hart Milman, D.D., Dean of St. Paul's. 3 vols. 12mo. New York: W. J. Widdleton.

A History of the Gypsies; with Specimens of the Gypsy Language. By Walter Simson. Edited, with Preface, Introduction, and Notes, and a Disquisition on the Past, Present, and Future of Gypsydom, by James Simson. 12mo. pp. 575. New York: M. Doolady.

On Democracy. 8vo. pp. 418; also, The Making of the American Nation; or, the Rise and Decline of Oligarchy in the West. By J. Arthur Partridge. 8vo. pp. 523. Philadelphia: J. B. Lippincott & Co.

An American Family in Germany. By J. Ross Browne. Illustrated by the Author. 12mo. pp. 381; The Race for Wealth. By Mrs. J. H. Riddell; All in the Dark. By J. Sheridan Le Fanu; Sir Brooke Fosbrooke. By Charles Lever; The Beauclercs, Father and Son. By Charles Clarke; Madonna Mary. By Thomas Oliphant. New York: Harper & Brothers.

Melibœus Hipponax. The Biglow Papers. Second Series. Boston: Ticknor & Fields. pp. 258.

The Poems of Alfred B. Street. New York: Hurd & Houghton. 2 vols. pp. 302, 338.

Flower-de-Luce. By Henry Wadsworth Longfellow. With Illustrations. Boston: Ticknor & Fields. pp. 72.

Maud Muller. By John G. Whittier. With Illustrations by W. J. Hennersy. Boston: Ticknor & Fields. 8vo. pp. 12.

The King's Ring. By Theodore Tilton. Illustrated by Frank Jones. New York: Hurd & Houghton. pp. 8. (Quaintly and tastefully illuminated; a beautiful fancy piece, with a moral.)

Reading without Tears; or, a Pleasant Mode of Learning to Read. Part Second. Sqr. 18mo. pp. 292. New York: Harper & Brothers.

Red-Letter Days in Applethorpe. By Gail Hamilton. pp. 141; Stories of Many Lands. By Grace Greenwood. pp. 206; A Summer in Leslie Goldthwaite's Life. By Mrs. A. D. T. Whitney. pp. 230. Illustrated. Boston: Ticknor & Fields.

Ned Nevins, the Newsboy; or, Street Life in Boston. By Henry Morgan. Illustrated. Boston: Lee & Shepard. pp. 424.

The Arabian Nights' Entertainments. A new edition, revised, with Notes, by the late Rev. George Tyler Townsend. Sixteen Illustrations. New York: Hurd & Houghton. pp. 583.

The Sanctuary: a Story of the Civil War. By George Ward Nichols, author of "The Story of the Great March." With Illustrations. 12mo. pp. 286. New York: Harper & Brothers.

Personal Recollections of Distinguished Generals. By William F. G. Shanks. 12mo. pp. 347. Illustrated. New York: Harper & Brothers.

The Life and Light of Men. An Essay. By John Young, LL.D. (Edin.) 12mo. pp. 497. Alexander Strahan, London and New York.

First Years in Europe. By George H. Calvert. Boston: William V. Spencer. pp. 303.

Morning by Morning; or, Daily Readings for the Family and the Closet. By C. H. Spurgeon. New York: Sheldon & Co. pp. 403.

TARRANT'S
EFFERVESCENT
SELTZER APERIENT.

This valuable and popular Medicine, prepared in conformity with the analysis of the water of the celebrated Seltzer Spring in Germany, in a most convenient and portable form, has universally received the most favorable recommendations of the medical profession and a discerning public, as the

Most Efficient and Agreeable Saline Aperient

in use, and as being entitled to special preference over the many Mineral Spring Waters, Seidlitz Powders, and other similar articles, both from its compactness and greater efficacy. It may be used with the best effect in all

Bilious and Febrile Diseases;

  Sick Headache; Loss of Appetite;

    Indigestion, and all Similar Complaints,

Peculiarly incident to the Spring and Summer Seasons.

It is particularly adapted to the wants of Travellers by sea and land, Residents in Hot Climates, Persons of Sedentary Habits, Invalids, and Convalescents.
With those who have used it, it has high favor, and is deemed indispensable.

In a Torpid State of the Liver, it renders great service in restoring healthy action.

In Gout and Rheumatism, it gives the best satisfaction, allaying all inflammatory symptoms, and in many cases effectually curing those afflicted.

Its Success in Cases of Gravel, Indigestion, Heartburn, and Costiveness, proves it to be a Medicine of the greatest utility.

Acidity of the Stomach, and the Distressing Sickness so usual during Pregnancy, yields speedily, and with marked success, under its healthful influence.

It affords the Greatest Relief to those afflicted with, or subject to, the Piles, acting gently on the bowels, neutralizing all irritating secretions, and thereby removing all inflammatory tendencies.

In fact, it is invaluable in all cases where a gentle Aperient is required.

It is in the form of a powder, carefully put up in bottles, to keep in any climate; and merely requires water poured upon it, to produce a delightful effervescent beverage.

Taken in the morning, it never interferes with the avocations of the day, acting gently on the system, restoring the digestive powers, exciting a healthy and vigorous tone of the stomach, and creating an elasticity of mind and flow of spirits which give zest to every enjoyment. It also enables the invalid to enjoy many luxuries with impunity, from which he must otherwise be debarred, and without which life is irksome and distressing.

Numerous testimonials from professional and other gentlemen of the highest standing throughout the country, and its steadily increasing popularity for a series of years, strongly guarantee its efficacy and valuable character, and commend it to the favorable notice of an intelligent public.

Manufactured only by TARRANT & COMPANY,
    278, Greenwich Street, New York.

STEINWAY & SONS'

GRAND, SQUARE, & UPRIGHT PIANO-FORTES,

are now acknowledged the best instruments in America, as well as in Europe, having taken Thirty-two *First Premiums, Gold and Silver Medals*, at the principal Fairs held in this country within the last ten years; and in addition thereto they were awarded a First Prize Medal at the Great International Exhibition in London, 1862, for POWERFUL, CLEAR, BRILLIANT, and SYMPATHETIC TONE, with excellence of workmanship, as shown in Grand and Square Pianos. There were 269 Pianos, from all parts of the world, entered for competition; and the special correspondent of "The Times" says:—

"Messrs. STEINWAY's indorsement by **the jurors is emphatic, and stronger and more to the** point than that of any European maker."

Among the many and most valuable important improvements introduced by Messrs. Steinway & Sons, in their Piano-fortes, the special attention of purchasers is directed to their PATENT AGRAFFE ARRANGEMENT, for which Letters Patent were granted them Nov. 29, 1859. The value and importance of this invention having been practically tested, during a period of nearly six years, by Steinway & Sons, in all their Grands and highest-priced Square Piano-fortes, and admitted to be the greatest improvement of modern times, they now announce that they have determined to introduce their "Patent Agraffe Arrangement" in *every Piano-forte manufactured by them, without increase of its cost*, in order that all their patrons may reap the full **advantage** of this great improvement.

Reasons for Purchasing a STEINWAY *Piano-Forte in preference to all others.*

FIRST. — *The fact* that they have been awarded the first premiums, both in Europe and America, by the most competent and inflexible of judges.

SECOND. — *The fact* that all their "scales, improvement, and peculiarities of construction," have been copied by a large majority of the manufacturers of both hemispheres, as closely as could be done without infringement of patent rights; *thus admitting their vast superiority over all others*.

THIRDLY. — *The fact* that a large number of manufacturers and "Associations" *profess* to make Piano-fortes *exactly like Steinway's*, or to have been in their employ as foremen or workmen, thus conceding their excellence in claiming an indorsement for their own instruments.

FOURTHLY. — *The fact* that, while the majority of the smaller makers manufacture their Pianos in several separate shops, **and** *purchase* the actions, some also the keyboards, and even the cases for their instruments, *ready made*, every portion of a "Steinway" Piano, from its incipiency to its completion, is manufactured in one immense building, under the immediate personal superintendence of the Messrs. Steinway (father and **three** sons), thus insuring perfect uniformity and unrivalled excellence.

FIFTHLY. — *The fact* that no Piano-forte with the **slightest possible** defect is ever permitted to leave the manufactory; and that every Steinway instrument *is warranted for Five years*.

SIXTHLY. — *The fact* that, in purchasing a Piano-forte, the established reputation of its maker should be relied on as strongly as its *apparent* quality, and far more than its first cost.

SEVENTHLY. — The immense working capital employed, which commands alike the choice of labor, the employment of the most skilful artisans, the selection and accumulation of materials of all kinds, and the thorough and lengthened seasoning process to which the lumber is subjected.

EIGHTHLY. — *The fact* that the unexampled success achieved by STEINWAY & SONS' PIANO-FORTES, in spite of all and every opposition, is admitted to be owing to their sterling and lasting qualities, which stand alike the test of time **and** trial.

NINTHLY. — *The fact* that the majority of the most eminent artists of Europe, and, with but few exceptions, the most celebrated pianists resident in America, prefer them for their own private and public use whenever they can obtain them; and their testimony is overwhelming, as will be seen by their certificate, signed by S. B. MILLS, ROBERT GOLDBECK, HENRY C. TIMM, F. L. RITTER, GEORGE W. MORGAN, THEO. THOMAS, MAX MARETZEK, WILLIAM MASON, ROBERT HELLER, WILLIAM BERGE, F. BRANDEIS, THEO. MOELLING, E. MUZIO, CARL ANSCHUTZ, A. H. PEASE, CARL WOLFSOHN, A. DAVIS, F. VON BREUNING, THEO. EISFELD, CARL BERGMANN, and many others.

STEINWAY & SONS,
WAREROOMS, Nos. 71 AND 73, EAST FOURTEENTH STREET (between Union Square and Irving Place), NEW YORK.

Published once in two months, at Five Dollars a year.

Nº CCLX.] New Series. [VOL. III.—Nº 2.

THE
CHRISTIAN EXAMINER.

MARCH, 1867.

CONTENTS.

ART.		PAGE
I.	CHRISTIANITY AND PSEUDO-CHRISTIANITY.—*E. C. Towne*	133
II.	LESSING.—*F. Tiffany*	161
III.	SCHENKEL'S CHARACTER OF JESUS.—*J. W. Chadwick*	186
IV.	HERBERT SPENCER AND HIS REVIEWERS.—*E. L. Youmans*	200
V.	CRETE AND THE CRETANS.—*H. J. Warner*	224

ART.		PAGE
VI.	REVIEW OF CURRENT LITERATURE	246
	Theology and Philosophy. Mansel's Philosophy of the Conditioned, 247; McCosh's Examination of Mill's Philosophy, 249; Miss Carpenter's "Last Days in England of the Rajah Rammohun Roy," 250; *Miscellaneous.* Woolbury's Ninth Army Corps, 252; Channing's Prize Essays, 254; Napoleon's Julius Cæsar, 254; Staunton's Great Schools of England, 256; Meyer's Vergleichende Grammatik, 260; Magill's French Grammar, 261	
	NEW PUBLICATIONS RECEIVED	263

NEW YORK:
JAMES MILLER, PUBLISHER,
522, BROADWAY.

BOSTON: JAMES P. WALKER, 26, CHAUNCY STREET.

PYLE'S
SALERATUS

AND

CREAM TARTAR,

GENERALLY ACKNOWLEDGED

The Best in the Market. Always full Weight.

In the New-England States, PYLE'S SALERATUS is superseding all others. Its purely wholesome character, and general efficiency in baking, are qualifications which the intelligent housekeeper readily discovers and appreciates. These articles are always put up full weight, and housekeepers realize a measure of economy in their use.

PYLE'S O. K. SOAP,

The best Household Soap in America,

Is made from pure materials, similar in quality to the best English and French soaps, and becomes very hard; therefore not liable to the unavoidable waste suffered in the use of common brown soap. By its use all bleached goods will retain the desired whiteness, which is not the case when ordinary soaps are used.

It is also a good Bath and Toilet Soap. Each pound is sufficiently rich in stock to make *three gallons of good soft soap* by the simple addition of water.

There is no exaggeration in these representations, and we can refer to the editors of nearly all the weeklies in New York, who are using the above articles; but we prefer that the practical housekeeper shall test them herself.

Sold by first-class Grocers generally.

JAMES PYLE, Manufacturer,

350, WASHINGTON STREET, NEW YORK.

THE
CHRISTIAN EXAMINER.

MARCH, 1867.

Art. I. — CHRISTIANITY AND PSEUDO-CHRISTIANITY.

In his volume entitled "Reason in Religion," Dr. Hedge opens his discussion of the position of Christ in the Christian Church with the following significant passage:—

"In the various attempts which, during the last half-century, have been made to construe the veritable image of Jesus from the ill-digested and often conflicting accounts of the four evangelists, no result is so conspicuous as the impossibility of any valid and final solution of that problem. The historical and legendary are so confused in these narratives, the genuine sayings of Jesus are often so undistinguishably blended with the comments and interpolations of his reporters, that criticism, incompetent to the work of elimination, can do no more than furnish an approximate and conjectural reconstruction.... It comes to this at last, that every reader must construct his own Christ from the fourfold record, according to his own impression of the verisimilitudes of the case. And, on the whole, the impression derived immediately from the record by a thoughtful reader, with no theory to support and no case to make out, is quite as likely to be correct as any obtained through a foreign medium.

"Were it possible to reproduce, with exactitude beyond dispute, the portrait of the true historical Jesus, the image, I suppose, would be found to differ widely from the Christ of the Church, or the Christ received by the great majority of Christians." — *Reason in Religion*, pp. 227, 228.

The interpretation of Christ and Christianity, which we are about to present, became matter of distinct and earnest conviction with us before we had been permitted to see any of the results of modern criticism, and when, as yet, our study of facts had not gone beyond the pages of the New Testament. The original traditional aspect of the matter with us had inspired us with implicit faith in Jesus as the ATONING GOD AND SAVIOUR of a sinful world. This faith was not at first disturbed by any direct results of study or of thought. Criticism had not yet touched for us the "fourfold record." Inquiry had not disturbed, in the least particular, our evangelical interpretation of that record. With the single exception of a consciousness of God, newly re-awakened and enlarged, every thing in us and around us conspired to persuade us of the truth of Orthodoxy.

We did not fall into unbelief at all. Our denials were not born of scepticism; and yet we did entirely throw off the yoke of tradition. Our attitude towards the Christian Church was completely changed.

This change, however, was no change of the inward life, save as growth is change. The supreme principle of our Christian faith, direct faith in God, was carried up to a degree which left far behind the subordinate parts of our faith. An indestructible conviction, that *for all things God will provide*, became our supreme rule of faith, replacing as such the old rule of Christ's words and of the Biblical catechism. It was a great overturning as to the outward setting forth of truth, and as to our outward relation to the Christian Church; but, as to the inward life of faith and the soul's relation to God, it was no more than a natural unfolding of pure belief. Belief in God, so much enlarged as to exclude every form of partial faith, was the law of faith under which we entered upon, and earnestly prosecuted, a diligent examination of the true significance, under God, of Christ and Christianity. This was our bias, our prepossession, our guiding principle. " A thoughtful reader, with no theory to support and no case to make out," says Dr. Hedge, is most likely to obtain a correct impression of what Christ in truth was. Does he mean just this? Is not a supreme prepossession of faith in God the best possible preparation for the study of God's word and work in Christ and Christianity?

From the first, we fixed our thought on the trial in the garden, as affording a key to the life and character of Jesus. It seemed to us necessary to penetrate the human experience of that thrice-repeated prayer, that "my will" need not be set aside by "thy will," and to divine the full significance of the fact that it was finally set aside. How was it that there was such agonizing effort at giving up this "my will"? and what was it which "my will" contemplated? Answer these questions, and it will be possible to have a well-grounded general opinion in regard to the life and character of the Christ of history, and from that to proceed to a distinct view of historical Christianity. If Jesus cherished a purpose which was not sanctioned in the will of God, and came in consequence into conflict with the purpose of *his* Lord and Master, we want to know what that purpose of Jesus was, and where it comes out in his life and teaching, and just how the subjection of this purpose to the will of God modifies for us the revelation of God in Christ and in historical Christianity. Our own conclusion — after ten years, during which we have distinctly contemplated and earnestly studied this question, while as yet few Christian scholars have been moved to raise it — is, that the mind of Jesus was divided between God's thought revealed to him by the Spirit, and a thought of his own suggested in his outward life; and that in general, while pure Christianity, as God designed and designs it, should be built on the pure thought of God, accredited Christianity during these eighteen centuries has been built, as to its form and history in the world, on just that in the mind of Jesus which was *not* true to the will of God. To the argument of this conclusion, or rather to a brief outline of the argument, we now invite attention. It need not be said, that the support, in our view impregnable, afforded to our position by the best results of modern criticism, cannot be shown in a short essay. We content ourselves with a mere sketch of the position itself, and to this invoke the Christian attention of our readers.

It must have been a matter, not of the few years during which Jesus lived in the little world of Galilee and Judea, nor even of a few primitive generations of Christian disciples, but of an extended course of history, to introduce Christian revelation to the human mind. Even if we assume that Jesus was, in his own character and life, and in his individual conception of the divine word and will, a perfect master of grace and truth, how could he utter the revelation which possessed his soul, surrounded as he was by Jewish doubt of the spiritual, and Jewish hunger for the material, manifestation of the divine presence? A glance at the circumstances under which the young carpenter of Nazareth * became to his little circle of disciples the lord of a Messianic dominion, whereof the glory was soon to break upon the world, more than suffices to make evident, that Jesus, if he truly had a perfect thought of the kingdom of God in the soul of man, was not suffered to possess that thought in peace.

---

* It is very instructive to see the lineaments of common humanity in the pictures of Jesus most recently drawn by eminent representatives of the advance of evangelical Orthodoxy. Through the veil of glory which Dr. Bushnell intends for the head of "very God" appear these lines of a human face: "He is simply the child of two very humble people, in a very mean provincial town." — "He goes into his work, therefore, as a merely common man, a Nazarene carpenter, respected for nothing, save as he compels respect by his works and his words." — "It does not appear that Christ grew at all on the public sentiment by means of his discourses. He only mystified a little the public feeling, and made himself a character about as much more suspicious and dangerous." — "His death takes away all confidence; ... the poor disciples are obliged to confess to themselves, if not to others, that their much-loved Messiah is now stamped as another exploded pretender; ... now that he is dead, every expectation is blasted. Even their profound respect, unwilling as they are to shake it off, and tenderly as they would cling to it still, is yet a really blasted confidence, now that he is dead under such ignominy." — *The Vicarious Sacrifice*, part ii. chap. iv.

Dr. Döllinger, "the great Catholic divine of the Continent," has, in a recent sketch of the ministry of Jesus, the following: "This young man, Jesus, was the son of a poor woman who lived in the little Galilean town of Nazareth.... He had lived, as the 'carpenter' at Nazareth, quiet and unobserved.... His immediate neighborhood had perceived nothing remarkable in him; so far from it, that, when he afterwards began to teach in public, his relations thought him mad, and wished to lay hands on his person." — *The First Age of the Church*, vol. i. chap. 1.

He was beset on every hand by the most subtle and tremendous temptation,— the spectacle of his people, of his own chosen even, agonizing with all the force of piety, patriotism, and personal desire for a Deliverer, who should come in visible glory on the earth; and, with an arm not wholly spiritual, should break the yoke of hateful bondage, purge the land of unrighteousness, and bring in material blessedness like a flood.

Through the fervent passion of Jewish piety there ran a signally false conceit. It was that the Lord of the universe had taken the Jew into special covenant relation with himself. And when, in his usual providence, the God of all the earth did not save the Jew from overwhelming calamity, this conceit took the form of confident expectation, that a special Deliverer would be in good time deputed of God to appear on the earth, and vindicate, against all its foes, the chosen race. Little by little, unwittingly, the pious Jew had ceased to believe, "The Lord is my shepherd, I shall not want," and had begun to look for a shepherd other than the living God. Instead of expecting the kingdom of God in holy spirit shed abroad in human hearts, and in heavenly providence overruling all the trouble of an evil world, he looked for a visible manifestation of that kingdom in the person and the reign of a Messianic king, at whose appearing the world should be no more evil to the chosen ones, and trouble should no more beset the holy race. The pure theism of the best religion of the ancient saints was displaced by a *Messianism*, in which the recognition of God in loving faith was postponed to a thoroughly Jewish expectation of a visible heir of David's throne.

Jesus, even if he were a man of absolute perfection, could not but wish to meet that expectation around which gathered all the piety of his people. Yet his best conviction, as far as we can judge from the imperfect biography in our hands, instructed him that the kingdom of God must be providential and spiritual, God's own exercise of control and care, God's own administration of life in the soul. Imagination, duly instructed in the mysteries and miracles of the life of God in the soul of man, may trace in mere outline the conflict in the mind of Jesus between his natural wish as a Jew and his best conviction as a Christ, or spirit-anointed soul; but, except to this extent, we have lost the most significant element in the life of the carpenter-Master of Christendom. The heavy Jewish mind, which the storm of earthly woe had so "pressed out of measure, above strength," invariably slept while the Spirit made intercession in Jesus with groanings that could not be uttered. Of such inner life as their Master had, the disciples knew little or nothing. Hence the record can tell us almost nothing. So much as this, however, we seem able to make out, — that Jesus was moved to commit himself to the hope of living among his people as their Deliverer, through whom the true kingdom of God should come; while yet there were times when this hope utterly forsook his soul, and he was compelled to see and to declare, that for him, as for previous would-be Messiahs, there must be a sudden and violent end, with no hope of Messianic leadership, except in some return in glory which the Father might vouchsafe to his broken people and their suffering shepherd. It is impossible to fix the details of the scene; but the main facts hardly admit of doubt, that the mind of Jesus was profoundly divided between the hope of a life of spiritual — not to say supernatural — kingship on earth, and anticipation of a death which should leave all in the hands of God; though not without some hope, or dream at least, of a throne borne on the clouds in some great day of God's visitation. The last days of the life of Jesus, if we can accept the record, furnish evidence which cannot be resisted. Much as the Master had admitted to himself, and had declared to his disciples, what the end must be, the hope of divine intervention to set up Messiah's kingdom had remained fixed in his heart; with such faith that this would yet prove God's will, and such fond desire that it might be provided for in the divine purpose, that even the cruel fact could not convince him, nor the undoubted fate pluck out his hope, until again and again, and yet again, he had prayed in a great agony "that the cup might pass from him."

Though we drop the veil reverently upon that hour in

which Jesus, pursuing the thought and purpose of his own mind, encountered in full career the will of God, and was forced by the clearest sense of duty to surrender the first aim and chief hope of his life, yet it is impossible not to see how this fact affects the transmission of revelation through the mind and life of Jesus. This surrender to which he was brought, and which he accepted, is the most significant fact of the life of the Christ. All that he did and all that he said must be viewed in the light of this closing scene. If Jesus had in life a thought and will not warranted in the hidden will of God; especially if he had this — as he had — in the most guileless exercise of natural faith and national religious expectation; and, still more, if he proved equal to entire self-surrender, and did relinquish, in view of the ignominious cross, his cherished hope of life, surrendering himself utterly to the will of God, — it is evident that THE FINAL DOCTRINE OF JESUS IS IN THIS LAST DOING OF THE WILL OF GOD, and that by this all that has gone before should be judged, and, if need be, *corrected.*

This surrender of Jesus at last to the will of God requires us to pass over whatever savors of his own will in his previous teaching, and to find his final doctrine, the doctrine sealed with his blood, in *the absolute removal of hope from every other object, and the absolute surrender of faith to God alone.* The confession of Jesus, that he was not sufficient unto himself, made and witnessed as it was, settles, as far as his authority can settle it, the futility of all faith which does not rest on God alone in absolute submission. Does not this final development of the life and teaching of the Master impose on us the necessity of interpreting all that went before, in the light of this last and most impressive lesson? Is it too much to say, that mere justice to Jesus may require us to modify his previous testimony, to make it agree perfectly with this final and most significant testimony? Are we not bound, in the high honor of discipleship even, instead of exalting the very words and will of Jesus, to suffer him to withdraw these in his great surrender, and so to take the story of his life, especially in the imperfect Jew-Christian record which we have, as the envelope or suggestion of revelation rather than as revelation itself? So far as Jesus ever wished to take revelation into his own hands, and to himself break for the world the bread of life, he found reason to give up that wish, and leave all in the hands of God. Shall we compel him to do what the divine purpose caused him to desist from? Shall we insist on his divine sufficiency, when he himself has confessed, that it was not in his will, but in the will of God overruling his own, to accomplish a perfect work for mankind? Are we not bound as honest Christians to accept the most serious and characteristic act of Christ, by which he acknowledged that it was not in him to know or to do the perfect will of God, except by surrendering his own aims, and leaving all in the control and care of the only God and Saviour? It may seem good to exalt Jesus as the Saviour; but is it true to Jesus, or to the truth of God revealed in the experience of Jesus? No matter what accredited authority may command, the authority of truth toward God, and of the true submission of Jesus himself to God, should outweigh with us all other. We must come to the truth of this matter, though it cost us as much as it cost our Galilean brother and teacher. By his sacrifice we are warned, that of us also may be demanded the uttermost sacrifice of cherished thought and pious purpose. If we allow ourselves to feel, "*It cannot be that profound Christian piety is in error*," we may resist, but we cannot alter, the truth. The cup which Jesus agonized before God to put away must be pressed to our lips also, however sincerely and earnestly our traditional feeling may resist the trial, until we become fully conscious that there is no supreme will or name but that of God.

If our position thus far be at all correct, we need hardly say that it is a great mistake to assume, that upon the death of Jesus certain apostolic men became fully possessed of Christian revelation, and transmitted it entire to mankind. They neither transmitted it nor possessed it, except in the imperfect fashion of men who themselves knew but "in part." To question the absolute knowledge of men "called to be apostles," or called to be any thing at all in the "apostolic age," is thought in many quarters extremely heretical. No doubt it is. The Orthodoxy which is most interested on this point virtually assumes, that any man who was an apostle, or who lived while any apostle yet lived, or whose early youth goes back far enough to barely touch the old age of an apostle, must have known all about Christianity; and that when it is evident that Jesus himself did not at first comprehend and attach himself to the whole will of God. This Orthodox assumption is quite unwarranted by facts. The chosen disciples of Jesus were very far from having a full comprehension of the burden of Christian gospel. If they apprehended some part correctly; if they, in part, caught the right spirit of Christian faith, — they yet utterly failed to receive Christianity in its purity and completeness.

A significant comparison may be made here between the regular "historical" apostles and their great rival, Paul. The former were overshadowed completely by the latter, in spite of the fact that they were the accredited depositaries of the story and teaching of Jesus. His comprehension of principle was superior to theirs, and it raised him far above them as a minister of Christian truth. Paul took his hint from the life of Jesus, and wrought it out in his own ardent thought; then he came forward, better possessed of Christian truth than were the apostles, who thought they had learned from Jesus himself. His own account of the matter is capable of no other explanation. He pursued a spiritual method in making himself acquainted with the substance of Christian Idea; and he boldly claimed for the results of his independent inquiry a value not shared by the gospel which Peter, James, and John believed themselves to have received directly from the Master. We need not decide the question between heretical Paul and Orthodox Peter and James. It is enough to point out, that Paul, the "inveterate rationalist," * did in fact

---

* "St. Paul, though disclaiming, as 'carnal wisdom' and 'the wisdom of this world,' the philosophic prepossessions of his time, is himself the subtlest of reasoners, — an inveterate rationalist, never more thoroughly in his element than when arguing the claims of Christianity on psychological grounds, or boldly rationalizing the Old Testament to rebut the scruples of his countrymen. The

overshadow, in the Christian world, the apostolic exponents of a more strictly "historical Christianity."

And, truly, how could we expect to find a correct "historical Christianity" in the apostolic age? If Jesus had been commissioned to give definite form to his faith, and had lived to set this forth distinctly and adequately; if he had been possessed of the lower logical, as well as of the higher spiritual, power, and had made any attempt to define and state in order and fulness the great elements of revelation; and if he had himself possessed a perfect thought of the will of God, and had perfectly presented it, — of what avail had it been? These Jews who alone heard Jesus were hopelessly entangled in their unspiritual conception of the kingdom of God. The best of them hoped to the end that he would "restore Israel." They interpreted every thing, including both Jesus and his teaching, in the light of its supposed relation to "Israel." *
Paul did somewhat better than the rest, because the historical Jesus was taken away. He was compelled to receive Christianity, in part at least, as a matter of spiritual conviction; and, so far as he attempted to take Christ on the historical side, he fell into great error. He was of the mistaken opinion, that Jesus had died in the character of a suffering Messiah, had risen in that character, and in the same would

---

authorities at Jerusalem — Bishop James, and Peter, and the rest — stood aghast, and no wonder, at this 'terrible child' of their communion; they spoke doubtfully of 'our beloved brother Paul' and the 'hard things' in his Epistles; they could not quote him without a caution: but who at this day doubts that Paul's idea was nearer the mind of Christ than the views of his Judaizing critics? Providence adopted it; it carried the age; Jewish Christianity decreased, Liberal Christianity increased, — and will increase." — *Reason in Religion*, pp. 210, 211.

* "Christ to them was the Beloved in whom God was well pleased, the national Messiah, — Son of God, not in the sense of generation, but in the sense of election and divine favor. God was in heaven, and man on the earth: nothing could bridge the distance between them. The risen Christ was gone to God, and would soon return to judge the world and establish his throne on the earth. This was the earliest doctrine concerning Christ, the Jew-Christian doctrine, the Christology of the apostles. . . . It was the doctrine of the first century. There is no Christian writing, whose date can be proved anterior to the close of that century, which recognizes a different doctrine, unless it be as a heresy to be repudiated." — *Reason in Religion*, p. 281.

return speedily to set up on the earth a Messianic kingdom. And in preaching as gospel "Jesus and the resurrection," the historical Christ crucified and risen, he erred from the real truth in Jesus, the faith in which Jesus died, *leaving all in the hands of God.*

Our own conviction on this point is firm, and it has this foundation. So far as we can see, if we permit ourselves to look at the fact, Jesus himself, in wishing, as far as he did wish it, to be historical, to live and build for God in human history on earth, got off the track of God's will, and only concluded and completed the obedience of his life by utterly giving up all expectation of becoming any thing in his own person between man and God. When he made a surrender which left God alone enthroned, his thought of historical Christianity, so to speak, — or, as it lay in his and in the Jewish mind generally, of an historical Messiahship, — was entirely given up. But his disciples took up this thought, partly of themselves, and partly from earlier suggestions of Jesus himself. In doing this, they wholly missed the closing lesson, and the grand lesson, of the life of their Master. They piously dreamed of what "must needs be" in the case of Jesus as Messiah; and, out of such story as was breathed on the air by common thought and common talk, they "constructed" an historical Christ, crucified, risen, ascended, and soon to return, — such a Christ as Jesus had no thought of when he said, "Thy will be done."

If it be necessary to recognize, on New-Testament evidence judiciously interpreted, that Jesus himself was not suffered to have his own will, but came to bitter grief in pursuing it, and was compelled to give up all to the will of God, it cannot be denied that the apostles, in following out the very thought which Jesus gave up, were not in the way of truth, and did not think or do as they would have done had they been awake to the meaning of the last and great experience of their Master. They followed Jesus the Jew, rather than Jesus the Christ. It was natural for them to do this, and in doing it to err sadly from the truth. That which Dr. Hedge says of faith, though inapplicable to sound faith, which ever has the inner light of pure idea, applies very well to the Jewish faith of the Christian apostles: —

"Faith is determined by accidental causes; it has no necessary relation to truth, — a strong persuasion, but no objective certitude. It embraces error as well as truth, and embraces it with equal affection.

"The office of reason in religion is not discovery, but verification and purification. Its function is to make and keep religion true and pure, by eliminating from the code of elemental beliefs the human additions and corruptions that have gathered around it. This faith cannot do: faith can only embrace, not discriminate; and, for want of discrimination, may soon degenerate and turn to monstrous superstition, as in all historical dispensations of religion it has done." *

The overshadowing "accident," in the case of the apostles, was Jewish Idea; and this, in its more spiritual aspects, may well have passed with them for truth, undistinguished from the real truth offered them in the best teaching of Jesus. All the more that these were Jews of piety and zeal, were they likely to bring with them into the sphere of Christian thought that Jewish thought which even Jesus did not give up until he *saw* the end right before him, and saw that this thought could not be the will of God. The "additions and corruptions" which gathered around the elements of pure gospel in the minds of the disciples should not surprise and need not perplex us. Faith could not do otherwise, while as yet it was without the law and order of experience and study. The warm hearts of these disciples, hungry and faint for thoughts of their Master and his kingdom, all unsuspicious that he had given up just what they were clinging to most passionately, could not but be fruitful of pious imaginings, rumors, and supposed "revelations," out of which to construct the story which put Jesus back into the place which he, with so much pains, had abdicated. Paul's account of his revelations shows in part, but amply, how the supplemental history of Jesus, and the prophecy of his return and his kingdom, came by way of "addition and corruption."

---

* Reason in Religion, pp. 207, 209.

In fact, we detect Paul in the very act of unconscious invention in at least one significant instance. There is a passage of Deuteronomy, containing radical doctrine, in which we read of "the commandment" as being "not in heaven, that thou shouldst say, Who shall go up for us to heaven, and bring it unto us, that we may hear it, and do it?" but as a "word very nigh unto thee, in thy mouth, and in thy heart, that thou mayst do it," "to love the Lord thy God, to walk in his ways, and to keep his commandments and his statutes and his judgments."* To a rational interpreter, this will be found re-affirmed in the first and great commandment given by Jesus. Not so to Paul, who was sincerely and ardently consecrated, not to God alone, as taught in the best thought of Jesus, but to Jesus in his Jewish character, crucified indeed, but also raised, and to come again in Messiah's glory on the earth. Supremely anxious to say, "Lord, Lord," to Jesus, and unconscious of the perfect way of doing God's will which Jesus had found in his last hour, Paul honestly wanders into this corruption of his quotation. "But what saith it? The word is nigh thee, even in thy mouth and in thy heart; that is, the word of faith, which we preach: that if thou shalt confess with thy mouth the Lord Jesus, and shalt believe in thine heart that God hath raised him from the dead, thou shalt be saved."† The fact here is undeniable. Paul brings in confession of Jesus as Lord, and faith in his resurrection, by way of corrupting and adding to a passage the clear sense of which is that saving faith consists in obedience of heart and life to God. He adds to the essential word of pure religion, as Jesus had stated it, this word of faith in the risen Jesus, through manifest misapprehension and mistake. Correct the evident blunder of Paul, and, instead of a doctrine of the Lord Jesus and his resurrection, we have a doctrine of God and of the surrender of heart and soul to God. This latter agrees with the best thought and the final example of Jesus: the former belongs to that Jewish thought which Jesus had made it the last and crowning victory

---

* Deut. xxx. 11-16.   † Rom. x. 8, 9.

of his life to discard. Here, then, we come out again to this important conclusion, that neither in those who were apostles before Paul, nor yet in Paul himself, was there a distinct utterance of pure Christian Idea, but only a certain crude grasp of it, — in Paul's case, a large and vigorous grasp, though still crude; and so, for the world, not a revelation, but only a suggestion to faith and study, of the exact truth of God and meaning of God in Christ and Christianity.

Let this be understood and accepted, not quarrelled with in pious anger. It is just as wrong to take the side of Paul's error as to indulge error and foster false notions in ourselves. In fact, we may say a thing more emphatic even than this. We may say that for a man to come to Jesus himself with "Lord, Lord," upon his lips, and take the side of that "my will" which he agonized to give up, is just as much sin and shame, if we could but understand, as any other going against the will of God. Jesus felt this deeply, bitterly even, if we may trust that part of the record which relates a sharp conflict of rebuke between himself and Peter. Compare what Jesus said to Peter when the thought of a Messiahship apparently was uppermost in his mind, with what he said to the same Peter when the other and more obedient thought was uppermost, — the thought of dying, and leaving all in the hands of God. Peter, in the first case, is made the chief of the Church under Jesus, of which Jesus is to be the Christ-king. This savors — does it not? — of that "my will" we are to hear of in the garden. At any rate, as far as Peter is concerned, the Master's judgment changes wholly when the thought of surrendering all possesses him. But this does not fit with Peter's view at all. It promises to end all that pre-eminence he had fixed his heart on. It takes for ever away his "Lord Christ." So he comes out against the sad conviction of the Master — "took him and began to rebuke him" — for giving up in that way. How Jesus blazes out upon him, as against incarnate temptation! Is it not plain how and why he does this? Peter's hopeful word brings up the very temptation against which Jesus is struggling, and to which it would be but too easy for him to yield, it so appeals to profound religious feeling, to undying Jewish faith in the "God of Israel." The soul of the Master has no lasting rest until the cruel event takes him out of the trial. At the last there is a great passion unconquered, the surrender of which completes the truth of this unsurpassed life. Talk of this man as furnished with more than a man's powers, when he goes bowed and crushed under the agony of his endeavor to find and to do the will of God, and only succeeds in the last and overwhelming access of his woe! It is mockery without parallel. What if Jesus did have a "my will," and did anticipate a kingdom for himself wherein Peter should stand next the throne? Did he not give up all that with a final *Get thee behind me?* And to the Church of Peter, or of Paul, or of any Disciples, which rebukes this giving up, and insists on the identical "my will" lordship, does not Jesus say for ever, "Get thee behind me"? Is there, can there be, truth in Peter when he takes up the very thought he rebuked the Master with, and builds a Church, not on the pure will of God, but on that "my will" which was given up while Peter and the rest slept? Must not the honest mind — sadly as it watches with the conflict and agony of the sinless Jesus, and painfully as it notes how little these forever-boasted-of disciples heeded what passed in their Master's mind — vigorously put away whatever has a taint of even that "my will" of the adorable Master, much more whatever savors in his apostles, not of the things that be of God, but of the things that be of men?

It may be very hard not to find the revelation declared. But if it is not declared in distinct terms and pure thought; if it is only suggested even in Jesus, and in his apostles is set forth undistinguished from striking error, — it is our duty to accept the fact, and be content to depend on such revelation as is accessible to our faith. This cross, exactly this, is undoubtedly the best means of grace and truth to our minds. It sends us to the Spirit, — to that true incarnation of divinity, the life of God in the soul of man. The spirit in Christianity, not its form and historical manifestation, is the true revelation; and this is with us to-day as with Jesus and Paul long ago. Dr. Hedge truly says:—

"The spirit which prays in any of us to-day, if the genuine fire of devotion is in us, is the same which discoursed in the Sermon on the Mount, and opened the eyes of the blind; which blew into the soul of Peter, and drove Paul like a rolling thing around the world, and built up universal Christendom, with its temples and its scriptures, its sanctities and its arts."*

If this is not all that the Christian Church has asserted, it is all which the spirit and providence of God established as the foundation of Christianity. The life of Jesus was a revelation, to penetrating faith, of the spirit of truth: it was not a revelation, for the undiscerning natural man, of the body and form of truth. If we have insight to perceive what the spirit of truth was, and what it directly implied, we may state at once the essential doctrine of Christianity; but, without this insight, even this fundamental dogma is beyond our reach. If we truly comprehend the obedience and faith of Jesus, we may define in terms of his faith the general rule of faith and life; but, if we do not comprehend aright his obedience and faith, nothing can save us from going wrong in our whole interpretation of Christian Scripture, however reverently we may hold it as our divine rule. In spite of all that we can do, we find ourselves forced back upon our own comprehension of the spirit, and our own development of the thought implied in the spirit of Christianity. Not only must "every reader," as Dr. Hedge says, "construct his own Christ" out of "the ill-digested and often conflicting accounts of the four evangelists," but every believing student must hear for himself the voice of God, in and through whatever voice of man may come to him. There is no other method of revelation. Dr. Hedge recognizes this fully in the following valuable statements:—

"Revelation is a thing of degrees; yet all revelation is essentially the same. All revelation is in man and through man. It is not an

---

* Reason in Religion, p. 308.

unearthly voice speaking to us out of the clouds; it is not an angelic apparition; but always the voice of a brother man that instructs and exhorts us. And that voice is not the revelation itself, but only its witness and declaration. The true revelation is internal. The only effectual knowledge of God is the private experience of the individual soul." *

"To the question, What is Truth?—the supreme question of the soul, on which hang the issues of everlasting life,—is there no expressed and unmistakable answer of God on which the soul may repose with the certainty of infallible truth, and there end the bewildering quest? No infallible oracle out of the breast. The oracle within, the answer of the Holy Ghost, which the listening, waiting soul receives in the inmost recesses of her own consciousness, is for each individual the high tribunal of last appeal. However desirable it may seem that infallible guidance from without should have been vouchsafed to our perplexity, however we may covet it and sigh for it, it has not been so ordained." †

To us it seems certain, that the final perfect obedience of Jesus, the faith which was fully developed in his last hours of trial, was the true Christian faith. If this be so, two things follow directly: *first*, that the example of Jesus in its perfection warns us to look, not to him as Lord and Saviour, but to the spirit and providence of the living God, the true Lord and Shepherd, the true Master and Redeemer of our souls; and, *second*, that so far as his example before the end suggests or warrants religious trust in himself, it comes short of perfection. We are for ourselves convinced, that the surrender of his own will to God, leaving all in the hands of God, was a manifestation of true Christian faith, the perfection to which through suffering he was brought. Viewed in the light of the ideal, or as the last step of the career of Jesus, this equally seems the very truth to which he attained. Love to God, the good Father of souls, is the spirit of Christianity. Loyalty to God our Father is the essential of discipleship in the Christian Church. If a would-be evangelist makes Jesus say, "I am the good shepherd," Christian

---

* Reason in Religion, p. 67.   † Id., p. 205.

revelation makes the instructed disciple reply, "The Lord is my shepherd." Even if Jesus himself hopes, and somewhat aims, to be on earth a "Lord-and-Saviour" Christ, with power delegated from God, Christian revelation declares to him that this is not the will of God, and that even he must give up all to the only "God and Saviour," the only and the sufficient "Lord and Saviour." Is not, then, the recognition by his disciples of Jesus as the Saviour based on a suggestion not warranted by the spirit of Christianity? Is not the interpretation of Christianity decidedly put wrong by the presence of this idea, that Jesus, in any divine sense, either as atoning God-man or as superhuman teacher, is the Lord and Saviour of man?

Dr. Hedge says of the original meaning of Christianity: "It expelled from the field of faith and worship all lesser personalities, and claimed the whole ground for the one eternal Person above all, and through all, and in all." He further points out, that "Christianity did not keep in this its first estate." But he* does not sufficiently bring out the fact, that ideal Christianity exalts, not merely the eternal Person who is all in all, but so exalts the GOD AND FATHER OF SOULS as to suppress the pretension of any other Saviour. He does not apprize us, that, in its original historical manifestation, this aim of pure Christianity was partially obscured by the natural Jewish opinion of a Saviour in the Christ. He does not make clear enough, that loving and loyal obedience to God involved in Jesus himself the surrender of his Messianic or ecclesiastic aim; and involves in the true disciple, not allegiance to the word or will of Jesus, but absolute allegiance to the discernible word of the spirit and the providential will of God. He too dogmatically asserts that the fulness of the Godhead was in Jesus. The fulness of the Godhead! It would not be in a race of Christs! It surely was not in the man who found his will, not God's will! No more did Jesus absolutely illustrate divine humanity. He did not even affirm it. "*I* and my Father are one" is in the intensest spirit of "my will;"

---

* See Reason in Religion, pp. 251-254.

but we need not accept this as coming from Jesus. We must certainly doubt the historical value of the gospel which puts this flagrant egotism into the mouth of Jesus. Nor is Jesus the life in which we are rooted by Christian faith. The living spirit of God, in which Jesus was rooted, is that life. And though Jesus suggests our ideal, he actually was something quite other than our ideal. He was a Jew, bound by Jewish preconception, and drawn unwittingly by Jewish spiritual hope out of the path of God's will. He was not in himself a revelation either of perfect humanity or of God, though he stimulates our conception of both. He *is* indeed a method, an example of the spirit of obedience, and, in his last hour, of the perfect act of obedience,— surrender of all to God. Dr. Hedge has an adequate recognition of this in the following: —

"When we recollect, and lay it to heart, that the one chief aim of the gospel is to reconcile and unite to God, to bring the soul into conscious relation and immediate contact with the Father, then all dwelling in inferior sanctities, all pre-occupation of mind and heart with lesser names, will be seen to be a traversing of that intent, and contrary to the doctrine of Christ. If 'the Son can do nothing of himself but what he seeth the Father do;' if the Son can give nothing but what he receives,— then why not go to the Father at once? why stop short of the infinite fulness? why kneel at the pool, when through the pool the everlasting prime Fountain invites every soul to full participation of the underived, supernal grace?" *

Is not this a question which admits of but one answer with all who have pure Christian faith in God? And does not this necessary Christian answer involve the entire suppression of faith in Jesus as *the* Son, the miraculous pool to which we must go for grace and truth? It was as Messiah, as ecclesiastic, spiritual vicegerent of God, that Jesus was called *the* Son of God. All that is given up from the moment we comprehend in what faith Jesus himself laid down his own wish and will, to take up in entire submission the will of God.

---

* Reason in Religion, p. 257.

Dr. Hedge assumes that Paul, on "the height of prophetic vision, foresaw the approaching deification of the Son of man; divined its reason and necessity in the counsels of God and the wants of the Church; and so announced, that Christ 'must reign till he hath put all things under his feet;'" and that Paul, further, "casting his inspired glance along the line of the Christian ages, foresaw that this deification would be temporary."* "The verification of the first part of this saying," he says, "has been the chief topic of the doctrinal history of the Church." And elsewhere (p. 239): "No doubt the general prevalence of this conception of Christ as God, an historical and human God, is justified by the moral and spiritual needs of mankind. I must suppose a providential order, a divine method and reason, in it."

Did Paul stand on the height of prophetic vision, cast his inspired glance along the line of the Christian ages, foresee the deification of Jesus Christ, and also foresee, what has not yet taken place, the end of faith in Jesus as the historical and human God? Dr. Hedge alleges no evidence that he did. There was no such evidence to allege. There is no shadow of evidence that Paul foresaw, in any particular, the course which Christianity was to run. On the contrary, so far as he tried to guess what the future would be, he completely failed. He looked for the speedy descent of Jesus "from heaven with a shout, with the voice of the archangel, and with the trump of God," when " the dead in Christ shall rise; and we which are alive and remain shall be caught up together with them in the clouds, to meet the Lord in the air."† Meanwhile, as to those who did not believe, Paul prophesies, that "for this cause God shall send them strong delusion, that they should believe a lie: that they all might be damned, who believed not the truth, but had pleasure in unrighteousness."‡

---

* Reason in Religion, p. 258.
† 1 Thess. iv. 16, 17.
‡ 2 Thess. ii. 11, 12. The fearful thought of this text may be modified in appearance by the more literal "judged" for "damned," as in the revised translation of Bishop Ellicott. The vulgar rendering, however, is more faithful to the thought of Paul. It alone carries forward the conception by which the

No: Paul did not so much as dream that there might be a line of Christian ages. He gave no glance in that direction. He literally built a castle "in the air," and rested his hopes for the history of Christianity on a wild Jewish dream. And he did this, in the moments when his mind was engaged with it, in the Jewish spirit, with a strong Jewish greed of blessedness for the saints, and vengeance for all others. If "Protestantism, in some of its communions," as Dr. Hedge says, "has given us, instead of an evangile or message of glad tidings, a bloody cartel of vengeance and of doom," it has done no more than Paul did in his least Christian thought, as in this vaticination upon the future of the unbelieving world. The "Christian ages," indeed, if God was to send strong delusion upon the unbelieving, that they might believe a lie and all be damned!

Dr. Hedge is too rational and candid to assume the *truth* of his supposition in regard to Paul's inspired glance. He makes it, confessedly, as a bare supposition. He admits that "Paul's mystic words" are of "uncertain import." Why, then, does he make so remarkable an assumption? It is, apparently, because of his view, that the deification of Jesus was a providential necessity, which Paul might well have foreseen. But, in all reason, we cannot think this "corrup-

---

unbelievers are made by God the victims of delusion and a lie. Moreover, by referring to a passage of the first chapter of this Epistle, according to which the Lord Jesus is to come "in flame of fire, rendering vengeance to them that know not God, . . . eternal destruction apart from the presence of the Lord," it will be seen that *in this thought*, though not in the general tenor of his teaching, Paul accepted, and adopted into "historical Christianity," one of the most vulgar and false conceits of the Jewish mind. Reuss, the discriminating historian of "Christian Theology in the Apostolic Age," shows that this doctrine of the eternal destruction of the "enemies" in hell, though appearing only in this passage of Paul's writings, entered well enough into his system; and that Paul did not, though choosing to dwell on the consoling side of the picture, ever hold, much less teach, the doctrine of the final restoration of all souls. That great truth came with a speculation of which Paul knew nothing. — *Histoire de la Théologie Chrétienne au Siècle Apostolique*, tom. ii. pp. 237–239.

We thus do Paul no injustice; and, if we did, we should only follow the body of the Christian Church, which has always, as M. Reuss remarks, regarded with special favor the dogma of the destruction in hell of all who do not believe.

tion" of Christianity "providential,"—as Dr. Hedge has it, "a necessary stage in the history of religion, necessary in the counsels of the Spirit, necessary in human experience." We utterly refuse to thus dignify the ignorance and error of man. We do not believe that the Providence which overrules us needs that we corrupt his revelation in receiving it. It was not necessary that Jesus should miss the will of God, through ardently cherishing a Messianic expectation of taking the kingdom upon his own shoulders; nor that the Jews who heard and tried to follow him should miss the final lesson of their Master's life, and blindly, wildly anticipate, that on an imagined resurrection and return to earth should yet be established the kingdom of their "Lord and Saviour Jesus Christ;" nor that Christian thought, stumbling helplessly out of the original confusion of undiscerning, all-embracing faith, should deify the Galilean son of Joseph. These things took place, not by the counsel of the Spirit, but through the ignorance of man; and, taking place, they were duly overruled. Had better things taken place, would not they have been overruled as well? It is inexact and untrue to say, that the worse thing was necessary, when the fact is that it was not at all necessary, though it took place.

In unfolding his supposition, Dr. Hedge says, that Paul "divined the reason and necessity, in the counsels of God and the wants of the Church," of the "approaching deification" of Jesus. He assumes that this was the best thing for the Church, and that God decreed it as such. He assumes even that Paul, foreseeing a "corruption" of Christianity, prophesied of it as a good thing, instead of prophesying against it as an evil thing. Could this be with an honest man? Could Paul contemplate a false thing as good? No doubt God could permit it; but is it not too much to say, that he provided error for a Church which wanted it?

The principle on which Dr. Hedge stands, for the moment, in this supposition in regard to Paul as a prophet, is a common, but we believe a false, principle with Christian teachers. It is that the Christian Church, from its foundation in Jesus Christ, through the Christian ages, is a direct product of the counsel of God, a specially divine manifestation in history. This principle is, in our opinion, the original "corruption" out of which so many further corruptions have sprung. Tradition, the Papacy, the divinity of a very human book, and the deification of the man Jesus, could not have postponed Christianity to Pseudo-Christianity for eighteen or twenty centuries but for this baseless conceit, that historical Christianity, the Christianity of men, is the express image of God's ideal, a divine interpolation in human history.

Jesus and his disciples lived under the shadow of the baneful Jewish opinion, that God was, or would be, exceptionally present with the Jews. Jesus himself did not escape the temptation to regard himself as, in some sense, the special historical representative in humanity of the kingdom of God; though he seems to have made a noble struggle to accept providential indications that this was not God's will after all, and though he did finally make a perfect surrender of all to God. The disciples knew nothing of their Master's conflict; their thoughts in this matter "savored of the things that be of men:" they could not watch with him, and knew nothing of his surrender. Pure Christianity was historical during the hour in which Jesus, honestly pleading for his own will, did yet give up all to the will of God. In that moment it came to its birth out of the heart of Jesus. But there was no disciple to understand. From the death of Jesus, Christianity was no more than a spirit: its truth was in men's hearts, but its word was not upon men's lips. The Jew spoke in Peter and John and James and Paul,—more in the three than in the fourth, but in all alike when the origin and nature of Christianity were in view.* They all clung

---

* In Matt. xviii. 3, we find Jesus telling the disciples explicitly, that they were wholly wrong in their spirit and conception of his truth. The disciples had been disputing who should be the greatest, so Mark tells us (ix. 84); and Jesus emphatically declares, that they—yes, *they, the chosen*, the then Church,—must be converted, or fail to enter the kingdom of heaven. This does not imply an outward rejection, for it is the chosen to whom it is addressed. It implies rather the perception on the part of Jesus, that, if these chosen disciples were not wholly changed in respect of that Jewish spirit of theirs, they would entirely fail to comprehend, and become possessed of, the true revelation and

to and started from the fatal Jewish preconception of an exceptional presence of God with a chosen *ecclesia*. Ecclesiasticism was their common method; ecclesiastical continuity, their common assumption. They all made the Church succeed the chosen people,—a people whose pretensions, *as an elect nation*, it has been the business of history to scout from the beginning,— it never having found its glory, not even in the long centuries before Christ; and its religion having grown under its humiliation, in its hour of agony and trial, never under the exaltation it coveted; in the breasts of its publicans, never in its Pharisees; in the heart of its defeated, never with its successful, Messiah. Blind to the fact that divine providence had unceasingly punished, never gratified, their nation's conceit of special glory in store for it with God, these Jew-Christians "divined," in an intensely Jewish spirit, the counsels of God and the wants of their Church. They did not once think of founding their Church simply on the presence of God with the race, on God's fatherhood and the brotherhood of man; but based it, instead, on Jesus, on an exceptional presence of God with this one individual,—a disregard of the spirit of Christianity, which buried pure Christianity, as far as the world at large is concerned, for not less than twenty centuries. So far from the historical gospel of the New Testament being "a divine interpolation of the Spirit in the secular text of history," as Dr. Hedge assumes, its characteristic exaltation of Jesus as "Lord and Saviour" was a human interpolation of the Jewish spirit into the true gospel of the Holy Ghost. And we point with confidence to the history of the Church, from the hour in which the disciples quarrelled over the chance of the chief seats in the kingdom, to prove that human fallibility, ignorance, and error

---

kingdom of God. That "except ye be converted, and become as little children, ye shall not enter into the kingdom of heaven," settles the pretensions of the apostles. It demands of them an entirely new spirit and conception, one that would cause entire self-surrender before the providence and spirit of God. There is no evidence that this conversion from the Jewish to the Christian conception ever took place: on the contrary, there is abundant evidence, that in all the apostles, even in Paul, the Jewish preconception remained.

have shaped the external form and movement, the ecclesiastical continuity, of the "Church of our Lord and Saviour Jesus Christ."

It is impossible to pursue at length the discussion of our theme in this direction, nor is it necessary. The actual Church of Christendom already lies under condemnation with all liberal intelligences. It is out of sentiment, and in the way of reverent evasion, that the condemnation is not pronounced in full. Dr. Hedge makes some points of this sentence, enough to indicate the position of things. He says:—

"For want of counsel and concurrence of reason in time past, theology has builded her house in vain."—"What a really scientific building is to a crumbling Gothic edifice, such is a rational theology to the rotten systems of the past."—"While we claim for the Christian religion the peculiarity of a dispensation of grace, it must be confessed, that the gospel has not been so received and so interpreted by the Christian Church. The grace that was in it was soon forgotten, and overlaid with dogmatic additions and ecclesiastical inventions. It would seem as if the Christian Church had made it her special aim to obscure and obliterate this characteristic trait of our faith,— to assimilate the religion of Jesus to other religions, by engrafting upon it a sacrificial, expiatory element, entirely foreign to its spirit." *

It is necessary to recognize that an unchristian "special aim," such as Dr. Hedge alludes to, has powerfully controlled, thus far, the historical or outward development of Christianity. This special aim has grown out of the interests or necessities of a scheme of human redemption, at the centre of which we find, as "the Saviour," "the Redeemer," *the Atoning and Judging Christ.* Dr. Hedge avers, that the more Orthodox forms of Protestantism have given us, instead of the gospel of grace, "a bloody cartel of vengeance and of doom." He is aware that this has been done in good faith, in the interest of Jesus as "the Saviour." If God has been

---

* Reason in Religion, pp. 215, 217, 841.

represented more as a devil than as a deity, it has been to demonstrate the necessity of "looking unto Jesus" as "the Redeemer." In fact, there is not the least room to doubt, that the "special aim" of our actual Christianity has been to exalt Jesus, to make Jesus the Lord and Shepherd of souls; and that, in doing this, it has subverted, as Dr. Hedge must admit, the true Christian faith, so far as its statements and its schools are concerned. How, then, can a Church be divine, in any peculiar sense, any more than all human history is divine, which thus fails to apprehend aright its own better nature, and has not yet grasped in idea, much less manifested in history, its own higher law?

And why should the Christian Church have been divine? Why should Jesus have been divine? The word of Christian gospel is that God is with men burdened with imperfection and deficiency, not that he is with perfect men. Christian apology should accept and must accept the task of showing that God was with Jesus, though he did bear the cross of human deficiency and imperfection; and that He is with the Christian Church, though it be only a company of erring men; with Jesus and with the Church, not because of what they were, but because in his own nature He is with his entire creation. Because we recognize that Jesus had in the living God a Lord and Master, a Shepherd and Saviour, and that the lot of Jesus in this respect is the lot of every soul, we can heartily consent to find that it has been a mistake from the beginning to put Jesus at the centre of Christianity, in the sense that he, rather than God, the Father of all souls, is the redeemer from guilt and the author of salvation.

In the course of our argument, we have had occasion to use, and somewhat criticise, some recent statements of Dr. Hedge. The volume in which these statements appear has been more than once the subject of remark in the "Examiner;" but, in one respect, we think full justice has not been meted out to this last and best of Dr. Hedge's contributions to the literature of our communion. We refer to the singularly fine poetic quality of Dr. Hedge's thought. The poetic form is absent, but it is not needed. The numbers of Tennyson could not render these grand intuitions of a believing soul more inspiring.

In the use of logic, Dr. Hedge is often unfortunate, not so much from any lack of logical power as from entire spiritual pre-occupation. The glory of the vision dims the eye of his understanding, while flooding heart and soul with ineffable light. He thinks less of the logical adequacy of the statement than of the spiritual value of his word. In simple statement, where there is no aim but to utter the intuition, Dr. Hedge is a master of expression. It is in utterances incidentally argumentative or critical that he gets very wide of the mark, through the absorption of his attention by the interior sense of his thought. If intending to argue or to criticise, Dr. Hedge will be found just and correct, though throwing no special weight into that form of intellectual demonstration. Usually he does not propose argument and criticism so much as revelation, the simple utterance of intuitions; and not infrequently, as it seems to us, his words do his real thought a serious injustice. And, manifestly, his opinions may sometimes assume, through the inadvertence of which we have spoken, a form and bearing not at all suited to do justice to the profound reason which lies behind them.

It is emphatically on the score of religious genius, as an exponent of pure reason, leaving out of view the processes of the understanding, that Dr. Hedge takes the highest rank as a teacher of divine truth. To make his eminence as clear to our readers as it appears to ourselves, it would be necessary to review some of the striking illustrations of religious genius or of poetic power in religion, and to point out the particulars in which Dr. Hedge has conformed to the standard of the great seers and singers of Christian belief. We have not space to do this, even if it were appropriate to append such a discussion to our article. It is in the sober ecstasy of believing reason that Dr. Hedge illustrates the advance which rationalism has secured to mysticism. To examine and illustrate this rational ecstasy, and to separate, in Dr. Hedge's invaluable essays, between the fruits of this and the quite worthless results of inadvertent reasoning, would be a delightful task. We cannot enter upon it here; but, to stimulate the reader to critical inquiry, we will give one example in each kind from the essay on "The Exorable God:"—

"George Müller prayed for pecuniary succor in his charities [that is, of course, begged of all the world, by praying publicly and with an ostentation of faith], and again and again received an answer to his supplications, in pecuniary supplies."

That is the husk of bad logic. Here is the pure thought:—

"The spirit and life of prayer is the consciousness of God, the feeling that we are his, that he is ours, that nothing but the voluntary aversion of our spirits can separate us from him. A feeling of Deity as the power by which we live, the light by which we see, the great reality, in the knowledge of whom is eternal life, and whose participation is the supreme blessing,—where this consciousness lives and burns, there is prayer, though not always expressed in words. For the soul, in its highest devotion, is content to repose in the thought of God, asking nothing, seeking nothing; its whole being concentrated in the one, unuttered desire, Thy will be done."

The rare poetic quality, that which belongs to thought which prophesies the hidden light of God's presence in the soul, is so full and effective in much that Dr. Hedge has written of "Reason in Religion," as to color richly and wonderfully his fine style. The plain prose "sings itself," in many passages, with beauty like that of Homer's, or solemn music like that of Milton's verse. Philosophy of the wisest and richest kind is the undertone of many of these strains. If any of our readers have not yet afforded themselves the pleasure of listening with Dr. Hedge to the epic story of man's wondrous faith in God, we urge them to resort at once to the suggestive pages of the volume we have imperfectly criticized in these brief remarks.

Art. II.— LESSING.

The Life and Works of Gotthold Ephraim Lessing. From the German of Adolph Stahr. By E. P. EVANS, Ph.D., Professor of Modern Languages and Literature, in the University of Michigan. Two volumes. Boston: William V. Spencer, 203, Washington Street. 1866.

WE bespeak a cordial welcome for these two handsome volumes. They present Stahr's "Life of Lessing" to the American reader in a shape which reflects great credit on their publisher. The work of translation has evidently been done as a labor of love, and is no mere piece of job-work. We feel it has cost more time and study than are ordinarily spent on a dozen volumes of equal size. With great precision in verbal rendering, it has at the same time an easy flow of style. The collateral sources of information have been carefully examined, and digested in notes which are a valuable addition to the work. It is no easy task to produce so good a translation as this. We owe a debt of gratitude to Professor Evans, for making accessible to the public the life of so grand a personality as Lessing. It will call attention to a man whose character and genius are so remarkable as to constitute it an epoch in every student's life to learn to know him. We trust the work will be widely bought and widely read. No thoughtful man can afford to do without it.

Gotthold Ephraim Lessing was born, on the 22d of January, 1729, in Kamenz, a city in Upper Lusatia, Saxony. He came of marrowy old German stock,— German in the best sense of the word, as predicated, not of geographical locality, but of certain sturdy-minded, honest-hearted qualities. No better birthplace could have been hit on for the man who was to rouse his nation to the consciousness of its own inherent resources, and shame it out of vassalage and servile imitation. For here were all about him those basal elements of character,

— simplicity, integrity, humanity, and piety, — which lie at the foundation of all enduring literature. Kamenz, of course, was no Eden. It had its full infusion of narrow, fierce, old-Lutheran dogmatism; but its dogmatism was of that up-and-down-right stamp which more enlightened men can at once smile at and respect, — smile at, because it is so exquisitely unconscious of any truth beyond its own horizon, and so implies no taint of cowardice or recreancy; respect, because it is so thorough-going and hot with honest love and hate.

Lessing's father was the deacon, and afterwards chief pastor, of the church in Kamenz. A fiery-hearted, brave, and consecrated man he was, a grand type of the old-fashioned Lutheran minister. It is plain to see he is of the sort of fathers that makes *men* of their boys, if the boys have any stuff in them to make men of. Heroic industry in study, an austere sense of right, contempt for wealth in comparison with knowledge, deep-rooted hatred of frivolity, — these virtues constituted the warp and woof of his character, and were illustrated under conditions which proved them at the farthest remove from sentimentalities. " With almost incomprehensible abnegation of the common enjoyments of life which are within reach of even the poorest mechanic, he sacrificed himself for the education of his children; endured all privations with cheerfulness, all want with firmness, all weariness with joyful tranquillity; and, notwithstanding his own penury, never sent a poor man from his door without alms."

The mother of Lessing was of less marked individuality. A humble, devout woman, overweighted with bringing her twelve children into the world and rearing them through painful poverty; one whose whole life was a prolonged strain of meekly-borne toil, cheered only by the hope of struggling through to see her ten boys all grow up, study, and become pastors! Poor woman! all that her Gotthold did of great and glorious in the world brought never a smile to relieve the sadness of her heart. A *pastor primarius* stood to her on the pinnacle of human aspiration; and to see her first-born son, after all the weary abnegation his education cost, dwindle down and down to mere critic, poet, tragedy-composer, — not so much as University Professor even, — was to her a bitter cup to drink. Many a stricken Scotch or New-England mother of fifty years ago knew all about her life-long sorrow.

As but the second child of a family of twelve, Lessing's boyhood escaped the pressure of the direful poverty which overtook the household farther on. Till the age of eight, he had a private tutor; and, at thirteen, the influence of a relative procured him a scholarship in the famous grammar-school at Meissen.

The school of St. Afra, at Meissen, was one of several which had been founded by an old Elector of Saxony, out of the proceeds of confiscated cloisters. Its righteous object was to make the funds enjoyed of yore by monks and nuns rear up a doughty race of Lutheran pastors, full-trained to confute the deadly heresies of the very Church whose money educated them, — a carrying the war into Africa, after the highest old Scipionian manner. Take it for all in all, it was a good school for a boy like Lessing. Narrow and dry indeed it was in aim and method, a fit machine to turn out class on class in the accredited pedantic shape; but it was a place where solid, conscientious work was done. Lessing himself affirmed in after-years, that, "if any thoroughness and accuracy of scholarship had become his portion," he owed it to the discipline acquired at this time.

Latin stood first in the rank of studies. It was Latin, alas! considered not as the gate of introduction to the splendid eloquence of Cicero, or the flowing beauty of Virgil, or the genial worldly wisdom of Horace; but Latin as the pedant's paradise, the school-boy's drill-field, the theologian's outfit, the versifier's treasure-house of longs and shorts. A silly, childish conceit at the ability, purchased by due waste of years, to write more or less imperfect Latin prose and metre, was the normal product of the school. A noble enthusiasm for the manners and literature of a mighty nation was a fanaticism whose outbreak was duly depressed under heaps of smothering ashes.

It is fine to see the impetuous spirit of the boy Lessing

re-acting against these pitiful conceptions, and working itself out into the clear perception, that Latin was made for man, and not man for Latin, — a heresy as monstrous at Meissen as ever of old in Judea the plea, that the sabbath was made for man, and not man for the sabbath. There was in the eager boy such a plus of physical and mental vigor; such super-abundant life, craving to meet with and rejoice in like life elsewhere; such ever-present sense that the men and the nations on earth who have thought wisely and acted nobly are the one great thing in the world's history, and that the use of knowing their languages is to enter into glorious companionship of spirit with them, and receive ever-new access of being, — that the young Samson burst contemptuously the pedantic withes which held the other boys so securely bound, and flung off adventurously after a nobler quest. He eagerly spent his spare time over Theophrastus and Plautus and Terence, writers whose theme is Man and Life, and wrote home to his mother that he had learned "self-knowledge" by reading comedies. His first essays at composition evince the same live spirit. He will have nothing to do with dead things. The phases of life through which he himself is passing, — these are what he wants to write about. We see no hunting after subjects. The subjects are hunting him, running him to his desk, demanding to work themselves out into the clear through him. He attempts a play of his own; and what does he choose for a theme? The death of Cæsar? The return of Regulus to Carthage? Not a bit of it. "The Young Scholar." And why? "A young scholar was the only species of fool with whom, at that time, it was not possible for me to be unacquainted. Grown up amongst such vermin, was it strange I directed my first weapons against them?" This is hitting the very bull's-eye. But better still even the words he wrote his mother about the effect of this self-same comedy upon himself: "I learned to know myself; and from that time I have certainly laughed at no one else more heartily." Here we have Lessing all over. As glad to have the truth hit him as hit any one else! Strike on, honest fellow, Truth; buffet the nonsense and pedantry out of me and out of every one. It is rare fun to see the dust and shoddy fly from the old coat, even though one be inside, and the blows feel through.

Evidently such a boy would exhaust the possibilities of a school long before he had completed its ordinary terms. A year and three months ahead of the time when his course was up, we find him restless to get away. "He is a horse that must have double fodder; we cannot use him much longer," wrote the rector to his father. Accordingly his importunity prevailed over the tenacity of established order; and, at the age of seventeen, he was permitted to enter the University of Leipsic.

Among the theologians connected with the University, there was not one of sufficient breadth and freshness to awaken interest in a youth of the stamp of Lessing. Among the classical professors, however, there were two, Christ and Ernesti, whose genius and enthusiasm stirred him to the centre. They were creative men both, heralds of a new dawn of glow and beauty breaking in upon the long night of obscurest pedantry; men who studied the art and literature of Greece and Rome, to rejoice in the life that had expressed itself in the philosophy, poems, temples, sculpture, laws, customs, of the two foremost nations of antiquity; men who studied these things to become more men themselves, and with a view to æsthetic culture and individual power of creation. In Christ, in particular, Lessing for the first time saw a rounded man,—no awkward book-worm, ignorant of the world, but one who had travelled widely, had acquired the bearing of a man of the world, and had learned to subordinate all study to purposes of life. Nor was the influence of Leipsic itself — "a whole world in miniature" to his unwonted eyes — less stimulating and amazing. Its aristocratic polish; its solid, burgher comfort; its literati, its vast book-trade, its journalism; above all, its theatre,—these, to the fresh, unhackneyed youth, opened up endless opportunities for culture and delight. At once, with clear-eyed outlook, he sets to work to adjust himself to his new position. His massive common-sense at once asserts itself, as all through life with him :—

"I left my study, and ventured out amongst my fellows. Great heavens! What a contrast between myself and them did I discover! A boorish bashfulness of manner, an ungainly clownishness of body, an utter ignorance of social customs,—these were the fine qualities which distinguished me. I read contempt in the demeanor and looks of my companions. I resolved, at whatever cost, to improve myself. I learned dancing, fencing, riding. I made such progress in these exercises, that even those who at first had wished to deny me all dexterity were compelled to admire me. My body became somewhat more graceful, and I sought society in order to learn life. I realized that books might make me learned, *but would never make me a man.*"

The centre of intensest interest, however, lay to Lessing in the Leipsic Theatre. He would sooner have eaten dry bread than have missed the play. He translated and corrected for the actors to gain the needed tickets. He frequented the representations, not for amusement, but for serious ends of study. The impulse to dramatic creation was already strong within him. Here was the Theatre as it was: he must understand it thoroughly. Every activity with him developed itself in connection with some real existence. He yoked himself ever to the present. Evolution, and not revolution, was the law he read as ruling all progression. The merits and the demerits of the plays themselves, the weakness and the strength of the actors, the tone and temper of the audience,—these he must learn to feel and comprehend through and through in the school of practical experience. He seemed to understand from the outset why it has held true in every age, that all great dramatic literature, the Greek, the Spanish, the English, grew out of a living stage, and learned its laws by the proof of trial. He felt that just as surely as war alone can breed soldiers, and stormy seas sailors, and public affairs statesmen, so the only school of the dramatist lay in the doing the thing itself, in the production of the drama face to face with the eyes and ears, the shouts, hisses, tears, hushed and expectant silence, of a sea of human beings.

This reverence for the infinite richness and tutelage of life itself, of the great restless, million-sided, marvellous world in which men live, is the grand peculiarity which makes

Lessing stand out in such striking contrast with the large proportion of his nation's leading men. He was a realist in the broadest and deepest sense of the word. Never a momentary disposition did he evince to retire into the depth of his consciousness to evolve the absolute idea of the camel. He took the hump-backed, knock-kneed, snow-shoed creature of the desert as he found him, in profound faith that the desert itself, with its shifting sands and stunted herbage and springless wastes, knew how to bring to bear a thousand-fold more cunning and persistent energies to turn out just the gaunt, long-suffering servant needed, than ever your philosopher, be the depths of his inner consciousness of the profoundest. The race-course to create racers; the fox-chase to create daring riders, bottom in horses, keen scent in hounds; the rivalries of yachtsmen to create flowing lines, and right-trimmed sails, and hardy handling in a heavy blow,— this was his philosophy. And this is the more remarkable when we reflect on Lessing's ceaseless quest after absolute perfection, after immutable laws of truth and beauty. These were the passion of his heart. But he knew that to reach them one must respect the conditions of their growth. They were to be studied in their richest earthly incarnations, not in vague and baseless theories. They were to be sought in the works of those whom they themselves had chosen, through personal endowments, and rare opportunities, and richest inheritance of slowly-ripened results, to reveal their fulness. They had descended to earth, and taken up their abode in the Parthenon at Athens, in the sculpture of Phidias, in the Iliad of Homer, in Æschylus and Sophocles and Shakespeare. There meet them; there study the shaping forces that made these men organs of truth and beauty; there learn to open the soul to the teachings of life, as these men did; there learn to believe, that you too live in the same rich world with them, and that the same elemental powers are at hand to mould and inspire you according to the measure of your capacity. If Lessing's life teaches any lesson nobly, it is the lesson of measureless scorn for the puling sentimentalism which affects to look on life and its providential teaching as too poor a barren to move to love and wonder,—of the self-centered vanity which assumes to be able to live on its own meagre personal resources, and to need no help outside itself.

Thus absorbed in a bright world of thought and emotion, time passed swiftly and profitably with the young Leipsic student. Alas! he was soon to be made cruelly aware, that there were other worlds of life whose existence he had lost sight of. Dame Rumor had flown abroad. She had alighted in the old parsonage, and gasped out her breathless story. Shrieks had greeted the dread recital. Their Gotthold! *their* Gotthold! was living in the vile society of comedians,— people too vile to have the right of Christian burial! His intimate friends were free-thinkers! He had written a play, and was to personate one of the characters in it on the public stage himself! There was wailing in every chamber, from the outraged father, the broken-hearted mother, the eleven children, the smallest even old enough to catch the feeling that Gotthold had done something dreadful. Here was the wreck of every hope. He that was to become *pastor primarius* himself, and help to make *pastores primarios* of the ten other boys, was worse than dead. He must be plucked from the pit at any cost. "Disobedience is learned in bad company: he will not obey an order home," cries the distracted mother. "God forgive us! we must resort to a lie; nothing else will do," responds the father. "Your mother is dangerously ill, and longs to speak with you before her death," writes the hard-pressed pastor,—as fair a case for the recording angel's blotting tear as Uncle Toby's oath; and off posts at once the true-hearted son, without stopping even for needful clothing, through the cold and storms of winter.

Lessing's visit to the old home in Kamenz produced a somewhat better state of feeling, though it could not bridge the gulf that had opened up between the family and himself. He did what he could to reconcile their minds to the change that had come upon him. The father saw that the son had preserved an unblemished purity of morals, and had made great growth in knowledge: the mother was somewhat consoled by a sermon he wrote for her, to show her he could compose one at any time. He agreed to take up the study of medicine, and also devote much time to philology, that he might become qualified for a professorship, should opportunity offer. But it was little after all he could do to heal their cruel disappointment. They worked their work; he must work his. And so he left them, and returned to Leipsic.

His stay there, however, was short. Leipsic was over and through for him. He had exhausted university life; the theatrical troupe had been broken up; and, worse than all, he had stood security for several actors who had decamped, leaving him to bear the brunt, and was in debt. Something must be done. He had no taste for professional life in any form, so he resolved on authorship. We find him, accordingly, shortly after in Berlin, his communications destroyed with all the established bread-and-butter vocations of college-trained men, — a Bohemian, if you choose to call him so.

A Bohemian, assuredly, in one of the badges of the tribe, — his poverty. "No money, no recommendations, no influential friends, no other weapons for his battle than his cheerful courage, his confidence in his own powers, and the discipline acquired through past privations!" An old friend and fellow-student, Mylius, shares his garret with him. His clothes are so shabby, that he cannot present himself to ask employment with any hope of success. A sad outlook, apparently. But we need waste no superfluous pity over threadbare clothing, when we see in it, or mayhap through it, a young man buoyed up with such hope and faith as Lessing knew. Forthwith we find him projecting and commencing, in association with Mylius, a quarterly review, entitled "Contributions to the History and Reform of the Theatre." It was to include, besides a philosophical criticism of the dramatic literature of all nations and ages, instruction on all matters pertaining to histrionic art, together with translations of the best Greek, Latin, English, Spanish, French, Italian, and Dutch plays. Such was the glorious hope that cheered the breast of a threadbare youth of twenty, in his garret. The scope and boldness of the inception are illustrative of the hardihood of Lessing's mind. And yet the abandonment of the enterprise, after the issue of the first few numbers, brings before us, in quite as marked a way, the lofty conscientiousness of the man. His collaborator, Mylius, had affirmed in one of the numbers that there was no Italian drama. *No Italian drama?* Here was the whole undertaking disgraced at the outset by an exhibition of the grossest ignorance. "If you are not better acquainted with the stage among other foreign nations than with that of the Italians, we have pretty things to expect from you," Lessing seemed to hear uttered in disgust by every competent judge. He would go no step farther in such association. His whole nature revolted from every form of pretence and assumption. No earnest Luther ever looked with hotter-burning abhorrence on greedy, foul-minded monk or pardon-vendor, daring to speak to the people in the name of God and holiness, than Lessing on shallow, pretentious, oracular ignorance, sacrilegiously leaping upon the throne of instruction, and tampering with the eternal laws of truth and beauty. To him, these laws of truth and beauty were matters of unspeakable moment. In their cause he would willingly endure poverty, wearing toil, the hate of cliques and parties. Absolute veracity, as the foundation-stone of the teacher's character, was the god he worshipped on bended knees. And, all through life, he broke away from the contamination of every kind of literary association with ignorance and pretence, with as chaste and wounded a horror as Hebrew Joseph from the hateful arms of the wife of Potiphar, even though in his flight he must leave behind him his only garment. Henceforth he would work alone.

For a year or more we find our friend earning his daily bread by such job-work as he could compass; yet finding time to push, with iron diligence, his own peculiar studies. He is beginning to make a name; and, at the age of twenty-two, we see him called to the editorship of a literary sheet, the "Berlin Journal."

The courage, originality, and fertility of his mind shone forth at once. While duly noticing the ordinary literature of the day, he shows his innate temper by grappling at once with the giants of the world of letters,—the giants alike by bulk of thews and sinews, and the giants by courtesy of their dwarf surroundings. Two great parties then divided in bitter feud the German literary world,—the followers of Klopstock and the followers of Gottsched; the party of vague, tumultuous license, and the party of narrow, pedantic rules. "Genius scorns rules," shrieked the one. "Genius is made by rules," shrieked the other. Lessing sides with neither party. Penetrating at once to the cause of the confused and bitter strife, he lays down the reconciling truth. There are eternal laws. Genius in its grandest flights is ever sublimely orderly; but genius takes its laws from no dry, digested code. Genius is vision; and each fresh creative mind sees farther into the eternal realms, and legislates anew:—

"What charms this soul, all souls must charm; what grieves it, saddens all: It holds the choices of the world within its subtle thrall."

This principle established, he lashes, with pitiless wit, alike the pedantic conceit of those who would stretch out a Shakespeare or a Molière on the Procrustes' bed of a Sophocles or an Aristophanes, and proceed to hack off every protruding member, indifferent alike whether it be winged-foot, or cunning hand, or majestic head, so only an accurate fit be made,—lashes alike this fool's proceeding, and the crude, uncultured ignorance which would hail with rapture every utterance of muddy, bombastic feeling, as glorious enfranchisement from the tyranny of law.

All the great qualities of the later acknowledged man appear in these youthful essays. From the first, his analysis is exhaustive, his wit brilliant, his art of presentation masterly, his style alternately trenchant, sportive, fascinating, annihilating. What a revelation, this last, to a nation with whom dulness and depth, attractiveness and emptiness, were regarded as one flesh,—the ban of God on all who should dare to put them asunder! Under Lessing's hand the driest work receives a notice all ablaze with wit and wisdom. Stupidity inspired his faculties as readily as genius, and was as instructive to the full. He would have seen a deep philosopher in the drunken sot, whose boast it was that he did more for the cause of temperance than all the lecturers; because he taught by example, and, reeling everywhere round the streets, gave men a chance to see with their own eyes what a beast drink made of man. Woe to the rancorous theological pamphlet which, in the name of the religion of peace, but added fuel to the flames of sectarian hate! Lessing would candidly admit its bitter spirit, but come to its defence with the maddening plea, that " the winning art of representing the yoke of religion as an easy yoke is so difficult, that not *every* theologian can possess it." To furious zealots contending for Churchunity he would cry out, " What gain! are two vicious dogs made good by being shut up in a single kennel?" — " To disarm the scoffer by a life controlled by the spirit of religion is a work which most people are unwilling to undertake, because the *Moravians* have made it the principle of their conduct." What an exquisite *non sequitur*, and yet what a commentary on the logic of sectarian strife! Such vermin would seem small game for a Lessing, were it not that he uses them as illustrations of broad principles, and finds them inciting cause to launch forth on a noble tide of justice, wisdom, and love. But he is quite as eager to join issue with Voltaire, Rousseau, or Diderot.

From the age of twenty-two to that of thirty-one, Lessing was mainly engaged with this work of purifying criticism. Still, with all this varied journalistic activity, he never loses sight of his deep, underlying purpose to fit himself, by careful training, for creative work, — for " doing the thing itself" as poet and dramatist, as well as showing how to do it as critic. He broke resolutely away at intervals from journalism, and spent the little money he had laid by in buying leisure to bury himself for months in study, and in opening up new vistas into wider realms. Literature as a trade he hated. The journalist's wont of living from hand to mouth, and cramming to meet the cry of the hour, was utterly odious to him. While his mind was full, he would write with delight; yet at the first sign that the springs were getting low, he would draw never another bucketful, but open up fresh communications with cloud and mountain and plain, and wait till the fountain was once more brimming. The ordinary plea of necessity for hack-work seemed never to weigh a feather with him. The necessity lay all on the other side. Never a man who had a profounder conviction that the "life is more than meat, and the body than raiment." To sit aloft where he could command a wide outlook, to feel his wings free to respond to every invitation to shady grove, or crystal stream, or far-off field gleaming in the sunshine, — this was his life-long, passionate love. He called himself "the bird upon the roof," and would consent to no cage, though its wires were of burnished gold. It stirs the blood of every reader of his life to feel the pulses of this Indian, Tartar, Arab love of freedom. He was full kith and kin, in this respect, with our own Concord Thoreau. It was such a noble freedom, too, he panted for, — freedom to give himself, heart and soul, to such lofty ends. And with what unflinching heroism he paid the price!

About the age of thirty-one, Lessing grew utterly tired of his Berlin life. A disappointment, the severest he had ever yet encountered, had left him entirely unfitted for his ordinary work. He had entered into a most advantageous contract with a rich young man of Leipsic to journey with him, as his Mentor, over Europe, and spend years in studying the best that Belgium and Holland and France and Italy had to offer. Now, for the first time, he felt he could secure that broad foundation of thought and observation which would fit him to instruct his nation. He started forth on his travels in a mood of perfect exultation. But war broke out. The project must be abandoned. The rich young man was ruined. Lessing must seek change and renewal in other ways. The opportunity came before very long, in the shape of an invitation to him from one of Frederic's generals, Tauentzien, then military governor of Breslau, to become his assistant. It offered fair compensation, change of scene, intercourse with new phases of human life; and he gladly accepted it. Lessing's bookworm friends felt that he had committed literary suicide. But he knew better. "I wish," he at this date entered in his diary, "to spin myself in for a time like an ugly worm, in order to come to light again a brilliant butterfly."

In Breslau, Lessing found what was far better for him than books and bookish men,— characters and events. His chief, Von Tauentzien, was himself a specimen of those burly forces, which, with locked horns and butting foreheads, were in those days pushing to crowd one another back, to run new lines for the map of Europe. The rough humor of his response to the Austrian general who had summoned him to surrender Breslau,— with the threat that elsewise not even the child in the womb should be spared, "I am not pregnant, nor my soldiers either;" and the heroic oath he and his officers swore, and justified by doughty deeds, to die man by man sooner than give up the city,— had already made his quality known. In daily intercourse with such a man, Lessing came in contact with that kind of mass and momentum of character which the energy of his own nature ever craved to encounter. As confidential adviser of one of Frederic's ablest generals, he was brought into intimate relations with a host of strong and active characters; he surveyed public affairs from a commanding height; he was admitted behind the scenes, and into the secret initiation of schemes that afterwards startled Europe; and "learned to know the relations of the world and of life on an incomparably grander scale than had been possible in his former literary career." Give a man with all this a seeing eye and a thoughtful brain, and a love of watching the varied play of life, and what can he ask better as one of his training fields for literary work? Nothing teaches like life. Of a somewhat similar experience, though immeasurably inferior in degree, even the ponderous Gibbon declares, that his own four months' drill in the county militia, in his youth, gave him more insight into the vast and complex military evolutions he unfolded in his "Decline and Fall," than all the books he had ever read.

Accordingly we find, that, with all his business and social engrossments, Lessing never studied harder, never created more vigorously. To his residence in Breslau we owe these two noble productions, the play "Minna von Barnhelm," and "The Laocoon."

"Minna von Barnhelm" is one of those dramatic pieces which keep themselves young and attractive from generation to generation, because they feed an enduring interest in human nature. It is a page out of life. Its characters are not personified qualities, but flesh-and-blood men and women. Even to this very day, Germany can boast no second comedy which so absolutely mirrors the national life. Its appearance constitutes an epoch in the literary history of the nation. It turned away attention from the old stock-subjects, traditional characters, and conventional rhetoric of the stage, and brought about a return to nature. It awakened a new consciousness of the infinitely rich and varied elements of pathos and fun and suffering and triumph and virtue and guilt, lying open in the common life all around us and within us. We learn more from it of how men thought and felt in the stern days of Frederic's wars than from volumes of ordinary histories. The tavern-keepers, the chambermaids, the officers' body-servants, the sergeant, the colonel, old Fritz himself, the loves of high life and low, of parlor and kitchen, are brought in vivid distinctness before us. It is the next thing to being there ourselves. Nay, we are there to all real intents. We lay the play down with thankfulness that the life of one more period is henceforth a reality to us. Nor is this all. It has added another figure to that Pantheon of human nobilities through which every aspiring mind loves to wander. In Major von Tellheim, the hero of the piece, we learn to know a man at once grand and of a distinctive cast of grandeur, — no mere lay-figure, on which are draped certain moral or professional generalities, but the culminating product of the most characteristic forces of the time, working through a high-strung, responsive soul. He is a brave officer, on whom unjust suspicion has fallen. He has descended, step by step, into humiliating poverty, when the frank-hearted young Saxon woman Minna, to whom, in brighter days, he had been betrothed, discovers him. To her warm, generous soul, the whole sad history is ended in that hour. She is rich: they will marry; they will be, oh, how happy! No: never while stain rests on him. He will link the destiny of no gentle soul with his dishonored name. It is the old tragical story of the proud soul that would rather live in hell, its honor acknowledged, than be happy in heaven, the least breath sullying it. And yet the character is absolutely original. It is a pride that stands on no mere beggarly points of conventional honor. There is in the man such towering sense of grand integrity, such absolute identification of personal qualities with all that is worthiest of salvos of admiration, that to sully his name means to him to sully eternal right and truth. He asks no favor; only justice. The whole world ought to, *shall*, see him as he is. The king himself must acknowledge himself in the wrong. We may call such pride a weakness, if we will,—a slavery, after all, to the vanity of human breath. But it rests on a self-confidence so supreme, on a wrath, that rectitude like his should be called in question, so righteously ablaze; its proportions are so grand, its trampling under foot the thought of home and happiness, and every form of joy, sooner than bring taint upon a gentle woman, is so heroic, that it affects us with the awe we feel in the presence of the bleak mountain and the desert ocean. There is such mass and power about it, that it becomes sublime. And we rejoice to feel, that, even in the dreary days of Frederic's wars, humanity took on such lordly shapes.

Lessing had nearly completed his "Laocoon," when he resolved to throw up his situation, and leave Breslau. He had spent nearly five years there; the war was over; henceforth the position meant but so much a year and routine work: he must be off for fresh scenes and pastures new. He left his post as poor as he had entered on it, with but one exception. He had made a large and choice collection of books. He might have acquired an ample fortune, as did his associates, in Breslau. He had known, before their public announcement, the various adulterations of the currency, to which Frederic from time to time was driven, and the various undertakings which would affect the value of stocks. He could have speculated with absolute certainty of large returns. But his sense of honor was too delicately scrupulous to permit of his using such knowledge; and he saw men growing rich all round him, without a murmur that conscience forbade him to do the same.

His Berlin friends cherished sanguine expectations that Frederic would recognize his worth, and offer him the now vacant post of Royal Librarian. This spurred him on to complete and publish his "Laocoon." The world gained much, but Lessing nothing. It is doubtful whether Frederic ever turned a page of it. His eagle eye blinked darkly when the question came of recognizing the grandest man in all his kingdom. Despising the literature of his own tongue, infatuated with the idea of the superiority of every thing French, too avaricious to be willing to pay a respectable salary, he sought out in France a second-rate man, and left Lessing to his poverty. And once more we find the foremost literary man in Europe earning his scanty daily bread by what chance job-writing he can obtain. The "Laocoon," however, was published.

It is a fragment after all, this "Laocoon;" but what a fragment! The immediate impulse to its composition seems to have lain in a single passage of Winckelmann's, in which a comparison is instituted between the famous marble group of Laocoon and his sons in the coils of the avenging serpents, and the well-known description of the same scene in Virgil. Winckelmann places the poet below the sculptor, and gives his reasons for so doing. They are more than insufficient to justify his judgment, and Lessing's keen eye pierced at once to the source of the confusion, — the carrying over into the domain of poetry, and erecting there as standards, the laws which hold true of sculpture only. Keeping clearly before him the fundamental truth which Goethe afterwards enunciated in the words, "Art should be discussed only in the presence of works of art," — a procedure ever spontaneous with Lessing, who hated the barrenness of naked abstractions, and gloried in the inspiring teaching of the living incarnations, — he proceeds at once to develop and illustrate his positions from "the eternal types of Homer and of Sophocles." What poetry can express, and what it cannot; what plastic art can express, and what it cannot; the limits, the power, the range, the glory of each, — this is his theme: and with what absolute mastery he handles it! Intellect, imagination, and heart are alike stimulated and charmed as we move along. What rarest union of keen analysis with glow of feeling! The accuracy of the surveyor, running his lines and angles with such precision, that the most imbittered litigants might as well think to dispute the parallax of the sun or moon as question them! The triumphant art of the landscape-gardener filling in the sharply measured tracts with a wealth of stately forests, and winding lakes, and stretches of velvet lawn, and gorgeous masses of flowering shrubs! Lessing does not give us the bare results of a hidden process. He carries us through the process with him. We become identified with him. So wonderfully vital in his style, so complete a revealer of the man himself, of the man all warm and eager and alive with the chase after truth, that a contagious sympathy seizes upon the reader, and teacher and taught, each shouts "Εὕρηκα!" at the same moment. Illustration upon illustration from the works of master-spirits help the dawning light of eternal principles to break in fulness upon our minds. We are taught by such as have authority. The scribes, with their frivolities and technicalities, are allowed no hearing. It is like studying naval tactics with Nelson at the Nile and at Trafalgar, or architecture in the presence of the Parthenon or York Minster. And when we lay down the work, we feel that the intellect has been fortified with foundation principles, our appreciation of beauty intensified, and that henceforth we are capable both of a deeper and a more enlightened admiration. We have learned, too, an invaluable lesson in method, which will help us in our private studies all through life.

A thoughtful reading of the "Laocoon" enables one to understand clearly enough the sacred importance Lessing attached to the vocation of the critic. We see how his deep sense of this partook of the nature of worship itself, and enter thoroughly into his stern indignation at all trifling profaners of such a calling. His countrymen call him their second Luther, and rightly. The two men are full-blood brothers in the spirit. In heroism, in power of wrath and love, in sense of moral obligation, in respect for the common people, in belief that the grandest truth is meant for the humblest being, in resolve to do battle ever against all enemies of the general good, they stand side by side, and tower head and shoulders above all others of their race. As were to Luther popes and princes and bishops God's enemies and nothing more, when they dared to veil the glory from above; so, too, to Lessing were the most potent names of Europe, when he found them barbarizing and corrupting the general taste, and robbing the world of the rich and perennial sources of joy and purification that lie waiting in the works of the long line of earth's exalted spirits. No matter from what quarter proceeded any hurtful criticism or noxious work of art, — from bosom friend in Berlin, or incense-reeking, servilely dreaded hierarch, Voltaire, in France, — he let fly at once his scathing bolt.

Frederic had rejected Lessing. But many months had not elapsed when he was called to a work which he hailed with rare delight. An effort was to be made in Hamburg to create a theatre worthy of the name. Ballets and all such fripperies were to be discarded. The production of a national dramatic literature was to be in every way encouraged. A journal was to be established in which every thing in each nightly presentation — the play itself, the actors, to their very gait and dress — were to be criticised from the standpoint of absolute principle. The audiences were to be trained to know the good, and reject the bad. He must come on, and take absolute control. And he went.

Of course the grand scheme came to nought. Generous and patriotic as was the spirit which prompted it, it was asking too much of human nature. No Rhadamanthus, like Lessing, could many weeks sit in judgment on thin-skinned mortals, without the accompaniments of a prisoners' bar, with flanking constables, to hold fast the victims, or a three-headed

Cerberus to keep the peace. But neither were constables, nor was Cerberus, in the contract. Lessing loved truth, and longed to be purified by it: the actors loved lies, and did not want to be purified at all. Lessing was dead in earnest, and regarded the theatre as a moral agency; the audiences cared only for sentimentalities, for excitement, for fun. But the experiment lasted long enough to give the world the noble series of papers which constitute the "Hamburg Dramaturgy."

The "Hamburg Dramaturgy" is a striking illustration of the fact before adverted to, that, in the hands of Lessing, an inferior work is made, through its very faults, to teach as pregnant lessons as a worthy one through its merits. In the light of the glaring contrast presented by the plays he so mercilessly dissects and exposes in all their nakedness to works deserving of our reverence, we are made to feel, as perhaps in no other way were possible, the informing spirit of the truly great. And yet they were not all vulgar names and reputations which Lessing riddled. He grappled hand to hand with such authorities as Corneille and Voltaire only the more eagerly, not because they were foemen worthy of his steel,— for they were but babies in his grasp,— but because they were vast powers of evil influence, corrupters of all Europe, Antichrists in the world of letters. A flattering French critic had asserted that Love itself had dictated Voltaire's "Zaire." "Gallantry rather," was Lessing's scathing answer. Here lay the root of the perversion. Gallantry mistaken for love, bombast for eloquence, monstrosity for sublimity, rant for earnestness, prudery for purity, shocking madhouse horrors for tragic interest,— these were what he saw the whole world gaping at, imitating, lauding to the skies. And yet the arch-corrupters, Corneille and Voltaire, had boasted themselves lineal descendants from the Greeks, renewers of Greek art, champions of the fundamental laws laid down by Aristotle!

It was an ill day for them when they had mentioned Aristotle. To them, Aristotle was a fetish, ignorantly worshipped. To Lessing, he was a grand lawgiver, reverenced because understood. There are few things in all criticism equal to the clear-sighted analysis Lessing makes of the famous dictum of Aristotle as to the purifying influence wrought by tragedy through sympathy and fear, and his remorseless application of the results obtained to the tragedies of Corneille and Voltaire. He shows that the passions to be purified through sympathy and fear are " our sympathy and our fear themselves."

When we rise from a thoughtful reading of a " Hamlet " or a " Lear," we feel that we have been carried into the very depths of this mysterious drama of humanity, in which we ourselves are likewise sufferers and actors. The entrancing joys, the terrible vicissitudes, the insoluble problems, the dreads, the hopes, the whole circle of thoughts and events which come sweeping in upon the human soul in life itself, have been brought to bear upon us. Our sympathies and our fears alike have been educated and been purified. Were *these first* too cold, they have been set aglow; were they excessive, sentimental, weak, the eternal connection of justice and discipline with suffering has toned and braced them. Were our *fears* too sluggish, our sense of immunity from evil too rooted, the awful realities of life have inspired a salutary dread. Were they too ready to startle and unnerve us, we have been shown the real calamities which overtake man, and the limits that hedge them in; and have been brought face to face with the compensations which attend them. It is salutary for man to have his fears and sympathies thus wrought upon and modified. It links him in with the great common fate of his fellows, and shows him how to bear himself. A very different thing is this, as the dramatist's end, from a gross sensation aim at creating horror by a hideous medley of ghastly atrocities, incomprehensible crimes, earthquakes, eruptions, fire, and flood. Such work as this he may leave to the agents of " Accident-Insurance Companies," who, to quicken the sense of human vicissitude and induce the purchase of policies, think to compass their object by heaping together in a single picture, lit up by a glaring conflagration, a frightful railroad collision, a runaway stage-coach plunging over a precipice, an annihilating steamboat explosion, and a whelming avalanche of snow from a roof. The dramatist has one work to do; the "Police Gazette" or the "Terrific Register," another. Corneille and Voltaire failed to perceive this delicate distinction. They robbed other departments of their inherent rights. They bodily stole the electrician's prescriptive claim to make man's hair stand on end, and insisted that it belonged to the drama alone.

The Hamburg enterprise had come to wreck. Again was Lessing compelled to strike his tent, and wander forth into the world. He stood, worse than penniless, — in debt. The matchless papers which had dethroned such potent idols, and were to break the abject thraldom to France in which the nation stood, from Frederic on the throne to every scribbler in his garret, had brought their author nothing but detraction and ill-will. They had been widely read, but in pirated editions. In this sad juncture of affairs, he received a call to Wolfenbüttel, as Librarian to the Duke of Brunswick. The salary offered was only a wretched pittance; but promises of a better place and an ampler support were freely extended by the prince. It was a bitter thing to Lessing to give up his liberty, and enter into service; but to the stress of poverty now was added the stress of love. In Hamburg he had met the first woman that ever won his heart, — Madame Eva König; and for her he must build a home. In an unhappy hour he accepted the position. And now began the dark days of Lessing's life. Henceforth it was to be one long, heart-rending tragedy. The prince was a hollow-hearted, shameless cheat. He wanted Lessing for the glory of having him; but he wanted the glory *cheap*. His money was for his pleasures and his mistresses; and other pay, the pay of broken pledges, must serve for the famous man.

All shapes of evil now accumulated on the head of Lessing, — poverty, hope deferred making the heart sick, utter loneliness in wretched Wolfenbüttel, a malarious climate, which ruined his constitution, and made him a martyr to chills and rheumatism. The disordered condition in which the affairs of Eva König had been left by her former husband necessitated that she should spend years in weary journeyings to and fro, and debarred all present hope of union. It is heart-rending to behold so grand a man for six long years plunged in such woes and humiliations. They are described with painful distinctness in the "Life of Lessing," and we are made to feel them in all their long-drawn anguish. And when at last a bright day dawns, and the two noble beings we have learned to love and venerate are united, it proves after all but a fitful gleam of sunshine. On Christmas Eve of the year 1776, his wife, to Lessing's unspeakable joy, bore him a son. In twenty-four hours the child was dead; and, in a few days, the mother followed. When anguish grows too oppressive to express itself through the common channels, it finds vent in strange and startling ways. To one who knows the human heart, could any serious language tell the tale of woe so movingly as these words, so full of the "wit of sorrow," he wrote to Eschenberg? —

"I seize the moment, when my wife is lying senseless, to thank you for your kind sympathy. My joy was only short. And I was so sorry to lose him, this son; for he had so much sense! so much sense! Do not think that my few hours of fatherhood have already made me such an ape of a father. I know what I say. Did it not show his sense, that they were obliged to draw him into this world with forceps? — that he so soon became disgusted with his new abode? Was he not wise in seizing the first opportunity to make off again? To be sure, the little hasty-head drags the mother also away with him; for there is little hope left that I shall save her. I wished, just for once, to prosper like other men; but it has fallen out badly for me."

And yet these years of sorrow and humiliation in Wolfenbüttel were full of enduring fruit. A tragedy, indeed, they were; but a tragedy which purifies every beholding soul, which forbids alike all emasculate sympathy and all craven fear. They were the years which witnessed the birth of Lessing's "Emilia Galotti," of "The Wolfenbüttel Fragments," of "The Controversy with Goeze," of "Nathan the Wise," of "The Education of the Human Race," — works full of an inspiration, a glow of beauty, a wit, a wisdom, a fire of passion, which awaken our amazement when we reflect against what pressure of misery their author was contending. The limits of a single article forbid all extended criticism of these. They are mainly theological in their subjects; but let no man who associates theology and dryness confound them here. He who would burn with indignation at bigotry, arrogance, and priestly tyranny, and shout for joy at seeing the representatives of these flayed alive, — let him read "The Controversy with Goeze." He who would feel with awe and gladness the guiding hand of God in human history, — let him read "The Education of the Human Race." He who would have his heart set aglow with divinest charity for all mankind, and live an hour at least in the Millennial Kingdom, — let him read and re-read, with ever-fresh delight, "Nathan the Wise."

It is hard to conceive a more exhilarating surprise than they would feel, who, long fed on the dry bran and stubble of ordinary theological literature, should open first upon the luscious pastures and sparkling waters of any one of Lessing's pamphlets on these subjects. No theologian by profession, he yet outweighs whole hosts of the foremost names in this department. Not that he is strong on every side. His nature had its limits. He lacked the gushing, lyric element, which, in the soul of his loved Spinoza, overflowed in joy and worship, and greeted the driest abstractions with the rapt adoration of St. Theresa. He is cast too much in the Stoic mould, is too born a gladiator, is too inflexible in fibre, to be swept and made musical by the divinest breath of the Spirit. There are intimations from on high, whose whispered secrets his ear was not framed to hear. But, his foot on his own native heather, he was a matchless man. No formal treatises, no ponderous bodies of divinity, have ever come down from him; but on every page he scatters seed-thoughts that have the germs of revolutions in them. He set a nation thinking. His Hercules' arms and his Hercules' club cleansed the Augean stables of rotten, infectious accumulations, and smote down the monsters who held the land in terror. His words are "half-battles." Every word is rammed with life. Every page comes hot from the heart of a man who cannot trifle, will press close to the soul of things. Truth as result, as dogma, as thing outside the present life of mind, has no attraction for him. The powers it sets in action; the thought, the love, the integrity, the reverence, the loyalty, it keeps in glowing, blissful play,—these are its worth to man. It reveals to him his nature; it glorifies his life; it makes it a joy and dignity to be. Lessing's own oft-quoted, yet still unhackneyed, words are full of this brave conviction:—

"Not the truth a man has stored up, or thinks he has stored up,—not this constitutes the dignity of the man, but the conscientious work he has done in getting at the truth. For it is not the possession, but the pursuit, of truth, which develops the powers. Possession breeds content, sloth, pride. Did God hold shut in His right hand all Truth, and in His left but the unquenchable thirst for Truth (although with the condition that I should ever and eternally err), and say to me, 'Choose,'—with all humility would I fall upon His left hand, and say, 'Father, give. Absolute truth is for Thee alone.'"

It is the contagion of this example, far more than any positive results he reached, which constitutes the worth of Lessing to the reader's mind. The spirit he brings to bear in all his investigations, the sense we gain of the ennobling influence on character of the devout and brave pursuit of truth,—these are what do us good. It is not clear in every case what were his own conclusions. In his "Life," by Stahr, there is too much special pleading to rope him in with some given consistent school. In the chapter especially in which is discussed Lessing's position in regard to immortality, there is an amount of "reading between the lines," of interpolating what the writer thinks ought logically to have been his thought, which leaves an unsatisfactory feeling in the mind. But, alike whether man lives but his earthly day, or is conscious heir of the eternal future, one spirit alone is to animate his life. He is to seek his reward in the blessedness of doing right, and not in any ultramundane bribe. This much is clear in Lessing's view, and this is the substance of what he urges.

The motto prefixed to the "Life of Lessing" tells the faithful story, "To go back to Lessing means to go forward."

No writings are more full of that perennial life which is the same yesterday, to-day, and for ever. They are instinct with the primal qualities, ever old and ever young, which animate all enduring literature. Once more we give a hearty welcome to the work, and thank Professor Evans for it. May it give an impulse to the study of Lessing's works, and bring him in as a power in our young, growing land! We need him. He will leave his life-long mark on every mind which shall give him hospitable greeting.

Art. III. — SCHENKEL'S CHARACTER OF JESUS.

The Character of Jesus Portrayed; a Biblical Essay, with an Appendix. By Dr. DANIEL SCHENKEL, Professor of Theology, Heidelberg. Translated from the third German Edition, with Introduction and Notes, by W. H. FURNESS, D.D. 2 vols. Boston: Little, Brown, & Co. 1866.

WE have here not merely two volumes, but two separate works, — one by Dr. Schenkel, and one by his translator. Nor is one by any means the echo of the other. Dr. Furness is not, after the fashion of most editors, continually bidding you stop just to admire this or that sentiment or argument in his author's book. When he agrees with Dr. Schenkel, he says nothing; but, when he disagrees, he bids you stand. And this he does so often, that, long before the reader reaches the end, he wonders why Dr. Furness translated a book so carefully, only for the sake of afterward refuting it at every step. It certainly seems very generous. But, after all the difference, there is a great deal in common between Schenkel and his translator. The London "Quarterly," in a recent article on the various lives of Jesus that have recently appeared, ascribes to Schenkel "a certain democratic twang." What the London "Quarterly" would be apt to characterize in this way, enemy of all progress as it is, would be very certain to attract a man like Dr. Furness, whose life has been divided

between two great enthusiasms, — one, for the redemption of
the slave from his bondage; the other, to redeem the character
of Jesus from the unworthy representations that have disfig-
ured it for so many centuries. In his own life, these two
enthusiasms cannot have been separated; and, in his previous
works, they often touch upon each other. But in Schenkel's
"Character of Jesus" he found them melted into one. In his
sympathy with the common people, Schenkel finds the root
of Jesus' consecration, the key of his divinest purposes. It
was probably this feature of his book that attracted Dr.
Furness, and induced him, in spite of much with which he
did not sympathize, to undertake the task that he has performed so handsomely. If we are not mistaken, Schenkel
will find this English rendering of his book more fine and
crisp than the original. We can scarcely imagine a greater
contrast than between the muddy current of Strauss's "New
Life of Jesus," in its English form, and the transparent clearness of Dr. Furness's translation. And yet we cannot but
think that Strauss's stream bears costlier freights upon its
bosom, and escapes at length into a deeper sea.

But so free is Dr. Furness to differ from the author he
translates, that these volumes should be carefully avoided by
that class of persons whose opinions are invariably those of
the last book which they have read; for they would be sure
to breed confusion in their tender minds. They should, at
least, wait a week or two after reading Dr. Schenkel's Essay
before reading the Introduction and the Notes, so that they
may accept, successively, entirely different views, and not be
pained by an attempt to judge between them. But the man
who thinks for himself, and tries to form his own opinions,
will rejoice at such a fund of provocation as awaits him here.
Upon the very threshold of the discussion, Dr. Schenkel is
opposed by his translator. When and by whom the Gospels
were written is the first consideration. To Schenkel it is all-
important. For the most part, Dr. Furness goes with him in
his investigations. But, when the work of destruction is
completed, and the Gospels have been assigned to a late
period, and in but one case out of four — and then only in

part, and doubtfully at that—to a disciple of Jesus, is he
alarmed at the result? Not in the least. For he has a touchstone
of his own by which to try the various accounts that
criticism has left not one upon another, and discover whether
they were over parts of the great living temple of the Galilean's
soul. The nature of this touchstone is thus indicated in
the closing paragraph of the book:—

"In concluding a labor which he has found full of interest, and
which he trusts is to serve the truth, the translator is free to confess,
that, with great respect for the learning and industry of German
critics and commentators, he is struck with the fact, that these eminent
and laborious scholars appear never to perceive *that the records
owe their existence to the reality of the facts recorded*" (vol. ii. p. 359).

"They look everywhere," he says (these German critics),
"but directly at the facts, to solve the secret of their having
passed into history." But Dr. Furness looks "directly at
the facts," and nowhere else. They are sufficient for his purposes.
They bear upon their faces the proofs that they are
genuine. But he cannot help seeing that there were many
reasons why they should not have been reported by the immediate
followers of Jesus. These men lived not in the past,
but in the future. The Jesus of their meditations was not
a Jesus of the past, but of the future. He was not so much a
glorious memory to his disciples as a glorious hope. Nothing
that he had said or done was of account, in comparison with
what he would say or do when he should come again in the
glory of his Father with all his holy angels. What mattered
it if words and deeds were not recorded, that were so soon to
be eclipsed? Why be so careful to report the beauty of a
few violets and anemones that had been nipped by not untimely
frost, when, in a little while, the Messianic summer
was to burst in a great tide of fragrant beauty over all the
land? It was not to be expected, therefore, that these men
would go about to write biographies of Jesus as soon as he
was dead. If, then, these facts must be reported, who should
report them? Dr. Furness's answer is original. The first records
of Christianity, he suggests, were written by half-con-

verts, half-followers of Jesus, lukewarm disciples, men of the Nicodemus sort, "neutral and uncommitted lookers-on." But, if any thing is certain, is it not that neither the Gospels as they now stand, nor the first memoranda from which they were compiled, were written by members of this class? Every line, every word of them, is written *con amore*. Whoever wrote them, whoever cherished the remembrances out of which they were written, must have been adoring followers of Jesus, undoubted converts to his teachings, in so far as they could understand them.

But this unique hypothesis, convenient as it would be, does not begin to be so sweeping as the principle, that "the records owe their existence to the reality of the facts recorded." But can this be allowed? Does the existence of these records imply the certainty that these events took place? Is it not possible to conceive of the genesis of these accounts from any womb but that of sober fact? Does not Dr. Furness allow, that Strauss is right in supposing that some of these accounts are mythical? If it was thought that the Messiah would do certain things, and if it was also thought that Jesus was the Messiah, was it not natural that those things that were expected of the Messiah should be ascribed to him? If part of the record can be thus accounted for, cannot another part be credited, as M. Renan supposes, to the play of highly wrought imaginations? How can the "naturalness" of any statement concerning Jesus attest its authenticity, until we know enough about him to determine what is "natural"? What is natural to one man is not natural to another. How shall we know that it was natural for Jesus to arouse the dead and rise from his own grave, until it has been proved that he did so? It certainly is not natural for other men, however good, to do such things. Dr. Furness says, "the manner in which they are told" proves that these stories are trustworthy. But, however fresh and simple and artless an account may be, if it involves the preternatural it is much easier to believe that we are dealing with a legend, notwithstanding all these traits, than that any thing so exceptional ever happened. Indeed, it is notorious that the popular imagination can invest a fiction with all the outward semblance of a fact. A village rumor, utterly without foundation, is thrice as natural in its form, as the most careful phrases of the historian. "Can a great man be concealed?" said Plato. But allow that great events must be recorded, and it does not follow that what claims to be the record of a great event, however natural, is strictly true. And hence, when Dr. Furness tells us that we ought to look "directly at the facts," he takes for granted every thing that criticism has been trying to discover for the last fifty years; viz., *What are the facts?* And, until we know more of this matter than we do at present, it is of the first importance to know when and by whom the first reports of Jesus and his work were written.

And to this part of his labors Dr. Schenkel has applied himself with a great deal of fairness and ability. His result is not very different from that of M. Renan, except that he assigns the fourth Gospel to a much lower rank of authenticity. Our nearest approach to Jesus is the "primitive Mark," of which the present Gospel by that name is an enlargement and exaggeration. This opinion is supported by various reasons, the most prominent of which, after the external testimony, are, that it has no literary aim, has much less of the legendary and miraculous, contains no fabled infancy, and no appearance after death. The estimate of Matthew is very similar to that of Renan and Réville. It is made up, principally, from the primitive Mark and the τὰ λόγια spoken of by Papias. It shows, unmistakably, a literary purpose. Its object is to prove the Messianic dignity of Jesus. His life is viewed as something fixed beforehand, from the beginning to the end. It addresses itself, throughout, to Jewish prejudices. Jesus acts in one way rather than in another, not from internal desire, but from external necessity, in order that some prophecy of the Old Testament may be fulfilled. The literary aim in the third Gospel is even more apparent than in the first. It leans as far from the historic perpendicular in favor of the Gentiles as the first in favor of the Jews. It gives us the various legends in their latest, and hence grossest, form. It is much more miraculous than the first Gospel, vastly more than the second. The legends of the infancy and the resurrection here assume their baldest form. The extra-Jewish features in the ministry of Jesus are much magnified, and the universal significance of his teachings everywhere made prominent. The arguments by which Dr. Schenkel seeks to prove that John did not write the fourth Gospel are the most masterly portions of his book. We should do injustice to their fulness and ability by attempting a synopsis of them. His own conviction on this point is complete; and he abides by it throughout his work, instead of using the fourth Gospel as if it were authentic, after having proved that it is not. The blunder of Renan is here continually before him. He fully realizes the impossibility of a consistent life of Jesus, that does not leave this Gospel out of the account. And, although his consequent success is far from complete, it is so much greater than it would otherwise have been, that we lament afresh that Renan did not feel at liberty to build with the material furnished by the first three Gospels; for, had he done so, the life of Jesus would have been written, as now we fear it will not be for many years to come.

And what is the conception of Jesus that Dr. Schenkel has discovered in the Synoptic Gospels? Certainly, it is a conception very different from that which the fourth Gospel has enshrined, and Christendom has always cherished. According to the fourth Gospel, there is no development of his religious or Messianic self-consciousness, no growth of his ideas. He is already at the first what he continues to be to the end. But the conception of the Synoptic Gospels involves the idea of development. By degrees, it is borne in upon his mind that he is the Messiah; not the Messiah of the Old Testament, not the Messiah that the Pharisees were looking for, but the Messiah, in a moral and spiritual sense, that was but barely hinted at in prophecy. By degrees, also, he widens the circle of his activity,— comes to the conclusion that it was not only "the lost sheep of the house of Israel" that he must try to save. And, when the idea of his work is fully formed in his own mind, it is only by degrees that he imparts it to his disciples, and by still slower processes that he communicates it to the adherents of the Old Theocracy.

The first resolve to enter upon a public career awoke in Jesus at the call of John the Baptist. It is here that the "democratic twang," spoken of by the "London Quarterly," first makes itself evident. "The third Gospel, by a fine allusion, lets us read in the soul of Jesus the moving cause of his wishing to be baptized: 'When *all the people* were baptized,' then Jesus also suffered himself to be baptized." It is a beautiful idea; but we should like it better, if, in this case, it did not seem to be a last resort, on the part of Dr. Schenkel, to save us from the supposition that Jesus had any sins to repent of. Dr. Furness does well to rebuke this prudery. From positive impurity or malice, Jesus may at this time have been free; but he was yet far short of his ideal of holiness. It was long after that he said to the young man who called him "good master," "Why callest thou me good?" But Jesus does not long remain with the Baptist. He resolves to do an independent work; concludes that John is doing, on the whole, more harm than good; and goes apart into the wilderness, to meditate upon the form of his mission and the methods by which it shall be carried on. The temptation which here awaits him is partly to misuse his working-wonder power, and partly to compromise with the theocracy. He triumphs over it, and goes back into the world to choose four disciples (at first) from the middle class, and begin a ministry characterized by two assertions and by two demands. The assertions are: 1. The time is fulfilled, i.e., the time of the old order; 2. The kingdom of God is among you, i.e., is waiting to be realized by spiritual appropriation of its benefits. The demands are: 1. For a change of heart; "he insisted on a life moulded in one way from within;" 2. Faith, not in his person, but in the possibility of a new life in the kingdom of heaven, whose presence he declared to be a fact.

The limits of an article do not permit us to follow Dr. Schenkel in the subsequent details of the career which he ascribes to Jesus. His fame grew rapidly, with little opposition. At first he did not consider himself the Messiah, but only a teacher of the people, the founder of a new era, the herald of the kingdom of God. The laws of this kingdom he unfolded with increasing clearness and boldness as the days went on. The necessary conflict between his purpose and the Old Theocracy became more apparent to him, and more evident to the hierarchy, with every word he spoke. At length he confesses to the disciples that he is the Christ. By what arguments he was convinced of this we are not told; but it was a turning-point in his mission. It bound the disciples to him more closely; it alienated, in like proportion, the Jewish theologues and priests. The impossibility of making any thing out of the old order growing stronger in the mind of Jesus, he resolves to break with it completely, to attack it with all the energy of his being. For this purpose he goes to Jerusalem. He is haunted with the idea of the suffering Messiah. To be this; to sacrifice himself; to crown his sacrifice with his death, and, dying, to drag down the tottering hierarchy into a grave thrice deeper than his own, — this from henceforth is his ideal. The latter part of Dr. Schenkel's work is loaded with this thought, and he applies it to the records with an ingenuity that is sometimes almost startling. Still Jesus does not go out of his way to irritate his enemies. There is no need for him to do so: the crisis comes full soon enough. A few days in Jerusalem are sufficient to bring all the fury of the hierarchy down upon his head. But every preparation has been made. Mary has consecrated him to death; at a last supper with his followers he has formally established the communion, the New Theocracy of which he is to be the Paschal Lamb, the only sacrifice. Then comes the cross, and then the grave; and then — Jesus is glorified.

"It is an indisputable fact, that, in the early morning of the first day of the week following the crucifixion, the grave of Jesus was found empty" (vol. ii. p. 313).

"It is a second fact, that the disciples and other members of the Apostolic Communion were convinced that Jesus was seen after his crucifixion" (vol. ii. p. 313).

"There is a third fact: the appearances of Jesus after his death, related in the Gospels, had substantially no other character than that which marked the appearance of Christ to the Apostle Paul upon his journey to Damascus. Paul mentions the appearance of Christ to himself among the other appearances related in the Gospels, as in every respect of a like description. Thence we may conclude, that the accounts in the Gospels which represent the risen Master as having a material body cannot be well grounded. From the account in the Book of Acts, it does not appear that Jesus wrought any effect upon the apostle through the organs of a material body. It was an appearance of light attended by a voice, which, according to this representation, was perceived by Paul. He himself describes his vision of Christ as emphatically an inward revelation of Christ: 'It pleased God to reveal his Son *in* him'" (vol. ii. p. 314).

In this portrait of Jesus, which Dr. Schenkel has sketched with such a loving hand and reverent spirit, there is less, far less, in the features than in the expression to make us feel that we are really looking at that blessed face. It is in what is incidental, rather than in what is essential, to his treatment, that the finest touches will be found, and the impression of severest truthfulness received. One thing he has proved conclusively, that a true Life of Jesus does not necessarily arise from a right estimate of the Gospels, however indispensable such an estimate may be to such a Life. It is also necessary to be without bias, without preconceptions. He that would write the Life of Jesus, though he need not be without hypotheses, must be content to drop them just as fast as he discovers that they are not justified by the reports which he accepts as genuine. And he must not be too anxious to make the record square with his hypotheses. It may well be doubted whether the application of these tests to Dr. Schenkel's method would not reveal a leaning on his part to certain modes of thought, so strong as to unfit him for the task which he has undertaken. Never was a book written more earnestly, in a more truth-loving and God-serving spirit. It shines at every page with a most perfect conscientiousness and purity of aim. But these qualities often consist with violent dogmatic leanings, that, in spite of them, are sure to tell upon the task in hand.

Such leanings Dr. Schenkel nowhere manifests. But he is haunted with the idea of the Church. He does not mean that it shall influence his studies of the life and character of Jesus; but it is very certain that it does. At times he seems half to suspect it; and, in his chapter on the Last Supper, it is painfully interesting to see him wavering between his preconception and the stubborn facts that do not willingly conform to it.

Dr. Schenkel's conception of Jesus appears to us much more formal, much more self-conscious, much more ecclesiastical, than it would have been could he have freed himself, upon the threshold of his work, from this idea of the Church. But it was so much a part of him, that he was not conscious of it any more than we are conscious of the muscles that we use most frequently. The result has been, that he has found in the New Testament what was not there until he had imported it. His portrait of Jesus is the portrait of a man who does every thing self-consciously, every thing for effect. He does nothing spontaneously. There is a *wilfulness* about him for which the Gospels furnish us no warrant. He acts for reasons from without, not by necessity from within. Dr. Schenkel complains that Matthew's Jesus is a fore-ordained and pre-determined character. But his own conception is but little better, — that of a *post*-determined character, that of a man who does every thing to-day with reference to something else that he will do to-morrow. He is always drilling his disciples, always initiating them into the formalities of his kingdom. He does not go right on, willing to die if death is incidental to his work. He keeps his eye for ever on the cross. His death is always in his thought. There is something very morbid about this. It takes very much from the idea that Jesus was as courageous as he was sensitive. It is not the part of greatness to think so much upon one's death. It does not seem like Jesus to think so much more of something that is to befall him than of the living word of truth which he can preach.

Instead of removing the dust that has concealed the portrait of Jesus from the world for eighteen centuries, that we may see the great original, Dr. Schenkel has hung up in front of it what he declares to be a copy; but it is a copy of his own idea, rather than a copy of the face that we would fain behold. Let the reader, when he has been swept along through these six hundred pages on the flood-tide of Dr. Schenkel's beautiful enthusiasm, retrace his course, and see how meagre are the facts on which the doctor builds his theory. And, of the facts that he is pleased to use, it is even more astonishing to see how many of them he distorts and whips, unconsciously enough, into his service. The candid reader will appeal from him to his translator very frequently; for Dr. Furness steadily opposes Dr. Schenkel's tendency to formulate the life of Jesus, and pleads very eloquently for a less intentional and more spontaneous conception of his character. According to Dr. Furness, he did not institute a communion; he lived a divine life; he lived it into others, and they, finding themselves possessed of it, were drawn together, and there was a communion whether they would or no; he did not go to Jerusalem to sacrifice himself, but to declare the truth of God, and to abide the consequences. Nor did the woman who anointed him do this in token of his death, as if she were embalming him before his time, but out of purest reverence and love; nor was the Last Supper with his disciples "only the last of a series of previously arranged acts, a solemn ending, in view of his death and of the formal institution of his Communion," as Dr. Schenkel says. He well says "only." It was a great deal more than that. It was an hour of tenderest emotion. The words he spoke were not the language of a ritual. They were a plea for human love; a cry for human sympathy; a prayer, that when his followers came, from year to year, to celebrate the Paschal feast, he might not be forgotten. That he meant to abolish this feast and institute another in its stead, or that he meant to symbolize the death of the old order, the record gives us no sign. All this, if not a great deal more with reference to the war that Jesus made upon the hierarchy, is to be credited, not to the Gospels, but to the prepossessions with which Dr. Schenkel entered upon his work.

Marked as the difference is between Dr. Schenkel and his translator, as to the amount of definiteness in the aims of Jesus, there is another question, not less interesting, on which they divide even more sharply. It is the question of the so-called miracles ascribed to Jesus in the Gospels. Of course Dr. Furness would insist, as earnestly as Dr. Schenkel, that the theological miracle is impossible; that there can be no such thing as a violation of natural law. Of course they are united in believing that the miracles of Jesus are not credentials, and do not make the truth of his teaching any truer or any more authoritative than it would otherwise be. They are also agreed that the miraculous accounts pertaining to the birth and infancy of Jesus have no historical validity. But there is still much room for difference. Schenkel allows that Jesus was possessed of healing power. With his estimate of the Gospels, he can do no less. But he does this only because he is compelled. He does not rejoice in doing it. He would certainly be better pleased if he could eliminate every atom of this wonder-working from the text. This he cannot do; but he does not go an inch further than he is compelled to go. And, when he comes to any thing of this sort that he feels must be historic, he still makes every possible allowance for exaggeration, and ascribes the largest possible proportion of the effect produced to "faith." The words of Jesus to the woman that had touched his garment, "Thy faith hath made thee whole," are the key with which he unlocks the majority of these accounts. He further imagines, that he can trace in Jesus a growing dislike of these wonders, and a limiting of them almost entirely to those afflicted with insanity. Very different is Dr. Furness's treatment of these same accounts. He fondles them most lovingly. He makes the most of them. It is scarcely necessary for him to suppose "faith" on the part of the diseased. The power of Jesus of itself is quite sufficient. What Dr. Schenkel trips over as lightly as he can, Dr. Furness dwells upon with constantly increasing admiration.

But, outside of these reports of sudden cures, Dr. Schenkel accepts nothing. The blasting of the fig-tree is a distorted parable. The miracle of Cana was no miracle: Jesus had provided wine in case the first supply should be exhausted. The Transfiguration points to a private conversation, in which Jesus told a few of his disciples of his relation to Moses and the prophets. Jairus's daughter was not dead; Jesus himself said so. The raising of Lazarus is in the fourth Gospel; and the fourth Gospel is not authentic. The stilling of the sea, — it was the stilling of men's fears. The feeding of the multitude was a spiritual feast. The resurrection of Jesus, — it was a purely internal experience, not an external fact: that his fleshly body ever rose again we have no reason to believe.

But Dr. Schenkel does not strengthen his position when he says that these accounts of miracle involve the idea of omnipotence, and gives this as a reason for rejecting them. Even Mr. Mansel has allowed that no bystander can testify to a miracle. He can only testify to certain exceptional appearances. He can know nothing of their essential character. It were well to keep the question on this plane, — to speak of the miracles of the New Testament as so many *phenomena*, and weigh the evidence accordingly. But the more remarkable the phenomenon reported, the more faithfully should we sift the evidence. We are by no means bound to believe the story of a resurrection on the same amount of evidence as would convince us that a certain man died on a certain day. But let us rest our incredulity upon the isolated character of the event, not on its impossibility. For, until we know all the laws of nature, scarcely can we say of any thing reported that for it to happen is impossible. But its unwontedness may furnish, on the one hand, a presumption against the truth of it; and if, on the other hand, we find that the report can be accounted for without supposing any, or scarcely any, basis in fact, we are certainly at liberty to disbelieve.

Dr. Schenkel's position will be attacked from two directions. It will be denied that miracles are violations of natural law, and hence impossible. And it is to be regretted that he has put the term *impossibility* where the term *improbability*, based on unwontedness, would have done as well.

But, again, it will be argued against him that he has not shown how these accounts arose, supposing that they do not point to actual occurrences. Nor can it be denied that many of his explanations of the genesis of these accounts are more curious than satisfactory. But the general principle, that it was natural that this parasitic growth of miracle should fasten itself to the living personality of Jesus, considering the time in which he lived and his relation to it, does not depend upon these explanations; it does not stand or fall with our ability to state exactly in what manner the blasting of a fig-tree, or the resurrection of a dead person, came to be regarded as a fact. It is enough to make it evident that such reports would naturally arise. If it is impossible to say in any case *how* they arose, it surely is not less impossible to state how Jairus's daughter arose from her bed, or Lazarus from his tomb; while the general probability is less a thousand times in the second case than in the first. Not but that Dr. Furness, while denying somewhat less confidently than Dr. Schenkel that Jesus had control over the powers of nature, thinks that nothing could have been more "natural" than that Lazarus should come forth at the command of Jesus. But when in this case, or in any other, we come down to particulars, it is invariably the verbal and circumstantial setting of the event, not the event itself, which is so full of naturalness. And this is only what we should expect.

We have spoken at some length of Dr. Schenkel's treatment of the miracles, because we feel that, on the whole, it is a great success. He has not been at the mercy of any particular hypothesis. Never did critic shun more carefully "the falsehood of extremes." Others may succeed better in showing us how these reports of miracle arose. As belonging to the history of opinions, it is a matter of no small importance. But of the Life of Jesus they can no longer be considered an essential part. Even such of them as survive the ordeal of criticism do not affect our estimate of his character. For to argue from his character to his miracles, as both Drs. Schenkel and Furness do, and then to argue back again from his miracles to his character, is manifestly absurd.

But these volumes are as significant in their omissions as in any thing that they assert. Where the Church affects to see a great mountain of dogma, Schenkel sees nothing of the sort. The idea of a Church, of a communion, does indeed pervade his book; but it is a Church without dogmas, without a ritual. Its only creeds are righteousness and love. So simple is its structure, that there seems to be no reason to suppose that Jesus ever took the pains to form it that Dr. Schenkel indicates. Such as it is, it might have grown — it must have grown — out of a heart like that which Jesus carried in his breast. But Dr. Schenkel's negative result is full of hope. It reconciles us to a great deal of passionate attachment to the person of Jesus, to consider, that, just in proportion as the Church discovers him in his real character, it must, if it is honest, cease to believe the pernicious doctrines it has cherished in his name. So much has been achieved already, that it seems not too much to hope, that, when his form shall be revealed in all its beauty, he will be seen, not sitting on a throne demanding homage, but looking up as Beatrice looked into the everlasting glory of another greater than himself. Then God grant that the great Church that he has led so long, following his gaze, as Dante followed Beatrice's in the wondrous tale, may see at length that vision of the Father ever present with his children, which flooded him with so much strength and peace!

Art. IV. — HERBERT SPENCER AND HIS REVIEWERS.

That the highest interest of man is to know the truth, and the highest prerogative of intellect to discover it, are propositions which, though questioned by none, are reduced to practice by few. Numerous causes — such as preconceived ideas, deference to popular belief, dread of inconsistency, party feeling, and bias of temperament — act powerfully to warp the judgment and mislead the intellect in the work of inquiry. So potent are these disturbing influences, that it becomes the highest discipline of the highest natures to guard against them. Even the most gifted minds are liable to be perverted in their action by circumstances commonly regarded as trivial. The great Newton, whose majestic intellect we are wont to think moved in unequalled serenity above the clouds of passion, was so disturbed by the collisions incident to discussion in the meetings of the Royal Society, that he desired the interchange of opinion to take the form of private conference, declaring that "what's done before many witnesses is seldom without some further concern than that for truth." But, while the attainment of truth is hindered by many causes, and we are hence bound to extend a large charity to opponents, there are certain excesses into which writers are prone to fall that we are not for a moment at liberty to tolerate. In these times, when no interests are too vital and no opinions too sacred to escape the assaults of destructive criticism, and when all grades and classes of thinkers are drawn into the vortex of controversy, the danger from over-zeal and over-timidity, as well as from less worthy motives, is greatly heightened; and we are required to insist, with redoubled emphasis, upon a rigorous circumspection in the treatment of adverse views. With the increasing seriousness of conviction and boldness of inquiry which mark our age, a higher standard of justice and honor, and a more thorough conscientiousness in the management of discussion, are to be imperatively demanded. Carelessness of statement, gratuitous imputation of evil motives, misrepresentations of meaning, and all the petty tricks by which a writer seeks to bring an author into reproach, should be sternly reprobated.

Among other ways in which a hostile critic may easily injure an author whose views he dislikes is that of picking out some real or apparent error or incompleteness of knowledge, and so presenting it as to carry an implication damaging to his works at large. An example of this has been furnished by the "North-American Review," in a reference to the pamphlet on the Classification of the Sciences : —

"In Mr. Spencer's subdivisions of mathematics, he has given a prominence to 'Descriptive Geometry' which might be regarded as arising from the partiality of the civil engineer for a branch of his own art, were it not that he says, 'I was ignorant of the existence of this as a separate division of mathematics, until it was described to me by Mr. Hirst, whom I have also to thank for pointing out the omission of the subdivision "Kinematics." It was only when seeking to affiliate and define "Descriptive Geometry," that I reached the conclusion, that there is a negatively quantitative mathematics, as well as a positively quantitative mathematics. In explanation of the term "negatively quantitative," it will suffice to instance the proposition that certain three lines will meet in a point as a negatively quantitative proposition, since it asserts the absence of any quantity of space between their intersections. Similarly, the assertion that certain three points will always fall in a straight line is negatively quantitative, since the conception of a straight line implies the negative of any lateral quantity or deviation.' The propositions selected by Mr. Spencer to illustrate what he calls 'Descriptive Geometry' are by no means peculiar to, or characteristic of, the art to which mathematicians have given this name. In the most elaborate and extensive treatises, no more is claimed for this art, than that it is an account, in a scientific order, of certain methods of geometrical construction useful in engineering and architecture, but inferior in scientific extension even to trigonometry, to which Mr. Spencer does not deign to descend. It is possible that Mr. Spencer has in mind certain propositions in the 'Higher Geometry' concerning relations of position and direction in points and lines: but these cannot be made to stand alone or independently of dimensional properties; and, if they could, they would be as appropriately named 'quantitative' mathematics as 'negatively quantitative.'"*

Must we then conclude that the writer who assumes to estimate a philosophical system like that of Mr. Spencer in the "North-American Review" is really unaware of the fundamental distinction between Science and Art? It would almost seem so. Ignoring the fact that Science is a statement of the relations among phenomena, and can include in its various divisions nothing more than the various classes of those relations, from which all practice based on knowledge

---

* North-American Review, April, 1865, p. 470.

of them is excluded, he actually supposes, that, by "Descriptive Geometry" Mr. Spencer means the art of plan-drawing! "Descriptive Geometry," in its scientific sense, no more means "certain methods of geometrical construction useful in engineering," &c., than "Geometry," in its scientific sense, means certain methods of earth-measuring. As from Geometry, which was originally a mathematical art, there has grown up a division of pure mathematics which has usurped the name of the art; so, beginning with the "Géométritric Descriptive" of Monge, in which theorems and their applications to drawing were mingled together, there has grown up a system of theorems which takes the name of "Descriptive Geometry," while omitting all mention of the practice which gave that name. If, because certain manufacturers and retailers are called "chemists," the reviewer had supposed that by "chemistry," as a branch of science, Mr. Spencer meant certain methods of preparing medicines and making dyes, he would have drawn an equally rational inference. He gains, however, by thus confounding science and art. It enables him to insinuate, by the quotation he makes, that Mr. Spencer, though educated as a civil engineer, was unacquainted with the branch of mathematical art which is especially familiar to engineers.* This insinuation it is unnecessary to meet: it disappears along with the reviewer's mistake on which it is based. It is needful only to point out what Mr. Spencer's admission really amounts to. Here, as in various places, Mr. Spencer has been careful to acknowledge aid derived from others; and, without stating that he was unacquainted with the propositions of "Descriptive Geometry,"† he candidly says he was not aware that they

---

* It is somewhat unfortunate for the writer's inference, that Mr. Spencer's first contribution to engineering literature (written before he was nineteen) is an account of a new and easier method of performing one of the most difficult problems of plan-drawing; namely, the delineation of the spiral courses of skew arches. See "The Civil Engineer and Architect's Journal" for May, 1839, p. 164.

† It happens, again unfortunate for the reviewer, that one division of "Descriptive Geometry" owes an original theorem to Mr. Spencer, which dates back to the time when he was seventeen; the theorem, namely, that the centres of the circles inscribed in all the triangles contained in any segment of a circle fall

had been grouped into "a separate division of mathematics." Why he was not aware of this is easily explained. The title, "Descriptive Geometry," has never been adopted in England for the subject to which it was originally applied by the French: its modern restricted use is known only to professed mathematicians, and, as it now turns out, not even to all of these. This candor of Mr. Spencer, however, the reviewer takes advantage of,— with what fairness we have seen. And then, showing the disingenuousness of his criticism, he seeks to ward off the charge of misrepresentation by saying "it is possible that Mr. Spencer has in mind certain propositions in the 'Higher Geometry' concerning relations of position and direction in points and lines." Indeed! it is possible that Mr. Spencer means that which, by his definition, he obviously does mean! Having first founded a charge of ignorance on a misrepresentation, the reviewer admits the possibility of another interpretation, which is, in truth, the only one Mr. Spencer's words will bear! There remains but to note the second clause of his last sentence: "But these [propositions in the Higher Geometry] cannot be made to stand alone, or independently of dimensional properties." To this the rejoinder is nothing else but a direct contradiction. If the reviewer asks for proof, we refer him to the recently published German work of Reye, entitled, "Geometrie der Lage." This will supply him with a whole volume full of propositions that wholly ignore "dimensional properties," are absolutely non-quantitative.

The readers of the "Christian Examiner" will remember an article which appeared in March of last year, entitled "Positivism in Theology." It is to this that most of the remarks we have to make will more especially apply. But first we offer a few words relating to the general plan of Mr. Spencer's system.

An early and thorough student of science in its various departments, and with a strongly philosophical turn of mind,

---

in the arc of a circle, which circle has its centre at the bisection of the arc of the complementary segment. This theorem he afterward published, with a demonstration, in The Civil Engineer and Architect's Journal for July, 1840, p. 224.

it was but natural that Mr. Spencer's attention should have been drawn to the necessity and possibility of a more perfect organization than had hitherto been made of the general principles of knowledge, so as to form a connected and comprehensive philosophy of nature. This inclination was entirely coincident with the great tendency of modern inquiry, which is towards the disclosure of universal interdependence, harmony, and unity in nature. The problem of philosophy, as conceived by Mr. Spencer, was to represent this order and unity in thought. As the system was thus to be a mental reflex of the truth of nature, it was inevitable that he should take for its central and controlling idea the largest principle of connection and action which science has revealed in the universe; and this he discovered to be the Law of *Evolution*. The principle thus shadowed forth in so many directions, Mr. Spencer has worked out with more precision and completeness than any other thinker; and, holding it to be a universal law of nature, he has made it the organizing principle of his philosophical system. With it, that system, as such, must stand or fall. But to this scheme, which is to comprise some ten volumes in its development, he has prefixed an Introductory Essay of a hundred and twenty-two pages, discussing the question how far philosophy can go, and where she must stop, the bounds of legitimate inquiry, the limits of the knowable and the sphere of the unknowable; and he has here made an earnest and able attempt to fix the basis of a reconciliation between religion and science.

This introductory part, however, is by no means an essential portion of the philosophical system. Had Mr. Spencer not entered at all upon the question of the connection of the knowable and unknowable, his system of philosophy would still have been substantially what it is. For it is a perfectly possible thing, without expressing any opinion concerning the *origin* of things, to propound generalizations respecting the universal *course* of things, the order of phenomena, the connection and succession of events, as known to us in time and space. The general doctrine of evolution may be enunciated and worked out in full detail, quite apart from all theological or ontological or metaphysical questions; and its truth or error is not in the least affected by the truth or error of Mr. Spencer's views respecting religion and science. Yet his critics have constantly committed the mistake of supposing, that, if they could throw doubt upon Mr. Spencer's doctrine regarding the relation of the Universe and its Cause, they thereby effectually disposed of his philosophy.

Now, so far as the philosophy proper is concerned, our reviewer has very little to say about it. He denies the adequacy of Mr. Spencer's method of inquiry to attain the result proposed, and carps at the law of Evolution. Mr. Spencer adopts the method by which modern knowledge has been created, — first, the establishment of data; second, generalizing from these data; third, verification of the generalizations. His idea is, that, when we have thus reached the most general truth attainable, we have also arrived at the highest unity of knowledge; or, that the process by which knowledge is created is competent also to "unify" it. Not at all, says the reviewer. "Mere generalization is powerless to unify knowledge" (p. 240). Now, what is unifying knowledge but reducing many facts to one fact? and what is this but generalizing? What is the highest unification of knowledge but the reduction of all facts to different forms of one fact? and what is this but generalization carried to its highest degree? To say that mere generalization is powerless to unify knowledge is to say that mere generalization is powerless to achieve generalization. Having thus, as he supposes, by a dash of his pen, discredited the grand tendency of modern intellect, what does the reader imagine he offers instead? He offers us the old file at which metaphysicians have been gnawing these thousands of years; and which will probably continue as sharp as at first, so long as this species of mental enterprise continues. "Its unity must be found in the equipoise and dynamic correlation of being and thought, which are welded into one in the act of knowledge itself." And, pray, what unification of fragmentary knowledges has ever been accomplished by that recipe?

Again, as to the fundamental conception of Mr. Spencer's philosophy. "Further, in assuming universal nebula as the homogeneous of progressive heterogeneity, Mr. Spencer really makes an enormous assumption opposed to facts. What sort of homogeneity is that which would exist among sixty-two chemical elements, probably differing in atomic shape, and certainly differing in chemical affinities and properties?" (p. 243.) It might be thought that, before a reviewer ventured so confidently to expose this "enormous assumption opposed to facts," he would have taken some care to acquaint himself with the current views of chemists on the matter in question. What is his authority for supposing, that the sixty-two chemical elements are considered as elements, in any other sense than as substances which we are at present unable to decompose? No chemist of any prudence, who bears in mind what Davy did with the alkalies, would commit himself to the assertion, that what we regard for convenience' sake as simple bodies are really simple bodies. On the contrary, chemists in general tacitly assume the great probability that all these bodies, which as yet resist our powers of decomposition, are really compound. The whole chemical notation is based upon an implied supposition of this kind. The endeavor to reduce the various atomic weights to multiples of hydrogen, involves the suspicion that the so-called elements are all built up out of some common unit. And various attempts have been made to represent the modes in which this original unit may be so grouped and re-grouped as to form atoms answering to the atomic weights of the different elements. Even the strictures that are passed, and legitimately passed, upon the belief that the atoms of other elements are multiples of the atoms of hydrogen, — strictures based upon the fact that the atomic weights do not exactly correspond with this assumption, — even these strictures are not supposed to tell against the belief that the various kinds of matter are built up of homogeneous units, but only against the idea that the atom of hydrogen is that unit. If hydrogen is compound, which we have now good reason for believing, the anomalies in the chemical scale no longer stand in the way of the belief in the fundamental homogeneity of matter. But the belief that the so-called elementary bodies are not really elementary is no longer merely suspected: it is proved as clearly as is possible without actual separation of the components. The phenomena of spectrum analysis render the assumption, that the so-called elementary bodies are really elementary, quite inconceivable. Were their atoms simple, each of them could produce only a single line in the spectrum. But each of them produces more than one, and some of them a great number. Even those of small atomic weight, such as nitrogen, have three or more lines; and those of higher atomic weights have some of them very many; as instance iron, which has eighty-three lines. Being produced by the absorption of certain ethereal undulations by atoms oscillating synchronously with them, it is impossible that the atom of a so-called element should produce very many lines, unless it were composed of very many atoms oscillating in different periods.

But, even supposing it were true that there are sixty-two elements, properly so called, and that, instead of beginning with absolute homogeneity, evolution begins with a form of matter that is to this extent heterogeneous, it by no means follows that the law of Evolution is untrue. Mr. Spencer has nowhere made the "enormous assumption" ascribed to him. He has himself pointed out, that the formula has to be taken with a qualification; that there is no such thing in nature as absolute homogeneity; that, save under unimaginable conditions, absolute homogeneity is impossible. And, to meet the fact rigorously, he describes the process of evolution as a transformation of the *relatively homogeneous* into the *relatively heterogeneous*, through a progressive increase of heterogeneity. All that is alleged is, that, with whatever stage of the process we begin, every further stage increases the degree of multiformity. Whether the first stage, as known to us, was or was not absolute uniformity matters not; and, as Mr. Spencer himself asserts that the first stage was not and could not be absolute uniformity, he will probably not feel much discomfited by the reviewer's statement, that nebulous matter consists of sixty-two elements, even were that statement an ascertained fact, instead of being an improbable hypothesis.

Again, the reviewer observes, "Exactly as much heterogeneity existed in nebulous matter as now exists in the organized Cosmos." This is to assert that there was exactly as much heterogeneity in the solar system when its matter was equally diffused through its space, giving two grains to a cubic mile, as now when condensed and differentiated into inhabited globes; and this is equivalent to saying, that there is exactly as much heterogeneity in the organic germ as in the developed adult. Hence the criticism, if valid at all, is valid against the law of Von Baer, or that radical conception of evolution which has been long since accepted by all scientific men.

But it is with the theological and metaphysical doctrines enunciated in Part I. of Mr. Spencer's work that the reviewer is chiefly concerned. The drift of his argument is to fasten upon their author the imputation of Materialism and (by implication) of Atheism. The reviewer repeatedly disclaims the design of exciting an *odium theologicum*. But what is the *odium theologicum*, if not an appeal to theological prejudice by branding certain doctrines with terms of reproach, in order to make them obnoxious? He well knows that the terms he applies to Mr. Spencer's philosophy are those of odium; and he recognizes this when he says, that, by certain parties, the imputation of holding such doctrines would be "shaken off with indignation and horror." He recognizes it again when he tells the religious sects, that, if these doctrines prevail, they are all but so many "cattle fattening for the shambles." Before passing to the examination of his position, we ask attention to the following extract from a leading English Orthodox review, which gives an excellent statement of the ground assumed by Mr. Spencer:—

"Why *cannot* some of our teachers learn, that, just so far as science is emancipated from scholasticism, it has to do with phenomena alone? The actuality underlying the phenomena is beyond all reach of human intellect; and no truly scientific man has even the shadow of a dream of finding it out. Ever near us, ever in us, the one Divine and omnipresent mystery of the world, it remains unchanged and insoluble for all the petty strivings of our reason to formulate in words the phases it presents, and transcends immeasurably the most transcendental analysis that man has been able to invent. Yet, when Descartes thought to find the seat of the soul in the pineal gland, many persons were honestly alarmed, and cried 'Materialism!' 'Atheism!' and so forth. And when Mr. Buckle transcribed, almost bodily, some pages from Comte, setting forth the somewhat overrated researches of Bichat into the theory of life, there was again heard the familiar cry. And now, when Mr. Spencer says that 'the deepest truths we can reach are simply statements of the widest uniformities in our experience of the relations of Matter, Motion, and Force; and Matter, Motion, and Force are but symbols of the unknown reality,' we are like, it seems, to hear again renewed the insensate anathema. A friend and brother reviewer writes to us, with all earnestness and some eloquence, to affirm as follows:—

"'The discourse of Mr. Spencer on the law of Evolution contains some admirable things; but the residuum of the whole is simply irreligious nonsense,—that, and no other. True, he tells us that his theory is "no more materialistic than it is spiritualistic, and no more spiritualistic than it is materialistic;" but what avails such a "bead-roll of unbaptized jargon," if he insists on formulating every thing in terms of Matter, Motion, and Force? It really is insufferable, puts one out of all patience. Why, if we may thus formulate a flower, we may thus formulate a Shakespeare. The one is no more and no less a phenomenon than the other. And if we may thus formulate a Shakespeare and a Socrates, Plato and the late United States, a railway engine and the mind which fashioned it, what remains — I almost shudder to ask it — what remains that we should not thus formulate our Lord himself? Nay, what is there to forbid the supposition, that the higher mode of being we attribute to what we call God may be but a different conditioning from any of those we have observed of Matter, Motion, and Force?'

"All of which, we feel assured, is thoroughly sincere, but is as completely mistaken as it is possible it should be. For what is proposed is *not* the possibility of formulating either flowers or steam-engines, Platos or Stephensons, ultimately and actually, but of formulating *only and exclusively the uniformities of the phenomena they present*. Themselves we are ignorant of; and, so far as science is concerned, always shall be. We can no more formulate their true

Being than we can create such true Being. We can take cognizance of the Matter, Motion, and Force by which they speak to us, only as these are in relation with other manifestations of Matter, Motion, and Force;' but it makes all the difference in the world to observe, that these terms are but the convenient and serviceable expressions of our ignorance, and are — in Mr. Spencer's own words, not sufficiently observed by our indignant friend — '*but symbols of the unknown reality.*'" *

The writer in the "Examiner" takes a different view. He says: —

"This doctrine is also implied in Mr. Spencer's attempt to formulate all phenomena in 'terms of Space, Time, Matter, Motion, and Force;' for, Space and Time being made the conditions of all phenomena, and Force their universal cause, phenomena without exception must be simply *motions of matter;* that is, changes of position among material wholes and parts, atoms and masses" (p. 241).

Where does he find it asserted by Mr. Spencer, that there can be no other manifestation of force to the human consciousness than under the form of motions of matter? Mr. Spencer recognizes as known to us in space and time the three forms of being, — Matter, Motion, and Force; and regards the first two as modes of the last. But does he therefore say that the last has no other modes? It is true that Mr. Spencer holds all evolution to be change of arrangement in these two modes of Force which we know as Matter and Motion. But what are the entire phenomena of evolution thus generalized? They are the phenomena of the objective universe as presented to the subjective consciousness, and as continually modifying the substance of consciousness by their presentation to it. Does this view imply that Mr. Spencer regards this *substance of consciousness* as either Matter or Motion? Has he not distinctly alleged, that the substance of consciousness is another mode of manifestation of Force, or of the unknowable source of things? What, then, becomes of the allegation that Mr. Spencer is bound to

---

* British Quarterly Review, January, 1868.

show that "all phenomena can be truly reduced to changes of position among atoms and masses," and that the phenomena of consciousness are not simply *accompanied by*, but *consist in*, such changes? This representation of Mr. Spencer's position is diametrically opposed to his own statement of it in the last chapter of "First Principles," where he argues that, by virtue of the relations of subject and object, those external manifestations of force which we call Matter and Motion must stand in eternal antithesis with that internal manifestation which we know as Consciousness; and that, though these antithetical modes are probably but different manifestations of the same unknowable Cause, yet they must for ever appear to us to be antithetically opposed to one another, as belonging to self and not-self respectively. By generalizing all phenomena as processes of Evolution and Dissolution (not Evolution only, as the reviewer carelessly states), Mr. Spencer generalizes only the changes of the *non ego* as they are phenomenally manifested to the *ego;* and he does not profess to say what these changes are in themselves, or what are in themselves the changes they produce in consciousness.

Again, the reviewer says, "Every mechanical philosophy, like Mr. Spencer's, touches only the surface of things; since mechanism is inexplicable, except through *dynamism*" (p. 243). Here Mr. Spencer's philosophy is represented as *mechanical*, as distinguished from *dynamical;* yet, if one term more completely than any other describes it, dynamical is the word. Does not Mr. Spencer, in his chapter on "Matter, Motion, and Force," resolve our experiences of matter and motion into experiences of Force conditioned in certain ways? Does he not, in his chapters upon the "Indestructibility of Matter and the Continuity of Motion," point out that all which we can prove to be indestructible in Matter is the Force it manifests, and that all which we can prove to be continuous in Motion is the Force it implies? And does he not, in his chapter on the "Persistence of Force," repeatedly and most emphatically dwell on the truth, that all other forms of being are resolvable into this form? Yet his system is actually described as one from which the idea of power is left out, — as mechanical, and not dynamical! The reviewer goes on to say, "Although Mr. Spencer has much to say about Force, he identifies Force with Unknowable, and thus empties his philosophy of all dynamism that is intelligible:" from which sentence, if it has any meaning at all, it is to be inferred that the reviewer does not identify Force with the Unknowable, but that to him it is knowable. Why, then, has he delayed so long explaining to us what Force is? Probably, by an "intelligible dynamism," he will say that he means the action of a personal God; but if this action is intelligible to him, as solving the problem of Force for the human intellect, he evidently has a new revelation to make, one for which the thinking world has been seeking these thousands of years.

In the next sentence, he goes on to say that Mr. Spencer "borrows largely from a source that is shut from every consistent empiricist, in taking from transcendentalism the idea of strict universality." Here is another instance of applying a wrong title, and then pointing out an inconsistency, on the assumption that that title is the right one. On what authority does he call Mr. Spencer "a consistent empiricist," — meaning, of course, an empiricist in the sense commonly given to the word? Does he not know, that, ever since he commenced publishing, Mr. Spencer has been an antagonist of pure empiricism? The antagonism was displayed in his first work, "Social Statics." It was still more definitely displayed in his "Principles of Psychology," where, in his doctrine of "the Universal Postulate," he contended, in opposition to Mr. Mill, that certain truths must be accepted as necessary. The controversy between the two, pending since that time, has been recently revived. In the "Fortnightly Review" for July 15, 1865, Mr. Spencer re-asserted and re-inforced the position he had before taken, that, even supposing all knowledge to be interpretable as having originated in experience, there are nevertheless certain truths which must be accepted as *a priori* before the interpretation becomes possible.

Again the reviewer says, "Force must be either a personal God, an impersonal entity, or a property of matter. Mr.

Spencer denies that it is a personal God." Where does Mr. Spencer deny that Force, or the unknown cause of things, is a personal God? So far from doing so, he distinctly says ("First Principles," chap. v.) that a personal God can neither be affirmed nor denied. Having asserted that Mr. Spencer denies that which he distinctly says cannot be denied, — that is, that Force, or the unknown cause of things, is a personal God, — he goes on to say, that "he ought to treat it as a property of matter, whereas he seems to regard it as an impersonal entity." This is diametrically opposed to a previous representation made by the reviewer himself, only two pages back, where he recognizes Mr. Spencer's doctrine as being, that Force is the universal Cause of which Matter and Motion are manifestations. If, as Mr. Spencer everywhere asserts or implies, Force is the ultimate unknowable Cause, manifested to us in the forms of Matter and Motion, under certain conditions of time and space, how is it possible for him to regard Force as "a property of Matter?" According to him, Matter cannot be known to us, except as the resistance of co-existent positions in space; it cannot be conceived, save as a statical embodiment of forces occupying space. If, then, when matter is conceived to be deprived of its forces, nothing remains, how can Force be conceived as a property of Matter?

Again, the reviewer says, —

"But Mr. Spencer has here fallen helplessly into a vicious circle. On the one hand, all phenomena can be formulated under a single law, because the materialist and spiritualist controversy is absurd: on the other hand, the materialist and spiritualist controversy is absurd, because all phenomena can be formulated under a single law."

Now, neither of the propositions said to constitute this vicious circle is anywhere to be found in Mr. Spencer's writings, either expressed or implied. What are the facts? Mr. Spencer carefully goes through in detail the various classes of phenomena, for the purpose of seeing whether they exemplify the law he alleges. He distinctly points out, that this law is a universal induction from the phenomena examined. And he then goes on to verify it, by showing that it is also a necessary deduction from the persistence of Force. Yet, though the greater part of "First Principles" is occupied with these inductive and deductive proofs, Mr. Spencer is made to allege this law, "because the materialist and spiritualist controversy is absurd"! Equally baseless is the other statement, that Mr. Spencer considers the materialist and spiritualist controversy absurd, "because all phenomena can be formulated under a single law." The very passage which the reviewer has just quoted gives Mr. Spencer's reason for calling them absurd, which is a totally different reason. Mr. Spencer's own words are: "The Materialist and Spiritualist controversy is a mere war of words, in which the disputants are equally absurd, each thinking he understands that which it is impossible for any man to understand."

Again, the reviewer says,—

" Recognizing the phenomenal diversity of matter and mind, and at the same time scouting their ontological diversity, to the inquiry *why* their ontological diversity must be denied, he has no sound answer to make. There is as great an assumption of knowledge in saying that there is no difference at bottom between matter and mind, as in saying that a radical difference exists " (p. 245).

Here Mr. Spencer is represented as making a great assumption for which he gives no reason; and yet he has given both special and general reasons. In his chapter on the "Correlation and Equivalence of Forces," he has pointed out that the modes of Force with which matter impresses us are transformable into the mode of Force which we know as mind; showing how there is an equivalence between the amount of an external agency acting on the senses, and the amount of consciousness produced by it in the shape of feeling; and how, conversely, there is an equivalence between the amount of consciousness which we experience in making a muscular effort and the amount of physical effect produced on an external object. In the very chapter from which the reviewer quotes respecting the absurdity of the materialist and spiritualist controversy, Mr. Spencer points out, that, if the transformation of external forces into the internal forces which we call feelings is an argument for the materialist, the transformation of these forces we call feelings into external physical actions is an equally good argument for the spiritualist. That the forces of the *ego* and the *non ego* are transformable into one another, is the evidence which Mr. Spencer assigns for the belief that they are but differently conditioned forms of the same ultimate Force. Yet this assimilation of them, the reviewer calls an assumption,—an assumption for which there is no better warrant than the opposite one. And this, too, in spite of the further reason distinctly assigned in other parts of Mr. Spencer's work; as in the chapters on the "Relativity of Knowledge" and the "Persistence of Force," where, after showing that mind and matter are alike inscrutable in their ultimate natures, or are manifestations of *something* unknown, Mr. Spencer concludes that they are manifestations of the *same* unknown, and are made to seem different to us by belonging, the one set to our consciousness, and the other set to existence out of our consciousness.

But, if the fact of the transformability of these inner and outer manifestations into one another goes for nothing with the reviewer, perhaps he will be able to furnish "sound answers" to the following questions suggested by the dualistic hypothesis. If mind and matter are not differently conditioned manifestations of *one* unknown cause, must there not be two unknown causes? Are these independent of one another? And, if so, in what manner are they made to work in harmony as they do? If they are not independent of one another, which of the two is the cause of the other? And in what relation stands the one that is caused to that which causes it? If the one which is caused is not itself a portion of that which is said to cause it, what is the nature of its being? According to the dualistic view, it must be the Creator of what are known as its manifestations. If it is a Deputy Creator, how does it derive its creative power? And must not the power by which it creates be a part of the power of that which created it? And is not this saying that it is itself but another form of the original unknown power of which it is the deputy? The reviewer must accept one of two conclusions: Either the two causes are independent, in which case we have what may be called Bi-theism; or one is dependent on the other, in which case the dependent one can but be a mode of manifestation of the other, and we are at once thrust back on the conception of a single Unknown Cause.

In a classification of the various types of philosophy, the reviewer says, —

"Is the organism purely the product of the environment? then we have empiricism, sensationalism, materialism." [And, after defining idealism:] "Are the organism and environment both products of some underlying and active unity? then we have identity or pantheism."

Under which of these heads does the reader suppose the reviewer classes Mr. Spencer? Of course, it will be said, under the last. Has he not been reproaching Mr. Spencer with Monism, and insisting on the truth of Dualism? and is not this the theory of Monism, that the organism and environment are both products of some underlying and active unity? Of course, then, the class which asserts this last proposition is that in which he places Mr. Spencer. Not at all. He puts Mr. Spencer in the first class, and then proceeds to show, on the strength of it, his inconsistency; asserts that Mr. Spencer makes his election in empiricism, but shrinks from the acceptance of its necessary implications. He then expends a couple of pages on the unscientific character of empiricism, all of which is supposed to tell against Mr. Spencer; though, as we have already seen, he has repeatedly repudiated empiricism, and though the reviewer's own definitions exclude him from the empirical school.

Again: —

"He (Mr. Spencer) sets aside the three theories of Theism, Atheism, and Pantheism, as equally claiming to comprehend the incomprehensible; and will not suffer 'religion' to use either of them as means or helps in the discovery of truth. Yet, by his own showing, the idea of Space, Time, Matter, Motion, and Force, which he allows science to use in her own investigations, are precisely as incomprehensible as the idea of God. What sort of consistency or impartiality is this?" (p. 253, 254.)

Theism, then, according to the reviewer, is not a truth, but a help in the discovery of truth. In this case, it is not clear what is his ground of quarrel with Mr. Spencer. Certainly, Mr. Spencer objects to Theism, Atheism, and Pantheism, only in so far as they claim to be *ascertained* truths; and if the reviewer regards them simply as convenient hypotheses, to be used as "helps in the discovery of truth," he will find it hard to point out in Mr. Spencer's work any demurrer to their being so used. Having first represented him, not as denying each of these theological formulas to be an ascertained truth, which he does, but as disallowing the use of it as a help to the discovery of truth, which he does not,—the reviewer proceeds to say, that Mr. Spencer is inconsistent in allowing science to use, in her own investigations, the ideas of Space, Time, Matter, Motion, and Force, which are precisely as incomprehensible. Now, if Mr. Spencer had used, or proposed that science should use, Matter, Motion, &c., as words severally standing for a positive theory, in the same way as Theism or Atheism does, there would be the inconsistency charged. But he does nothing of the kind. Over and over again he asserts that they are to be used as *symbols* of things unknown; that all which science can do is to simplify the equations expressed in these symbols; and that, when it has reduced the equations to their lowest forms, the unknown quantities are unknown quantities still.* Where, then, are the alleged inconsistencies? Mr. Spencer rejects the atheistic or the theistic idea, in so far as it claims to be *a piece of definite knowledge;* and he equally rejects every idea of Matter or Force which pretends to be a piece of definite knowledge, having elaborately shown that every such idea ends in absurdity. If the proposition that the universe has resulted from the act of a Creator, and every other proposition professing to be an explanation of the universe, had been described by Mr. Spencer as inadmissible; and if he had then accepted such a proposition as that matter consists of atoms, or that it is composed of unextended monads, or that it is

---

* See First Principles, chap. xvii.

made up of centres of force,—he would have assumed for science a liberty which he denied theology. But, while he rejects as unthinkable every proposition respecting the nature of the universe in general, he equally rejects as unthinkable every proposition respecting the nature of matter. While he admits that we are obliged to use, for the purpose of investigation, the conception of matter as formed of units, yet he expressly points out that such conceptions, being merely the product of our own forms of thought, must not be understood as corresponding to the reality; and he takes just as much care to show that such a conception, if supposed to represent the reality, brings us to contradictory absurdities, as he takes to show that the conception named Atheism or Pantheism, if supposed to represent the reality, brings us to the same result.

Perhaps it will still be said, that, as Mr. Spencer admits an hypothesis respecting the constitution of Matter to be used by science, and holds as valid the conclusions thereby reached, he ought to admit the legitimacy of the hypothesis of Theism as a means of reaching possibly valid theological conclusions. The reply is, that the conclusions proposed to be reached in the two cases are of totally different orders, and claim to be truths in totally different senses. The only truths proposed to be reached by this hypothesis respecting the constitution of matter are *constant relations of co-existence and sequence among phenomena;* whereas the truths proposed to be reached by one of these theological hypotheses are *truths concerning noumenal existence underlying phenomena.* The propositions which science aims by such means to establish, pretend only to express *the order among the manifestations of the Unknowable;* whereas the propositions which theology aims by such means to establish, pretend to express *the nature of the Unknowable itself.* Relative truth is the assigned end in the one case; absolute truth in the other. Yet Mr. Spencer is called inconsistent, because the method of inquiry which he admits as legitimate in the one case, he considers illegitimate in the other.

The reviewer goes on to say in the next sentence, —

"And further, when we find him identifying the Unknowable with the scientific idea of Force, and predicating of it Unity, Omnipresence, and Causation, at the very same time that he denies our right to predicate of it any attributes at all, what shall we say of such surreptitious and ostensibly disallowed predications?" (p. 254.)

Let us take by itself the first clause of this sentence. In it Mr. Spencer is represented as identifying the Unknowable with the scientific idea of Force. Now, inasmuch as the scientific idea of Force, as understood commonly, and as understood even by men of science, is supposed to be something of which we have a conception, Mr. Spencer is here made to appear as identifying the unknowable with something that is conceivable. But the identification which he makes is exactly the reverse of this. Already, in his chapter on "Ultimate Scientific Ideas," he has shown that the scientific idea of Force, when pushed to the last result, is not an idea at all, but the sign of something unknown; and, in his chapter on the "Persistence of Force," he takes especial care to insist upon the truth there arrived at, that the Force which science postulates in all its inquiries and conclusions is no one of the forces for which science has a name; but that what is tacitly postulated by the doctrine of the persistence of force, is really that Unknowable Cause of which the forces dealt with by science are manifestations. The reviewer's proposition should thus be inverted. He should have said that Mr. Spencer merges the scientific idea of Force into the Unknowable; and, had he said this, the sentence would have had a quite contrary implication. The difference is as great as that between saying of any one that he identifies morality with good manners, and that he identifies good manners with morality.

Turning to the criticism on Mr. Spencer's treatment of the question of Religion and Science, we again find the reviewer making his points by misrepresentations. He sets out by distinguishing between two meanings of the word "religion;" saying, truly enough, that "while religious knowledge, supposing it to exist, is what we more properly call theology, religion is a term more properly confined to the emotional and moral phenomena which reciprocally cause, and are caused by, the consciousness of our relations to God." If for the word "God" we read "Unknowable Cause," this is the meaning given to the word "religion" all through the first part of Mr. Spencer's work. The reviewer, however, makes it appear that Mr. Spencer means by religion what is more properly called theology; and thereupon proceeds to evolve inconsistencies from his argument. He does this by the help of a certain quotation which seems to bear the alleged construction, but which a moment's thought shows does not bear it. The sentence is, "Every religion is an *a priori* theory of the universe." Now, it might have been thought sufficiently clear, that any one who speaks of an individual religion, either singly or as one of a number, means a system of theology. Current usage has established a wide distinction between "religion" spoken of without reference to any creed, and "a religion," as Catholicism or Mahometanism, which becomes individualized by virtue of its creed. But the reviewer has overlooked this very plain distinction. He has dealt with the sentence as though it ran, "Religion is an *a priori* theory of the universe." This is a proposition of an entirely different meaning, — one which probably nobody would make, and totally at variance with the whole tenor of Mr. Spencer's argument. Yet it is on the strength of this reading that the reviewer goes on to manufacture a page full of incongruities. He might have been excused for this misconstruction, had there been no passage showing that it could not be the right one; but he ignores the repeated proofs that by "religion" Mr. Spencer means the emotional state produced by the contemplation of the Unknowable, and deliberately asserts in the teeth of them that by religion Mr. Spencer means theology, or the intellectual theory of religion.*

We close these remarks, which might easily be extended to a much greater length, with some passages in a private

---

* The reader may verify the foregoing by reference to pp. 17, 44, 98, 100, 107, of "First Principles."

letter of Mr. Spencer to the writer, on the ethics of reviewing, which seem so appropriate here as perhaps to justify the liberty of publication:—

"I am not inclined to quarrel with the intolerance which limits itself to hard words. Denunciation of something held to be wrong commonly implies strong attachment to something held to be right; and, whether this something is right or not, the feeling enlisted on its side is a good one. Whoso is indifferent when he hears denial of what he mistakes for the truth, would be an equally indifferent defender of the truth itself, did he hold it. If absolute toleration were possible, society would dissolve. Were there no reprobation of any opinions, there would be no reprobation of the actions dictated by those opinions; vice would be as respectable as virtue, and order would become impossible. Any one who says toleration should be unlimited, commits himself to more than he intends; as he will find on taking an extreme case. Suppose there grew up among us a sect like the Thugs of India, with whom assassination is religious duty. Suppose that their doctrine was tolerated to the full, and no one spoken the worse of for becoming a convert to it. Suppose that, thus unhindered, the sect grew and ramified throughout society, assimilating to itself all who had enemies to be revenged on, or wished to get rid of men standing in their way. Would not the organization, by facilitating murders, be a gigantic evil? and would not the universal sense of insecurity be an additional source of misery? Nay, worse. To treat such a doctrine with toleration implies toleration of murder itself; for, detestation of the doctrine being merely a reflex of detestation of the act, the one cannot cease without the other ceasing. And, if there were no detestation of murder, the punishment for murder would not be enforced; since a law becomes inoperative when there is no public feeling to support and aid the agency for executing it. Clearly, then, the welfare of mankind, necessitating intolerance of certain kinds of conduct, necessitates intolerance of the opinions which justify such conduct. Had you heard the strong words I have used to those who defend our doings in Jamaica, you would see that I can be intolerant enough myself upon occasion; and I should be ashamed were it otherwise.

"But, you will say, the doctrines which we thus cannot allow to be denied without manifesting reprobation are moral principles which directly underlie social life, and we resent any thing antagonistic to them, because it endangers human welfare; whereas the theological intolerance in question concerns certain propositions," which may be admitted or rejected, without affecting the laws of right conduct. The reply is, that those who defend these propositions so warmly, contend that belief in them also underlies human welfare, — underlies it, indeed, more deeply than any other. I have no hesitation in accepting as perfectly sincere their professed conviction, that, in the absence of a revealed will of God, there could be no moral law. And hence it seems to me quite natural, and indeed quite proper, that they should be intolerant of doctrines opposed to one which they think all-essential. That the laws of right conduct are deducible from the laws of life, as limited by social conditions, is a conception entirely alien to their way of thinking, and practically incredible to them. In the absence of such a conception, the choice is between the guidance they have, or no guidance at all; and, very rightly, they cling to that which they have. Their intolerance is but the correlative of their allegiance to the highest truth they see.

"Beyond this justification for theological intolerance, there is a deeper justification. The attachment of a society to its creed is the mark of a certain fitness between the two, — not simply an intellectual fitness, but a moral fitness. The rewards and penalties of the existing religions, described as definite and inevitable, are far more operative on minds in a certain stage of progress than those which science discloses as arising by the necessities of things, but in ways that are difficult to trace, and contingent in detail, though inevitable on the average. Hence it is best for the old to live on as long as it can, yielding inch by inch only as fast as the new grows up to replace it; and men's attachment to the old is the measure of its remaining vitality, and of the still continued need for it.

"'Are, then,' you will ask, 'all these displays of intolerance to pass unnoticed?' I do not say that. Though the spirit which prompts them is defensible, it does not follow that the ways in which this spirit is manifested are defensible. The dishonesties and stupidities of criticism may be condemned while saying nothing against the feeling of antagonism which the criticism shows. Judging from those I have seen, your religious journals in America are less unscrupulous than those we have here; but their criticisms contain plenty of gross misrepresentations and deliberate perversities, and for these they may very properly be held to account."

Art. V.—CRETE AND THE CRETANS.

Kreta. Ein Versuch zur Aufhellung der Mythologie und Geschichte, der Religion und Verfassung dieser Insel, von den ältesten Zeiten bis auf die Römer-Herrschaft. Von KARL HOECK, Dr. Professor der Universität Göttingen und Secretär der Königl. Bibliothek. [Three volumes.] Göttingen: Bei Carl Eduard Rosenbusch. 1823–1829.

Reise nach der Insel Kreta im griechischen Archipelagus im Jahre 1817. Von F. W. SIEBER. [Two volumes.] Leipzig und Sorau: Bei Friedrich Fleischer. 1823.

Travels in Crete. By ROBERT PASHLEY, Fellow of Trinity College, Cambridge. [Two volumes.] Cambridge, Pitt Press; and London, John Murray. 1837.

Travels and Researches in Crete. By Captain T. A. B. Spratt, R.N., C.B., F.R.S., Honorary Member of the Archæological Institutes at Berlin and Rome. [Two volumes.] London: John Van Voorst. 1865.

CRETE may be regarded in many respects as the garden of Greece; for it is capable, if civilized and cultivated, of producing, in vast abundance, corn, wine, silk, oil, honey, and wool. "The land is stocked with game," says Gordon, "the sea with fine fish; fruit is plentiful, and of a delicious flavor." The southernmost land in Europe, with an extreme length of one hundred and sixty miles and a breadth varying from six to forty-five miles, it contains an area of about four thousand square miles. Its northern coast is deeply indented, and affords numerous roadsteads; but the mountain chain that runs the whole length of the island fronts the sea, on its southern side, bleak and precipitous; and its southern coast is therefore almost inaccessible.

The climate on the uplands, which are rapidly drained of the rain, has always been famous for its excellence; the heats of summer being tempered by the north wind, while the warmer breezes that reach the island from Africa, meeting and driving back the cold air that draws down from Europe, soften the harshness of winter. One of the names, indeed, the ancients gave the island was *Æria*, by reason of its balmy air and splendid climate. Moreover, if a spot were to be sought for with the mildest, and therefore the best, climate, it would naturally be found in Crete. Excluding the polar circle, such a spot would be midway between the first and sixty sixth or seventh degree of latitude; that is, about latitude 33½°; and Crete lies between 34° and 35° north latitude. Its northern coast, indeed, being washed by the Ægean, and its southern by the Libyan Sea, Crete lies just where the three continents of Europe, Asia, and Africa meet; and it possesses, therefore, all the climatic advantages of those continents without being subjected to any of their disadvantages. In the winter, there is only rain; while the summer, by reason of the lofty snowy summits of its mountains and the cool sea-breezes, is a perpetual spring. As early as December, you find hyacinths and narcissuses and jasmines. Orange-blossoms perfume the air the whole year; and, with no north wind and no sirocco to strip the trees of their leaves or blast the freshness of their verdure, the lemon, olive, palm, laurel, cyprus, pomegranate, oleander, and myrtle never lose their foliage or their fragrance. Well might the ancients term the mountain from which they looked down upon this laughing landscape of forest, meadow, green glen, and sparkling rill, with the lower mountain-sides all golden with the broom or blood-red with the ilex,—well might they call it *Ida, I have seen!*

The summer vegetables, being such as are peculiar to hot climates, rest in the winter; when the hardier vegetables of Northern Europe grow all through the island in perfection, ripening in May, and resting in turn until revived by the autumnal rains. The quince-tree, so common in our own rougher climate, received its name from Cydonia, the district in Crete where it was indigenous. According to Pliny, every thing grew better in Crete than elsewhere. Homer praises its Pramnian wine: and it was famous for aromatic shrubs and medicinal herbs; among others, the *dictammon*, so celebrated among physicians, naturalists, and poets. The island, moreover, was free from all wild beasts and all noxious animals;

though the Cretan dogs could vie with the hounds of Sparta, and Sieber states that there are still wild horses on Mount Ida, who can only be caught by being driven into the gorges, and there arrested by the lasso; while the Cretan *agrimi*, or wild goat, is supposed to be the origin of all our domestic varieties.

There is no month in the year without its green leaves, and brilliant flowers, and esculent fruits, and fragrant shrubs. By every wayside fountain you will find a great plane-tree overshadowing the crystal water, — such a plane-tree as that under which, as the legend was, Zeus first embraced Europa with his love, in memory of which event the tree never afterwards lost its leaves. No wonder that the ancients called it *Macaronesos*, or the "fortunate isle;" or that Hippocrates sent his patients there to be cured.

The hill-sides and the mountains are fragrant with red and white and blue thyme flowers; and, along the streams in the valleys, you may pluck at any time a myrtle blossom or the laurel. In every field you will find a shady *bosquet* of orange, citron, and almond trees, interrupting with their bright tints the running gray of the olive groves that make the background of the landscape. The hollows of the rocks you lie in are carpeted with the dictammon, whose blossoms perfume the air; and here and there, among the roses and myrtles and sweet-smelling thyme, rises the tall palm far above the garlanded trees at its feet, its stately crown swaying in the air with the zephyrs that glide forth from the thickets where bubbling fountains have cooled them; while everywhere you hear the hum of bees busy at their work of making the choicest honey of the Old World, and now and then, clear and sweet, above the notes of countless songsters, the voice of the kaja-bulbul, so famous in Turkey for its melody and plumage as to command a price of a hundred dollars.

It was perhaps because they found in Crete alone a nectar worthy of them, that the gods chose to be born there. The water of Crete, too, seems to have obtained the reputation of being of the best; and it is still the custom to set before the stranger, on his arrival, in gracious token of their hospitality, — first honey to eat, and then water to drink.

But, above all things, it is the olive-tree, with its silver leaves glittering in the sunlight, that most impresses one in the landscape. On every hill-side and plain spread countless groves of them, with gray old trunks, twenty to twenty-five feet in diameter, that have withstood the desolations of a thousand years, but are falling now before the torch and axe of a foe more barbarous even than the Mongol who called himself the scourge of God, and boasted of having butchered two-thirds of the inhabitants of the countries he had traversed: for the Turk slays all human beings, man, woman, child, sparing neither age nor sex; and, as if with a fanaticism that would take its revenge on nature for having furnished sustenance to the accursed Ghiaour, lays his profane hand on the very bosom of Mother Earth, and would smite her with impotence, if his power but equalled his rage.

With such natural advantages, it is obvious that, in the movement of civilization westward from Asia, the island of Crete, from its geographical position, must have played a considerable part; and, though there is a good deal of controversy as to the character of the service it rendered, there can be none as to the fact of its participation in the original creation of the Greek myths: for at the very threshold of the gorgeous temple of fiction that enshrines them, stands the majestic form of Ζεὺς κρηταγενής, the Cretan-born Jove.

The island of Cythera, says Curtius, as the southernmost prolongation of the mountain chain of the Peloponnesus, together with Crete, bounds the Ægean Sea, and forms the beginning of the Mediterranean for voyagers from the East. Crete was, therefore, in the most ancient times the point of departure for those adventurous navigators who struck out boldly into the waste of waters that rolled on, unbroken and with scanty harbors for refuge, up to the shores of Sicily, — waters that were swept by quite other winds from those the timorous mariner was familiar with, as he ran from isle to isle in the Ægean. For a long period, however, it is probable that the rocky promontory of Malea formed the limit beyond which the Phœnician navigator did not venture into the unknown West; for there was an ancient proverb, which could have been applicable only to those coming from the East, "Beyond Malea, forget your home." But there can be little probability, that, as some writers have affirmed, Crete was the isle of Kaphthor mentioned in the Old Testament, from which the Kaphthorim migrated into the southern part of Canaan; for the course of migration was all the other way.

The very name, indeed, of Crete seems to have been derived from the glittering whiteness of its mountains, as seen afar from the sea; for *Creta*, though doubtless an original word, was afterwards applied not merely to chalk, but to a sort of argillaceous earth; whence our word *cretaceous*, though, in point of fact, there is not a particle of chalk, Sieber states, in the geological formations of the island. The name also of *Candia*, by which the island was known among the Italians, — though never at any time used by the inhabitants, who have uniformly adhered to the name of Crete, which has come down to them from the days of Minos, — may perhaps have had a similar origin, from *candida*, "white," shortened by the Venetians into Candia, and by the English merchants into *Candy;* from which latter word imaginative etymologists have derived the common designation for the sweet products of the confectioner's art. The true derivation, however, of the name Candia is probably quite different, and goes back perhaps to the time of the Saracen invasion of the island, during the reign of the Emperor Michael, in the ninth century. The word *khandax* signified a fortified place or camp, *megalokastron*, such as was established where the town of Candia now stands; and when, as was often the case, the camp changed into a town, the appellation *par excellence* of Khandax, or *the camp*, went along with it, and became Candia with the Venetians, when they took possession of the island, early in the thirteenth century.

It is difficult, if not quite impossible, to construct a theory wholly satisfactory as to the period or extent of the relation between Crete and other Hellenic countries; though no one can so much as take up the handbooks of ancient mythology without perceiving, that, very early in the history of both, there was an important influence exercised by the one upon the other. Many of the most ancient myths will be found to centre in Crete, as many of the earliest inventions were ascribed to the superior genius of its inhabitants. It was the Idæan Dactyli, Δακτύλοι, so called from the skill of their fingers, who discovered the art of smelting ores and of fashioning useful tools from metals; and it was the Curetes of Crete who were the first to tame domestic animals, and to institute social feasts and moral order, as well as to invent the sword and lance, and to introduce architecture and music and the dance, and the use of corn and oil and wine. Aristotle says that Crete seemed by its geographical position to be destined for supremacy over Hellas, separated as it is by only a short sail from the Peloponnesus and the Triopian promontory of Asia; and Herodotus and Thucydides both recognize its naval supremacy in the days of Minos: so that, whether Dorians came from Greece to receive it, or Cretans went to Greece to diffuse it, there can be no doubt that the Cretan mythology exerted a great influence upon the Hellenic, nor as little, it seems to us, that the Asiatic, Phrygian doctrines exerted a great influence upon the Cretan.

From the earliest times, the Cretans were, next to the Phœnicians, the great sailors of the Eastern Mediterranean, familiar with all the ports of the Asiatic coast, as with all the islands of the Ægean; so that it is extremely probable, that, while by their own early progress in civilization they softened the grosser features of the Asiatic worship, they were also the busiest agents in diffusing the ideas that underlay it, — ideas which afterward, developed or recast by the profounder Greek mind and clothed in luxuriant forms by the Greek imagination, dominated in part the whole Hellenic mythology. And it is for the reason that it was in Crete, that this fusion of the Asiatic mind with the Greek began, without being completed, that so many traces are found there of doctrines which never became Hellenic. The Cretan conception of Zeus in particular seems to have retained its original character, long after the Hellenic conception to which it probably gave birth had obtained a much higher and purer form.

Creuzer, as is well known, derives the worship of the Cretan

Zeus from Phœnicia, where he was called Moloch; and unquestionably the Cretan Zeus does exhibit evidences of an Asiatic, Phrygian origin. The labryinth, the temple grottos, the idols figured with the attributes of bulls, all indicate that Crete was an original seat of Egyptian and Phœnician colonists. And it was no doubt this blending of Egyptian and Phœnician ideas that gave rise to the mythological system of Uranus as the heavens, and of Kronos as the God of time, and the father by Rhea ('Ρέα, the flowing; that is, the humid elements), of Zeus, which was the prevailing system in Greece. Whether the whole worship of Zeus was originally, in its essence, nothing but the Phrygian worship of the sun and moon, afterwards lost in the legends that wreathed it so wantonly, may be more doubtful. But, however that may be, Zeus seems to have been early conceived of as the bull-god, the sun-bull, as Jupiter-Moloch; while his daughter Dictynna was figured as the moon, throwing rays of light (from δίκειν), appearing again also as Britomartis, or "the sweet virgin," or as Pasiphaë, that is Πασιφαεσσα, "the All-illuminating." For the leading idea attached to the Syro-Phœnician goddess was always that of the fertilizing moon and the fruitful earth, especially in the case of Astarte; and the symbolical representation of Diana Luna, as exhibited in the worship of her all along the Persian Gulf, and in many parts of Asia Minor and Central Asia, was under the form of a woman riding upon a bull, with a crescent-shaped veil over her head. And it was doubtless an image of that sort which suggested to the lively imagination of the Greeks the fiction of the carrying off of Europa from Phœnicia by Zeus in the form of a bull. The very word Europa, indeed, reminds one, by its obvious derivation from εὐρύωψ, of the broad-faced full moon. Homer and Hesiod, as Hoeck remarks, knew nothing of Asia and Europe as geographical terms; with Homer, the Asian fields are but a trifling bit of territory on the banks of the Cayster, the application of the name becoming extended as the Greeks obtained further knowledge of the country. The name Europa, as that of a continent, first occurs in the hymn to Apollo, where it is applied to the Peloponnesus and the islands, as distinguished from what was afterwards continental Greece. Herrmann conjectures that the word Asia is of Hellenic origin; but the word Europe, as Buttman imagines, was Oriental, for εὐρωπός signifies in Euripides *gloomy*, — a meaning which could only have arisen in Asia where the word was applied to the West, in distinction from the country in which it was first used.

According to Voss, the infant Zeus, whom the Cretans first adopted from Phrygia, was the same as the many-titled Zeus Hyes, who, when the Hyades rise in the spring-time, sent down the fructifying rain upon the earth, — the Assyrian god Adad, figured with the attributes of a bull. For as the same writer maintains, *Jehova Sabaoth*, the Only One, whose gracious power Jeroboam indicated by the same form, that of a bull, passed from Thapsacus into Phrygia, and thence to Assyria; whence he found his way to Egypt and Hellas, lifting the Chaldæan thinkers of Babylon, as well as the Ionian poets of Smyrna, to the conception of one God. But the diffusion of this purer faith, Voss argues, offended the Phrygian and Ionian priests of polytheism; and thenceforth in the mysteries they represented the popular gods as attributes of the One God, while they invented the myths for the mere purpose of deceiving the people. Speculation of this sort, however, is somewhat too ingenious; and we pass on to the more probable fact, that in the days of Minos, — who, notwithstanding all the legends in which he is enveloped, was undoubtedly an historical personage, ruling over Crete and the islands of the Ægean, together with the south-western coast of Asia Minor, a contemporary of Moses, from whom he is said to have borrowed many of his institutions, — in the days of Minos, we say, the religion of Zeus, as the Supreme God, had established itself in Crete, together with certain branches of the Asiatic worship of the moon. But, as the Cretans made progress in civilization, their conception of Zeus made progress also; and, as we read the mythologies, there was a conflict always going on between the gross ideas they had received from Asia, and the purer thought to which the Greek mind naturally tended.

From time immemorial, the fundamental principle of life

seems to have been figured in Asia under the form of a male, man or bull or what not; and hence the worship of the Supreme Being was orgiastic, traces of this gross worship being found everywhere, from the banks of the Indus and the Ganges to the shores of Italy, from the Caucasian Highlands to the desert wastes of Africa. Almost all Hellenes, says Strabo, ascribe to Dionysos and Apollo and Hecate and the Muses and Demeter and Zeus all orgiastic, Bacchic ceremonies, as well as all mysteries that involve a secret doctrine. And in Crete, in particular, the worship of Zeus was wholly orgiastic; for just as the Satyrs played the chief part in the worship of Dionysos, so the birth of Zeus, that is the revival of nature in the spring-time, was celebrated by young persons, — called in Phrygia, Corybantes; and in Crete, Curetes, — with the wildest dances and songs, and clang of symbols and drums. And the myth of Rhea having originally commanded this dance to be performed, arose no doubt, as Hoeck suggests, from the perception of the fact, that the dance, wild and inharmonious as it may have been, is found everywhere to accompany the worship of nature. The orgies in the worship of the goddess of Hierapolis, and of Comana, of the Scythian Artemis, and of the Ephesian Diana, were always accompanied with music and dancing.

But from this gross Asiatic conception the Aryan races were always endeavoring to free themselves; for the word for God is common to them all, the root of it, *div*, meaning light, being the basis of the Indian *devas*, of the Persian *dæva*, of the Greek θεός, of the Latin *deus* and *divus*, of the Lithuanian *diewas*, of the Irish *dia*, and of *tivar*, the term in the Edda for gods and men. And as in Phrygia the idea of the Great Mother was monotheistic, so the idea of Zeus as the Supreme God of nature was monotheistic in Crete. At what period, however, this great step was taken in the conception of Zeus, which made him the primal cause of the intellectual, instead of the mere ruler of the physical, world, cannot of course be determined. The ancient myth represented Kronos as having destroyed the earlier children of Rhea; so that, when the latter gave birth to Zeus, she concealed him at first in the hollow of a mountain, and then gave him to the Curetes, who carried him to the recesses of Mount Ida, where they brought him up; that is, Kronos was originally a god to whom human sacrifices were offered, children probably, as was the case with Moloch in Phœnicia. But the divine infant had to be saved, and so recourse was had in the myth to a stratagem. Kronos swallowed a stone instead of his child; that is, there was originally an aërolite, probably worshipped as a fetish, the worship of which was abolished by the purer idea of Zeus at last gaining ground; these myths marking the phases of the struggle that was ever going on in the Greek mind to emancipate itself from its Asiatic thraldom.

But if there was a birth of Zeus — that is, a revival of nature in the spring-time — to be celebrated, there was a death of Zeus to be commemorated; for in nature there is death as well as life, — death of the year brought on by the hastening hours. If there is joy in life, there is also sorrow. In the tumult of his ecstatic orgies, the nature-worshipper inflicted a bloody wound upon himself, enduring what the god endured; whence the myths of mutilation and of death in Hellas. While other Hellenic countries, however, broke away from this conception of Zeus as identical with the physical world, and ascended to the conception of him as the primal cause of intellectual and immortal life, the Cretans seem never to have banished wholly the original inferior conception, for they are found always clinging to this idea of the death of Zeus, and they persisted in showing his burial-place long after belief in his death had been abandoned in Greece.

Yet so strong was the recollection of the influence of Crete on Athens, that it was reserved for one of the most touching of Greek myths, that of Theseus and Ariadne, to consecrate the gradual breaking of the bond that once bound them together, and to keep ever present to the Greek mind this memory of the triumph of Ionic religion and morality over the grossness of Asiatic nature-worship. In Plutarch's time there was at Delos a sacred dance called *Geranos*, which Theseus is said to have been the first to introduce, upon his return from the conquest of the Minotaur in Crete, the involutions of it being in imitation of the intricacies of the labyrinth. But, as the grossness of the Asiatic worship died away in Crete itself, the monster that typified it, half-bull, half-man, died too. The Athenian, however, could never forgive the Cretans for laying claim to their protecting goddess, Pallas Athene; and, if the Cretans deserved to be called liars for their falsehood in asserting that Zeus had died, much more did they deserve to be called so for their audacious presumption in asserting that Athene was not native to the heavens that arched so blue over Attica. But the Athenians seem to have been troubled how to express their disgust; for they could invent no more ingenious fiction than that the owl, the bird sacred to Pallas, invariably died when carried to Crete, which of course would not happen if Crete had been the birthplace of its protectress.

Again, according to the Cretan legend, there lived, in the time of the Curetes, a race called Titans, who, wherever encountered in Greek mythology, present the idea of hostility, — an idea, indeed, which Herrmann has found in the name itself, — of hostility as exhibited in the destroying elements of nature or in the wild passions of man. The Cretans applied it originally to a tribe or part of the population that opposed the worship of Zeus; and it might have been applied in a certain sense to those who thus bestowed it, — for the Cretans seem not to have ascended much above the human conception of the Supreme Being, so to speak, as identified with nature, and so a partaker of the sorrow and the death that pervade it; and it was for this reason that, when Euhemerus appeared, at a long subsequent period, with his destroying doctrine that the gods were only deified men, — a doctrine that for several centuries excited nothing but horror in the religious mind of Greece, as one may see from the terms in which Pausanias speaks of its author, — there was no country so well prepared to receive and cherish it as Crete. And hence, doubtless, arose in great part the evil reputation which the island had ever afterwards among the Greeks.

St. Paul says in his Epistle to Titus, — whom the Cretans affirm to have been their first archbishop, having been left there by St. Paul himself, to set in order the things that were wanting,* — "One of themselves, even a prophet of their own, said, The Cretans are always liars, evil beasts, slow bellies." The Church Fathers thought he meant Epimenides; but Epimenides lived in the seventh century before Christ, at a time when the activity of the Cretans in war and the chase would at least rebut a charge of laziness. Hoeck cannot trace the reproach back farther than Callimachus, who was perhaps a contemporary of Euhemerus, in the third century before Christ; and whose enmity to the Cretans arose probably from the fact, that it was upon their testimony that Euhemerus relied when he placed the burial-place of Zeus in Crete. But so permanent did the stigma become, that the very word κρητίζειν (to Cretize) came to be synonymous with ψεύδεσθαι (to lie). Ὁ Κρὴς τὸν Κρῆτα meant "Birds of a feather flock together;" and Κρὴς πρὸς Αἰγινήτην was equivalent to "diamond cut diamond."

The special falsehood, however, charged against the Cretans seems to have been throughout, as we have indicated, that of pretending to exhibit the burial-place of Jove, the supreme god, who could never die; though, according to the myths universally prevalent in Greece, there was a time when he came into being. Arcadia, Messenia, Bœotian Thebes, and the Phrygian and Trojan Ida, all claimed to have been his birth-place; but the belief that he was born in Crete, that is, that the original conception of him came from that island, was general throughout Hellas. The Cretans, however, as we have seen, never wholly abandoning this original conception of him as the god of nature, if they were allowed to show where he was born, were perfectly consistent when they also claimed to show where he was buried: for as nature is mortal, and the green leaves wither in the autumn breeze, so the god of nature was subject to mortality; and if he were born, so

---

* Of whom the present archbishop, of course, claims to be the regular successor, in an unbroken line of succession from the apostles, though we fear he would hardly rebuke anybody sharply now, — certainly not a pagan; being quite occupied with preserving his dignities, which are not much to be sure, but still something for a bishop; to wit, the triple crown, the right to make his autograph in red ink, and to ride on horseback into the capital.

did he also die. Hence the burial-place of Zeus was regarded in Crete, even down to a late day, with a reverence similar to that in which the tomb of Mohammed is held at Medina, and the sepulchre of Jesus at Jerusalem. Pashley says it was venerated even down to the fourth century of our era, when the Theodosian persecutions put a final end to the pagan worship; while, according to Pococke, the Cretans in the last century still asserted that there came such a wind from it that no one could enter therein. The grave of Zeus was united with his birthplace, says Welcker, as the symbol of the yearly disappearance of the life of nature; and he recalls a curious passage in an old writer, hitherto overlooked, in which mention is made of the sacred cavern in Crete where Rhea is said to have given birth to Zeus, which it was permitted to no one, either god or mortal, to enter. At a certain period of the year, however, in the spring, a great flame was seen to arise from the cavern, the sign of the bloody birth of Zeus; whereupon the bees took possession of the place, in order to nourish the child. This symbol of a flame, as indicating the fructifying element of nature revived each year, is found also in the worship of the Thracian Dionysos; and in our day the Greek Church has transferred this ancient pagan symbol of resurrection to the sepulchre of Jesus at Jerusalem, where the festival of Easter Monday, so often described by travellers, forms one of the most disgraceful exhibitions of superstition to be witnessed in Christendom. But there is consistency even in superstition; and, as the central stone of the Church of the Holy Sepulchre is the central point of the earth, the flame which rekindles nature is properly flashed down from heaven there.

Thus conceiving Zeus as born a mortal child, the luxuriant imagination of the Cretans would naturally dwell upon his childhood and bringing-up. But imagination is not the basis of religion; and what the Cretans mainly reverenced under these flowery myths was the great human fact of regeneration, physical and moral, which underlies the mortality of earth. Hence if they crowded around the sacred cave in the jagged hill-sides of Ida, to pay their joyous homage to the supreme god who, taking mortal form, had been born a mortal child, it was with no blinder faith than that which, in the Middle Age, accepted the miracles of birds singing the praises of God, and of flowers spontaneously opening to adore him; with no more childish reverence than that the pious Roman Catholic exhibits to-day, as he gazes upon the beautiful procession of the Holy Infant carried on high in a crib (*præsepe*) through the splendid nave of Sta. Maria Maggiore, on Christmas Eve, in Rome, — the symbol now, as the mythological child was so long ago in Crete, of the yearly revival of nature and the regeneration of human life.

But when the rest of the Greeks had outgrown this limitation of the conception of Zeus to physical nature, it is as little surprising that they rejected the myth of the death of Zeus as that the Cretans adopted the doctrine of Euhemerus, though the real doctrine of that philosopher probably did not go so far as was asserted in ancient times. An acute French writer, the Abbé Foucher, maintains that he was in no sense an atheist, but, as appears from a passage in his writings preserved by Eusebius, merely made a distinction between the two classes of gods, — the one eternal and immortal, such as the sun, moon, stars, winds, and all things of an ethereal nature; the other born of the earth, who had attained divine honors through the service they had done mankind, such as Hercules, Bacchus, and the rest, of which terrestrial gods the histories on the one hand, and the mythologies on the other, gave diverse accounts. It was with this passage, moreover, preserved by Sextus Empiricus, that the work of Euhemerus, "surnamed the Atheist," probably opened. "When men lived without law and order, those among them who excelled in bodily strength and in intelligence compelled the others to defer to their will. And, in order to conciliate the admiration and respect of their fellows, they attributed to themselves superior and divine power; whence it came that several of them were regarded and honored as gods."

The writings of Euhemerus, of course, made a great noise. Ennius translated them into Latin, and Varro, the most learned of the Romans, adopted the principles they taught; and the

Church Fathers naturally made frequent use of them in exposing the absurdities of the pagan mythology. But Euhemerus was probably no more an atheist than Anaxagoras and Socrates, who recognized the same distinction between immortal gods, divine by nature (so to speak), and deified heroes, — a distinction, moreover, which was admitted by the Neo-Platonists, and openly professed by the Stoics. Cicero says of the system of Euhemerus, that it supposes the immortality of the soul; and that great men would not have been deified after their death, if there had not already been a belief that the souls of men subsisting after death were eternal and perfect beings.

Uranus, obliged for some reason to expatriate himself from Egypt or Phœnicia, took refuge in Crete. His civilizing arts softened the people he found there; and, Kronos (Saturn) following in his footsteps, the inhabitants were so enchanted with the sweet life thus opened to them, that they adored the latter as a god, and called his reign the age of gold. The end of it, however, did not correspond with the beginning; for Titan, his brother, had consented to give place to him, only on condition that he should not bring up a son, in order that at Saturn's death the empire might revert to the former. Saturn, therefore, faithful to his oath, devoured his children; that is, slew them as fast as they were born. But Jupiter, Neptune, and Pluto escaped his cruelty; Ops, or Rhea, their mother, having deceived her husband, and secreted them among the rocks of Mount Ida. Titan, believing that he had been deceived, seized his brother and threw him into prison. Jupiter, however, as soon as he was grown up, delivered his father, and re-established him upon his throne. But, Saturn having soon afterwards begun to entertain projects hostile to his son, the latter banished him, and Saturn went to the coasts of Hesperia (the West), and spread abroad there the arts of Crete; whence the fable that Jupiter had driven out his father, and relegated him to Tartarus; that is, the Western regions of Europe, which, in their ignorance, the Greeks believed to be the realm of darkness. The Titans thereupon claimed their rights, but Jupiter overcame them, and drove them to the caverns of the mountains; which gave rise to the fable, that Jupiter had plunged them into the abysses of the sea, and kept them there by the weight of enormous mountains.

Jupiter's subjects afterwards began to be unquiet. The passions of men broke loose, and, finding that they needed to be restrained by force, he established penal laws; whence the fable that Astrea had quitted the earth, and that Themis had taken her place. The silver age then began, and the blessings which Crete enjoyed became noised abroad. Other Hellenic countries desired to participate in them. Yielding, therefore, to the universal request, Jupiter travelled through Greece, and was everywhere received as a god, establishing salutary laws and correcting abuses. Being accompanied in his travels by his family, Juno conceived an affection for Argos; Apollo settled at Delphi, where he became famous for his skill in divination; Neptune taught the Greeks navigation, Mars war, Mercury eloquence; Pluto instituted funeral rites; Ceres introduced agriculture; and so on. At length Jupiter returned to Crete, and died there; and on his tomb they inscribed these words, Τοῦ Διὸς τάφος (Tomb of Jupiter), or, according to Euhemerus, Ὁ Ζεὺς τοῦ Κρόνου (Zeus, the son of Kronos). All his legitimate children having been left in Greece, Crete was devised to Minos his son by Europa, daughter of a king of Sidon, whom he had carried off in a maritime expedition to that country.

Such, according to the Abbé Foucher, is the explanation of the myths given by the Euhemerists; and it is evident, as the Abbé remarks, that from the time of Cadmus the Greeks were persuaded that Greece was originally inhabited by gods; or rather, as Cicero says, that mankind had peopled the heavens with gods, the greatest of whom did but leave earth to inhabit Olympus. The Cretans, as we have seen, held on to this original belief that the gods were men; and therefore, in showing the burial-place of Jupiter, were so far from being "liars," that they were quite remarkable for their adherence to the truth. The allegorists attempted to confute them, by pretending that the tomb ascribed to Jupiter was originally the burial-place of Minos, the inscription having been at first, Τοῦ Μινῶος τοῦ Διὸς τάφος (The tomb of Minos, the son of Jupiter); but that, in course of time, the two first words were effaced, leaving "the tomb of Jupiter;" whence the legend of his burial in Crete. But this assertion is destitute of proof, besides being contradicted by the immemorial traditions of the island. The Cretans, it is said, were liars (*semper mendaces*). Perhaps they were in those degenerate days, when the universal corruption of the ancient world was blighting the conscience alike of Roman and Greek; but the early wonderful development of law, art, and religion in Crete, forbids the attaching of that stigma to them at any other than a very late period, when it made little difference what particular epithet was employed to designate them or anybody else. And, moreover, however mendacious a people may be, they are not apt to lie against their own interest and without motive, as the Cretans would have done if this particular charge of falsehood about Jupiter's burial-place could be sustained against them; for it was to their honor to have had for a king one who was recognized by all Hellas as supreme over heaven and earth. Hence, as the Abbé Foucher says, to have lied to a purpose, they ought to have proclaimed, that, after having governed them for a time, Jupiter had been ravished into heaven, as the Romans asserted was the case with Romulus. But the Cretans, faithful to the truth, preferred rather to make the humiliating avowal that their protecting god had not been able to save himself from death and the corruption of the grave.

"Zeus shall not thunder any more, because he has long been dead," was the scoffing interpretation by Lucian of the inscription on the tomb of the god. And Lucian was right, though he meant only to be witty. The true Zeus, the majestic conception of the one Supreme Being who presides over nature and the course of time, ruling the winds and the waves and the spirit of man, did die in Crete, as it passed on to Greece. Yet how pure the Cretan conception of Zeus originally was, is proved by the head of him which Captain Spratt obtained in the island, and which, according to that writer, was not only remarkable for its majesty and benignity and serenity of expression, but for its striking resemblance to the head of Christ in Leonardo da Vinci's "Last Supper;" with the difference only that the great Italian artist's representation of Christ is the youthful presentment of the Greek conception of Zeus.

We have thus been at some pains to look a little into a charge that is sometimes brought against the Cretans, because it makes part of the general charge of worthlessness that is sometimes brought against the whole Greek race in modern times, especially at critical moments like the present, when the struggle so long deferred for the liberation of the whole Greek race seems impending.

Of the ancient history of Crete, however, we have no time to say any thing, nor to allude to the question whether its famous institutions came from Sparta or served as a model for the Spartan, which they so much resembled. The Cretans are found, all along the course of ancient history, taking part in the great Hellenic festivals, and carrying off prizes at the Olympic and Nemean games. The most ancient combat indeed was said to be that in which a prize was offered to one who should be adjudged to have chanted best the hymn to Apollo; and it was taken by Chrysothemis of Crete. Herodotus records the bravery of the Cretan soldiers whom Idomeneus conducted to Troy; and his comrade Meriones won the first prize in archery, at the funeral games in honor of Patroclus. The flourishing period of Crete, however, so long preceded the great struggle of Greece with Asia, that the island plays no part in that memorable drama. Civil dissension had done its ruinous work among its inhabitants; and they were only too ready, when the Oracle at Delphi bade them give no aid to the Greeks in the contest with Xerxes, to heed its voice and fold their arms.

Yet, with all their faults and vices, the Cretans have in all ages shown a wonderful degree of vitality and courage. The various states of Crete were so isolated, that even the names of the months were different in the different cities; yet, when assailed by foreign enemies, they so laid aside their domestic quarrels, and gathered with such zeal in defence of their common country, that the endearing term *mother-land* (μητρίς) arose first among them; and hence also came the word *syncretism* (συγκρητισμός). And, when its ancient fame had tempted the ambition of the Romans to include it in the vast sweep of their conquests, they found it any thing but an easy task to overcome the resistance of the Cretans. The Roman general was confident of success; but he soon found out his mistake, and was severely punished for his arrogance. The Cretans intercepted a great part of his fleet, took his soldiers prisoners, and hung them at the yard-arm. But it was a fatal success; for Rome never pardoned a defeat.

The Cretans had an ancient custom of marking every fortunate day of their lives with a white stone, and every evil day with a black one; and then, throwing these stones into their quivers, they reckoned the number of days they had lived by the number of white stones. They must have used a very black stone indeed to mark the day when the Roman eagles were descried again from the mountain-tops, glittering in the sunlight on the distant sea; for though they made a desperate defence, and compelled the Romans to buy their victory with the blood of their bravest legions, yet fortune was against them. Fate was riding roughshod over the ancient world; and they who had led on the purple dawn of Hellenism were the necessary victims of its incomplete development. The first care of the Romans was to abolish the laws of Minos, and establish those of Numa; for Strabo says that in his time the Cretan institutions were already no longer in force, because the Romans had compelled them to adopt theirs.

The Cretan archers and slingers appear as mercenaries in Greece and Asia. Pausanias saw their tombstones, on his way to the Academy, next to those of Thessalian horsemen. And the Sfakiots, the brave mountaineers of Crete, still uphold the reputation of their ancestors, whose true descendants all the testimony agrees they are. Secluded in their mountain homes, they have preserved not merely the unmixed blood and the haughty carriage of the ancient Cretan soldiers, but a good many of the ancient customs. In Belon's time they still carried the bow and quiver; but they appear with them now only on festive occasions, when they assume the old national costume, and dance the old Pyrrhic dance invented by their fathers untold centuries ago, — the dance that was held in such honor, that it was equally disgraceful and equally an offence against the law to desert the ranks of the dancers and the line of battle in the face of the enemy. In Savary's time, the Sfakiots, when they executed it, were clad in the ancient costume, — a short robe, tightened round the waist by a girdle, with breeches and buskins, and quiver on their shoulder, and bow in their hand, and a long sword at their side. According to Mr. Pashley, the dress of the peasant still resembles that of antiquity; for he still wears the boots described by Galen, and the short cloak mentioned by Eupolis and Aristophanes. And even the dialect of the Sfakiots still exhibits peculiarities that have probably come down from the days of Minos; for, however long the tide of foreign conquest, Roman or Saracen or Italian or Turkish, may have submerged the lowlands, it has never swept up to the mountain retreats of this ancient and hardy tribe. Their dialect, indeed, is claimed by some to have an affinity with the Doric. One of the most competent judges of modern times, the late Colonel Leake, pronounces it to be genuine Hellenic, in a state of extreme corruption; while the accurate German traveller, Sieber, infers the purity of their descent, not merely from their isolated position, but especially from the great similarity in their physiognomy.

So, too, the marriage festivals among the Cretans at the present day still exhibit the beautiful symbolism of the ancient life. They decorate the walls of the bride's chamber, says Captain Spratt, with loaves of wheaten bread, as an omen of plenty and peace; and upon the pillows of the nuptial bed they lay three wreaths, woven of leaves of thorn and myrtle and orange: the thorn as an emblem of long life and endurance under its cares, and the myrtle and orange-leaves as a token that the love of husband and wife should be as lasting and as fragrant as the evergreens. And when the priest says, in concluding the marriage ceremony, " Glory and honor to you who are crowned," they throw cotton seeds, and myrtle and orange-leaves, upon bride and bridegroom. And, as they pass the house of the bridegroom's mother, the bride dips the little finger of the right hand in a pot of virgin honey, and makes four crosses on the door with it, in token that her love is as holy and sweet and strong as this symbol of her faith. And then they present her with a pomegranate, which she throws down, scattering its ruby-colored fruit upon the floor, as a token of her desire that her house may be filled with as many goods as there are seeds thus scattered. And finally they enter the bride's house; and the bride and bridegroom, taking their seats side by side upon the couch at the end of the room, the young virgins gather around them, and sing songs in praise of the happy and honored pair. Has Theocritus described any thing more idyllic?

So, too, the old Cretan institutions sanctioned solemn friendships between male friends and also between female friends, and the Greek Church does the same to-day; the spiritual relationship thus established being held so sacred, that marriages cannot take place between those immediately connected with the contracting parties. And if the Cretan peasants still have their superstitions, they are quite harmless compared with many that desolate Italy and Spain and other Catholic countries. If they still cherish the memory of the Cretan labyrinth as one of the seven wonders of the ancient world, and naïvely believe that these seven wonders correspond to the seven sacraments of the Christian Church; or if they people the fountains with holy virgins, as their fathers did with the Naiads, — it is surely a much less baneful fancy than the necromancy and kindred delusions that prevail in New England at this moment.

If any thing, however, were wanted to refute the charge of degeneracy so often brought against the modern Greeks, it would be the terrible earnestness with which the Cretans are now struggling to conquer their independence. We have already alluded in these pages to the Revolution of 1821, which resulted in the establishment of the present Hellenic kingdom, as well as to some of the political events which have since occurred; and we have nothing now to add to what we have said as to the character and vitality of the Greek genius.*

The history of the present struggle may be embraced in a few words. It began in April of last year, when, unable to endure any longer the unheard-of tyranny of the Turks, the Cretans assembled, and addressed a memorial to the Sultan, imploring relief, and showing that for the two preceding years the taxes they had been forced to pay into the Ottoman treasury exceeded the revenues of the island. The Sultan replied after three months, by landing a body of thirty thousand Turkish-Egyptian troops. During July and August, there was no collision; but when, on the 31st of August, Mustapha Pacha landed on the island with instructions to refuse all concessions on the part of the Porte, the Christians collected their forces, and, taking a solemn oath to obtain their liberty and be united with Greece, or die in the attempt, went into the conflict with a calmness and intrepidity which challenges comparison with any thing recorded in the annals of man. And now for about five months and a half, up to the moment when we write these words, they have never quailed before the deadly task they have set themselves. They have seen their wives and children massacred, and their houses and fields burned and laid waste; and they have fought on, with God's voice only to cheer them.

The Minotaur was once a fabulous animal in Crete: he is fabulous no longer. Half bull, half man, he stalks to-day, raging with the fury of ten thousand fiends, over that doomed isle, trampling all things, man, woman, child, orchards, olive groves, meadows, under his brutal hoof. Once and again the tribute of the choicest youths and maidens of matchless beauty has been offered up to him, but only to whet his insatiable appetite and to fire his godless lust. It remains but for some brave Theseus to slay him. And let us hope that he will appear, — on board an iron-clad, and with a Spencer rifle, — for the beautiful Ariadne, the beaming, radiant goddess, —

---

* See Christian Examiner for May, 1862, and July, 1864.

Aridela, as the Cretans called her, — the white-winged genius of liberty, waits to give him the key to the labyrinth, and conduct him to the monster's lair; that so in the beast's blood the bond may be for ever severed which, binding Asia with Europe, leagues together in an infamous union the aspiring intellect and the purer hope of the West, with the filthy vices and the sodden despair of the East.

The long struggle by which the Turks conquered Crete from Venice cost them so many lives, that the island has been known among them ever since as the Mussulmans' grave. It will be so indeed, if, as all the signs indicate, the Cretans succeed; for Islam, once dead in Crete, will have received its death-blow in Europe. "The man who has not learned to die for liberty is unworthy the enjoyment of it," was the dominant idea of the ancient Doric race; and the Doric race colonized Crete.

ART. VI. — REVIEW OF CURRENT LITERATURE.

THEOLOGY AND PHILOSOPHY.

WHEN, two or three years ago, Mr. Mill made his celebrated attack on the philosophy of Hamilton and its defenders, it was a matter of curious interest, apart from the points in controversy, to see how he would maintain himself in that comparatively unfamiliar field. The listener pricked up his ears, at hearing the logician, the political economist, the student of positive science, discourse so confidently of metaphysics as taught by Plato, Kant, or the more modern masters. The reader rubbed his eyes at statements respecting Hamilton's opinions and arguments, which seemed to show that we had all been under a delusion in giving him credit for any consistent method, or any genuine learning, or any intellectual discernment. We felt a certain painful and perplexed interest to know what could be said in vindication of so great a name. There was a deliberation, a confidence of conviction, a decision of utterance in Mr. Mill's assertions, which made it seem impossible that his charges could be groundless, while his great reputation as a thinker commanded much reliance, beforehand, on his judgment. At the same time, one felt that the attack was tentative, not decisive. It was playing at fence with buttoned foils, — nay, with only an imaginary opponent. As if doubtful of his argument, Mr. Mill wished his adversary were still living, to strike back in his own defence. This conflict in the field of metaphysics was only an episode among more serious tasks, an occupation for the leisure hours of one whose real business is to instruct the practical mind of England. The challenge was thrown down, as it were, in the mere love of intellectual encounter. Only once the foil is exchanged for a rapier, and the contest becomes vindictively earnest, — where he deals with a living antagonist, and bursts out in his famous protest, declaring he would "go to hell" rather than consent to certain inferences of a metaphysical theology. But, on the whole, the review is chiefly valuable as an able exposition of the psychological method which Mr. Mill adopts, as contrasted, point by point, with that of his opponent; and, to one whom his method does not wholly satisfy, there is little damage done to Mr. Mill's great reputation, if his attack is shown to have proceeded from lack of quite understanding the doctrine he controverts.

We have read with much interest the defence which Mr. Mansel has volunteered for the system so confidently challenged.* In explanation of his title, he begins by quoting Plato's statement of the problem of "the unconditioned;" that is, to ascend, by methods of reasoning, to an absolute First Principle, from which all actual existence may be derived by the process of deduction. The positivist denounces such a problem as both impossible and illegitimate. Sir William Hamilton affirms that its solution is impossible to the human reason, hence his "Philosophy of the Conditioned;" but that the *existence* of an absolute First Principle is a necessary postulate for our reason, and even more for our faith, since Christianity has rendered it impossible for a theist to think of the Absolute or the Infinite except as identified with God himself. He seeks "a sphere of belief beyond the limits of the sphere of thought." His position is, "that we *must believe*, as actual, much that we are unable (positively) *to conceive* as even possible."

---

* The Philosophy of the Conditioned; comprising some Remarks on Sir William Hamilton's Philosophy, and on Mr. J. S. Mill's Examination of that Philosophy. By H. L. MANSEL. (Reprinted, with additions, from The Contemporary Review.) London: Alexander Strahan. pp. 184.

The language in which Hamilton vindicates his position, and particularly that in which he deals with his theories of Perception, Knowledge, and Belief, is often barbarous and harsh. Mr. Mill, generally affecting plain clear English speech, may be excused for a little impatience at the Hamiltonian nomenclature. But it would seem that he has not been as scrupulous to ascertain its meaning as he might. In one case, Mr. Mansel shows that he "actually mistakes the position which Hamilton is opposing for that which he is maintaining" (p. 108). In another case (p. 90), the entire argument is shown to turn on the assumption that "the Absolute" or "the Infinite" is used as a name of God, which is as far as possible from Hamilton's meaning; and again (p. 114), on what we might call an invincible ignorance, that, "what the mathematician calls infinite, the metaphysician calls indefinite." The "real battle-ground," the "diametrical antagonism," of the two systems, is shown (p. 58) to be the controversy between free-will and fatalism; and Mr. Mill is distinctly charged with belonging to "that school of materialism which Sir W. Hamilton denounces as virtual atheism" (p. 57). But Mr. Mansel does not rest his case on opprobrious names. "Mr. Mill," he asserts, "has, throughout his criticism, altogether missed the meaning of theories he is attempting to assail" (p. 63). And this charge is what he undertakes to sustain by abundant citation and argument.

It is very instructive, and to some of us a little consoling, to find men of such eminence still at fault as to the very meaning of the terms they employ in their wordy warfare. One cannot help suspecting that the real ground of argument lies back of the theories of the several schools, and that the antagonists differ quite as much in their motive as in their method. Hamilton seeks a religious foundation for his philosophy, at least one that will justify him in assuming certain maxims of *faith* — that is, of belief independent of the reason — among the first principles of it. He will, apparently, have a method that shall leave unmolested the sectarian creed in which he has been bred. He is, covertly, a theologian, full as much as a philosopher: the theory he vindicates must be in harmony with pious feeling, no less than with the rational understanding; and apparently it can be made to justify a doctrinal system against which common sense and the moral nature enter, alike, a vehement protest.

With Mr. Mill, philosophy is a matter of pure science, and the science he adopts is of another school. His style of thought and his moral sympathies are both enlisted against the current orthodoxy, which Hamilton implicitly defends; and, in assailing the highest contemporary names of English metaphysics, he is doing battle for free thought against a despotic theology which he abhors. Mr. Mansel seems to us not quite candid, in his plausible statement of man's imperfect comprehension of the Divine purpose in creation, when he cites it to rebuke the vehemence of Mr. Mill's protest. At least, he must know that Mr. Mill *means* in that protest to repudiate a conception of the Divine government, — once identified with the very name of Christianity, and full of terror to the ignorant even now, — which no intelligent man dares any longer state in its full atrocity. The controversy interests us even more as a theological than as a metaphysical one. Yet our sympathies in it are divided. For, while human nature itself protests against that monstrous system of mental tyranny and religious terror from which the processes of modern thought are effecting our deliverance, human nature also protests against that drift towards Fatalism — a godless or else a divine necessity — which the courses of positive science seem to indicate so strongly.

Dr. McCosh's argument, in the same general direction as that we have been reviewing,* differs from it in being more of the nature of a general treatise, and less a vindication of particular opinions. It is "a defence of fundamental Truth," not strictly a defence of Sir William Hamilton, from whose system it expresses free dissent. In style, too, it is less combative and personal. It has a more direct and express acknowledgment of Mr. Mill's services and eminence in kindred lines of thought. The Introduction, in particular, is very winning by its tone of fairness and candor; and in many points its criticism is keen, sagacious, and valuable. Mr. Mill's theory is stated quite explicitly at the outset; viz., "that we can know nothing of mind except that it is a series of sensations aware of itself, or of matter except that it is a possibility of sensations." Probably, Mr. Mill would not complain of this statement, which is given almost in his own words; though his reviewer follows it, almost immediately, by a citation, carefully registered under twenty-four different heads, of arguments, phrases, and positions, in which, from an ample maga-

---

* An Examination of Mr. Mill's Philosophy; Being a Defence of Fundamental Truth. By JAMES McCOSH. London: McMillan & Co.

zine of first principles, Mr. Mill appears to select at will whatever will suit the purpose of his argument, whatever his theory may say to the contrary. In short, Mr. Mill is convicted of the most honorable fault that can befall a reasoner,—an intelligence too broad and rich to be a consistent materialist, and too masculine to shrink at inconsistency of phrase when he would declare realities of things. In spite of a theological motive apparent here and there, and something of narrow prejudice in dealing with the "positive" school,—as where it speaks of Comte as "a rabid atheist,"—and an appeal to consequences and tendencies which hardly becomes the single search for truth, the book is a fair, able, and valuable study of the subject it treats: it is honestly and seriously religious; and it considerably mitigates the impression produced by the author's ponderous scheme, published fifteen years ago, in which the moral and physical order of the universe were expounded from the point of view of Scotch Presbyterianism.

J. H. A.

MISS CARPENTER'S deeply interesting memorial* refreshens recollections that were growing dim by the lapse of a generation. It is just fifty years since the name of Rammohun Roy—then somewhere between thirty and thirty-five years old — was becoming known as the zealous defender of the Divine Unity against the superstitions of Hindoo Polytheism. In 1833 he died, near Bristol, England, in a circle of friends to whom he was greatly endeared; leaving a reputation as wide and pure, perhaps, as any Christian thinker of the century. We are greatly indebted to this volume for reviving and revindicating that reputation now. It was prepared by the editor as one of the tasks preparatory to her present visit of charity in India; and at the special request of four young men, natives of that country, who have been pursuing their studies in England, and who propose, on their return, to publish the completest biography possible of their illustrious countryman.

Ever since the age of fifteen, when he made a journey into Thibet for the sake of understanding the religious customs there, Rammohun Roy had been powerfully attracted to the study of religious truth at the fountain-heads of sacred tradition. His father, whose death

---

* The Last Days in England of the Rajah Rammohun Roy. Edited by Mary Carpenter, of Bristol. London: Trübner & Co. Calcutta: R. C. Lepage & Co. pp. 255.

left him ample wealth and leisure, seems to have favored this strong bent. At an early age, he was already master, not only of the several Hindoo tongues, but of Arabic (which he studied as a living tongue) and Persian; and, from the ancient Sanscrit lore, he had published (in 1816) a compilation of passages to prove, as the primitive faith, his favorite theory of the unity of God. Hebrew and Greek he also learned, in order to study Christianity in its original documents; and, having acquired sufficient knowledge of English, he took a zealous interest in the translation of the Scriptures then in preparation at Calcutta. We believe we are correct in saying, that his discussions and arguments, during this work, had a decisive influence in converting at least one English missionary — the learned and eminent William Adam — to Unitarian views of Christianity. The unbiassed testimony of a highly educated Brahmin in favor of a free and undogmatic interpretation of the Testament was reckoned at that time a very important contribution to Unitarian literature. Many of our readers will recollect the volume, republished in this country, containing his compilation of the moral instructions of the gospel, entitled "The Precepts of Jesus, the Guide to Peace and Happiness" (first published in 1820), together with his tracts, or appeals to his countrymen in his own defence. And, with perhaps a little wavering as to the more strictly dogmatic and supernatural elements of faith, he was frank and positive in declaring himself a Christian believer to the end.

But, a Hindoo by birth and a high-caste Brahmin, the object he had most at heart was the good of his own countrymen; and for their sakes, as well as for that of his family, he was solicitous never to forfeit the privileges of his rank and birth. At his death, the thread denoting his caste was found about his body; and at his burial, in a private estate apart from any Christian cemetery, no funeral service was held, nor were any words spoken, lest they should prejudice the jealously guarded birthright. The religious animosity of his countrymen he had braved for years, and even the bitter hostility of his own mother, who (we are informed) once attempted his life by poison. But he would not put any obstacle which could possibly be avoided between his mind and theirs. Accordingly, his influence was early and powerfully felt for good among them. It was one of the strongest agencies in abolishing the *suttee*,— the burning alive of Hindoo widows; it was used, along with the generous employment of his private wealth, in establishing schools, and otherwise combating native ignorance and superstitions; it is one of the powerful agents now in inspiring the efforts of a younger generation.

Of large frame and noble features; of gentle and winning manners; of a delicate courtesy in the society of women, and eager affection to little children; of unvarying serious demeanor, somewhat tinged with melancholy; fluent and eloquent in the gift of speech; appealing to the imagination also by the rich and scrupulously elegant oriental costume which he never abandoned, — Rammohun Roy left a singularly deep and strong impression wherever he was met in personal intercourse. His visit to England in the spring of 1831, and his residence there until his death in September, 1833, of which this volume is the special record, was occasioned partly by his interest in the study of European life and politics, as well as by the hope of doing larger service to his people on his return. It is very grateful and touching, at this interval, to recall the cordial and thorough appreciation with which he was welcomed everywhere, and the genuine love and affection he inspired. Those who knew him personally then do not speak of him now without a peculiar emotion of veneration and esteem. And a larger circle of a younger generation will be glad to find in this fresh memorial a testimony to perhaps the purest native worth and nobility that we have known in the records of British India, and an encouragement to the best hopes that have been entertained for that ill-starred population.

MISCELLANEOUS.

THE War of the Union presents so vast a field of interests and operations, that many years must elapse before the records are sufficiently collated, the facts sufficiently digested, to furnish and perfect the materials for a thorough and complete history of this eventful section of American national life. No war, it is likely, was ever so copiously documented; but the very abundance of the documents embarrasses the task of the historian, whose obligation to the truth compels him, so far as possible, to examine, compare, and sift them all, in order to a final trustworthy judgment.

Meanwhile, therefore, an important service is rendered by the special contributions of competent witnesses and chroniclers whom personal experience or private interest has induced to elaborate single and select portions of this wide field. Of such contributions, we have met with none more weighty and every way satisfactory than Mr. Woodbury's faithful and laborious monograph.*

---

* Major-General Ambrose E. Burnside, and the Ninth Army Corps. By AUGUSTUS WOODBURY. Illustrated with Portraits and Maps. Providence, 1867.

As chaplain of the First Rhode-Island Regiment, the author had abundant opportunity of becoming acquainted with General Burnside, who entered the military service of the war as colonel of that regiment; was afterward invested with the charge of a brigade; then received, in acknowledgment of his brilliant services, the commission of major-general of volunteers; and was finally promoted to the chief command of the Army of the Potomac. Whatever may be thought of his management in this latter capacity, — a position which was thrust upon him against his inclination, — there can be but one opinion as to the soldierly and moral qualities of this distinguished officer, than whom the war evoked no purer patriot, no truer, nobler spirit. His merits and services are set forth by Mr. Woodbury with a friendly and admiring, but not unduly biassed, pen. Indeed the book, both in what relates to General Burnside and other officers, and in sketching the operations of the Ninth Army Corps, is eminently temperate and calm. It is the tone of the thoughtful, self-possessed historian, not that of the advocate or partisan. Due credit is given where credit is deserved. Failures and incompetence are not glossed over, but neither are they made the occasion of bitter invective. The record is instinct with manly, Christian sentiment, but remarkably free from morbid sentimentality.

The chief value of this work consists in the carefully studied, thoroughly comprehended, and luminously described, operations and achievements, — the marches, sieges, battles, captures, of the war, — so far as the Ninth Army Corps had part in them; and that corps was concerned in many of the most important. The descriptions are illustrated with plans and maps, enabling the reader to form a correct and adequate idea of each operation. The roster of the corps is given in full, so far as practicable; and the whole is supplemented with a careful and minute index, without which no work of the kind is complete.

It is a thorough piece of work; and all who but glance at these pages, especially all who have had experience in book-making, will appreciate the labor and pains it must have cost. We congratulate Mr. Woodbury on having accomplished so arduous a task, and we cordially recommend his work to all who are interested in studying the details of the most gigantic struggle for national existence against treason and rebellion which history records. F. H. H.

We have received copies of two essays * on widely differing themes, which bear the titles below, and possess an interest independent of their intrinsic value as discussions of the subjects they severally handle. They are the productions of a young fellow-countryman, who has had the unusual honor of winning in the University of Oxford two prizes assigned to excellence in departments of study so distinct that pre-eminence in both implies, not only rare intellectual ability, but breadth of scholarship and completeness of training equally rare. Their author — the son of the Rev. William H. Channing, well known in this community, and grand-nephew of the late Dr. Channing of world-wide repute — has lately, as we learn, been elected Fellow of University College at Oxford, and charged with the responsible office of preparing the select young men of that College for " honors in greats," as it is technically called; that is, of training students who intend to compete for honors at the great examination.

The first essay, on one of the most obscure and most interesting of psychological problems, — the nature of instinct and its relations to organic and to intellectual life, — after stating the popular conception of this form of psychical action, and comparing the views of modern philosophers, Des Cartes, Leibnitz, Condillac, Hume, and others, concerning it, proceeds to analyze the operation of the faculty so named, discriminating its action from that of mere organic mechanism on the one hand, and of pure intelligence on the other, and reaches the conclusion that instinct is a special determination of the vital force; a psychical power, original, distinct, spontaneous, and unconscious in its action; the immediate "response to the natural adaptations and the natural conditions of each creature." The analysis displays a good degree of metaphysical acumen, as well as great clearness and vigor of presentation. The incidental illustrations are pertinent and striking.

The second essay is of greater significance and more conspicuous ability. It discusses, with a show of learning, which, judged by the standard of American university acquirements, seems prodigious, the bearings of the speeches of Greek orators, which have come down to us on the facts of Grecian history; introducing this topic

---

* 1. Instinct. A Prize Essay read in the Theatre, Oxford, June 21, 1865.

2. The Greek Orators considered as Historical Authorities: the Arnold Prize Essay, for 1866. By FRANCIS ALLSTON CHANNING, B.A., late scholar of Exeter College.

with a brief review of the nature and history of Greek oratory of their time. The conclusion arrived at is, that, "down to the wars with Philip, they throw little light on the more important events of Greek history.... Still, the full details given by the orators of the internal events of Athens, at some of her most critical moments, are of great value. They complete the scanty information of contemporary historians, and afford more ample materials for judging the strength and weakness of Athenian institutions. In the time of Philip, all the interest of Greek history is gathered around the decisions and the movements of Athens; and, for this period, the orators are the best authorities, as they were the chief actors in the events they describe." The amount of classical research which illustrates the discussion of this topic is very remarkable; but the ease of handling, and the solid maturity of judgment in so youthful a scholar, are still more so.

The gratification afforded by these essays would be complete, if the author could find, in his native land, a sphere of action worthy his attainments, and suited to his powers. F. H. H.

THE second volume of Napoleon's "Histoire de Jules César"* brings the history down to the outbreak of the civil war in the year B.C. 49. This volume does not differ materially in character from its predecessor. The *motive* of the work, to uphold the dynasty of the writer by the aid of one of those fallacious parallels in which history so abounds, is perhaps kept rather more in the background than in the first volume; and, probably, whatever original material the emperor has finds its place chiefly in this volume. The notes on the Gallic War, and the appendices, are very valuable.

One is astonished, however, to find so little of worth in the body of the work. It is the fruit, no doubt, of great labor. The events of the period are carefully arranged by years, with great fulness of detail, and with a fidelity which may sometimes be called slavish, but which, at any rate, makes certain chapters a very useful guide to the student. Even those portions of the work which invite most temptingly to widen the verge of inquiry, and give some of the results of modern investigation, are as meagre as any. In the chapter on

---

* Histoire de Jules César. Par S.M.I. NAPOLÉON III. Tome deuxième. New York: D. Appleton et Cie., libraires-éditeurs 443 et 445, Broadway. MDCCCLXVI.

the state of Gaul, hardly any authority is cited but Cæsar,— the chief and most indispensable of all, of course, but who imperatively needs illustration and expanding.

On page 47, for example, the author states, in a matter-of-fact way, — almost translating Cæsar's very words, — that each state, each canton, and each family, was divided into two parties. What was the nature of these parties,— whether religious, political, personal, or national,— he takes no pains to inquire. In a few words, he gives the bare facts as to the rivalry between the Ædui and Sequani, but tells us nothing of the relation which this bore to the sacerdotal institutions of the Gauls, or the sense of national unity which was beginning to make itself felt among them; nothing of the degree in which this particular rivalry exerted an influence in the remoter parts of Gaul, or was connected with similar rivalries there; nothing of the connection it had with the parties in the individual cantons and private families,— obscure points, to be sure, which can be investigated only by following out slight hints and isolated statements in ancient writers, but, for this reason, all the more interesting and deserving of consideration. But it is not the way of this imperial author to concern himself with any thing but the commonplaces of history.

Mr. Staunton's work on the great schools of England* contains information which very many will be glad to have in so convenient and attractive a form. In regard to the history, organization, and peculiarities of these schools, he has left little to be desired; although a foreigner would like explanation, now and then, upon points perfectly clear to an Englishman. Matters of professional detail,— as systems of instruction, methods of recitation, character of text-books,— he hardly notices at all; and, consequently, we find little in the volume which will be of much practical service to us in America: for, much as we might learn from the English methods of instruction, the organization of their public schools is something entirely foreign to our usages and needs, and has few features which we should care, or have it in our power, to copy.

It is therefore with a view to gratify a praiseworthy curiosity, rather than to draw practical lessons, that we shall copy, from the work before us, some of the most interesting facts as regards these

---

* The Great Schools of England. By Howard Staunton. London: Sampson Low, Son, and Marston, Milton House, Ludgate Hill. 1865.

schools. We in this country are most familiar with the fame of five of these, — Eton, Winchester, Westminster, Harrow, and Rugby, — unless, indeed, a kindly memory of Colonel Newcome has given the Charterhouse the next place to Rugby in our affections; and, with the exception of Westminster, these mentioned are the largest of all the schools, — Eton far the largest of all; and Harrow next, being a very little larger than Rugby.

A feature which belongs to nearly all of these schools is that they have two classes of scholars, — *Foundationers* and *Non-Foundationers*. The Foundationers are those for whose benefit the school (or college, — as Eton, Winchester, and Westminster, are called) was originally designed: they are educated free of charge, or at a small expense. The Non-Foundationers are the outgrowth of a provision for the instruction of *filii nobilium* and others, additional to the college proper. The Non-Foundationers (called *Oppidans* at Eton, and *Commoners* at Winchester) compose the *school* as distinguished from the *college;* and, so enormously have these establishments grown beyond the idea with which they were originally endowed, that, whereas the school was at first only an appendage to the college, the college is now, in every case, a mere appendage to the school. The Foundationers at Eton number 70; the Non-Foundationers, 770: the Foundationers at Rugby, 61; the Non-Foundationers, 402: the Foundationers at the Charterhouse, 44; the Non-Foundationers, 92. We all remember the foot-ball match in "Tom Brown," between the "School-House" and the "Whole-School." This was, perhaps, between the Foundationers and the Non-Foundationers.

We think we can give a better notion of the constitution of these schools by taking up one of them more in detail; and, for this purpose, we shall select Rugby, not only because it ranks with Abbotsford and Rydal — almost with Runnymede and Stratford on Avon — in the affections of educated Americans, but because it is, no doubt, the most liberal and progressive of all these schools.

It is well known, that the term "Sixth Form" means, in England, precisely what "First Class" does here. Of course, however, in a school of four hundred and sixty-three scholars, there must be practically more than six forms or divisions, each form being supposed to be under the charge of one master. These forms are therefore divided and subdivided. The Fifth and Sixth Forms compose, in the Classical School at Rugby, the "Upper School," divided into the following classes: *Sixth Form, The Twenty, Fifth Form,* and *Lower Fifth,* — one hundred and eighty-seven scholars in all. The Middle School, of two hundred and fifty-five scholars, is divided into *First* and *Second Upper Middle* (each with two parallel classes, doing the same work), *Third Upper Middle,* and *Lower Middle* (also in two parallel classes). The Lower School, of forty-eight scholars, is divided into *Remove, Lower Remove,* and the four lower forms under one master. This is the division of the Classical School, which is, of course, the main work of the institution : the numbers of the classes appear to be taken from the returns of a different year from those given in the former statement. The main divisions of the Mathematical School correspond with these, and contain the same boys ; so that no boy can be promoted in mathematics, unless he is in the classics : they are, however, subdivided into " sets," according to the needs of this department. The subdivisions of the Modern-Language School correspond more nearly with those of the Classical. The function of the Natural-Philosophy School appears to be to furnish a substitute for the modern languages : it teaches, it would seem, only chemistry and electricity.

The time allotted to these various branches is, for the classics, seventeen hours a week ; mathematics, three ; modern languages, two ; besides time for preparation, and private tuition in mathematics. Every scholar studies mathematics through his course ; also French, to which German is added as soon as he has attained sufficient proficiency in French. We do not find any statement of the relative weight of these various studies in making up the rank of the boys at Rugby ; but, at Winchester, where mathematics receive more attention than at any of the others, they amount, in the estimate, to one-fourth, and the modern languages to one-eighth, of the grand total.

The school hours at Rugby are less in amount than at most of the others, on account, we suppose, of the *tutorial system,* of which we shall speak presently. They are three hours before dinner, and an hour and a half after dinner. At Winchester, where the tutorial system is in a very slightly developed form, and at Westminster, where it has been given up, the hours are more nearly like those of our schools, but differently distributed ; at Winchester, from 7 to 7½, from 9 to 12, and from 3 to 6. Outside of these, there appear to be no regular study hours, except for particular classes. The vacations at Rugby are seven weeks at Christmas, and eight in the summer ; at Winchester, sixteen days at Easter, six weeks and a day or two at Midsummer, and five weeks and a day or two at Christmas, besides any number of holidays at one time and another. The other schools generally resemble Winchester, in this respect, rather than Rugby.

The tutorial system, spoken of above, is nearly peculiar to Eton, Harrow, and Rugby: as it is found in its most complete form at Eton, we shall describe it as it exists there. The school work at Eton is insignificant, compared with the out-of-school work. Each boy, on coming to the school, is assigned (by arrangement with his parents) to one of the masters as a tutor, who continues in this relation to him throughout his entire course. He thus has the advantage, at once, of coming into contact with the mind of each teacher, as he advances from one class to another, and, at the same time, of having the influence of one superior mind constantly working upon his. With this tutor, he makes his preparations for the school-recitations; and his exercises are corrected in detail by the tutor, before being handed to the master of his division. Besides this work, the boy has, with his tutor, what is called " private business," — that is, extra instruction, on work selected by the tutor. For instance, the only Greek taught at Eton is that of Homer: the scholar reads the other Greek authors with his tutor. The tutorial system, at Harrow, is very much the same as at Eton: at Rugby, it is somewhat subordinate, and the "private business" is with large and very promiscuous classes. The advantage of this, as stated by Dr. Temple, the head master, is, that the tutor, in this way, comes in contact with members of the whole school, and becomes acquainted with all the work that is going on in it.

The salaries paid in the Greek Schools of England are munificent, when compared with our best endowed schools and colleges. The head master of Rugby receives, in salary, fee, profits of boarding-house, &c., £2,957. 8d.; the highest assistant, £1,617. 6s. 6d.; and the lowest, £286. 13s. 4d. There are, in all, thirteen classical, three mathematical, and two modern-language assistants, besides one for natural philosophy.

Mr. Staunton's introductory remarks are judicious and progressive. He has enhanced the value of his book by adding a copy of the recommendations of the commissioners appointed to examine the condition of the schools, — both the general recommendations and those for the special schools. These gentlemen are in favor of a limited degree of progress: they are willing to concede something to the modern languages and the sciences; and, within the narrow bounds in which they shut themselves, their ideas upon education are, in the main, good.

It is a curious indication of the backward condition of educational discussion in Great Britain, that, just at the time that we in this country are becoming convinced of the harmfulness of prizes and medals in our schools, these commissioners advise the introduction of the system of prizes into the schools in question.

The detailed account of the ten great endowed schools (numbering, besides those already mentioned, St. Paul's, Merchant-Tailors', Shrewsbury, and Christ's Hospital), the principal features of which we have described above, occupies much the largest part of the book. But Mr. Staunton has wisely added an appendix, containing a brief account of the principal *Proprietary Schools*, in which we may see the results of the more liberal tendencies of English education. Of Marlborough and Cheltenham, we in this country know at least the names from Matthew Arnold's "French Eton." Their peculiarity consists in the fact, that they have a *Modern School*, especially designed to fit for the army and navy, which teaches history, mathematics, science, Latin, &c. (Greek only optional, if at all), by the side of the Classical Department, which is modelled upon the great public schools. Of all these, "Alleyn's College of God's Gift at Dulwich," founded in the reign of James I., and recently re-organized; and the school at Rossal, for clergymen's sons and others, — are the most liberal, and nearest to the American ideal of a good school. They are, for instance, so far as we have observed, the only ones of the fifteen schools treated of in this volume which make the English language and literature a distinct and prominent object. The "Modern School" at Rossall is divided into the Military, Naval, Civil-Service, Civil-Engineering, and Mercantile Classes, in each of which special subjects are taught in addition to the general course.   w. f. a.

Those, and we believe they are many, who, without being acquainted with the Oriental languages, which are essential to a complete understanding of comparative philology, wish yet to learn the latest results of the investigations in this field, especially as regards the relation between the two classic tongues which are accustomed to form the groundwork of a liberal education, will find in Leo Meyer's "Comparative Grammar of the Greek and Latin Languages"* pre-

---

* Vergleichende Grammatik der Griechischen und Lateinischen Sprache. Von Leo Meyer. Zweiter Band. Berlin: Weidmannsche Buchhandlung, 1865. 12mo. pp. 628.

cisely the help that they want. His task he declares to be "to ascertain the condition of the language, and especially to determine the forms of the language, at the time when the Greek [which, it must be understood, is a younger language than Latin] was developed as from a common fundamental form (*Grundform*), which itself may have been very far removed from the condition of the oldest original language" (vol. i. p. 21). We find, therefore, comparatively little of the Sanscrit and other Oriental tongues in these pages, but also, with the exception of the introduction, very little *reading*. It is close, hard study of dry details, such as any one must work through, in order to rise to the perception of great principles, in any department of science.

WE have at last a French grammar formed upon a sensible plan, such as is now adopted almost universally in regard to the ancient languages, — a systematic arrangement, with progressive exercises from the very start.* That such progressive exercises were imperatively demanded, is proved by the popularity of the Ollendorff system, of which this is the single good feature. The confused and purely empirical arrangement of all books prepared upon this system has produced disastrous results in the community, in a superficial and slipshod knowledge of all languages usually studied. To acquire idioms and phrases, when one already knows the groundwork of the language, it may, to be sure, be used with very great advantage; but by itself, used by average teachers and with average pupils, we hold that it cannot produce either sound scholarship or accurate habits of mind. It has already been discarded as worthless in the ancient languages, but has held its ground until now in the modern languages, especially French, whose simplicity of structure and resemblance to English enable it to be studied by this method with less disadvantage. We hope, however, that this excellent book of Mr. Magill's will do something to redeem the study of French likewise.

A SERIOUS student is apt to be impatient at the presenting of any grave and large topic under the form of lectures for popular delivery: the set artificial divisions, the demands of an audience, the constraints

---

* A French Grammar. By EDWARD H. MAGILL, A.M., Sub-Master in the Boston Latin School. Boston: Crosby & Ainsworth, 1866. 12mo. pp. 287.

of time, the temptation to by-play, are so many violations of that natural order so essential to the right understanding of it. But this form has not only its convenience or its necessity to plead for it, but also its positive advantage. For every topic has its salient points, which rhetorical treatment may bring into the needed relief; and every extended history, in particular, is capable of a certain special handling, symmetrical and half imaginative, which makes the best form possible of presenting it to those who are not serious students, and may even be of service to those who are. And the readers of Grote or Thirlwall or Finlay — of Mure or Gladstone or Professor Blackie — will not be indifferent to the publication of the two handsome volumes of the late President Felton,[*] which, for the general public, make the best available introduction into the wide field with which they deal.

President Felton's qualifications for this task were as rare as they were generally recognized. A scholar, a teacher by profession and long practice, a traveller with special enthusiasm for the scene of his story; a man of infinite *bonhomie* and of considerable native humor; of wide acquaintance with general literature and considerable experience in affairs; of warm personal feelings and active interest in living politics, — he seems to meet the public mind at every point, as a fit interpreter of the history, the literature, and the public life which he had made it the chief occupation of his mind to study, and the chief labor of his life to illustrate. We have not space to anticipate now the sketch of his labors which we hope to give hereafter; and can only direct our readers to his volumes, with the assurance that they will find in them that best satisfaction, — results presented in an attractive form, with the indorsement of earnest, genuine, faithful scholarship. The volumes consist of four courses of a dozen lectures each: first, on the Greek Language and Poetry, including a preliminary sketch of recent philological studies; second, the Life of Greece, — social, domestic, political, and religious; third, Constitutions and Orators of Greece, giving, by the way, such notices of the history as are essential to a right understanding of them; and, fourth, Modern Greece, commencing with the Macedonian ascendency, and ending with the revolution of forty years ago, and a picturesque account of the land and people in these latter days.

J. H. A.

---

[*] Greece, Ancient and Modern: Lectures delivered before the Lowell Institute. By C. C. FELTON, LL.D., late President of Harvard University. Boston: Ticknor & Fields. 8vo, 2 vols.

NEW PUBLICATIONS RECEIVED.

The French Manual: a New, Simple, Concise, and Easy Method of acquiring a Conversational Knowledge of the French Language; including a Dictionary of over Ten Thousand Words. By M. Alfred Havet. 12mo. pp. 300.

Joseph II. and his Court: An Historical Novel. By L. Mühlbach. Translated from the German by Adelaide De V. Chaudron. Illustrated. 8vo. pp. 343. New York: D. Appleton & Co.

Lectures and Annual Reports on Education. By Horace Mann. 8vo. pp. 571. Cambridge: Printed for the Editor.

Thoughts Selected from the Writings of Horace Mann. Boston: H. B. Fuller & Co. 16mo. pp. 240. (Compact and handsome, skilfully exhibiting much of what is most characteristic in the thought and style of the writer.)

The Posthumous Papers of the Pickwick Club. By Charles Dickens. With original Illustrations by S. Eytinge, jr. Boston: Ticknor & Fields. 16mo. pp. 464. (Diamond edition.)

The Works of the Right Honorable Edmund Burke. Revised edition. Boston: Little & Brown. Vol. XI. pp. 445. (Containing Report and Speeches on the Impeachment of Warren Hastings.)

The American Conflict: a History of the Great Rebellion of the United States of America, 1860–65. By Horace Greeley. Hartford: O. D. Case & Co. Vol. II. 8vo. pp. 872.

Whom do you Worship? A Popular Treatise on Reasonable Religion. By Henry A. Abraham. 12mo. pp. 44. New York: James Miller.

The Claverings. A Novel. By Anthony Trollope. Illustrated. pp. 211.

Two Marriages. By the Author of "John Halifax, Gentleman." 12mo. pp. 301.

Bernthal; or, The Son's Revenge. From the German of L. Mühlbach. 8vo. pp. 96.

American Leaves. Familiar Notes of Thought and Life. By Samuel Osgood. 12mo. pp. 380.

Annals of a Quiet Neighborhood. By George MacDonald, M.A. Author of "David Elginbrod." 12mo. pp. 381.

Kissing the Rod. By Edward Yates.

Rachel's Secret. By the Author of "The Master of Marton."

Lizzie Norton of Greyrigg. By E. Lynn Linton.

Cradock Nowell: A Tale of the New Forest. By Richard Doddridge Blackmore. 8vo. pp. 218. New York: Harper & Brothers.

The Women of The Gospels. The Three Wakings, and other Poems. By the Author of "The Schönberg-Cotta Family." 12mo. pp. 275.

The Brownings: A Tale of the Great Rebellion. 16mo. pp. 310.

The Brewer's Family. By Mrs. Ellis. Author of "Women of England," &c. New York: M. W. Dodd. 16mo. pp. 325.

The Constitutional Convention; its History, Powers, and Modes of Proceeding. By John Alexander Jameson, Judge of the Superior Court of Chicago, and Professor of Constitutional Law, &c., in the Law Department of the Chicago University. New York: C. Scribner & Co. 8vo. pp. 561.

The Service of Sorrow. By Lucretia P. Hale. Boston: American Unitarian Association.

Laboulaye's Fairy Book. Fairy Tales of all Nations. By Edouard Laboulaye. Translated by Mary L. Booth. With engravings. 16mo. pp. 363.

Beginning French. Ahn's & Belezi's Systems. New York: Leypoldt & Holt. 16mo. pp. 124.

Principia Latina. Part II. A First Latin Reading Book. Containing an Epitome of Cæsar's Gallic Wars, and L. Homond's Lives of Distinguished Romans, &c., &c. By William Smith, LL.D; and Henry Drisler, LL.D., Professor of Latin in Columbia College, New York. New York: Harper & Brothers. 12mo. pp. 375.

The Great Rebellion; its Secret History, Rise, Progress, and Disastrous Failure. By John Minor Botts, of Virginia. The Political Life of the Author vindicated. New York: Harper & Brothers. 12mo. pp. 402.

Greece, Ancient and Modern. Lectures delivered before the Lowell Institute. By C. C. Felton, LL.D., Late President of Harvard University. Boston: Ticknor & Fields. 2 vols. pp. 511, 549.

Remarks on Classical and Utilitarian Studies, read before the American Academy of Arts & Sciences, Dec. 20, 1865. By Jacob Bigelow, M.D. Boston: Little, Brown & Co. pp. 57.

The Tent on the Beach, and other Poems. By John Greenleaf Whittier. Boston: Ticknor & Fields.

The Life of Jesus, according to the Original Biographers. With Notes. By Edmund Kirke. Boston: Lee & Shepard. pp. 297. (Slightly but skilfully modernized in phrase, and arranged according to Robinson's "Harmony." The notes illustrative, not critical.)

Joubert: Some of the Thoughts of Joseph Joubert, translated by George H. Calvert. Preceded by a Notice of Joubert, by the Translator. Boston: William V. Spencer. pp. 163. (A book of rare refinement and insight of the moral sense, tastefully and agreeably presented.)

A Child's Book of Religion, for Sunday-schools and Homes. Compiled by O. B. Frothingham. Boston: James P. Walker. (The most varied, suggestive, and agreeable hand-book of religious instruction yet compiled.)

TARRANT'S

EFFERVESCENT

SELTZER APERIENT.

This valuable and popular Medicine, prepared in conformity with the analysis of the water of the celebrated Seltzer Spring in Germany, in a most convenient and portable form, has universally received the most favorable recommendations of the medical profession and a discerning public, as the

Most Efficient and Agreeable Saline Aperient

in use, and as being entitled to special preference over the many Mineral Spring Waters, Seidlitz Powders, and other similar articles, both from its compactness and greater efficacy. It may be used with the best effect in all

Bilious and Febrile Diseases;

Sick Headache; Loss of Appetite;

Indigestion, and all Similar Complaints,

Peculiarly incident to the Spring and Summer Seasons.

It is particularly adapted to the wants of Travellers by sea and land, Residents in Hot Climates, Persons of Sedentary Habits, Invalids, and Convalescents.

With those who have used it, it has high favor, and is deemed indispensable.

In a Torpid State of the Liver, it **renders great** service in restoring healthy action.

In Gout and Rheumatism, it gives the best satisfaction, allaying all inflammatory symptoms, and in many cases effectually curing those afflicted.

Its Success in Cases of Gravel, Indigestion, Heartburn, and Costiveness, proves it to be a Medicine of the greatest utility.

Acidity of the Stomach, and the Distressing Sickness so usual during Pregnancy, yields speedily, and with marked success, under its healthful influence.

It affords the Greatest Relief to those afflicted with, or subject to, the Piles, acting gently on the bowels, neutralizing all irritating secretions, and thereby removing all inflammatory tendencies.

In fact, it is invaluable in all cases where a gentle Aperient is required.

It is in the form of a powder, carefully put up in bottles, to keep in any climate; and merely requires water poured upon it, to produce a delightful effervescent beverage.

Taken in the morning, it never interferes with the avocations of the day, acting gently on the system, restoring the digestive powers, exciting a healthy and vigorous tone of the stomach, and creating an elasticity of mind and flow of spirits which give zest to every enjoyment. It also enables the invalid to enjoy many luxuries with impunity, from which he must otherwise be debarred, and without which life is irksome and distressing.

Numerous testimonials from professional and other gentlemen of the highest standing throughout the country, and its steadily increasing popularity for a series of years, strongly guarantee its efficacy and valuable character, and commend it to the favorable notice of an intelligent public.

STEINWAY & SONS'

GRAND, SQUARE, & UPRIGHT PIANO-FORTES,

Are now acknowledged the best Instruments in America, as well as in Europe, having taken *Thirty-two First Premiums, Gold and Silver Medals*, at the principal Fairs held in this country within the last ten years; and in addition thereto they were awarded a First Prize Medal at the Great International Exhibition in London, 1862, for POWERFUL, CLEAR, BRILLIANT, and SYMPATHETIC TONE, with excellence of workmanship, as shown in Grand and Square Pianos. There were 269 Pianos, from all parts of the world, entered for competition; and the special correspondent of "The Times" says:—

"Messrs. STEINWAY's indorsement by the jurors is emphatic, and stronger and more to the point than that of any European maker."

Among the many and most valuable important improvements introduced by Messrs. Steinway & Sons, in their Piano-fortes, the special attention of purchasers is directed to their PATENT AGRAFFE ARRANGEMENT, for which Letters Patent were granted them Nov. 29, 1859. The value and importance of this invention having been practically tested, during a period of nearly six years, by Steinway & Sons, in all their Grands and highest-priced Square Piano-fortes, and admitted to be the greatest improvement of modern times, they now announce that they have determined to introduce their "Patent Agraffe Arrangement" in *every Piano-forte manufactured by them, without increase of its cost*, in order that all their patrons may reap the full advantage of this great improvement.

Reasons for Purchasing a STEINWAY Piano-Forte in preference to all others.

FIRST.— *The fact* that they have been awarded the first premiums, both in Europe and America, by the most competent and inflexible of judges.

SECOND.— *The fact* that all their "scales, improvement, and peculiarities of construction," have been copied by a large majority of the manufacturers of both hemispheres, as closely as could be done without infringement of patent rights; thus admitting their vast superiority over all others.

THIRDLY.— *The fact* that a large number of manufacturers and "Associations" *profess* to make Piano-fortes *exactly like* Steinway's, or to have been in their employ as foremen or workmen, thus conceding their excellence in claiming an indorsement for their own instruments.

FOURTHLY.— *The fact* that, while the majority of the smaller makers manufacture their Pianos in several separate shops, and purchase the actions, some also the keyboards, and even the cases for their instruments, *ready made*, every portion of a "Steinway" Piano, from its incipiency to its completion, is manufactured in one immense building, under the immediate personal superintendence of the Messrs. Steinway (father and three sons), thus insuring perfect uniformity and unrivalled excellence.

FIFTHLY.— *The fact* that no Piano-forte with the slightest possible defect is ever permitted to leave the manufactory; and that every Steinway instrument *is warranted for five years*.

SIXTHLY.— *The fact* that, in purchasing a Piano-forte, the established reputation of its maker should be relied on as strongly as its *apparent* quality, and far more than its first cost.

SEVENTHLY.— The immense working capital employed, which commands alike the choice of labor, the employment of the most skilful artisans, the selection and accumulation of materials of all kinds, and the thorough and lengthened seasoning process to which the lumber is subjected.

EIGHTHLY.— *The fact* that the unexampled success achieved by STEINWAY & SONS' PIANO-FORTES, in spite of all and every opposition, is admitted to be owing to their sterling and lasting qualities, which stand alike the test of time and trial.

NINTHLY.— *The fact* that the majority of the most eminent artists of Europe, and, with but few exceptions, the most celebrated pianists resident in America, prefer them for their own private and public use whenever they can obtain them; and their testimony is overwhelming, as will be seen by their certificate, signed by S. B. MILLS, ROBERT GOLDBECK, HENRY C. TIMM, F. L. RITTER, GEORGE W. MORGAN, THEO. THOMAS, MAX MARETZEK, WILLIAM MASON, ROBERT HELLER, WILLIAM BERGE, F. BRANDEIS, THEO. MOELLING, E. MUZIO, CARL ANSCHUTZ, A. H. PEASE, CARL WOLFSOHN, A. DAVIS, F. VON BREUNING, THEO. EISFELD, CARL BERGMANN, and many others.

STEINWAY & SONS,

WAREROOMS, Nos 71 AND 73, EAST FOURTEENTH STREET (**between** Union Square and Irving Place), NEW YORK.

Published once in two months, at Five Dollars a year.

Nº CCLXI.]　　　New Series.　　　[Vol. III.—Nº 3.

THE

NOTICE.

During the absence of Rev. Dr. BELLOWS in Europe, communications may be addressed to the Corresponding Editor, Rev. J. H. ALLEN, *Cambridge, Mass.*

All matters of business should be referred to the Publisher.

JAMES MILLER,
522, *Broadway, New York.*

VI. PHASES OF PRIMITIVE CHRISTIANITY.—*E. E. Du Bois* . . 342
VII. THE INCARNATION 355

Trustees' Report, 321; Marie's King Rene's Daughter, 392; Weeks' Poems, 392.
NEW PUBLICATIONS RECEIVED . . . 393

NEW YORK:
JAMES MILLER, PUBLISHER,
522, BROADWAY.
BOSTON: JAMES P. WALKER, 26, CHAUNCY STREET.

STEINWAY & SONS'

valled excellence.

FIFTHLY. — *The fact* that no Piano-forte with the slightest possible defect is ever permitted to leave the manufactory; and that every Steinway instrument *is warranted for Five years*.

SIXTHLY. — *The fact* that, in purchasing a Piano-forte, the established reputation of its maker should be relied on as strongly as its *apparent* quality, and far more than its first cost.

SEVENTHLY. — The immense working capital employed, which commands alike the choice of labor, the employment of the most skillful artisans, the selection and accumulation of materials of all kinds, and the thorough and lengthened seasoning process to which the lumber is subjected.

EIGHTHLY. — *The fact* that the unexampled success achieved by STEINWAY & SONS' PIANO-FORTES, in spite of all and every opposition, is admitted to be owing to their sterling and lasting qualities, which stand alike the test of time and trial.

NINTHLY. — *The fact* that the majority of the most eminent artists of Europe, and, with but few exceptions, the most celebrated pianists resident in America, prefer them for their own private and public use whenever they can obtain them; and their testimony is overwhelming, as will be seen by their certificate, signed by S. B. MILLS, ROBERT GOLDBECK, HENRY C. TIMM, F. L. RITTER, GEORGE W. MORGAN, THEO. THOMAS, MAX MARETZEK, WILLIAM MASON, ROBERT HELLER, WILLIAM BERGE, F. BRANDEIS, THEO. MOELLING, E. MUZIO, CARL ANSCHUTZ, A. H. PEASE, CARL WOLFSOHN, A. DAVIS, F. VON BREUNING, THEO. EISFELD, CARL BERGMANN, and many others.

STEINWAY & SONS,

WAREROOMS, Nos 71 AND 73, EAST FOURTEENTH STREET (between Union Square and Irving Place), NEW YORK.

Published once in two months, at Five Dollars a year.

Nº CCLXI.]   **New Series.**   [VOL. III.—Nº 3.

THE
CHRISTIAN EXAMINER.

MAY, 1867.

CONTENTS.

ART.	PAGE
I. WESTERN EMIGRATION AND WESTERN CHARACTER.— A. D. *Mayo*	265
II. GEOGRAPHY OF PALESTINE.— *C. H. Brigham*	282
III. MADAME RÉCAMIER AND HER FRIENDS.— *W. R. Alger*	299
IV. MAURICE DE GUÉRIN.— *J. H. Sinter*	328
V. SOCIAL EMULATION, AS A FEATURE OF AMERICAN LIFE	335
VI. PHASES OF PRIMITIVE CHRISTIANITY.— *E. E. Du Bois*	342
VII. THE INCARNATION	355

ART.	PAGE
VIII. REVIEW OF CURRENT LITERATURE	371
Theology. Castelli on Ecclesiastes, 371; Galletti's Rationalism, 372; Brugsch, Aus dem Orient, 373.— *Geography and Travels.* The Turks, the Greeks, and the Slavons, 378. Dixon's New America, 380.— *Poetry and Art.* Whittier's Tent on the Beach, 382. Samson's Elements of Art Criticism, 384; Palgrave's Essays on Art, 385.— *Miscellaneous.* Alger's Genius of Solitude, 389; Cornell University Trustees' Report, 391; Hertz's King René's Daughter, 392; Weeks' Poems, 393.	
NEW PUBLICATIONS RECEIVED	393

NEW YORK:

JAMES MILLER, PUBLISHER,

522, BROADWAY.

BOSTON: JAMES P. WALKER, 26, CHAUNCY STREET.

PYLE'S
SALERATUS

AND

CREAM TARTAR,

GENERALLY ACKNOWLEDGED

The Best in the Market. Always full Weight.

In the New-England States, PYLE'S SALERATUS is superseding all others. Its purely wholesome character, and general efficiency in baking, are qualifications which the intelligent housekeeper readily discovers and appreciates. These articles are always put up full weight, and housekeepers realize a measure of economy in their use.

PYLE'S O. K. SOAP,

The best Household Soap in America,

is made from pure materials, similar in quality to the best English and French soaps, and becomes very hard; therefore not liable to the unavoidable waste suffered in the use of common brown soap. By its use all bleached goods will retain the desired whiteness, which is not the case when ordinary soaps are used.

It is also a good Bath and Toilet Soap. Each pound is sufficiently rich in stock to make *three gallons of good soft soap* by the simple addition of water.

There is no exaggeration in these representations, and we can refer to the editors of nearly all the weeklies in New York, who are using the above articles; but we prefer that the practical housekeeper shall test them herself.

Sold by first-class Grocers generally.

JAMES PYLE, Manufacturer,
350, WASHINGTON STREET, NEW YORK.

THE
CHRISTIAN EXAMINER.

MAY, 1867.

Art. I. — WESTERN EMIGRATION AND WESTERN CHARACTER.

At the close of the Revolutionary War, the vast region bounded by the Alleghanies, the Ohio, the Mississippi, and the Lakes was a wilderness. The early attempt at French colonization had failed. The thirteen old colonies had resigned their misty claims of dominion in the far-off country, in favor of the new government. As early as 1790, this whole area was dedicated to Freedom by the new Congress of the United States; and an untrodden world invited a new experiment in human affairs. Then began that most wonderful movement of modern times, which, under the name of Western emigration, in seventy-five years has created five great States, rejuvenated the three most powerful of the older colonies, and planted therein a population of nine millions. Since that day, the people of the United States have come into possession of a vaster region, between the Mississippi and the Pacific, and organized it into seventeen free States and territories, containing a population of three millions. The close of the war of the Rebellion beheld this entire district inhabited by twelve million people, and bound together by a common devotion to American institutions. And, what is vastly more important, this population, gathered from the whole world, shows unmistakable signs of crystallizing into a new and decided Western character.

A Western character; for, although these twelve million people exhibit great diversities of origin, culture, and opinion on the one hand, and on the other are yearly becoming more thoroughly American, they at present exhibit positive traits of character as the result of the peculiar conditions of Western life. We propose in this article to consider, in a general way, this interesting spectacle of Western emigration and Western character.

At the outset, we may dismiss, as not pertinent to our inquiries, the very small class of persons on whose character an emigration to the West has produced no marked impression. In every Western community we find a few individuals, sometimes a respectable little clique, who, dwelling bodily amid the scenes of our New World, have spiritually never strayed beyond their place of nativity. The stubborn old English, Scotch, or North-Irish gentleman, who, after fifty years of Western-American friction, still carries London, Edinburgh, or Belfast in every stamp of his obstinate foot; the jolly German student, from whose vision the cloud-land of his meerschaum obscures the whole universe, save his own complacent "Ego," and who, even amid the opening thunders of the Judgment morning would call for his "lager" and be a "Philister;" the run-down French aristocrat, trying, with a sort of comic desperation, to keep his feet planted in the tracks of his forefathers; the Southern swashbuckler, who wears his hair long, rants in as insolent defiance of modern ideas, and chews his plug-tobacco as frantically, as if the Southern Confederacy were in full blast; the slow Pennsylvanian farmer and his more moderate wife, who, on the broad plains of Central Ohio, seem yet to abide in one of the dimples of father Alleghany's hands; the dear old Quaker lady, whom God keeps, as she is, as a model of essential womanhood; the trim Yankee housekeeper, dying slowly with her daily toil of washing the dirt from the surface of the great West, and dreaming o'nights of going to glory by the way of Worcester, Mass.; the New-York swell and the Philadelphia exquisite, whom even the splendors of Chicago cannot persuade to take down their harps from the willows; the gentlemanly University master of a select school of young ladies or gentlemen, who lives a sort of spectral existence amid our noisy realities, pleasantly indifferent to what we think of him or his classic scheme of life, since, happen what may, old Harvard and Yale will abide, — all these, and yet other phenomena, exist to confirm the fact, that nothing on earth is so enduring as a fixed conceit of human self-sufficiency. Most of these people are useful citizens in their own sphere of labor, and, even when goaded into chronic irritation by the annoyances of our barbarism, a picturesque feature in our Western human scenery. Many of them would occupy positions of high respectability in an old civilization. But here they are never at home; and their despairing existence is the most melancholy feature of Western life. We can look on the wreck of a thousand brave souls who believe in the destiny of the New World more fervently for every failure of their own to grasp its prizes, with enthusiasm, compared to the feeling with which we contemplate this class of strong men and women, slowly dying of spiritual scurvy, amid boundless opportunities which they have not the heart to touch.

The Germanic and British peoples, and their American descendants, are the great emigrating races of the modern world. So great is their breadth and versatility of nature, that they can at once furnish the noblest conservatism to sustain great empires at home, and send forth every variety of the radical character to found new civilizations in virgin lands. Out of this progressive region of the European and older American life has come the vast majority of our Western people. Few of this great number can abide in such a land without being greatly changed. Every State and locality has impressed its own features for a time upon the Western district it has colonized. But, underneath all these local influences, the general type of Western character is slowly developing. It is not an exclusive type of character, content to remain under the ban of provincialism. Indeed, it is the beginning of the distinctively American character; and will never rest content till it has reconstructed the South-west to the Gulf, overflowed the Alleghanies, and borne back the new life of the mighty West towards the rising sun.

The first great emigration under the auspices of the new American republic was from New England to Central and Western New York. The New York of the Revolution was the valleys of the Hudson and the Mohawk; and there an order of society had been established as aristocratic as Virginia itself. The country was chiefly parcelled out among its Dutch, English, North-Irish, and Scotch landholders, while great masses of tenantry were little in advance of the present poor whites of the South. As a consequence, New York was full of Tories during the war; and many a blatant copperhead of Manhattan and the Catskills, during the last six years, has only voiced the principles of his tory or cowboy grandfather. Such a country as Eastern New York, at the beginning of this century, was no home for the eager youth of Yankeeland, whose faces were set toward the great West. The Albany Dutchman smoked his pipe with placid wonderment on the stoop of his Pearl Street gable-ender, as he beheld the mysterious procession of emigrant wagons creeping towards Schenectady; and to-day, in Albany, the valley of the Mohawk goes by the name "Out-West." The Yankees struck Central New York at Utica, and flowed on in a resistless torrent, till they filled the whole inviting region to the Pennsylvania and Canadian borders on the south and north, and the Lakes upon the west.

Western New York is New England amplified and mollified by the rich and varied life of the greatest American State. It is more decided in its progressive American tendency than any portion of New England, save Maine, Vermont, and Eastern Massachusetts: indeed, Connecticut has been kept in an enfeebled, half-neutral condition, by this prodigious drain upon her youthful radical population. While the people of Western New York are lacking in the fine literary culture and English style of refinement so much prized in Boston, they have a weight of manly and womanly character, a breadth of thought and feeling, especially in public affairs, and a swinging onward movement almost unknown east of the Hudson. It is the grandest people in these United States, and has sent forth, and is still sending, more men of mark to the West than all other portions of the Union. With one hand it holds the chief American city from rushing to swift perdition, and with the other it grasps the new West. Here, on the first camping-ground of the Western emigrant, was struck the key-note of our new American order of character and social affairs.

From Western New York the tide of Western emigration skirted Lake Erie, throwing out an affluent down the western slopes of the Pennsylvania and Virginia Mountains, greatly changing Pennsylvania and Western Virginia. Here it is largely mingled with Scotch, Irish, Southern, and Pennsylvania elements. It has marched irresistibly along a path, almost identical with the fortieth parallel of latitude, to the Pacific, and there turned the flank of slavery and barbarism in California and Kansas, each of which was in succession the political Five-Forks of the slave power. In this way, Northern Ohio, Indiana and Illinois, Michigan and Wisconsin, were largely peopled. Though blended somewhat through all these regions with a scattering emigration from the South, and in certain localities almost a new Ireland or Germany, the Northern radical element has always been the foundation of society in this region.

From Eastport to St. Paul, one general type of the American character prevails, above the fortieth parallel of latitude. The inhabitants of this region, though in different states of progress and culture, represent all the essential attributes of that grand middle-class of Great Britain, to which free society owes its greatest debt of gratitude. It is the most intellectual people in the world; though its intellect has so far been chiefly occupied in regions of industrial, political, and social life. It bears within its latent deeps the new literature, philosophy, science, art, and religion of the republic. It is laying broad foundations for the education of the whole people, and its University of Michigan excites the admiration of Harvard itself; while its magnificent foundation of Cornell University, at Ithaca, awakens great hopes of something new in our university life; and in Oberlin, Antioch, Galesburg, and other rising colleges, it is solving the problem of the united university education of the sexes. From this region went forth the early movement against slavery, and its vote was united for Fremont in 1856. In religion it occupies the liberal wing of every American Church. Out of it came the theological and philanthropic agitation which divided every great American Protestant Church, save the Episcopal, before 1860.

Every good idea moves through our human life dogged by a black shadow; and it is not strange that this most progressive, intellectual, and energetic order of Northern society should be exposed to all the dangers of radicalism in its most extreme and varied forms. This region of our country has given birth to a multitude of excitable and unbalanced spirits, who have published their opinions in perfect freedom during the last twenty-five years. The system of popular lectures, the press, the convention, have given every facility to this class of agitators; and the lively interest of the masses of the people has always secured a large hearing to every public teacher who did not add to his radical extravagance the conservative grace of stupidity. The prolonged agitations in the churches have also bred destructive fanaticisms and desolating scepticisms, which have alarmed many good men for the existence of the Church itself. The political life of this district is never stagnant; for every month some new monster makes the sea of popular opinion "boil like a pot of ointment." Business is perpetually sounding the deeps and scaling the heights of speculation. And even the family is assailed by strange theories of marriage, which threaten to dissolve society itself. There is no doubt that the charge of the whole world is true, — that this portion of America is the battle-ground of all possible and impossible theories of human affairs.

But the enemies of the radical North, in their estimate of its tendencies, fail to discover the grand, distinctive characteristic of this remarkable people, — *its deep faith in the spiritual and moral side of human life.* There never was a people on this earth who believed so firmly in the spirituality and immortality of man, the justice and perpetual providence of God, and the eternal distinction between right and wrong, as this. They inherit this faith from their ancestors, the noble middle-class of Great Britain, who represent the most profound religious faith of the northern European races. This faith is a part of the spiritual furniture of every native-born Northern boy or girl. It may be dormant for long periods in whole classes or communities: indeed, the intense activity of the mental and executive faculty often gives it no opportunity to awake. Our people love to think, discuss, and work, for the pure enjoyment of the thing. Hence people whose volume of life is smaller, and whose religious sentiments lie nearer the surface and are more easily excited, declaim against us as a prosaic, materialistic, and irreligious race. But let some deep and searching experience penetrate below the region of thought and work, and unseal the deep fountains of his native faith, and this Northern man starts up, a hero, a reformer, a martyr, or a saint. The gorgeous ritualism of the old European churches is now but a thicket of thorns which he overleaps, or tears through on his swift flight to his God. His intellect is kindled by the great fire below it, and flashes a startling light into the face of every accepted theory of life, in complete faith that all truth can bear the strongest illumination. He knows himself too well to fear the full indulgence of his head and hands, while his soul takes hold on the everlasting realities.

This faith in spiritual things is at once the fountain of perpetual life, and the protecting providence of the Northern people. For want of it, the South, and all southern nations, are vibrating continually between the wildest fanaticisms, and utter despotism. A South-Carolina secessionist, an Italian priest, an Austrian nobleman, knows by experience the danger of free thought among his own people. They see how a new idea maddens the popular mind, and speedily ultimates itself in a social anarchy, the very image of the infernal world. They suppose a people which thinks so intensely and freely as the radical North must be in a state of spiritual, social, and civil delirium. But they do not know this great Northern soul, that, amidst its fiercest flames, is cooled by breezes from that high zone of life where God and man abide together. This portion of the United States is not only the home of radicalism in theory, but of the finest order in actual affairs. When its people have come to the end of their speculations, and begin the real work of life, they throw away nothing essential that has been gained by the toils of the past. They are deliberate in legislation, firm in administering justice, and practical in all their ideas. Mr. Phillips argued twenty years to persuade this people that it was a sin to vote and hold office under the government of the United States. He was the most popular orator of the North; but we never heard of an Abolitionist who was not glad to hold any office that Father Abraham could be induced to give him. Jackson Davis, the trance "media," and the advocates of every form of no-religion, have had the field clear to do their best; but there is no community that can be kept out of the churches when a saintly and eloquent man stands in the pulpit: and the Northern Church was never so active and really influential as now. Business, education, amusement, domestic and social life, are all moving towards a firmer basis. The pecuniary honesty, the solid learning, the domestic purity, the abiding cheerfulness of this republic, are emphatically to be found north of this line of demarcation. There is more gross sensuality in the homes of the poor Southern emigrants in Southern Indiana and Illinois, than in all the country above the fortieth parallel of latitude: indeed, most of the disorders, spiritual and social, in this region, can be traced either to Southern or European emigrants from lands of civil and religious despotism.

It is true that, socially, this region of the West is still somewhat crude, unformed, and stern. The aristocratic society of the South-west, including as it did but few elements of social refinement, ripened far more quickly; and, ten years ago, was the most attractive west of the Alleghanies. But it built on a class and not on man, and went down into the awful gulf of rebellion, from whose smoking deeps now emerge the ghastly spectres of defunct gentility which yet gibber and squeak in faded drawing-rooms, and turn the heads of soft young people of ample means in the cities of the West. Meanwhile our Western social life moves slowly, because it is building the new temple of republican society; more anxious now to lay its foundations deeply, than to overload a thin wall with ornaments that will bring it to the dust. Every observing man, who travels from Maine to Minnesota, must admire the gradual but constant growth of a beautiful social refinement in city and country. There are villages in New York, Michigan, Northern Ohio, Indiana, and Illinois, from which the visitor goes away with a new comprehension of human kindliness, and a refinement born of the heart. This inevitable movement is slowly shaping our American society; and neither the fashionable insanity nor the mimicry of foreign follies among the wealthy snobs of our cities will materially arrest its progress.

This Northern radical people will become the ruling power in American affairs. It has already captured the great line of central cities from Philadelphia to Leavenworth. It is moulding the entire population between the thirty-eighth and fortieth parallels of latitude to its own ideas. It is now the only concentrated power in the Union. While Cincinnati, Louisville, and St. Louis wrangle and hesitate, and never gather themselves up for one grand effort, the whole array of Northern towns, from Albany to St. Paul, are the well-organized division of a host that goes on conquering and to conquer. It already holds the republic beyond the Mississippi, save Texas, in the grasp of its ideas. It rules, as permanent ruling has always been done, — not through numbers, but through breadth and force of character. It is not afraid even to offer universal amnesty and universal suffrage through Mr. Chase, or forgiveness and forgetfulness of the whole past through Mr. Seward, as its final programme of policy. It will at last repudiate the weak devices of those who recommend a re-organization of the South through a centralized military power. The Secretary of State, the Chief Justice, General Grant, and Abraham Lincoln, know most of the radical North. It only asks an opportunity to get at the rest of the country with its ideas; and, once marshalled on the decisive field, it has no fear of the result.

Even were there any danger to American institutions from the radical North, it would be averted by the peculiar order of society that prevails between the thirty-eighth and fortieth parallels of north latitude. This region includes New Jersey, Southern Pennsylvania, Delaware, Northern Maryland, and Northern Virginia of the old States. Even before the emigration to the North-west, it struck the valley of the Ohio at Marietta and Cincinnati, and has poured a tide of emigration through Western Pennsylvania, West Virginia, Southern Ohio, Indiana, and Illinois, to the western boundary of Missouri. To this was added a decided Southern emigration, especially west of Ohio. For fifty years, the more progressive classes of the poor, and the liberal wing of the old Virginia and Kentucky families, have poured into the valley of the Ohio, and blended readily with the elements there found. A somewhat sparse emigration from New England and New York has also come in. On the heels of this has marched the great army from Germany, which has crowded the cities and swarmed upon the fields of this beautiful and fertile country. The Irish are less numerous, in proportion, than in the more northern cities. None of these elements of population, save the Northern and a portion of the German, are remarkably progressive; and, altogether, this belt of the Union contains the most irreconcilable population in the land; fully justifying the saying of the old Cincinnati judge, who always prefaced his charge to the jury with the sage remark, "Gentlemen of the jury, we live amid a very *hotorogenous* population."

This emigration has furnished to the West several elements, most valuable as foils and complements to the more radical North. The patient and plodding industry and invincible economy of the New-Jersey and Pennsylvania people have made a garden of vast districts, and piled up large accumulations of wealth. The tempestuous speculations which have desolated so many of the more enterprising Northern communities have been less violent in this region of sober industry. The opportunities of the Ohio Valley have also favored the growth of that legitimate manufacturing interest which is now the only reliable basis of prosperity for any inland city. There is no region of this country more blessed with comfort than this; and, when an elevated public spirit does finally awake, it will find a plethoric treasury in the accumulations of the last half-century. As yet, the higher forms of enterprise, in the way of donations for matters of great public utility and refinement, are not largely developed here. In Cincinnati, Louisville, and St. Louis, the persistent efforts of a few Northern men have secured a good system of public schools. But the general standard of education through all this region is far below the more northern latitudes. The colleges are drooping and second-rate; art and music, public lectures, and the higher grades of theatrical entertainment, meet a comparatively frigid encouragement. There is far less stir of ideas than in Michigan, Western New York, Northern Ohio, Indiana, and Illinois, among the masses. In politics this region has been for years the debatable ground of the Free States. The Germans of Cincinnati and St. Louis have saved those cities to freedom; and, in a few localities, the same spirit early achieved a triumph. But, up to the period of the war, this district was a reliable ally of the slave-power in any emergency. The treason of the North, outside the Irish Brigade and its American officers in a few cities, was found in this belt of population; whole reaches of South Ohio, Indiana, and Illinois being really as favorable to the rebellion as Tennessee, Missouri, or Kentucky: and on every election day the old battle rages anew. The churches are characterized by a lack of interest in theology. While generally adhering nominally to the oldest of "old-school" creeds, there is far less theological bigotry than in the new-school churches of New England. Christian institutions represent far more the social than the religious tendencies of the people of Cincinnati, St. Louis, and the country adjacent. There is not a first-class theologian or preacher in this whole area, between Pittsburg and Leavenworth. The leaders in the churches are men like Purcell, McIlvaine, Eliot, Clarke, and Post; admirable in social and executive capacity, but with no extended reputation as thinkers, writers, or preachers. A religion of the emotions, passions, and social sentiments, which warms the surface or explodes into revivals, leaving the will and practical life yet unchanged, is the most popular faith.

But in social life — as far as relates to the pleasant intercourse of families, neighbors, and friends, and the whole region of social amusement, general mingling of acquaintances, and an open-armed, affectionate hospitality to strangers — this district is a charming contrast to the radical North. There is a far greater portion of life given to making life agreeable than among the more intense peoples along the Lake shores. Wealth pours out in unstinted measures for personal indulgence, expensive and luxurious living, and foreign travel. As long as man desires to live for the sake of a genial "good time," these cities and villages, like Philadelphia, which they greatly resemble, are the most charming places in the West. The country, too, is far more attractive, and the climate more agreeable, than farther north.

But, so far, the most refined social life here runs in the aristocratic channels worn by the Southern leaders of society. The South gave the social law to Cincinnati, Louisville, St. Louis, and the valley of the Ohio. Almost every wealthy family has a Southern wing; and, before the Slave States plunged into rebellion, this region was a social suburb of the South. The law of Southern society is the exaltation of a family to permanent power, with no care for the corresponding elevation of the people. To build up a great family, connect it with other old and powerful families, educate the children abroad, and select its society from the aristocracy of the whole land, is its ideal of social life. All public spirit is subordinate to family aggrandizement; and, while men of vast wealth and high culture are spending fabulous sums on their family estates and foreign travels, great public institutions languish. With greater established wealth, social refinement, and expensive living than any Western city; with numbers of its rich citizens dwelling and travelling most expensively abroad,— Cincinnati has no large public library, no permanent gallery of art, no respectable theatre, no safe large hall for music or popular entertainments, no association with pluck to sustain a course of scientific or popular lectures, no literary periodical, and no concentration of its able and educated people to do any good thing. All good and great plans finally near the rim of this maelstrom of a luxurious sentimental life, and go down into the paradise of Catawba and oysters. The war has made a terrible inroad upon this old aristocracy of the valley of the Ohio. Too many of its leading families were rebel, or divided, to be forgiven. The people have already decreed its reconstruction, and when that comes a broader foundation will be laid; and, while we lose nothing of our present delightful social sentiment, we shall not make our refinement the silken covering of our selfishness, and contempt for the rights of man.

Out of this region has come, however, a large proportion of the eminent statesmen, jurists, and commanders of the West. Grant and Sherman and Sheridan, Logan and Oglesby, Rosecranz and Burnside, and their brilliant crowd of companions in glorious deeds; the Ewings and Shermans, Corwin, Stanton, Chase, Morton, Lincoln, Speed, Benton, — are by birth or education the growth of this region. With the exception of Cass and Douglas, both New-England men, no man of large proportions has yet got into national politics from the North-west. And while in war the bravery of its soldiery was eminent, neither the North-west nor Western New York produced a first-class general, save McPherson. The North-west swarms with acute lawyers, shrewd politicians, and able, agitating, radical statesmen of secondary calibre; but, somehow, the slower, less exciting society of our central region seems better adapted to the growth of those massive men who can calmly comprehend great interests of state, and put forth tremendous energies in organizing and leading men. The rampant individualism of the North-west breeds a personal conceit of infallibility unfavorable to greatness. The radical fever in the blood keeps the spirit lean, hectic, fiery, ready to put on wings and fly away into the future millennium; but not quite able to deal wisely with the present aspect of this mixed America.

The North-west, in its relations to the central region, reminds one of a splendid, eager, overpowering lover, battering away at the heart of a somewhat sleepy, but deep-souled and large-hearted maiden, who, alternately charmed and offended, at last surrenders, and becomes the wife of a man who is sure to come out at fifty a far nobler specimen of massive manhood than otherwise he could have been. The spirited cities and communities of the Lakes by turns ridicule and denounce our slow and undemonstrative region of the valleys; but the Lakes will end by marrying the valleys. Already Northern politics have revolutionized "Egypt," lifted up Indiana into a leading State, and sentenced the Pendletons and Pughs of Ohio to political exile. Northern ideas of industry, education, and society will follow. When this union of these States is complete, the Western character will be far more weighty, deliberate, and genial than now. May a good Providence speed that wedding-day!

In this final crystallization of the Western character, the German element of our population will doubtless be influential. Especially will the great masses of honest, industrious, kindly, slow but broad and deep-souled German farmers and mechanics and laborers, be a vast mine of healthy life, out of which can be drawn treasures of private and public worth. Even the Catholic Germans, who are the lowest of all, are not so obstinately wedded to the hierarchy that they will refuse to blend finally with the best elements of our population. The German Jews are often as genuine Americans as they " to the manor born." The Protestant German people are generally intelligent, industrious, economical, and virtuous as men can be who live chiefly in the realm of material comfort and social enjoyment. The complex despotisms of Central Europe have done their work upon them; for there is something in German despotism so subtle, elaborate, and persistent, that it seems to paralyze whole regions of the human mind.

The worst result of this Central European order of society on its subject masses is this paralyzing of the spiritual nature. Our German emigrants are now the most grossly materialistic of the American people. They live in this world as if there could be no other, and treat their bodies as if they were only the temples of a refined nervous organization. But this is a transition state. The thunders, lightnings, and earthquakes of our new Western life will split this stolid crust of materialism; and out of these good-natured, moderate, stingy, prosaic Hermanns and Minnas, will come the poets, the artists, the singers, the statesmen, and the saints of the West. They have no new ideas to give us; but their moderation, patience, and kindliness will be a fine atmosphere to pour around our fierce, restless intellectualism, and lunatic haste to build the millennium. The able men who represent this section of our German population are already among our most valuable citizens, and largely influential in our public, social, and religious affairs.

The least influential class of Germans will be that crowd of wild, long-haired, beer-drinking philosophers, who, on the strength of temporary residence inside a German University and banishment for revolutionary tendencies, put on Continental airs, and regard themselves as the legislators for the future American society. The headquarters of this tribe seems to be the State of Missouri; but they have active allies in all the cities and villages of the West. They are so near materialism and atheism in their central philosophy, that a wise man does not care to analyze the residuum of spiritual nature they leave in the crucible, to learn whether it be the soul or the sediment of the universe. In politics they are the wildest of impracticables, and were a sharp thorn in the side of long-suffering Abraham Lincoln during the war. Their political idol was John C. Fremont,— a romantic, miscellaneous French *savan*, accidentally made candidate for President and Commander-in-Chief in the West. Their social theories are admirably accommodating; their ideas of education, amusement, labor, the organization of society itself, ranging through all the varieties of communism.

Their personal conceit is of that boundless kind which only cholera or cold lead can abate. Now and then, one of these men can be caught and caged in Western society, where his learning or special skill can be made available. But they are almost useless for any work that demands respect for the spiritual realities, or the common sense even of the worldly American mind. They naturally affiliate with the Wendell-Phillips and Anna-Dickinson school of American reformers, though far more impracticable than they. Over their meer-schaums and their wine, in their obscure societies, they convince each other they are the breeze that blows the ship of Western society towards the "radicallissimi" millennium. But they are the barnacles and seaweed that will be scraped off the keel when the good ship is put in dry dock for repairs.

The grand mistake in all their estimate of American Society is their omission to recognize a spiritual nature in man, together with the religious, moral, social, and civil obligations flowing therefrom. Whatever may be true of this peculiar people, the American people are endowed with souls, and recognize the logical consequences of this fact. The Western American people cannot live this German socialistic life, because that is constructed on the idea that man is only a clever animal. Men who believe this can do a multitude of things as the end of existence, whose charm is dispelled by the suspicion of a nobler origin and a vaster destiny. Our people cannot guzzle beer, smoke in gardens, or roll on the grass with their sweethearts, wives, and babies on Sunday, because they believe that on one day an immortal being ought to live a higher life of the soul than he can easily achieve in the toil and unrest of the other six. They cannot be infinitely jolly, and full of careless, sensuous delight in their families; because they believe themselves responsible for the civilization of a mighty people, and do not see how all the social twittering and chirping in creation is to bring this about. If they were less bothered by an old American notion of honesty, they might come into some of the radical notions of property which titillate the boozy brains of these philosophical economists in the absence of pocket-money. They believe in teaching Young America to read and write the English language, confident that the Western mind will plough its way to a wisdom which shall overtop the learned folly of a thousand universities. The fact is, this clique is no faithful representative of the nobler side of Germany. To the real philosophy, the matchless criticism, the varied scholarship, the music, the theology, of the German mind, the West will make all due acknowledgment when its day comes. It will absorb as much of the charming geniality and catholic kindliness of its social life as can be blended with our own. But for this lager-beer brigade of atheistic anarchists it has only the regard of an express train, that thunders through a drove of mad bulls, leaving a few spots on the track to illustrate the result of an actual measurement of social forces.

Up to the present day, the Western character, thus forming from manifold combinations of the richest elements in the world, has been completely developed only in industry, politics, war, and the beginning of the people's school, church, and social life. The vast majority of large-minded men — the men who, in older communities, would be scholars, divines, statesmen, literati — are engrossed in business. Business in the West is nothing less than the shaping of a new empire into a fit area for the experiment of the largest civilization yet seen upon the earth. In politics, the broad foundations of mighty commonwealths are being laid, in which humanity can expand into a true American manhood and womanhood. The people's common-school will finally absorb all other forms of education, and culminate, as in Michigan, in free universities, which can command the largest culture of the age for every child. In war, it has made one demonstration which has written a new chapter in human history, and turned the eyes of the world on the people beyond the Alleghanies. But, beyond this, the Western character has not been fully developed. Its day for literature and art has not appeared. Its social life is the broadest and most genial in the world, but still fluctuating and crude, with great sloughs of coarseness and sensuality; and it doth not yet appear what it will finally become. Its organized religion represents its social far more than its religious life. But all things come in their order: "first the natural, afterward that which is spiritual;" and our children will see the West we only behold in vision, and recognize in it the most characteristic American life, and the broadest and highest organization into human affairs of the American Declaration of Independence and the Saviour's Golden Rule.

Art. II.—GEOGRAPHY OF PALESTINE.

The Comparative Geography of Palestine and the Sinaitic Peninsula. By CARL RITTER. Translated and adapted to the use of Biblical Students. By WILLIAM L. GAGE. 4 vols., 8vo. pp. xiv., 451, 418, 396, 410. New York: D. Appleton & Co. 1866.

FOUR solid octavos upon the Lands of the Bible, attractive to the eye by the bright color of their covers, by their luxury of paper and type, by the name of their author, and by the charm of their subject, which, worn as it is, never fairly becomes wearisome to a student of the Bible! Shall we not find in these the last word concerning the sacred soil, and the wise and final decision of the numerous disputed questions? Will not this work of the acknowledged master in geographical science,—the great organizer of the chaos of voyages, journals, and letters in all tongues,—will not this work bring an authority which we may implicitly trust, a verdict which cannot be set aside? That expectation is not realized. These full volumes, interesting as they are, settle hardly any important Biblical question. They give the best literature of the subject; but they leave readers to judge for themselves among the conflicting accounts and opinions. We are left more uncertain than ever, after the discussion of Ritter, whether the Serbal of Lepsius may not be the Sinai of the Exodus, and the traditional claim of the Mount of Moses be discredited. The place of Golgotha is still undetermined. We are at liberty still to find a site for Cana in Galilee, and to conjecture the place of Capernaum by the seaside. Elijah's abode is not yet identified; and even the discussion of the vexed questions of Tarshish and Ophir, exhaustive as this seems, does not give full satisfaction. The evidence for India preponderates, but not enough to exclude reasonable doubt.

The work of Ritter is rather the material for a geography of the holy lands, than a systematic treatise. It brings together the accounts of the best writers, ancient and modern, but does not fuse them into a scientific and positive statement. We learn what Greek and Hebrew, Arab and Christian, have said about the sites and the legends; but we have not a regular work of a new writer, built solidly and squarely from this foundation of conglomerate. And, in addition to this intrinsic defect of the work, there are several incidental defects in the translation which is here given. It is not a translation of the full work, but is abridged by the translator; and we are not satisfactorily informed on what principles the omitted matter has been left out. Neither the author nor the translator seems to have visited any of the regions which they describe; the knowledge which they have of the sacred lands is all at second-hand, — from reading, and not from journeying. Neither of them, too, is acquainted with the Arabic language, — an accomplishment indispensable in the thorough treatment of Arabian themes. There are no maps to illustrate the geographical details; and in these studies, for all but the fewest readers, accurate maps are essential to comfortable study. There are perpetual references in the text to statements and descriptions elsewhere given and in other works. And, as the original work was published fifteen years ago, no account is taken of the numerous important books which have appeared in the interval, except in the slight and frequently irrelevant notes of the translator. In the account of Jerusalem, for instance, hardly any use is made of the investigations and discoveries of Barclay, in the streets, caves, and water-courses, which he has so patiently explored.

Among those whom the translator includes as "too well known to the reader to require specification," is Sepp; yet neither the text nor the notes of these volumes show any actual acquaintance with the discussions of Sepp: indeed, it does not appear that the editor of these volumes has ever read one chapter of the voluminous and original work which he describes as so "well known." The same thing may be said of his acquaintance with numerous other works noted in his catalogue. There are also occasional annoying typographical blunders, which show carelessness of proof-reading.

But, with all these incidental defects, and with the original composite structure of the work, the thanks of Biblical students are due to the industrious editor of these volumes, for giving them, in such excellent, idiomatic English, a work of so much interest and value, — a work which condenses so well the substance of a Palestinian library. No matter if it does not settle the disputed questions: it does what is better, in bringing before us the land in its various aspects of winter and summer, sunshine and shade, beauty and ruin. With no attempt at fine writing or picture-painting, it brings before us a gallery of pictures, a series of panoramic views, more vivid and life-like than the fancies of such writers as De Saulcy, Lamartine, and Chateaubriand. Ritter makes the dry narrative of some writers that he quotes graphic, and tones down the imagination of other writers. If he does not interpret all the wonders and solve all the puzzles of Palestine and the Peninsula, he gives the land its proper relief and proportion before the eye; shows how the mountains stand, how the plains lie, and what hides in the caverns; shows the rocks and the men as they are now, and as they have been for thousands of years. The combinations of Ritter leave a picturesque effect, quite as real as the descriptions of Stanley; and he rounds off into graceful shape the accurate measurements of Robinson, who is his highest authority and his most trusted guide. The American scholar goes in the centre and at the head of that group of scholars and observers which the reader follows all through these volumes. When Ritter differs from Robinson, he apologizes for his temerity.

One would think, in the abundance of books which have been written about the Holy Land, by travellers, by naturalists, by pilgrims; by men of every name, faith, and nation; credulous and sceptical, prosaic plodders and poetic dreamers, — that the whole territory, shore and plain, hill and hollow, must have been described, leaving no foot of ground neglected. Yet this careful summary of the German geographer shows us the larger half of Palestine still waiting to be interpreted, — a *terra incognita*, within twenty miles of the sea, as real as the unknown region of inland Africa. Here is a country not larger than New Hampshire, and not unlike New Hampshire in its general shape and some of its physical characteristics, which, with its history of four thousand years, and all that has been written about it, cannot be pictured on a chart so surely as the State of yesterday. To read the four hundred works and more that have been written on Palestine in the last fifteen years, would take four years of close application; yet, at the end, one would not have gone over half of the land. And even of what seems to be explored, comparatively little is really told or known. Almost every one who has "walked about Zion," and uttered his impressions of the ancient city of God, adds his regret that his view has been so imperfect, and that he has seen and learned so little. Not one in all the books about Jerusalem, not all of them together, perfectly tell what is to be seen above ground there, much less what excavations anywhere would reveal. With all that has been written about the aqueducts and pools and cisterns, it is still uncertain how water was supplied to Solomon's temple, and where the water goes to that comes by the aqueduct now. After all the descriptions, a mystery hangs over the sacred land, even where it seems best known, as heavy and as dense as the mist upon the mountains of Moab and the Sea of Sodom. Neither the legends of piety nor the conclusions of science can dissolve that mystery.

It seems a disgraceful confession, after so much has been written about Palestine, so much money spent in travel there, that so little should be accurately known about it; that hundreds of travellers should go, one after another, along these short ways and through these small towns, and yet should show us their pathway only over a silent waste. How easy it would be to fill these chasms, to survey these vacant spaces, and to bring this confusion into order! Every traveller who goes through Palestine hopes and expects to help in removing this obscurity; to see something that no one else has seen; to make some new, if not some important, discovery. Only the fewest, however, seem to themselves to have discovered any thing; and most regret at the end that they did not see what others have seen. Even those who have made original observations are mortified to find that their views have been anticipated, and that their conclusions are doubted. The public opinion of the religious world almost settles it, that Palestine shall be an unknown land, and that exact science shall not get hold of this domain of ancient faith, over which reverence spreads an impenetrable golden cloud. Many who go there with the scientific spirit, to find truth and get knowledge, strangely find that this vanishes in the atmosphere of the land. They are careless of the inquiries that they came to make, and surrender themselves to the necessities of their position. They find that the knowledge which seemed so easy to gain is in fact extremely difficult, and they soon cease to trouble themselves about the questions which had invited them. Not one in a hundred of the Protestants who go to Jerusalem makes any investigation upon the spot of the site of the Holy Sepulchre, or vexes himself by reading the controversy of Robinson with Williams. Not one in fifty of those who cross the plain of Gennesaret stops to find among the rubbish the ruins of the cities of which Jesus spoke the doom. They quarrel with the Arabs at Medjdal, but make no effort to find the house of Mary in Magdala.

But there are many reasons why the multiplied narratives of travellers in the sacred land give no large increase of exact knowledge. In the first place, very few travellers stay long in the land; they go almost as quickly as they come, and hardly set foot in any of the cities before they arrange the plan of their departing. Economy of time and money compels to this hurry. The dragoman, hired in Egypt for the whole voyage, is paid for a specified number of days, and holds his victim close to the contract. Delays and excursions derange this contract; camel-men and mule-men refuse to obey orders, and curse their employer; and the care is to get through safely, rather than to make the journey profitable. Most of the published "tours" in Palestine have been of hardly more than two, four, or six weeks of stay in all the land, — from Dan to Beersheba. Jerusalem is described from the experiences of two or three days; Nazareth, from the impressions of a single night. It is preposterous to suppose that in this short time any thing new or valuable can be learned; that this mere passage of a fortnight's length, even though it be at so slow a pace, can acquaint the voyager either with scenery or people. A comfortable supper at the Carmelite convent, and a bath upon the beach, are by no means sufficient to show the "excellency" of the flowery mountain of Elijah's miracle. A swift walk through the bazaar of Gaza, and along the walls of Askelon, does not instruct very thoroughly in the lines of the Philistine land. And a halt of half an hour at the head of the Dead Sea, with a dragoman trembling in fear of Arab robbers and urging you to make haste and be off, does not make you competent authority on the height of those hills or the quality of those waters. In Italy or Germany, travellers take their own time, alter their plans, and stay as long as they please. It is not so easy to do this in Syrian travel. Then, again, it is difficult to find escort and protection, except upon the beaten routes of travel. The guides are afraid to try experiments, to go on any side-paths, or to venture on uncertain ways. There may be monsters in the caverns; there are, almost certainly, robbers and assassins. When a traveller goes into these "by and forbidden paths," he does it at his own risk and peril. The danger of these side excursions is doubtless exaggerated; but the bravest Frank cannot impart his own courage to the cautious natives or dispel their fears. There are regions in Galilee that no dragoman could be brought to traverse for love or money. He would as soon agree to show the way to

Ararat, as to go around the Lake of Tiberias. Few travellers are prepared to take the risk of these journeys without some escort, and they must pass these tempting breaks in the hills, because they cannot go through them alone. If twenty men, resolute and fearless, strongly armed, could go together, they might perhaps get guides for an eccentric and zigzag progress, might climb all the hills, visit all the wadies, explore all the tombs and caverns, and find the name of every village. But the travellers of this kind go by *twos* and not by twenties. The large parties are those who prefer to keep to the regular paths, and see the things that the handbooks show them. It is vexatious to an enthusiastic traveller, who comes to Palestine determined to explore the land faithfully and traverse it in every direction, to find that no one will guide him in any new way, or will go with him on any venture. The first words that he hears are warnings of danger and advice to keep in the regular track. The site of Shiloh is hardly a mile from the path between Bethel and Shechem; yet how few travellers on that path turn aside to see the place where was the earliest sacred city of Israel! It is only a sign of rashness to attempt these side excursions, which take time and bring peril. Only on the highways of Syria is a traveller safe; and these highways are few.

Moreover, the tastes and habits of the residents in Palestine do not assist scientific study of the land. Neither Jew nor Greek, Moslem nor Christian, cares any thing to settle questions of archæology or to construct anew the map of Canaan. You find no science of the land in the houses, or in the shops, or in the cloisters. The Greek monks in Jerusalem only care to know the way to the convent in St. Saba: the Latin monks are satisfied to direct pilgrims to the fords of the Jordan. It is impossible to make the dull Hebrews, who mumble rabbinical lore in the schools of Tiberias, comprehend your curiosity about the Sea of Galilee. Indeed, it is amazing to these people that sane men should go travelling in this solitary region for mere purposes of knowledge. They suspect some end of trade in this wandering. The Arabs have no word to describe the scientific traveller. If he is not a hadji (a pilgrim), whose religion brings him to the shrines, he must be a howadji (a merchant), who is seeking to buy or sell. A few of the monks and a few of the dragomen have borrowed some of the facts of the guide-books; but the most of them are utterly unconcerned to know more of the land and its history than belongs to their ecclesiastical legends or their daily routine. Moslem archæology in Palestine is summed up in the sacredness of Omar's mosque, and in the confession that Mohammed is the prophet of God. Christian archæology only keeps the local tradition. All that the monks of Nazareth can tell you about their city is the site of Mary's house, of Joseph's workshop, of the meeting-place of the disciples, and the Rock of Precipitation. The sacredness of the land, to the Samaritans, is all centred in their ancient synagogue, their yellow parchment-roll, and their altar on Gerizim. It is hopeless to ask for direct information from any class. Where they really know what you want to know, there will be a lie on their lips as they answer you.

Ignorance of the language spoken in Palestine is another effectual hindrance to travellers in attempting to study the antiquities of the land. Except in the few cities which are already quite well known, the Arabic is the universal dialect; and, to strangers, the Arabic is as unintelligible as Chinese or Choctaw. Very few of those who can read the literary language, and have mastered the flowing characters, can understand the jargon of Arab gutturals as they break harshly from the throat of a peasant or a Bedouin. Not one in fifty of the writers who would tell us something new about the land, could hold a conversation of five minutes with the natives of the land, on any important topic of history or fact. The Arabic is a very difficult language to learn thoroughly. Dr. Smith, who had made a study of it for thirty years, told us, even when his Arabic translation of the New Testament was nearly completed, that he was not at all satisfied with his knowledge of the language, and that he was every day learning some new words and phrases. Yet, without this power of talking directly with the people, it is impossible to learn much of their antiquities and their traditions, or to connect the natural features and productions of the land with the Biblical story, with the fauna and flora of the ancient Hebrews. How else can any one find the rose of Sharon, the lily of the valley, the unicorn, the conies (that feeble folk), and the dragons in their clefts? How else shall the sites of towns be identified? The main connection between the ancient and modern ages, between the former and present races, is in the words of similar sound. The Arabic names are all that tell of the famous villages of Canaan, and the cities renowned in the story of Israel. With this key, Robinson was able to unlock some of the closed doors, and to find some of the lost places. And this is the only key worth much in exploring the land. The language is the only fossil relic of much value in reading the former ages there.

Add to these the other hindrances in the way of travel: the climate, for half the year so hot and debilitating; the wretched roads, if indeed the bridle-paths through ravines and over rocks and precipices may be called roads; the absence of all wheel carriages, making it difficult to transport the instruments and conveniences of scientific study; the hostility of the people, sheikhs and rabble alike, sometimes breaking out in acts of violence; the lying directions, which turn a traveller upon the wrong track; the extortions, which wear out his patience; the combined annoyance of the laziness, dulness, brutality, and falsehood which he finds all around him, — and the wonder is rather, not that so little is learned, but that any thing is learned. Then, in digesting the fragments of information, there is infinite perplexity in harmonizing these contradictory stories, and finding the truth. No task can be more perplexing than the task of sifting out the local traditions of Palestine, and deciding what and how much to believe. It will not do to take extreme ground on either side, — to believe every thing that you hear, or to believe nothing that you hear, — to resolve, with the Rev. George Williams, that all legends of the Church are trustworthy, and must be maintained at any rate; or with the good Dr. Robinson, that the convents are the centres of lies, and that the Church repeats a story is a good reason for doubting it. The only safe theory about the matter is, that a good deal of the tradition is true, and a good deal is false. How much then, is true, and how much is false? Shall the Jewish tradition of the synagogue on Mount Zion be rejected as readily as the tradition of the house of Caiaphas on that hill? Shall the site of the Tanner's home at Joppa be treated like the rock of Andromeda in that harbor, and be slighted as no better than a Pagan fable? Shall the genuineness of Jacob's well be doubted, because the ruins of a church are scattered around its curb-stones?

The chief reason, however, why more has not been learned about Palestine in these constantly repeated narratives of travel is, that there is not really much interest, either of the men who journey or of the public who read their narratives, to know any thing more about the land. The Jewish, Christian, and even the scientific world are quite content to let the larger part of the territory stay in the obscurity that covers it, and leave it as a possession to the rude Arab tribes. They have no anxiety to find all the hills and valleys, towns and cities, that were noted in those wars of Joshua and Jehosaphat, or to identify the modern with the ancient names. They are as indifferent to this useless restoration of the old Hebrew order, as they are to the stories themselves in the Hebrew record. Before men will earnestly investigate the topography of the land of the tribes, they must get more zeal in studying the story of the tribes. The Bible Society tells, in its annual statements, in how many scores of tongues, at the cost of how many thousands of dollars, its millions of copies are printed. Yet in what book is so much matter printed only to be utterly neglected and wasted? Year by year, the churches are called to contribute their money for Bible-printing and distribution; while the members know, that one half at least of what they so send forth they will not read themselves, and no one will read with any interest. How many, in Christian churches, understand, or care to understand, four-fifths of the Hebrew prophecies,— those "burdens" of Moab and Tyre and Ammon; what Joel and Jeremy and Nahum and Zechariah have written of promise or of woe? How many read with pleasure the annals of the Hebrew kings after Solomon's time, much less the chronicle of the wars of Joshua? Except as part of the "proper lessons," would any one hear, even in the church, the details of the books of Leviticus and Numbers? By far the larger number of those who read the Bible pass over these details as tedious and not edifying. The stories of the Patriarchs; of the residence of Israel in Egypt; of Moses and Sinai; of Samuel, Saul, David, and Solomon, — are really the substance of all the historical part of the Old Testament which is cared for by Christian readers. A few add to these the stories of Samson, Gideon, the later kings, Ezra, and Nehemiah. In the prophecies, a few pages of Isaiah, Ezekiel, and Micah are found sufficient for profitable use. Next to the Book of Psalms, perhaps even more than the Book of Psalms, the Book of the Old Testament which is most completely used is the sceptical Book of Ecclesiastes. In spite of the seeming irreverence of the wish, not a few, we must think, have longed, in their use of the Bible, to have an *abridged edition*, which should retain what is instructive and pleasant to read, and leave out wholly what is dry, obscure, and repulsive. We heard a Christian mother once say, that, if she supposed that her daughters would read all that is in the Bible, she should not dare to put it into their hands; that she felt safe in giving it to them, because there was so little of it that they would care to read.

This want of interest in the details of the Hebrew story naturally implies want of interest in the details of the Hebrew land. The interest of most who read and write about the land is a Christian interest; and this interest has only a few centres. Pure physical science cares no more about Palestine than about Australia: indeed, not so much; since Australia is so much larger, newer to the world of science, and so much more curious in its abundance of species. The only scientific question of first importance in Palestine is the formation of the Jordan valley and the Ghor, from Mount Hermon to the salt hill of Usdum; how this strange chasm came, — whether from sinking or breaking, whether worn by the rush of waters, or torn by outburst of fires; whether there was ever an outlet to the Red Sea, across the sand or under the sand. That is an attractive question to men who care nothing about the wife of Lot, the grotto of Elijah, or the house of Zaccheus, and have no interest in the pilgrims' bathing place, or the battle at Gilboa. But, except this prime problem, all other questions of physical science which the sacred land suggests are of secondary moment. Did the sea ever come close to the walls of Gaza? Was the Kedron ever a running stream? How extensive were the forests three thousand years ago? Are the caves mostly natural or artificial holes in the rock? Were there ever lions in the land? Such questions as these, interesting as they may be to Biblical students, have no special charm for geologists or naturalists, who have been accustomed to the larger regions, where there are coal formations, fossil remains, and glaciers in the clefts of the hills. It is impossible to make of Palestine a country so interesting to the naturalist as Norway or Switzerland. Except for its one great scientific problem, and apart from the religious associations which seem to consecrate, and so to dignify, all that belongs to it,— the sacred land would not specially attract the feet of scientific wanderers.

It is a religious interest, and now mostly a Christian religious interest, that draws the travel and sustains the charm in Palestine. Some Jews go there; and in a few places — Jerusalem, Safed, Tiberias, Nablous, Hebron — they have communities: but among these Jews there is no spirit of inquiry, and they make no effort to re-instate their history, even in the place of their habitation. The Jew on Mount Zion has to get the Christian to show him the probable site of the citadel of David, and the place where Solomon was crowned. When a Jewish traveller visits the land to-day, he goes not to study its antiquities, but to see his brethren, to learn their circumstances, and to carry them relief. Sir Moses Montefiore and Leopold Frankl, baronet and poet, made no effort to find where Melchisedek had his palace, or where Deborah sung her song.

The Christian interest in Palestine is fastened mostly to those spots which are in some way connected with the story of Christ,—Bethlehem, Nazareth, the Sea of Galilee, the place of baptism at Jordan, Cæsarea, Philippi, Jericho, Bethany, Jacob's well, the Mount of Olives, and the city of Jerusalem. When one has seen these, he seems to have seen most of the sacred land that is worth seeing: he has seen what he went there to see. These are the points round which his impressions of the land are gathered. Interesting no doubt, but of secondary interest, are the spots which hold tradition of the heroes in Hebrew history; the tomb of Abraham at Hebron, the tomb of Rachel, the tomb of Joseph, the cities of the Philistines, the city of Ahab and Herod in Samaria. But it is utterly impossible to awaken in Christian hearts much zeal for discovering the localities of Israel in the days of the Kings or the days of the Judges, much less of the Jewish wars of the Maccabees and in the Roman dominion. The questions about Michmash and Gibeah and Timnath and Bethshan seem tedious and unprofitable. But for the song of the prophetess, Kishon, that mighty river, would have no more charm than any sluggish brook; and the command of Joshua to the moon and sun will not turn a Christian traveller from his path to find the valley of Ajalon. The same indifference which Christian readers feel in the Biblical narrative of these things, is manifest when they are on the ground and come into the neighborhood. This indifference is no sign of slender faith or lack in piety. It is as characteristic of Catholics as of Protestants, and is rather the sign of strength in faith. The man who seeks most diligently for the "well of David" in Bethlehem is he who has very moderate confidence in the legend of the Nativity.

Part of this indifference is due, no doubt, to the feeling which separates Jesus so widely from all who came before him, from all the men of his race, and treats him not as a Nazarene Jew, the son of human parents, but as the Saviour of all men and nations, miraculously born. If the new Gospel has abrogated the old Law with its traditions, and has made a new epoch in the history of the world and its religion, it seems needless to trace the ways and monuments of that old history. We may separate the Palestine of Jews from the

Palestine of Christ and his followers, as we separate in our
editions the Old Testament from the New Testament, — may
reserve only some small parcels of the land which seem to
fasten themselves to the spirit and prophecy of Christ's story,
just as we sometimes bind the Psalms in a volume with the
Gospels and Epistles. If Jesus were only another Joshua,
only a Jewish leader and deliverer, the same heed might be
given to the earlier as to the later of the names. But the
work and memory of the Son of God in the sacred land
suffer in Christian hearts no rival, whether warrior, king, or
prophet. We look unmoved upon the hill of Elijah or Saul
or Gideon, when we have walked upon the Mount of Olives.
Of what use to follow the chariots and spearmen of those
armies of Israel, when we have seen Calvary, where was
fought the great conflict of Satan with God, and the world's
redemption was accomplished in the death of the perfect
Saviour? The cell of Socrates in Athens does not spoil the
enjoyment of the Parthenon and the Pnyx, for a worshipper
of the sage; but the footprints of the Christ in Palestine
obliterate the impressions of the teachers who went before
Him. The real history, the history which has enduring
worth, seems to begin with Him, and that which came before
to be half mythical.

And yet it is curious to note, in solid works of Biblical
geography, how large a portion is given to those investigations
for which most readers care so little. Appended to this work
of Ritter are *eighteen* columns of Scripture "texts," referred
to in the four volumes. Of these, but little more than *two*
columns are of texts from the New Testament; while *nearly
ten* columns are taken from the Pentateuch and the Books of
Joshua and Judges. Putting out of view the first volume, —
which is devoted to the Sinaitic Peninsula, where, of course,
all the texts must be taken from the Old Testament, — in the
other three volumes at least three quarters of the references
are to passages in the earlier Hebrew history. This may show
us how small a portion of the land the Christian story covers.
The Apostolic Christian history gives almost no help to one
who would arrange the Scripture geography. In the sixteen

hundred and seventy-five pages of these volumes of Ritter, there are only *four* references to *all* the Epistles together, not one to any Epistle of Paul, and only twenty to the Book of Acts. If the geography of the land were reduced to the New-Testament narrative, to what John and the Synoptics have written, it would have, indeed, meagre proportions. Where, then, would be all the land of the Philistines and the plain of Sharon? Where would be the whole province of Judea, south and east of Bethlehem? Where, except in a single spot, would be the whole central province of the land,— the hills of Ephraim and the plain of Issachar? The immense disproportion between the circumstances and the work of the Saviour of the world appears more strikingly, when we consider how small a part of this small land on the Mediterranean shore was really known and visited by the Emanuel of Galilee, how small a surface saw the signs of the great salvation, in what narrow place "the fulness of time" brought its fulfilment.

And yet, on the other hand, it is the New-Testament story which the aspect of Palestine to-day best illustrates. The Christian traveller finds what he goes there to seek,— the footprints of his Lord. While most of the Jewish story is effaced and lost there, the Christian record has its clear sign in Judea and Samaria and Galilee. The relics of the Judges and the Kings and the Prophets are few and obscure; but everywhere the Evangelists seem to repeat their word. When one stands upon the Mount of Olives, it is hard, even in imagination, to see here the centre and crown of Solomon's glorious realm; but it is easy to see the city as the Saviour saw it, and to feel all the force of his sad lament. Judah has no dwelling-place now upon the hills of Judea; and you find Jewish customs in their freshness and vitality more in the cities of Europe than in the cities of Canaan. In Amsterdam, in Prague, in Frankfort, in Vienna, even in Rome, there is as much of the Old Testament as in the city of Jerusalem. The justice of the cadi's court there is not according to the statutes of Moses; the merchandise of the bazaars is not in the Jewish style of traffic; the dress, language, manners, of the Hebrew race there are not those of the ancient day. The geography and antiquities of Palestine, which are most trustworthy as well as most interesting, are the Christian geography and antiquities. Making all allowance for monkish lies, the Palestine of the time of Christ, narrow as it is, stands out in better relief than the Canaan which Joshua gave to the tribes: the Roman province, with Pilate and Herod for rulers, appears now in the Pachalik, — half Turk, half Arab. Christians have *a home* in the land, possessions which they hold securely; and these possessions are monuments of the first time of their faith. But what home have the Jews in the land of their fathers? what secure possession has Israel, either in Shiloh or Bethel or Jerusalem, either on the hill or on the plain? His monuments are only in the harsh names of a hostile faith.

We would not be thought, in these remarks, to undervalue the labors of those who have set themselves so patiently to discover and to explain the Jewish geography of the sacred land. We rather welcome any addition of this kind to our knowledge, however slight it may be. The laborers deserve praise all the more that their work has so little sympathy. The multiplication of books about Palestine cannot keep back the tendency to join this land to the other lands of the world, instead of viewing it as a land separate and apart. In Ritter's work, Palestine is only one chapter, and by no means the best or most satisfactory chapter, in his great "Erdkunde," his universal geography. We bring the history and place of the Holy Land into the history and place of civilization, and take it along with the ancient empires. We do not care for the scrutiny which shall show how God had his special abode on these hillsides and in these cities, and how the Infinite Creator was fastened to the narrowness of a Semitic tribe; but we receive thankfully any thing which shall show the habitation and development of that great idea which has given us the spiritual Father of our Christian faith. It is a commendation of the work, as the editor of these volumes suggests in his preface, that it is written by a Christian believer. Ritter's faith, nevertheless, was not a literal Bibliolatry, that found in the Scripture records a word of God unlike and apart from all other teaching of science or Providence. There is no Biblical cant in his investigation. Porter, in that beautifully printed, but most hasty, superficial, and self-sufficient description of "Syria's Holy Places," recently published, gives a long catalogue of what he calls "texts of Scripture illustrated," in his narrative. It is only weaving into the narrative passages of Scripture, selected from their seeming aptness, leaving the pietistic impression of some peculiar work of God in the destruction of these forsaken cities. These perpetual quotations from the Prophets are insufferably wearisome, and take from the work its scientific credit. A geographer of the Holy Land justifies his Christian intelligence and sincerity better in showing what time and change, the natural forces and the natural laws, have done there, than in awakening echoes of lost prophetic voices, though these were once the word of Jehovah. It will not do to show on the face of the land any other influence, whether in deluge or fire, or the ravage of war or the fall of kings, than the influence of the elements and of the passions of men everywhere and in all lands. The "*comparative* geography" must be that which compares not only the face of the land with the visions of Ezekiel and Isaiah, but with the face of other lands, — with China and India and Persia and Egypt and Greece; the laws of Moses with the laws of Brahma and Confucius and Menu and Lycurgus. It is the best service to get for Palestine its proper place in universal geography and history.

The theory of Ritter is the wise theory, that the physical conditions of the land make the characteristics of any people, and that the Jews were no exceptions to this general rule; that Israel was made God's people by its dwelling-place, and not by arbitrary choice. We cannot close this notice of his work more fitly, than in repeating this true and beautiful passage from the introductory chapter of his second volume: —

"Within the narrow limits of Palestine we must look for the foundations of that kingdom of truth, as well as of error, which has now become a subject of historic inquiry; we must trace the latest results to their primitive causes in the geographical conditions of the country: for even here there is opportunity for such agents as the soil under man's foot, and the atmosphere over his head, to have influence. If every garden plot owes a part of the rapid progress in flowering and in fruitage to the skilful and careful hand of the gardener, cannot every land in God's wide creation trace, under His wise direction, some measure of mutual action and re-action between the country and the people who inhabit it? Our historians have many things yet to learn; and even yet they continue to fall into one-sided speculations, which betray them and lead them astray. But here is one elemental truth: history does not lie in a domain adjoining nature, so to speak, but actually within the bosom of nature; history and nature are at one, as God looks down upon them from his canopy of stars. In studying the human soul, the mode of its training, the way of its working, — and that is history, — we cannot leave out of our view the outward field in which it finds its home, the world where it meets the phenomena which it investigates. In spite of the self-confidence of that pretence which science sometimes makes in the person of some of her votaries, — of finding all that she needs in the soul of man and in a mere world of subjective realities, — we may assert, that a close study of the outward world, as the soul's training-place, is the only true key to history."

Art. III. — MADAME RÉCAMIER AND HER FRIENDS.

Memoirs and Correspondence of Madame Récamier. Translated from the French and edited by ISAPHENE M. LUYSTER. Boston: Roberts Brothers. 1867. 16mo, pp. xxii., 408.

WE have here the two octavo volumes of the original French, admirably re-arranged, condensed, and translated into faithful and elegant English. Nothing of the original which is important, instructive, or entertaining, has been sacrificed. Yet the Messrs. Roberts Brothers, whose publishing house is distinguishing itself for the valuable and handsome books it issues, offer the work to the public, in a single charming volume, at less than a third of the cost of the original. It is one of the best books of the kind ever produced, full of an interest both fascinating and edifying. As a book of culture in the art of noble character and noble manners, we wish it might be thoughtfully read by every intelligent woman in our land. It would do a world of good, if, as is supposed, the choicest examples have a contagious power to impart their traits to those who gaze on them. We thank Miss Luyster for the graceful performance of her fine task, and trust she will win honor and remuneration.

Julie Bernard was born at Lyons, in 1777; was married, when fifteen, to the wealthy banker, Jacques Récamier, at Paris; and died there in 1849. In 1859, her memoirs and correspondence were edited by her niece, Madame Lenormant. We cannot but deeply deplore that this copious collection contains so little from the pen of Madame Récamier herself: the brief and rare specimens of her composition preserved are of such choice merit, that we must deem the destruction of her manuscripts, by her own order, a great loss to the reader. But a score of her most illustrious contemporaries have left descriptions of her and tributes to her, from which a satisfactory knowledge of her character may be gained.

The life of Madame Récamier is interesting in a pre-eminent degree, on account of the warmth, elevation, and fidelity of the friendships which filled it. Her personal loveliness and social charm made her a universal favorite, and gave her an unparalleled celebrity. But, full as her career was of romantic adventures, rich as it was in brilliant associations, its key-note throughout, its strongest interest at every point, is friendship. Unlike those of so many of the famous women of France, her friendships were as remarkable for their rational soundness, purity, and tenacity, as for their fervor. They were free from every thing morbid or affected. An adverse fate forbade the love to which she seemed destined by her bewitching beauty and grace: and a certain divine chill in the blood, a stamp from Diana in the senses, turned all the warmth of affection upwards into the mind, to radiate thence in her face and manners, and to make her a high priestess of friendship. The pure and wise Ballanche, who idolized her, said that she was originally an Antigone, of whom people vainly wished by force to make an Armida.

Her nominal husband is supposed by some to have been in reality her father; the marriage being merely a titular one, to secure his fortune to her in case of his death by the guillotine, of which he was then in daily dread. Deprived of the usual domestic vents of affection, her rich heart naturally led her to crave the best substitute, friendship. And her matchless personal gifts, together with her truly charming traits of character, enabled her permanently to win and experience this in a very exalted degree. Reserving her many deep friendships with women for mention on a later page, we proceed to speak first of her memorable friendships with men, — friendships which it is refreshing and delightful to study. Her three principal friends were Montmorency, Ballanche, and Chateaubriand; all three original and extraordinary characters, and all three worthy — in spite of some drawbacks on the part of the last — of the extraordinary devotion she gave them. The letters of these three possess extreme interest. Especially, those of the first named are the unique monument of an affection whose purity and delicacy equalled its vivacity and depth.

Matthieu de Montmorency was one of the noblest of the nobility of France, alike in birth and in spirit. In his youth a voluptuous liver, he had afterwards undergone a genuine and solemn conversion. While in Switzerland, the news of the guillotining of his brother gave him such a shock, that it revolutionized his motives and his life. The gay, impassioned, fascinating man of the world became an austere and fervent Christian. The rich sensibility he had formerly spent in amours and display, henceforward ennobled by wisdom and sanctified by religion, lent a singular charm of tenderness and loftiness to his friendships. The memory of his own errors gave a gracious charitableness to his judgments; his sorrow imparted an incomparable refinement to his air; his grave and devout demeanor inspired veneration; his sweet magnanimity drew every unprejudiced heart. He had long been a fervent friend of Madame de Staël, when the youthful virgin-wife, the dazzling Julie Récamier, formed an engrossing attachment to that gifted woman. Drawn mutually to this common goal, the fore-ordained friends soon met. He was then fifty years old; she, twenty-three. Her extraordinary charms of person and spirit,— her dangers, exposed, with such bewildering beauty and such peculiar domestic relations, to all the seductions of a most corrupt society, awakened at once his admiration, his sympathy, and his pity. An increasing intimacy revealing her irresistible sweetness of disposition, her many gifts and virtues, Montmorency found himself ever more and more drawn to her by the united bonds of reason, conscience, and affection. He undertook not merely to be her friend in the ordinary pleasures of sympathy, but, as a Christian, under the eye of God, sincerely and profoundly to befriend her. From that moment until his death, his devotion, though once severely tried, never faltered nor slumbered. He was to her more than a father and a brother; he was her guardian angel, as pure in feeling, as watchful to warn, to restrain, to encourage, to support, and console. For many years, through trying reverses of fortune, he visited her every evening. For many years each had a vital share in all that concerned the other; and, when he died, it was as if a large part of her being had been suddenly torn out of her soul, and transferred to heaven. The letters that passed between them form one of the most delightful and impressive records ever made of Christian friendship,— a record in which wisdom and duty are as prominent as affection.

Pierre Simon Ballanche, one of the most delicate and philosophical of French authors, most disinterested and affectionate of men, the perfect model of a friend, was born at Lyons in 1776. He was first introduced to Madame Récamier, in 1812, by their common friend, the generous and eloquent Camille Jordan. Ballanche, in an enthusiastic attachment to a noble, portionless young girl, had suffered a disappointment so deep, that it caused him to dismiss all thoughts of marriage for ever. He sought to ease the burden of rejected love by letting the sadness it had engendered exhale in a literary work. This exquisite work, called "Fragments," Jordan induced Madame Récamier to read: he also described to her the refined and magnanimous character of the author. Thus prepared, and aided by her own keen discernment, she immediately detected his choice talents, his rare vein of sentiment, his abiding hunger for affection. Ballanche was a philosopher of solitude, a poet and priest of humanity, — spending his days far from the crowd and uproar of the world, — his proper haunt the summits of the loftiest minds, the mysterious cradle of the destinies of society. His soul was an Æolian harp through which the music of the pre-historic ages played. Chastity and sorrow were two geniuses who unveiled to him the destiny of man. His philosophy, so redolent of the heart and the imagination, amidst the material struggles and selfishness of the time, has been compared to a chant of Orpheus in the school of Hobbes. The friendship which Madame Récamier gave this lonesome, sad, expansive, and lofty spirit, was as if a goddess had come down from heaven on purpose to minister to him. She brought him the attention he needed, the sympathy he pined for, the position and praise which were so grateful to his sensitive nature. She strove to win for him from others the recognition he deserved, to call out his powers, and to show off his gifts to the best advantage. Ballanche was timid, awkward, ugly, with no wealth, with no rank; but, in the sight of Madame Récamier, the treasures and graces of his soul were an intrinsic recommendation far superior to these outward advantages, and she was ready to honor it to the full.

Never was kindness more worthily bestowed; never was it more gratefully received. "I often," he says, "find myself astonished at your goodness to me. The silent, weary, sad man, whom others neglect, you notice, and seek with infinite tact to draw him out. You are indulgence and pity personified, and you compassionately see in me a kind of exile. Together with the feeling of a brother for a sister, I offer you the homage of my soul." From that time he belonged to her, and could not bear to live separate from her. Under her appreciation and encouragement, he expanded like a plant moved from a chill shade into the sunshine. His devotion was entire, and sought no equal return. It was simply the natural expression of his gratitude to her, his admiration of her, his delight in seeing her and being with her. His love for her, like that of Dante for Beatrice, was a religious worship, a celestial exhalation of his soul, utterly free from every alloy of earth and sense. For thirty-four years, he was almost inseparable from her. He removed to Paris, that he might look on her every day. Wherever she travelled, abroad or at home, he was one of her companions. At her receptions of company, the fame whereof has gone through the world, he was invariably an honored and active assistant. And, despite his deformed face, and uncouth appearance and bearing, he was a great favorite with all the favored guests at the Abbaye-aux-Bois. To those who really knew him, his large, beaming eyes and noble forehead, his disinterested goodness, his literary and philosophical accomplishments, his modest unworldliness and attentive sympathy, redeemed his physical blemishes, and covered them with a radiance superior to that of mere beauty. The letters of Ballanche to Madame Récamier are charming in their originality. His praise of her is marked by an inimitable grace of sincerity and refinement: —

"Your presence, so full of magic, the sweet reflection of your soul, will be to me a powerful inspiration. You are a perfect poem; you are poesy itself. It is your destiny to inspire, mine to be inspired. An occupation would do you good; your disturbed and dreamy imagination has need of aliment. Take care of your health, spare your nerves: you are an angel who has gone a little astray in coming into a world of agitation and falsehood."

What a reading of her inmost heart through her envied position, what matchless felicity of representation, in this picture of herself sent to her in one of his letters! —

"The phœnix, marvellous but solitary bird, is said often to weary of himself. He feeds on perfumes, and lives in the purest region of the air; and his brilliant existence ends on a pyre of odoriferous woods kindled by the sun. More than once, without doubt, he envies the lot of the white dove, because she has a companion like herself."

In his high estimate of her talent, he tried to persuade her to undertake a literary work, — the translation and illustration of Petrarch, which she actually began, but left unfinished.

"Your province, like my own," he writes, "is the interior of the sentiments; but, believe me, you have at command the genius of music, of flowers, of brooding meditation, and of elegance. Privileged creature, assume a little confidence, lift your charming head, and fear not to try your hand on the golden lyre of the poets. It is my mission to see that some trace of your noble existence remains on this earth. Help me to fulfil my mission. I regard it as a blessing that you will be loved and appreciated when you are no more. It would be a real misfortune if so excellent a being should pass merely as a charming shadow. Of what use is memory, if it does not perpetuate the beautiful and good?"

This league of lofty friendship, of endearing intercourse and service, held good while a whole generation of mortals came upon the stage and disappeared; and it throve with growing validity in the latest old age of the fortunate parties. Ballanche believed, after the death of his mother, that he saw her, several successive mornings, enter his room, and ask him how he had passed the night. This ocular illusion affords us an affecting glimpse of his heart. He wrote to his friend, "Antiquity confides its weariness and grief to us, without doubt, to beguile us from our own." — "Had Orpheus never met Eurydice, his existence would have remained incomplete; and, in place of the cruel grief of her loss, he would have known another grief not less intense, — solitude of soul." — "I am alone, and the solitude weighs heavily upon me. Permit me to solace myself by talking a moment with you." — "I protest to you in all sincerity, that my one absorbing thought is my warm feeling of friendship for you. I have need to be assured by you, and that as often as possible, that this sentiment shall not end in unhappiness for me. The thought of that is an agony which terrifies me. You are so kind, you have so much sympathy for all unhappy persons, that I fear it is through pity and condescension that you show kindness to me." This expression was in the year 1816; but all such uneasiness soon vanished, and he learned to rely on her sincere cordiality with a serene assurance which was the richest luxury of his life.

In 1830, Ballanche, publishing his chief work, the "Palingénésie Sociale," dedicated it to Madame Récamier, in a form whose delicacy and fervor made it one of the most exquisite pieces of praise ever paid in letters. Alluding to Canova's portrait of Madame Récamier, in the character of the celestial guide of Dante, he says:—

"An artist enveloped in a grand renown, a sculptor who has just shed so much glory on the illustrious land of Dante, and whose graceful imagination the masterpieces of antiquity have so often exalted, one day, for the first time, saw a woman who seemed to him a living apparition of Beatrice. Full of that religious emotion which is the gift of genius, he immediately commanded the marble, always obedient to his chisel, to express the sudden inspiration of the moment; and the Beatrice of Dante passed from the vague region of poetry into the domain of substantial art. The sentiment which dwells in this harmonious countenance, now become a new type of pure and virgin beauty, in its turn inspires artists and poets. This woman, whose name I would here conceal, whom I would veil even as Dante does, is endowed with all the generous sympathies of our age. She has visited, with the select few, the haunts of lofty minds. Here, in this seat of imperturbable peace, of unalterable security, she has formed noble friendships,—those friendships which have filled her life, which, born under immortal auspices, are sheltered alike from time, from death, and from all human vicissitudes. I address myself, then, to her who has been seen as a living apparition of Beatrice. Can she encourage me with her smile,—with that serious smile of love and of grace, which expresses at once confidence and pity for the pains of probation, for the burdens of an exile that should end,—sweet and calm augury, wherein is revealed, even in the present, the certainty of our infinite hopes, the grandeur of our definitive destinies?"

When the good Ballanche was taken dangerously ill, Madame Récamier had just undergone an operation for cataract, and was under strict orders from the physician not to leave her couch. But, on the announcement of the condition of Ballanche, she immediately rose, and went to his bedside, and watched by him until his last breath. In the anxiety and tears of this experience, she lost all hope of recovering her sight. Her incomparable friend received the supreme hospitality at her hands, and was buried in her family tomb,— leaving, in his works, a delightful picture of his mind; in his life, a perfect model of devotion. The removal of this soul, echo of her own; this heart, wholly filled by her; this mind, so gladly submissive to her influence,— could not but leave a mighty void behind. For, notwithstanding the wondrous array of gifts, attractions, and attentions lavished on her, her deep sensibility and interior loneliness made her often unhappy. She would sit by herself, in the twilight, playing from memory choice pieces of the great masters of music, the tears rolling down her cheeks. Friendship was more than a delight: it was a necessity to her.

De Tocqueville pronounced an exquisite eulogy by the grave of Ballanche, in the name of the Academy. La Prade, in the funeral address he delivered at Lyons, the birthplace of the deceased, said, "There was in his mind, in its serenity, its charming simplicity, its tenderness, something more than is found in the wisest and the best. His virtue was of a divine nature: it was at once a prolonged innocence and an acquired wisdom. Serene and radiant as his soul may now be in the mansions of peace, we can hardly conceive of it as more loving and more pure than we beheld it on this earth of infirmity and of strife." What a delight it is to contemplate the relation that bound two such spirits together, — the measureless treasures of inspiration, solace, joy, it must have yielded to them both! Sarah Austin, who was in Paris at the time Ballanche died, and an intimate of the illustrious circle of friends, says, "I shall never forget the sort of consternation, mingled with sorrow, which this death caused. Everybody felt regret for so pure and excellent a man, but yet more of grief and pity for Madame Récamier, whose loss was felt to be overwhelming, and entirely irreparable." Ampère says, in his cordial and glowing memoir of Ballanche, "While he was composing his 'Antigone,' Poetry appeared to him under an enchanting form. He became acquainted with her, of whom he said that the charm of her presence laid his sorrows to sleep; who, after being the soul of his most elevated and delicate inspirations, became in later years the providence of every moment of his life." Ballanche himself often assured Madame Récamier, that the ideal of the "Antigone" of his dreams was revealed to him by her, and that, in drawing this perfect portrait, he had copied largely from her. "It was only through Eurydice," he writes, "that Orpheus had any mission for his brother-men. If my name survives me, as appears more and more probable, I shall be called the Philosopher of the Abbaye-aux-Bois, and my philosophy will be considered as inspired by you. This thought is my joy. I am now entering on the last stage of my life: however prolonged this stage may be, I know well what is at the end of it. I shall fall asleep in the bosom of a great hope, full of confidence that your memory and mine will live the same life." Fortunate friends! happy in their living union immaculate as heaven, happy in the grateful admiration and love of all fit souls who shall ever read of them!

> And if he grieved because his words, his name,
> The breath of after-ages will not stir,
> 'Tis but because he would impart his fame,
> And share an immortality with her;
> So might there, from the brightest, holiest flame
> That e'er did martyrdom of heart confer,
> Two shadowy forms of Truth and Friendship rise,
> To seek their home together in the skies.

Pervading and earnest, however, as were these attachments of Madame Récamier to Montmorency and Ballanche, the crowning passion of her life was her friendship for Chateaubriand. This grand writer and imposing person has described his first meeting with her:—

"I was one morning with Madame de Staël, who, at toilet in the hands of her maid, twirled a green twig in her fingers while she talked. Suddenly Madame Récamier entered, clothed in white. She sits down on a blue-silk sofa. Madame de Staël, standing, continues her eloquent conversation. I scarcely reply, my eyes riveted on Madame Récamier. I had never seen any one equal to her, and was more than ever depressed. My admiration of her changed into dissatisfaction with myself. She went out, and I saw her no more for twelve years. Twelve years! What hostile power squanders thus our days, ironically lavishing them on the indifferences called attachments, on the wretchednesses named felicities!"

But it was in 1817, at a private dinner in the chamber of the dying Madame de Staël, that their real acquaintance began. The literary fame of Chateaubriand was then greater than that of any living man. He was a lofty, romantic, melancholy person, with a superb head and face, polished manners, and a grand vein of eloquence. Nothing was so deeply characteristic of Madame Récamier as her enthusiasm for brilliant minds, noble sentiment and conduct. It was this that had so fascinated her with Madame de Staël. The sure proof of the ideal nature of her attachments, their freedom from sensual ingredients, is this ruling stamp of reverence and loyalty. Those whom she admired the most enthusiastically she loved the most passionately. It could hardly fail that her imagination would be captivated with the chivalrous and imposing Chateaubriand, especially at such an affecting time. "He seemed the natural heir to Madame de Staël's place in her heart." Speaking of this overwhelming sentiment, thirty years later, she said, " It is impossible for a head to be more completely turned than mine was: I used to cry all day." Montmorency and Ballanche were greatly distressed, and not a little mortified and jealous. It was not that they had fallen into a lower and narrower place in her affection, but that they saw Chateaubriand installed in a higher and larger place. They feared that her peace would be wrecked in wretchedness by an intimate connection with one so discontented and capricious,— a sort of spoilt idol, a hero of *ennui*, filled with causeless melancholy, voracious of praise, querulous, exacting, his own imperious and inevitable personality ever uppermost. In vain they sought to warn and dissuade her from the new attachment. Montmorency seems to have fancied that the passion was not friendship, but love; and faithfully, with solemn energy, he adjured her, by all the sanctions of religion, to guard herself. He soon learned his error, and gracefully apologized: —

"When I read your perfect letter, lovely friend, remorse seized me, and now fills my soul. I am deeply touched by the proofs of your friendship, and by the triumphs of your reason. I am, for friendship's sake, proud of the exclusive privilege you accord to me of admission and consolation, and impatiently long to go and exercise the sweet right. Pardon me my letter of this morning. Adieu. Persist in your generous resolutions, and turn to Him who alone can strengthen them and reward them."

The friendship of Madame Récamier and Chateaubriand became more absorbing and complete, and was destined to endure with their lives. "It was," Madame Lenormant says, "the one aim of her life to appease the irritability, soothe the susceptibilities, and remove the annoyances of this noble, generous, but selfish nature, spoiled by too much adulation." Her steady moderation, moral wisdom, beautiful repose, and sweet oblivion of self, were an admirable antidote to his extreme moods, uneasy vanity, and morbid depression. Communion with her serene equity, her matchless beauty, her inexhaustible tenderness, the experience of her constant homage, soothed his haughty and mordant, but magnanimous and affectionate, nature, and were an infinite luxury to him. An admiring recognition is almost a necessity for those highly endowed with genius. And Madame Récamier's intense faculty of admiration, with her self-forgetting devotedness, exactly fitted her for this ministry. Chateaubriand became the first object of her life. Modifying her habits to suit his tastes, she made him, instead of herself, the centre around which every thing was to revolve. She devised endless means of lending an interest to his existence. She listened to every thing he wrote. She drew into her parlor, to meet him, all those persons who could interest or amuse him, or in any way give him pleasure. She diverted attentions from herself to him with exhaustless skill and generosity.

Such jealousy as can find a place in natures so noble is

easily to be traced in the letters of Ballanche and Montmorency. Chateaubriand calls Ballanche "the hierophant" or "the mysterious initiator," "the man the most advanced at the Abbaye-aux-Bois." Ballanche, in turn, calls Chateaubriand "the king of intelligence." But Madame Récamier's wonderful sweetness and discretion invariably restored the interrupted harmony. Nor, indeed, did she allow the superior attraction to cast her old friends in the shade. Several years after the death of Montmorency, which happened in church on a Good Friday, Chateaubriand wrote to her thus: "Yesterday I believed myself dying, as your best friend did. Then you would have found one resemblance at least between us, and perhaps you would have joined us in your heart." Five years after their first meeting, Chateaubriand, then ambassador at Berlin, writes to her, "That I shall see you in a month, seems a kind of dream to me." Twenty-five years later, two years before his death, he writes to her at a watering-place whither she had gone for her health, "Do not hasten back. I pass my time here in Notre Dame. It is well occupied; for I think only of you and of God." The persistence of an affection so profound and so pure as that of Madame Récamier bore its proper fruit, and ended by subduing Chateaubriand. Gratitude, respect, veneration, struck their roots to the very bottom of his heart. Little by little his self-occupied personality yields, and at last he writes to her, "You have transformed my nature." When she was alarmingly ill, in the winter of 1837, he, together with Ballanche, might be seen in the cold mornings, — "his beautiful white hair blown about by the wind, his physiognomy the image of despair," — in the court of the Abbaye-aux-Bois, waiting for the doctor to come out. He then writes, "I bring this note to your door. I was so terrified yesterday at not being admitted, that I believed you were going from me. Ah! remember it is I who am to go before you. Never speak of what I shall do without you. I have not done any thing so evil that I should be left behind you."

She recovered, and devoted herself more than ever, if possible, through the years of his mental decay, to alleviate and disguise the sad changes that came over him. Blindness began their separation before death came. Nothing can more emphatically bespeak her divine self-abnegation than the fact, that, for a long time after she had become perfectly blind, a dislike to trouble others with her infirmities led her to conceal the misfortune from her general acquaintance. Her eyes kept their brightness, and her hearing was most acute: she recognized, by the first inflection of the voice, those who drew near. The furniture was carefully arranged, always in the same way, so that she could move about confidently; and many persons, when she spoke of her "poor eyes," never dreamed that she had actually lost her sight.

After the decease of his wife, Chateaubriand besought Madame Récamier to marry him. She refused, on the ground, that, if she resided with him, the variety and pleasure his daily visits brought into the tedium of his existence would be destroyed. "Were we younger," she said, "I would gladly accept the right to consecrate my life to you. Age and blindness give me this right. I know the world will do justice to the purity of our relation. Let us change nothing." During his last sickness, he was as unable to speak as she was to see. She had the fortitude to undergo two operations on her eyes in the hope of looking on him once more; but in vain. By his bedside when he expired, she felt the sources of her life struck. She came from the room with no outward sign of distress, but clothed with a deadly paleness, which from that hour never left her. Her niece wrote at the time to a friend in England: —

"Those who, during the last two years, have seen Madame Récamier, blind, though the sweetness and brilliancy of her eyes remained uninjured, surrounding the illustrious friend whose age had extinguished his memory, with cares so delicate, so tender, so watchful, — who have seen her joy when she helped him to snatch a momentary distraction from the conversation around him, by leading it to subjects connected with that past which still lingered in his memory, — those persons will never forget the scene. They could not help being deeply affected with pity and respect at the sight of that noble beauty, brilliancy, and genius bending beneath the weight of age, and sheltered, with such ingenious tenderness, by the sacred friendship of a woman who forgot her own infirmities in the endeavor to lighten his."

History scarcely affords a finer instance of the ministrations of womanhood to soothe the woes and supply the wants of man than is exhibited in the relation of Madame Récamier and Chateaubriand. His egotistic and restless mental activity; his exaggerated, perturbed, and gnawing self-consciousness; his despairing view of men; his alienation from the spirit of his age, — made him most lonely and unhappy. Meanwhile, his ardent poetic susceptibility, his soaring imagination, his impassioned tenderness, his knightly sentiments, his religious feeling, pre-eminently fitted him to enjoy the moral homage, the delicate, sympathetic attentions, of a woman crowned with every exalting attribute of her sex. He appreciated the prize at its full worth. When nothing else could any longer interest him, her charm retained its pristine power. When beyond his threescore and ten, he writes to her thus, at different times: —

"Other things are old stories: you are all that I love to see." — "I am going to walk out with the lark. She shall sing to me of you: then she will be silent for ever in the furrow into which she drops." — "I have only one hope graven on my heart, and that is, to see you again." — "Cherish faithfully your attachment to me: it is all my life. You see how my poor hand trembles; but my heart is firm." — "I have but one thought, — fidelity to you: all the rest is gone."

For many years, — even after his noble faculties were broken, and he had lost the use of his limbs, so that he was forced to be carried into her room, — he passed the hours of every day, from three to six, with her. Amidst the ordinary hatreds, miseries, and indifferences of society, is it not indeed instructive and refreshing to see this example of a spotless friendship still yielding, in extreme old age, the interest, the solace, the happiness, which every thing else had ceased to yield?

Chateaubriand devotes to Madame Récamier the eighth volume of his "Memoires d'Outre Tombe." He recognizes, in her serious friendship, a support for the weariness of his life, a remuneration for all his sufferings.

"It seems, in nearing the close of my existence, as if every thing that has been dear to me has been dear to me in Madame Récamier, and that she was the concealed source of my affections. All my memories, both of my dreams and of my realities, have been kneaded into a mixture of charms and sweet pains, of which she has become the visible form. In the midst of these 'Memoirs,' the temple I am eagerly building, she will meet the chapel which I dedicate to her. Perhaps it will please her to repose there. There I have placed her image."

During the few months that she survived their loss, Madame Récamier often spoke of Chateaubriand and Ballanche together. Repeatedly, if the door chanced to open at the hour when these two friends had been accustomed to enter, she started; and, on being asked the reason, replied that at certain moments her thought of them was so vivid, that it amounted to an apparition. Only three days previous to her death, she received M. de Saint Priest, and took great interest in hearing him read the eulogy on Ballanche which he was about to pronounce before the Academy.

Besides these three chief friends, Madame Récamier had many others well deserving of separate mention. Paul David, nephew of her husband, was a most devoted and inseparable companion of her whole life. When she lost her sight, he used to read to her every evening. He was a poor reader, and, perceiving that she was sensitive to this defect, he secretly took lessons, at the age of sixty-four, to improve his elocution. Junot and Bernadotte were her ardent, lasting friends, always delighted to serve her. Her rare graces, and her generous goodness to Madame Desbordes-Valmore, disarmed the prejudices and won the heart of the gifted but misanthropic Latouche. The Duke de Noailles, who, under the envelop of a chill manner, concealed a conscientiousness of judgment, a constancy and delicacy of feeling, in strong sympathy with her own nature, was admitted to the rank and title of friend; "a serious thing," says her biographer, "for her who, more than any one in the world, inspired and practised friendship in the most perfect sense of the word." He held a place in her esteem like that held by Matthieu de Montmorency. One of the latest and warmest of her friends was the brilliant and high-souled Ampère, introduced to her by Ballanche, who had been an intimate friend of his father, and who now loved the son with double fervor, — a debt which the grateful young man repaid with interest in a noble tribute to his memory. Never did a mother feel a deeper solicitude in the prospects of a darling son, or exert herself more devotedly to further his success; never did a son more thoroughly idolize a beautiful and good mother, than was realized between Madame Récamier and Ampère. Solely to please her, this most entertaining and most courted man in Paris devoted himself not merely to her, which would have been easy, but to Chateaubriand, which was difficult. Nothing can better illustrate her irresistible charm. And nothing can better illustrate the coarseness and ignorance of many of our critics, than the presumption with which one of them, in 1864, speaking of Ampère's funeral, says, "He was one of Madame Récamier's many lovers, and was bitterly disappointed at her refusal to marry him after the death of Chateaubriand!"

Such were the few principal men who penetrated to the centre of that select circle, in whose outer ranges of general benevolence the right of citizenship was granted to so many choice figures. Among the more distinguished of these latter may be named Benjamin Constant, the Duke de Doudeauville, De Gerando, Prosper de Barante, Delacroix, Gérard, Thierry, Villemain, Lamartine, Guizot, De Tocqueville, Sainte-Beuve. Surrounded by such persons as these, in the humble chamber to which, on the loss of her fortune, she had betaken herself, she presided like a priestess in the temple of friendship, ever pre-occupied with *them*, their glory her dominant passion, never herself seeking to shine, but only intent to elicit and display their gifts. Was it not natural that they should, in the humorous phrase of Ballanche, "gravitate towards the centre of the Abbaye-aux-Bois"?

Margaret Fuller, after seeing an engraving of Madame Récamier, writes in her journal, —

"I have so often thought over the intimacy between her and Madame de Staël. It is so true that a woman may be in love with a woman, and a man with a man. I like to be sure of it; for it is the same love which angels feel, where —

"'Sie fragen nicht nach Mann und Weib.'"

Of the friendship of women, perhaps none is more historic than this. A large selection from the correspondence was published, in 1862, by Madame Lenormant, in connection with a volume called "Madame de Staël and the Grand Duchess Louise." It is impossible to read these letters without being struck by the rare grace that reigned in the union of which they are the witnesses, and being affected by the sight of a friendship so faithful, a confidence so entire.

The first meeting of these celebrated women took place when Madame de Staël was thirty-two, Madame Récamier twenty-one. Among the few existing papers from the pen of the latter is a description of this interview: —

"She came to speak with me for her father, about the purchase of a house. Her toilet was odd. She wore a morning gown, and a little dress bonnet adorned with flowers. I took her for a stranger in Paris. I was struck with the beauty of her eyes and her look. She said, with a vivid and impressive grace, that she was delighted to know me; that her father, M. Necker, — at these words I recognized Madame de Staël! I heard not the rest of her sentence. I blushed, my embarrassment was extreme. I had just come from reading her 'Letters on Rousseau,' and was full of the excitement. I expressed what I felt more by my looks than by my words. She at the same time awed and drew me. She fixed her wonderful eyes on me with a curiosity full of kindness, and complimented me on my figure in terms which would have seemed exaggerated and too direct if they had not been marked by an obvious sincerity, which made the praise very seductive. She perceived my embarrassment, and expressed a desire to see me often on her return to Paris; for she was then going to Coppet. It was then a mere apparition in my life; but the impression was intense. I thought only of Madame de Staël, so strongly did I return the action of this ardent and forceful nature."

Madame de Staël was a plain, energetic embodiment of the most impassioned genius. Madame Récamier was a dazzling personification of physical loveliness, united with the perfection of mental harmony. She had an enthusiastic admiration for her friend, who in return found an unspeakable luxury in her society. Her angelic candor of soul, and the frosty purity which enveloped her as a shield, inspired the tenderest respect; while her happy equipoise calmed and refreshed the restless and expensive imagination of the renowned authoress. There could be no rivalry between them. Both had lofty and thoroughly sincere characters. They were partly the reflection, partly the complement, of each other; and their relation was a noble and blessed one, charming and memorable among such records. "Are you not happy," writes Madame de Staël, " in your magical power of inspiring affection? To be sure always of being loved by those you love, seems to me the highest terrestrial happiness, the greatest conceivable privilege." Again, acknowledging the gift from her friend of a bracelet containing her portrait, she says, " It has this inconvenience : I find myself kissing it too often." In 1800, Madame Récamier had a brilliant social triumph in England: "Ah, well, beautiful Juliette! do you miss us? Have your successes in London made you forget your friends in Paris?" Madame Récamier was the original of the picture of the shawl-dance in " Corinne;" and her friend says of her, in the " Ten Years of Exile," " her beauty expressed her character." The following passages, taken from letters written in 1804, show how the intimacy had deepened: —

"For four days, faithless beauty, I have not heard the noise of the wind without thinking it was your carriage. Come quickly. My mind and my heart have need of you more than of any other friend." — "I have just seen Madame Henri Belmont. People say that all beautiful persons remind them of you. It is not so with me. I have never found any one who looks like you ; and the eyes of this Madame Henri seem to me blind by the side of yours." — "Dear and beautiful Juliette, they give me the hope of seeing you when I return from Italy ; then only shall I no longer feel myself an exile. I will receive you in the chateau where I lost what of all the world I most loved; and you will bring the feeling of happiness which no more exists there. I love you more than any other woman in France. Alas! when shall I see you again?"

The friends passed the autumn of 1807 together at Coppet, with Matthieu de Montmorency, Benjamin Constant, and a brilliant group of associates, amidst all the romance in which the scenery and atmosphere of that enchanted spot is steeped. One day they made a party for an excursion on Mount Blanc. Weary, scorched by the sun, De Staël and Récamier protested that they would go no farther. In vain the guide boasted, both in French and German, of the spectacle presented by the Mer de Glace. "Should you persuade me in all the languages of Europe," replied Madame de Staël, "I would not go another step." During the long and cruel banishment inflicted by Napoleon on this eloquent woman, the bold champion of liberty, her friend often paid her visits, and constantly wrote her letters:—

"Dear Juliette, your letters are at present the only interest of my life." — "How much, dear friend, I am touched by your precious letter, in which you so kindly send me all the news! My household rush from one room to another, crying, 'A letter from Madame Récamier!' and then all assemble to read it." — "Every one speaks of my beautiful friend with admiration. You have an ethereal reputation which nothing vulgar can approach." — "Adieu, dear angel. My God, how I envy all those who are near you!"

When an envious slanderer had greatly vexed and grieved Madame Récamier, Madame de Staël wrote to her, "You are as famous in your kind as I am in mine, and are not banished from France. I tell you there is nothing to be feared but truth and material persecution. Beyond these two things, enemies can do absolutely nothing; and your enemy is but a contemptible woman, jealous of your beauty and purity." — "Write to me. I know you address me by your deeds; but I still need your words."

In 1811, Madame de Staël resolved to flee to Sweden. Montmorency, paying her a parting visit, received from Napoleon an instant decree of exile. Madame Récamier determined, at any risk, to embrace her friend before this great distance should separate them. The generous fugitive wrote, imploring her not to come: "I am torn between the desire of seeing you and the fear of injuring you." No dissuasion could avail; but no sooner did she arrive at Coppet than the mean soul of Napoleon sought revenge, by exiling her also. The distress of Madame de Staël knew no bounds. On learning the fatal news, she wrote, —

"I cannot speak to you; I fling myself at your feet; I implore you not to hate me." — "What your noble generosity has cost you! If you could read my soul, you would pity me." — "The only service I can do my friends is to make them avoid me. In all my distraction, I adore you. Farewell, farewell! When shall I see you again? Never in this world."

Throughout the period of their banishment, the friends kept up an incessant correspondence, and often interchanged presents: —

"Dear friend," writes Madame de Staël, "how this dress has touched me! I shall wear it on Tuesday, in taking leave of the court. I shall tell everybody that it is a gift from you, and shall make all the men sigh that it is not you who are wearing it."

In return, some time later, she sends a pair of bracelets, and a copy of a new work from her pen, adding, "In your prayers, dear angel, ask God to give peace to my soul." In another letter she says, "Adieu, dear angel: promise to preserve that friendship which has given me such sweet days." And again, —

"Angel of goodness, would that my eternal tenderness could recompense you a little for the penalties your generous friendship has brought on you!" — "You cannot form an idea, my angel, of the emotion your letter has caused me. It is at the extremity of Moravia that these celestial words have reached me. I have shed tears of sorrow and tenderness in hearkening to the voice which comes to me in the desert, as the angel came to Hagar."

What a rare and high compliment is contained in the following passage:—

"You are the most amiable person in the world, dear Juliette; but you do not speak enough of yourself. You put your mind, your enchantment, in your letters, but not that which concerns yourself. Give me all the details pertaining to yourself."—" The hundred fine things Madame de Bigne and Madame de Bellegarde say of you and me, prove to me that I live a double life: one in you, one in myself."

When Napoleon fell, in 1814, Madame de Staël hurried home from her long exile. The great news found Madame Récamier at Rome. In a few days, she embraced her illustrious friend in Paris. Close was their union, great their joy. It was absorbing admiration and devotion on one side: absorbing sympathy, respect, and gratitude, on the other. The power and charm of Madame Récamier were not merely in her ravishing beauty, imperturbable good nature, and all-subduing graciousness, but in her mind and character as well. Madame de Staël, who was a great critic, and no flatterer, says to her:—

"What a charm there is in your manner of writing! I wish you would compose a romance, put in it some celestial being, and give her your own natural expressions, without altering a word."—" You have a character of astonishing nobleness; and the contrast of your delicate and gracious features, with your grand firmness of soul, produces an incomparable effect."

The last letter written by the dying authoress to her friend concluded with the words, "All that is left of me embraces you." The survivor paid the pious rites of affection to the departed with the devotion which had marked their whole relation. And when, years afterward, on the loss of her property, Madame Récamier betook herself to the Abbaye-aux-Bois, in her humble chamber, where she was more sought and admired than ever in her proudest prosperity, the chief articles to be seen, in addition to the indispensable furniture, were, as Chateaubriand has described the scene, a library, a harp, a piano, a magnificent portrait of Madame de Staël by

Gérard, and a moonlight view of Coppet. Madame de Staël had once written to her: "Your friendship is like the spring in the desert, that never fails; and it is this which makes it impossible not to love you." Death caused no decay of that sentiment, but raised and sanctified it. Her translated friend now became an object of worship; and she devoted her energies, without stint, to extend and preserve the memory of the illustrious authoress.

The self-forgetting sympathy of Madame Récamier, the magical atmosphere of loveliness she carried around her, obtained for her many warm friendships with women no less than with men. Far foremost among these was Madame de Staël. But others also were very dear, and claim to be named. The widow of Matthieu de Montmorency was extremely attached to her, wrote her touching letters, took every opportunity to see her. Madame de Boigne, too, was joined with Madame Récamier in a relation of respect and affection truly profound and vivid. This lady was herself greatly distinguished for her beauty, as well as for her voice, which was compared with that of Catalani. She was much impressed by the noble behaviour of Madame Récamier at the time of her husband's bankruptcy, and, by her delicate attentions, secured the most grateful love in return. Their earnest and faithful affection lasted until death. A novel, entitled "Une Passion dans le Grande Monde," in which Madame de Staël and Madame Récamier are the two chief characters, was left by Madame de Boigne at her death for publication. It was published in 1866, and has produced quite a sensation.

One of Madame Récamier's sweetest friendships was with the accomplished and charming Elizabeth Foster, Duchess of Devonshire, the fame of whose exquisite loveliness traversed the earth. The duchess said of her friend, "At first she is good, then she is intellectual, and after this she is very beautiful," — a striking compliment, when spoken by one herself so dazzlingly gifted, in relation to an admired rival. The order of precedence in her charms, however, was differently recognized by men. They were subdued successively by her beauty, her goodness, her judgment, her character. The Duchess of Devonshire had known all the romance and the sorrow of life. Her experience had left upon her a melancholy which attracted the heart almost as quickly as it did the eye, and lent to her something pensive and caressing. Although a Protestant, she had formed, during her long residence in Rome, an entire friendship with the Cardinal Consalvi, the prime-minister and favorite of Pope Pius VII. through his whole pontificate. These two beautiful women, as soon as they met, felt, by all the laws of elective affinity, that they belonged to each other. The death of the Pope was followed in a few months by that of his Minister and friend. During the illness of Consalvi, Madame Récamier shared all the hopes, fears, and distresses of the duchess. And when the fatal event had befallen, and the Cardinal was laid in state, and the romantic and despairing woman would go to look on her dead friend, she accompanied her, deeply veiled, through the crowd, and kneeled with her, amidst the solemn pomp, in tears and prayer, beside the unanswering clay. The duchess was struck to the heart by this irreparable loss. All that a devoted sympathy could yield to soothe and sustain, she received from Madame Récamier. And when, soon after, unable to speak, she lay dying, she silently pressed the hand of this faithful friend as the last act of her existence.

Madame Récamier retained to the last her enviable power of inspiring affection. Madame Lenormant says that the Countess Caffarelli found her, in her age and blindness, watching by the deathbed of Chateaubriand. Drawn by her singular goodness, she sought to share with her in these holy cares. She became the loving and beloved associate of the final hour. This admirable person worthily closes the list — the rich and bright list — of the friends of Madame Récamier.

In her youth, the first wish of Madame Récamier was the wish to please; and she was, no doubt, a little too coquettish, not enough considerate of the masculine hearts she damaged, and the feminine hearts she pained. The Duke de Laval said, "The gift of involuntary and powerful fascination was her talisman." Not, sometimes, to make a *voluntary* use of that talisman, she must have been more than human. As years and trials deepened her nature, she sought rather to make happy than merely to please. She always cared more to be respected than to be flattered, to be loved than to be admired. Admiration and sympathy were stronger in her than vanity and love of pleasure: reason and justice were strongest of all. Her judgment was as clear, her conscience as commanding, her sincerity, courage, and firmness as admirable, as her heart was rich and good. When Fouché said to her, in her misfortunes and exile, " The weak ought to be amiable," she ininstantly replied, " And the strong ought to be just." Her exquisite symmetry of form, her dazzling purity of complexion, her graciousness of disposition, her perfect health, her desire to please and generous delight in pleasing, — composed an all-potent *philtre*, which the sympathy of every spectator drank with intoxicating effect. She discriminated, with perfect truthfulness, the various degrees of acquaintance and friendship. She made all feel self-complacent, by her unaffected attention causing them to perceive that she wished their happiness and valued their good opinion. Ballanche tells her, " You feel yourself the impression you make on others, and are enveloped in the incense they burn at your feet." Wherever she went, as if a celestial magnet passed, all faces drifted towards her with admiring love and pleasure. By her lofty integrity, her matchless sweetness and dexterity, as by a rare alchemy, she transmuted all her fugitive lovers into permanent friends. Her talents were as attractive as her features: little by little her conversation made the listener forget even her loveliness. Saint-Beuve says, "As her beauty slowly retreated, the mind it had eclipsed gradually shone forth, as on certain days, towards twilight, the evening star appears in the quarter of the heaven opposite to the setting sun." Her voice was remarkably fresh, soft, and melodious. Her politeness never forsook her: with an extreme ease of manner she had a horror of familiarity as well as of all excess and violence. Her moderation of thought, serenity of soul, velvet manner, were as unwearying as reason and harmony.

Without pretence of any sort, she hid, under the full bloom of her beauty and celebrity, like humble violets, modesty and disinterestedness. At the time of her death, Guizot, when a distinguished American lady asked him what was the marvel of her fascination, replied, with great emotion, "Sympathy, sympathy, sympathy." She had none of that aridity of heart which regular coquetry either presupposes or produces. Deprived by destiny of those relations which usually fill the heart of woman, she carried into the only sentiment allowed her, a tender ardor, a faithfulness and delicacy unequalled; and the veracity of her soul joined with her singular discretion, gave her friends a most enjoyable sense of security. Ballanche called her "the genius of devotedness;" and Montalembert named her "the genius of confidence."

From the most dangerous and deteriorating influences of her position, she found a safeguard in active works of charity. Her pecuniary generosity, in her days of opulence, was boundless. She seemed to feel that every unfortunate had a right to her interest and her assistance. "Disgrace and misfortune had for her," avowed one who knew her entirely, "the same sort of attraction that favor and success usually have for vulgar souls; and under no circumstances was she ever false to this characteristic." The fine taste she had for literature and art, the great pleasure she took in their beauties, the natural grace and good-will with which she expressed her admiration, furnished precisely that kind of incense which authors and artists love to breathe. Old Laharpe, who in her young days had derived the deepest solace and delight from her attention and praise, wrote to her, "I love you as one loves an angel." The readiness with which the word "angel" rises to the lips of her friends is striking. Almost every one of them applies the word to her on almost every occasion. Madame de Krüdner writes to her, "I shall have the happiness, I hope, dear angel, of embracing you to-morrow, and talking with you." All seemed instantly to recognize something angelic in her expression. It was in her disposition as much as in her appearance, — apparently in the latter, because in the former, as Ballanche said to her, —

"In you, thought, taste, and grace will ever be united in one harmonious whole. I am fascinated at the idea of so perfect a harmony, and want the whole world to know what I so easily divine. It will be your mission to make the intrinsic character of beauty fully understood, to show that it is an entirely moral thing. Had Plato known you, he need not have resorted to so subtile an argument. You would have made him alive to a truth that was always a mystery to him; and that rare genius would thus have had one more title to the admiration of the world."

There was something celestial in her motions, that suggested the undulations of a spirit, rather than joints and muscles; and made her soul and flesh one melody. As to her heavenly temper of goodness, there is but one voice from all who knew her. She accorded to the sufferings of self-love a pity and kindness seldom shown to them. She had the sweetest faculty for dressing the wounds of envy and jealousy, soothing the lacerations of rivalry and hate, assuaging the bitterness of neglected and revengeful souls. For all those moral pains, or griefs of imagination, which burn in some natures with a cruel intensity, she was a true sister of charity. To the rest of her winsome gifts she added, according to the unanimous testimony of the witnesses, this rare and resistless quality, the power of listening to, and occupying herself with, others, — the secret both of social success, and of happiness without that success. "She said little," De Tocqueville avers, "but knew what each man's *forte* was, and led him to it. If any thing was said particularly well, her face brightened. You saw that her attention was always active, always intelligent." Lamartine said, "As radiant as Aspasia, but a pure and Christian Aspasia, it was not her features only that were beautiful: she was beautiful herself. Sarah Austin affirmed, "It was the atmosphere of benignity which seemed to exhale like a delicate perfume from her whole person, that prolonged the fascination of her beauty." And Lemoine declared, in his eloquent obituary notice, "In the hearts of those who had the honor and the happiness of living in constant intercourse with her, Madame Récamier will for ever remain the object of a sort of adoration which we should find it impossible to express." The only fault her friends would confess in her was the generous fault of too great toleration and indulgence. To dwell unkindly on this is as ungracious a task as to try to fix a stain on a star.

Arrayed in her divine charms; armed with irresistible goodness and archness; enriched with equal wisdom and uprightness, every movement a mixture of grace and dignity; protected by an *aureole* of purity which always surrounded her; walking among common mortals, "like a goddess on a cloud,"— she made it the business of her life to soften the asperities, listen to the plans, sympathize with the disappointments, stimulate the powers, encourage the efforts, praise the achievements, and enjoy the triumphs, of her friends. No wonder they loved her, and thronged around her alike in prosperity and in adversity. To appreciate her character is a joy; to portray her example, a duty. She was a kind of saint of the world.

The only fault Sainte-Beuve can find with the spirit of the society she formed, and governed so long with her irresistible sceptre, is that there was too much of complaisance and charity in it. Stern truth suffered, and character was enervated, while courtesy and taste flourished: "The personality or self-love of all who came into the charmed circle was too much caressed." One can scarcely help lamenting that so gracious a fault is so rarely to be met in the selfish and satirical world; that the opposite fault of a harsh carelessness is so much more frequent as to make this seem almost a virtue. Cast in an angel's mould, and animated with an angel's spirit, her consciousness vacant of self, vacant also of an absorbing aim, ever ready to install the aim of any worthy person who came before her, she was such a woman as Dante would have adored. It seems impossible not to recognize how much fitter a type of womanhood she is for her sex to admire than those specimens who spend their days in publicly ventilating their vanity, feverishly courting notoriety and power; or those who, without cultivation, without expansion, without devotion, without aspiration, lead a life of monotonous drudgery, with not a single interest beyond their own homes.

All who have written on this most admired and beloved woman have had much to say of the secret and the lesson of her sway. One ascribes her dominion to a skilful flattery, another to a marvellous tact, another to an indescribable magic. But really the secret was simple and obvious. It was the refined suavity and womanliness of her nature, the ineffable charm of a temper of invincible sweetness and kindliness, a ruling " desire to give pleasure, avert pain, avoid offence, render her society agreeable to all its members, and enable every one to present himself in the most favorable light." Let the fair creatures made to adorn and reign over society add to their beauty, as Sarah Austin observes, the proper virtues of true-born and Christian women, — gentleness, love, anxiety to please, fearfulness to offend, meekness, pity, an overflowing good-will manifested in kind words and deeds, — and they may see in the example before us how high and lasting its empire is. This is the true secret revealed, the genuine lesson taught, by the rare career we have been reviewing.

After this glorious example of the moral mission of woman, — glorious despite its acknowledged imperfections, — it is not necessary to deny the common assertion, that men have a monopoly of the sentiment of friendship. Neither is it necessary to expatiate on the great happiness this sentiment is capable of yielding in the comparatively narrow and quiet lives of women, or to insist on the larger space which ought to be assigned to the cultivation of it in those lives. The moral of the whole subject may be put into one short sentence, namely this: The chief recipe for giving richness and peace to the soul is, less of vague passion, less of ambitious activity, and more of dedicated sentiment in the private personal relations.

> How little matter unto us the great!
> What the *heart* touches, — that controls our fate.
> From the full galaxy we turn to one,
> Dim to all else, but to ourselves the sun;
> And still, to each, some poor, obscurest life
> Breathes all the bliss, or kindles all the strife.
> Wake up the countless dead; ask every ghost,
> Whose influence tortured or consoled the most?

> How each pale spectre of the host would turn
> From the fresh laurel and the glorious urn,
> To point where rots, beneath a nameless stone,
> Some heart in which had ebbed and flowed its own!

Art. IV.—MAURICE DE GUÉRIN.

The Journal of Maurice de Guérin. With an Essay by MATTHEW ARNOLD, and a Memoir by SAINTE-BEUVE. Translated by EDWARD THORNTON FISHER. New York: Leypoldt & Holt. 1867.

THIS Journal, which is at last brought out in an American edition, extends only from July, 1832, to October, 1835, and covers that period of Guérin's life which was embraced between his twenty-second and twenty-fifth year. Thus the work is brief. But brevity was no imperfection in Guérin: his writings rather resemble those paintings which his countrymen most admire,— works in miniature and surprising in accuracy. And this Journal, though it contains a record of no more than three years, yet presents Guérin at a time when his powers were freshest, most self-developed, and free from the influences of Parisian society,— the most heated, over-worked, and exaggerated of all societies; when, consequently, his faculties could labor without restraint, and thus appear with all their natural interest.

The Journal begins with Guérin at home in Languedoc; it transports us, after a few entries, to La Chênaie, on the edge of the forest of Coëtquen, in Brittany, where M. de La Mennais was residing and conducting his school. He remained there till September, 1833, when the school was broken up; and, after leaving La Chênaie, passed some time in Brittany, with friends whom he had met at the residence of M. de La Mennais. In February, 1834, he went to Paris; and from that time he appears in new surroundings, and with a character, externally at least, changed. Guérin lived about five years after he went to Paris, and died, at the age of twenty-nine, in 1839.

His Journal stops with 1835, as before said; and all that we know of him thereafter is occasional writings, and the notices of a few friends. But we know enough to assure us, that he did not always preserve that fresh susceptibility to natural impressions which was and is his chief charm. Not that he became debauched or dissipated, or at all deficient in the qualities of a gentleman; but it was precisely by gaining those qualities which allowed him to shine in *salons*, and to hold his own in repartee and social intercourse with men of wit, that he lost some of his original prestige,— that simple love of nature and thraldom to its charms that had separated him from the mass of conventional men, and given him the quality of " distinction " which Mr. Arnold claims for him.

The Journal, then, shows him in his best period: it presents the fullest account, and exhibits the most marked and striking contrast, of those two qualities which have been pointed out as Guérin's characteristics, and as giving him his individuality. The first was his power of painting nature; the second, his habit of introspection, and his most rare and admirable gift of stating clearly and justly the results of his observations. We do not wish to do again the work which M. Sainte-Beuve and Mr. Arnold have so excellently done,— emphasize these statements of Guérin's peculiarities, and establish them by quotations from his writings. Whoever would see the process by which the result is reached, may find it worked out at length in those essays, or, still better, the original material in the book itself. But there are two remarks which we wish to make upon these topics, and which we think necessary to a right comprehension of Guérin's character, and in referring him to his proper position.

In the first place, when it is said that Guérin was peculiarly alive to the life of nature, and that he not only felt and enjoyed its changing forms, but possessed the power of reproducing the influences that moved him, and idealizing them while reproducing them, it is not to be supposed that he was unique in this characteristic, or that he was the Coryphæus of a school that had never before existed. It is a cause of lamentation with French critics, that so few poets in their nation have attempted the poetry of fireside and domestic life, or have been happy in a simple and lifelike rendering of nature. Whoever will take the trouble to look at M. Sainte-Beuve's "Causeries," will find, in that which serves as preface to a series of essays upon Cowper, the question stated, and the names and the works of the writers reviewed, who have made attempts in this department of poetry. The list is surprisingly small; and the opinion which Sainte-Beuve pronounces upon the result of their labors, supported as it is by the testimony of others well qualified to judge, will show us what a void there has been in French literature, and will prepare us for whatever transports Frenchmen may manifest, when they meet with writings fitted to supply the national defect. Now it is this condition of French literature, undoubtedly, which accounts for part of the enthusiasm with which Guérin has been received. His writings, imperfect and fragmentary though they are, have shown that it was not a natural defect of the French taste and imagination, that suffered no classics in the sphere of simple and hearty country life; and that, in the homes of educated and noble-souled *châtelains*, there could dwell as pure and wholesome family affections, as in an English home might afford a theme for the pen of a Wordsworth or a Cowper. It is this which has given French critics so much joy; for Guérin, with his unaffected love of nature, his openness to its moods and aspects, though a prose-writer, is essentially a poet. His poet-nature would be disputed by few; and hence his countrymen can appeal to him, when French taste and French naturalness and simplicity are called in question.

It is this reservation which, while allowing Guérin all merited honors, must be borne in mind, when one reads the somewhat exaggerated notice by Mr. Arnold. Maurice de Guérin has certainly "distinction;" he possesses some rare qualities: "there is much to be gained from his book for poetry, much for the elevation of the soul, and much for the contemplation of nature." But, though he has distinction, he is not pre-eminently distinct from others. What qualities he has, he shares with many of our English writers; and, though he is well worthy, judged only by the promise he showed, to take his place by their side, yet he does not surpass them: he may be their equal, but he is not their superior. Even limiting his specialty to what Sainte-Beuve in another Essay restricts it, — " to the sentiment, not so much of details, as of the sacred *ensemble* and universality of nature; a sentiment of the origin of things and the sovereign principle of life," — yet no one would say, that, even compared with sole reference to this capacity, he surpasses Wordsworth or Keats; and, if you prefer to find his power, as most readers will, in the minute descriptions of the external world, there are pages of Cowper, both in prose and in poetry, equal to what Guérin has written. And, even looking away from the great models of poetry, and confining our comparisons to our own land, there are touches in Hawthorne's writings which equally proclaim the master, and which equally show a mind open to whatever aspect nature may put on. The extracts from his Diary, lately published in the "Atlantic Monthly," are the writings which, in this respect, most nearly resemble Guérin's; and the relative powers of the two artists, as exhibited in lines equally private and equally unintended for publication, admit of curious comparison. Making all the allowance that maturity and immaturity of powers may demand, it will be seen that both the writers are artists, and that both enjoyed gifts differing very little in quality.

The second point to which we would direct attention is the state of Guérin's moral constitution during the time noted by the Journal, or at least until the period when Guérin left M. de La Mennais' care, and had hanging over him the necessity of moving out of his seclusion, and solving the problem of the sphere of his faculties, and the course to be taken for their development. For somewhat more than the first year which this Journal records, and hence for the whole of Guérin's previous life, one stage of which we see end and another begin in these pages, he was like those sea-weeds which he somewhere describes, sending down their tendrils into the water that supports them, and from which they draw their sustenance, while yet they have no fixed root, and are driven along at the mercy of the waves. Moral power—will, the faculty of separating one's self from disturbing accidents and living in a world of calm, holding one's self well poised and collected—was unknown to him, and without ground in his experience. He was conscious of this defect; and he displays, in the analysis of those of his feelings which relate to it, all that keenness and accuracy of observation which we perceive in his descriptions of outward nature. And hence, when you read his Journal and find his inner self there portrayed, you see that you have before you a being without moral energy, and yet of so full sympathy with the life of birds and beasts and the fashions of the earth and sky, that he appears to be but a part of nature, and you can almost understand what he means, when he talks of "that mysterious breath that pervades all intelligences." And when you analyze, with what power you can, your own disposition, you feel that you, too, have something in you that connects you with lower forms of life. You almost doubt whether your superiority to the brute is so absolute as you have imagined. You are led to reason from one case to all, and to suspect that the moral nature in man is not fixed and perfect through all periods of his life, but that it grows with his growth; and that, coming forth from the sensuous and unreflecting life of childhood or brutehood, it increases with more or less success, and in different individuals with different degrees of development. Thus Guérin leads you to think, that, if to many men there were given as great a power of self-examination as he possessed, there might be discovered many of the now missing links between the brute and the human creation; that thus the moral nature might be exhibited in its growth, and a more perfect harmony and development be manifested in the different orders of living beings. And Guérin, by his want of will and his subjection to that emotional and sensitive part of his nature, which for so many years held authority over him, seems himself to be one of those links binding us to lower forms of life by our feelings and our passions, but uniting us to higher forms by our possibilities of progress. And it is not long, in fact, before you see the germs of a will and of a moral energy starting up in him, and manifesting themselves by cries of regret, by longings and stern resolutions. But this Journal, so short a way does it take us, does not exhibit him as travelled so far towards perfection, that the moral powers can be recognized in him in their fulness. His subsequent letters, and the accounts of his friends, show him in a state where he has made a nearer approach to calmness, and obtained some mastery over his impulses and his feelings. But yet there were reasons imbedded in his physical constitution, that forbade his attaining perfection in this part of his nature; and the progress that he did make, was, it is to be feared, not without hurt to his freshness and simplicity.

These are the reflections which have occurred to us upon reading Guérin's remains, and the Essays of Sainte-Beuve and Arnold that introduce them. In making them, we have not wished to injure the reputation which the name of Guérin has obtained with those — we fear too few — who know the rare and amiable qualities of the brother and sister; nor have we wished to exalt any thing English or American at the expense of any thing French, but rather, while emphasizing the true claims of the brother to admiration, to throw the true light upon his character, and bring him into relation with other names which we have learned to venerate.

We are glad that his Journal is now put into an English dress, and that thus the circle of his readers may be widened. Mr. Fisher has made his version with an accuracy that leaves little room for question; but there is a want of harmony between different parts of the work, and for which not Mr. Fisher but the French editor is responsible. We do not know how it has happened, but Sainte-Beuve seems to have had access to more abundant sources than M. Trebutien. Page 43, compared with page 100, shows Sainte-Beuve's quotations to be fuller than the text, — a strange reversal of custom; and the sentence omitted from the text adds something to the description. Page 44, again, has two paragraphs more than page 101. But the difference between Sainte-Beuve's quotations and the Journal is shown still more strikingly in that form of his preface which he has published in the fifteenth volume of his

"Causeries." The discrepancy relates to the records for Dec. 8 and 20, 1833, a part of the present publication which, as those familiar with the book know, is perhaps of greatest interest; and yet Sainte-Beuve's new preface has a number of striking passages or little turns of expression that are wholly ignored by M. Trebutien, and, of course, by his American translator. Sainte-Beuve quotes a paragraph or two, and apparently omits more, that are found neither in his original preface nor in the published Journal. We pass over these; but we wish to call attention to two or three additional details that he has given to the description which Guérin has written of his life at M. de La Morvonnais'. They seem to us curious and of interest. To what is said on page 104, " the subsequent walk, a sort of greeting and adoration that we offer to nature," Sainte-Beuve quotes, in addition, " for it seems good to me, after having worshipped God directly in the morning prayer, to bend the knee to that mysterious power that he has given for the adoration of a few,"— a mystical sentence, but perhaps of importance in deciding Guérin's theological position. Again, to " dinner announced . . . by a gentle voice," the new preface adds, " that calls us from below,"— a little detail; but the whole passage is taken up with the *menus détails* of Morvonnais' housekeeping. So the Journal speaks of " the crackling fire of dry brush around which we draw our chairs just afterwards;" but, instead of "just afterwards," Sainte-Beuve adds, " after that sign of the cross which bears to heaven our rendering of thanks." Neither Sainte-Beuve nor M. Trebutien speak of " various readings" to Guérin's Journal; and these discrepancies are somewhat strange. Some of them, however, may perhaps be accounted for by the remark of the French critic, that " the present edition bears, on many a page, the marks of the religious scruples of Guérin's friends."

Art. V. — SOCIAL EMULATION, AS A FEATURE OF AMERICAN LIFE.

New America. By WILLIAM HEPWORTH DIXON. Philadelphia: J. B. Lippincott & Co.

MR. DIXON'S vivacious and entertaining story deals — as we have remarked elsewhere — mainly with a few phenomena, mostly abnormal, in the social and religious life of this country, which are doing their part to shape out a "new America," differing, in many most important features, from what is familiar and old. We shall not attempt, at this time, to discuss the general character of that revolution whose germs and elements he seeks in the chaos of new opinions and strange experiments; but rather to trace the influence of a single motive, — perhaps more potent than any other single one in effecting those more superficial changes which strike every traveller's eye, and perhaps equally important with any other in affecting the tone and quality of our people's moral life. We mean the motive of social emulation, to which the strength and the weakness, the safety and the danger, of our American life are largely due, — a motive never before so active and wide-spreading in its operation as now and here.

Nowhere but in a young, prosperous country, uncrowded, with undeveloped and unlimited resources, could this principle have the sway it possesses among ourselves. In older nations, emulations are confined within narrow bounds. A certain spirit of contentment, born of circumstances that promise but doubtful prizes to ambition or rewards to effort, captivates the heart weary with observing the restlessness and forward-pushing desires of our own people. But, where this moderation or contentment prevails, we find feeble and dispirited energies, unawakened or drowsy powers, and a fixed mediocrity of affairs. Old abuses go uncured. Permanent inequalities prevail. Along with unknown and unused resources, there is needless poverty, stereotyped dulness and thinness of life.

Doubtless, no state of society is so picturesque as one in which broad contrasts are produced by unequal laws: on one side, a lofty aristocracy; on the other, a meek and dependent vassalage. None is so saintly in seeming as that in which a showy asceticism, accompanied with a sentimental devoutness, produces faces and costumes which are the delight of artists and the awe of ritualists. And, besides the picturesque effect, there is often an advantage more substantial. A noble condescension in the high, or a tender reverence in the low; the loyalty of an implicit faith, or that order of graces which flows out of the relations of widely-contrasted classes of society, — cannot be had where the exalted of yesterday are brought low to-day, and the low of to-day are lifted up to-morrow. Still, justice is the only permanent foundation of political or social life. All legal or artificial inequalities are curses and wrongs. The freest nation, the most equitable law, has the surest guaranty of its stability and happiness.

Social emulation is the whip that stirs the slothful faculties and drowsy desires of that constitutionally idle animal, man. It is to this, in great measure, we owe our swift growth in wealth and civilization. No man is willing to be poorer, less favored, less respectable, than his neighbors. He must be as well clothed and as well appointed as they; his family must be as well dressed and housed as theirs; he will not be content with less of educational advantage, or religious privilege, or opportunity of literary culture, or facility of communication with the world at large. The railroad system of this country, that miracle of energy, wealth, and engineering skill, is due but in small part to immediate needs of commerce, or hope of pecuniary profit. Farmers have mortgaged their lands to invest in roads that merely increased their sense of being in direct relations with the centres of life, and not behind the times; and this emulation has provoked and sustained enterprises of the most hopeless financial character. Take the Baltimore and Ohio Road, for example, — running directly across the bed of numerous torrents, or laid in rocky troughs, or raised on huge embankments, or lifted on stilted tressels, — here heaving an expensive bridge, there diving into a tunnel bored through a granite mountain.* Contemplating the poverty of the region and the costliness of the road, one is dumb with wonder at that ambitious rivalry which would not allow Pennsylvania or New York to frame the only bonds between East and West, but compelled Maryland and Virginia to this herculean and magnificent task, at any cost to their resources. In the West, social emulation is the great civilizer. It bridges the Mississippi; it occupies the banks of the Colorado and Columbia; it carries schools, churches, colleges, all the comforts and refinements of the oldest parts of this country, into the newest Territories and States. Michigan claims the largest American university, most munificent in endowment, and most generous in plan. St. Louis is at this hour rebuilding the largest and most sumptuous hotel in the world, destroyed by the recent conflagration; is building an Episcopal church, perhaps the costliest on the continent; has the finest building for a Polytechnic Institute to be found in America; the noblest Post-office and City Hall; and has grown, in the last thirty years, from fourteen thousand inhabitants to upwards of two hundred thousand. Chicago, even more energetic and restless, rivals New York in bustle and stir, and in its vast territorial extent. With its elegant churches, its convenient and expensive school-houses, it looks in parts like a city hundreds of years old; while in other parts a mere collection of extemporized shanties. The best models of New-England schools, with the best teachers, are already scattered over Michigan, Ohio, Illinois, Wisconsin, Minnesota, and California. No Eastern churches that we have seen are as thoroughly equipped for parish uses and religious charities, as are found in Illinois, Missouri, and California. The social element is so predominant in Western piety, that the churches almost uniformly provide for every gratification and development of that feeling, — some even including arrangements for exhibiting tableaux and semi-dramatic

---

* Sixteen of these tunnels we counted, on a recent journey, in a few miles. The melting snow, followed by a bitter frost, had decked the sides of those rocky excavations with frozen stalactites of enormous proportions. A fringe of colossal circles hung from the opposite walls of the gleaming way, and, as the sun got power, melted into noisy cataracts, and echoed the thunder of the train.

shows, while furnishing all possible accommodation for parish parties. The same spirit of emulation improves domestic architecture, introducing water and gas and side-walks into the remotest towns. A lecturer in a Western village finds himself indebted for his flattering audience to the attractions of the novel gas-illumination; and, being eagerly solicited to repeat his address in a certain place, presently discovers that the anxiety is not to hear him, but simply to prevent Oshkosh from receiving any privilege which Fond du Lac may not enjoy. Frivolous as the motive may seem, it is a powerful spring of improvement in our whole new country. It first did its work in the East, where town academies and turnpikes were built fifty years ago under its inspiration; and is now transferring its domain to the West, where it is working its miracles of civilization with a rapidity and success that no less universal or less immediate motive could rival.

But it works for evil too, as well as good. The extravagant fashions, the late hours, the expensive living, the high prices, travel as fast and as far as schools and churches. The fast driving, the gold-gambling, the gaudy drinking-houses, the gift-enterprises and showy weddings, the mania for piebald costumes, propagate themselves with telegraphic speed and American universality. If at Leavenworth and Omaha we find the newspapers, the gas-works, the paved side-walks, the stone fronts, the schools and churches of the Eastern cities, we still more surely find in their streets the Broadway saloons, and on their pavements the identical millinery of the metropolis. We find every vice of older civilizations blooming with hot-house luxuriance out of their fresh soil. The latest fashions flourish almost in sight of the desert and the buffalo; snatches of Italian opera or quotations from Emerson may be broken short by the whoop of the wild Indian, or the bark of the prairie wolf; and at the crossings of the ways we meet just as idle, over-dressed, and frivolous young men and women as we may see sauntering in the sun of any bright afternoon, up and down our city avenues.

In an era in which social emulation is the characteristic and unchecked passion, the landmarks of reason and piety are lost in the deluge of imitation and rivalry. What is good and what is bad spread as by contagion. The common school and the church are borne on the same universal tide which floats into every region the follies and extravagances and fashionable vices of the day. Religion is built up in stone and mortar with prodigious outlay; while its moral and spiritual foundations are undermined by ribaldry and unseemly jesting about all sacred things in the very columns that advertise the Sunday topics of the pulpit. The mania for hospitals, asylums, and reading-rooms spreads like an epidemic, and with it the passion for horrible exhibitions, in which the contortionist risks his life to amuse the fears and thrill the nerves of the spectators; or women exhibit their coarse immodesty to the vulgar gaze, while people of standing will eagerly applaud some lottery scheme, thinly disguised by the sacred name of charity.* Microscopic science informs us that two opposite currents run in the same slender tubules of the lungs: one setting out and carrying off the carbonic acid; the other setting in, charged with pure oxygen, death and life thus flowing in the same channel. And so it is with the current of social emulation, with this difference, that the tides here mingle, and both run one way.

One great peril of American society is the lack of manly, independent thinking, and individual conscience. Personal aspiration gets lowered to a popular standard. An average and compromised pattern of character is thrust on us by a tyrannical, hasty, and unreasoning public opinion. Things go by tides and rushes and sweeping floods; to colonize Califor-

---

* At the time of the drawing of the Crosby Opera-house lottery, it was said that hardly a town in the Western country was not largely interested in the exciting scheme. One poor-looking man in the cars was heard to speak of having a hundred and seventy chances in it. It was talked of more than the recent snow-storms, or Southern Reconstruction, or the prospects of spring wheat, or the renewal of the Canadian treaty, or even the price of lots in the new streets of a city that hopes and boasts of its ability to make New York a second-rate place in a generation more. The excitement of a passing fever would have been of no great moral account, if it had not illustrated the immense craving for speculation, the terrible gambling propensity, which, in the haste to be rich, has led to so much of moral debauchery and commercial ruin.

nia, to occupy Colorado and Montana; to drive railroads over mountain-chains, whose bases are hot and sandy, and their summits lost in clouds and snows, or across deserts whose borders are in different climates. Already Chicago, by superior energy, has managed to secure no small portion of the trade due west from St. Louis, and naturally belonging to it, which that city is now striving to regain, by driving her Pacific Railroad to the Rocky Mountains, before the northern line shall reach them. If we knew all the legislative lobbying; all the rash heat and haste; all the efforts to procure Federal aid to some of those local enterprises; all the hard feeling, the false and treacherous bargaining, involved in such emulations,—we should see that whatever blessings follow them, as contributions to the opening and settling of the country and the increase of its wealth, they tend to degrade and demoralize the generation that handles them, and to undermine justice, fairness, and open dealing.* Is there not, East and West, a growing disposition to think *success* the proof of merit, and almost the test of right? If a man has public spirit (as it is called); if he is successful in his schemes, and helps forward the external prosperity of his community,—he may gamble like a German prince, outwit all his contemporaries with his sharp practice, and still stand at the head of society (so called), and even be found taking high ground in regard to the company he keeps, so that none but persons of the very highest social standing can hope to enjoy his acquaintance: and yet hardly a person will be bold enough to smile at the gigantic jest, or to rebuke the fantastic absurdity.

It is often too easily assumed, that no direct rebuke of the popular temper can have any effect; that fashion is mightier

---

* We lately travelled along the line of a canal in Ohio, in which the neighboring farmers had invested, twenty years ago, their little earnings. A railroad company, wishing to avoid its rivalry in freighting, had lately bought up just enough of the stock of the canal to control its direction; and this direction had closed the canal, making the stock absolutely worthless, and robbing all the smaller holders of the whole value of their property in it. Nobody seemed to think it any thing but a "smart" transaction, in which cunning and address had triumphed over the sleepy trustfulness of the poor farmers along the line.

than conscience or the truth; that the world will and must have its way; that the aspiring heart and the consecrated will must retire into privacy and strict seclusion, if they would indulge their morbid, sanctimonious ways. The average life of the times says, "These are not times for such delicate moralities;" and indeed some tender souls have been foolish enough to talk of Protestant nunneries and monasteries as the only hope of modern piety.

But this is a cowardly retreat before a powerful, yet after all a very vulnerable, and by no means unconquerable, enemy. The social emulation of our people — now coarse, now refined; now avowed, now secret — is a spirit not to be exorcised, but to be instructed; not to be done away, but to be purified and restrained. It is to be defecated of its taint by the sturdy criticism of those who still believe in the might of truth, the sanctity of goodness, and the power of prayer and holiness, and in the possibilities of a Christian life. Courage, moral courage, is the great want of American society. It is cowardice among men and women who know better; cowardice in the pulpit and the press, cowardice in society and on the platform, in the home-circle and in the world, that leaves folly, extravagance, and wickedness their unchallenged arena. Would that we had a few moral leaders, — not men aiming at a cheap capital of religious repute by becoming extravagant and professional censors of what they do not understand, but men of conviction, intelligence, and moral standing; who, instead of going apart and disdainfully leaving the great tide of humanity to its own course, saving only their own feet and skirts, would boldly go into the stream, and preserve, by wisdom, justice, and piety, the costly freight it bears! The country has too much education and too much aspiration, not to value, not to heed, not to follow, better counsels than it receives. A great heart of courage is a real power in the world. A few genuine leaders of public sentiment might greatly change the aspect of American society. Our people are as apt for what is good as for what is bad. Their external circumstances, especially in the West, are favorable to large, strong, generous views. This tendency is now abused to encourage latitudinarianism of morals, rudeness of manners, and laxity of opinion. But, after all, the largest and most generous views are really the divinest, noblest, purest. The great region of the West, gigantic in its features, is breeding a physical race, worthy to be the shrine of a nobler spirit and a grander faith. We believe the impurities will settle, the perilous fires slacken, the folly abate, under principles vital and ever active at the heart of our society. But, meanwhile, can a single generation afford to wait the gravitation of events? Are we willing personally to be only tools spoiled in making a civilization which is to be worth something a hundred years hence? Individual character is the immortal end of our existence; and only atheists and infidels are prepared to build up civilization on the ruins of generations whose follies, vices, and sins are counted on to prepare the soil, filling with their refuse the deep quagmires which are thus to become the foundations of future stableness.

Art. VI. — PHASES OF PRIMITIVE CHRISTIANITY.

First Historical Transformations of Christianity. From the French of Athanase Coquerel, the Younger. By E. P. EVANS, Ph. D., Professor of Modern Languages and Literature in the University of Michigan. One volume. Boston: Wm. V. Spencer. 1867.

AGAIN we have to thank Professor Evans for an excellent translation of a book eminently adapted to the wants of candid and inquiring minds. This time it is a thoroughly religious work that is offered us; the "First Historical Transformations of Christianity," by Athanase Coquerel, the younger, — a man who, like his illustrious father, has distinguished himself not less by his acquirements as a scholar and his eloquence as a preacher than by his fearless declaration of unpopular truths, and his brave endurance of such forms of persecution as the church and the world still tolerate for the punishment of heretics and innovators.

The treatise — contained in one small volume of less than

three hundred pages — traces the various transformations which Christianity has undergone at the hands of its adherents, from the time immediately succeeding the death of Christ to the close of the fourth century. It displays great learning and careful research, and yet avoids all those technicalities and scholastic digressions which render so many church histories incomprehensible and uninteresting to the general reader. The simplest mind can understand and enjoy the plain statements, the reasonable conclusions, of this little book; the keenest intellect must admire the wonderful simplicity of its diction (which is the perfection of art in style), the cogency of its arguments, and the irresistible *naïveté* displayed in the declaration of its most startling positions, which, in many instances, contain, in a single terse sentence, as calmly laid down as though it were an axiom or an undisputed fact, a clear solution of points which have filled volumes with unprofitable discussion, and embittered the minds of hundreds of men who have allowed prejudice to falsify history. With great liberality of thought, our author is reverent toward all that is true in every phase of religious sentiment; and, under his skilful handling, the abnormal developments of Christianity, which we recognize in the form of dogmatic creeds, enfeebling superstitions, and spiritual tyrannies, are presented, not as miraculous institutions, having fixed conditions, which cannot be accommodated to the progress of humanity, but as the natural sequence of events, the unavoidable result of traditionary influences: thereby enabling us to fear them the less, and to escape from their injurious bondage the earlier.

The treatment of the theme is so methodical, that it would be unjust to the author not to follow the same arrangement in our notice of its excellencies. And, while we do this, we shall, in order to avoid continual reference to the text, present a faithful, though brief, summary of the contents of the work in our own words.

No one can deny, that a new and very strong impulse has recently been given to religious inquiry, and to critical investigation of the authority of existing creeds and forms of worship. This activity is met by renewed zeal, on the part of long-established religions, in defence of their doctrines and practices. Islam, no less than Christianity, seems animated with fresh vigor; and, in Christianity, both Popery and Protestantism are on the alert. The tendency everywhere is towards larger liberty: the conflict is caused by the effort of conservatism to restrain the progress of free thought.

It is undeniable also that every individual has an interest in these great questions, and a right to examine their conditions, and their bearings upon human welfare. With the diffusion of education, they demand more general study: they cannot be ignored. Ecclesiastical prohibitions cannot keep them hidden; carelessness and selfish ease cannot escape their intrusion. Many deprecate the free discussion of opinions on spiritual subjects, imagining that, because old creeds are trembling to their fall, religion itself is in danger of being overthrown. This is because the world has so long been trained to believe that religious knowledge must always be abstract and vague, not subject to the same laws of reason which govern other departments of human thought. But, in our days, men are beginning to venture to study religion in the light of history; and whoever does this with an unprejudiced mind and a fearless heart will be in no danger of losing sight of God, the infinite and absolute, or of that sentiment in man's nature which responds to His eternal and immediate presence.

Religions, like every thing else under the law of material and moral nature, are constantly undergoing modification. When a religion ceases to obey this law of change, it is a proof that it no longer contains any element of improvement for the world, any power over the consciences of men: it is dead. But while a religion retains life, it may be modified in several ways: it may develop in conformity with its nature and thus increase in strength, or contrary to its nature and thus become constantly weaker, or there may be at once elements of decay and of prosperity in its changes, so that the result is neither wholly beneficial nor utterly injurious. Religion is so fruitful in ideas, and admits of such great variety of sentiment, that, of widely different beliefs, each may contain true principles, and be deserving of respect and attention on account of its own peculiar contribution to the sum of human improvement: therefore, in view of these facts, and for the sake of historical impartiality, it is most correct to characterize the various modifications of the Christian religion as *transformations*, because this word does not imply prejudgment of their results, as the word *deviation* or *development* might seem to do.

The three great transformations of primitive Christianity are Roman Catholicism, the Greek or Russian Church, and Protestantism. But as these transformations cannot be understood without a survey of the work of the Founder of Christianity, and as even this was in some degree dependent on what preceded it, it will be necessary first to glance at the condition of the world before the coming of Christ.

No religion can properly be said to have been created by any individual, or by any body of men, or by any people. The religious sentiment is innate with every human being. There is an aspiration towards the infinite in every soul, and the conviction of its affinity with a superior power becomes stronger and more satisfactory with every new development of its own capacities. If this instinctive feeling be nurtured in a reasonable and healthful manner, it ennobles the whole nature; but, if it be perverted, it corrupts every thing: in any case it is the most powerful expansive force in the moral world, and must continually work either rapid progress or cruel devastation. Religion distorted and vitiated has always been the bane of true liberty; and it is on this account that many earnest men have revolted entirely from all acknowledgment of religious claims, and have declared themselves atheists.

Some religions have grown up, like languages, from the contributions of many souls for a long period of time: others bear the distinct impress of individual thought, the prevailing influence of some gifted man, wise enough to understand the wants of his time and strong enough to satisfy them. But in such a case the work of the Founder never remains precisely as he left it: if he was too far in advance of his age, his followers necessarily retrograde to more comprehensible ideas; if he stood but little above the ordinary level, he is soon surpassed.

When a people has developed gradually and harmoniously, its religion will also unfold from low and coarse outlines to a form of symmetry and beauty. Such a religion was Grecian polytheism,— particularly interesting to us from its direct influence upon the foundation of Christianity; while the religions of India and Scandinavia had no part in either the intellectual or spiritual agitations of that era. The natural development of the polytheism of the Greek is sufficiently and beautifully illustrated by tracing the course of one of their favorite divinities.

Far back in the legendary ages, the shores of Greece were settled by wanderers from the distant East. These brought with them the impulse — which is that of all infant and uncultivated minds — to worship those great powers of nature, so necessary to their existence, and yet so entirely beyond their control. One of these meteorological divinities, who was called *Herakles*, the "Glory of the Air," as the restorer of fine weather after storm, and therefore conqueror of the evil spirits of the tempest, became, in the modification of Greek thought, the divination of *force* in the human body, — *Hercules*, subduer of wild beasts and monsters; and, at a later day, after this noble race had discovered that moral strength is superior to physical energy, the same Hercules is chosen as the type of human struggles after perfection. Seated at the branching of two roads, he is invited by Wisdom on the one hand, and tempted by Pleasure on the other, and decides heroically for virtue, in spite of all the allurements of vice. This was the highest idea of which polytheism was capable; and no effort of after-times to extend its provisions or deepen its influence by giving a symbolical meaning to mythological characters was able to attain more than a brief and spasmodic success.

But all this while philosophy had been developing its various systems, and had arrived at the same result with polytheistic religion, although by a different method. With reference to the origin of Christianity, it is commonly urged by Christians, that, when Christ came, the world was weary of vain imaginings, and fully realized a spiritual need which nothing but his scheme of redemption could satisfy. This is true; but the inference generally drawn from the fact is not correct. It was not because the Pagans of Greece and Rome were sunk so low in ignorance and crime that a new salvation was demanded, but because they had reached such a point of intellectual culture and spiritual enlightenment, that the old religion, though modified and expanded to its utmost capacity, no longer possessed any purifying or elevating power. The human race will always be indebted to Greek philosophy for the early discovery of many important truths, and for the correct, though only partial, recognition of the capacities of the soul. Socrates, Plato and Aristotle, Zeno and Epicurus, with many others, gradually and successively approached the secret of moral life and happiness; while a host of illustrious characters exemplified in their own conduct the best thought of their age.

And, to strengthen these ennobling influences, a kind of alliance was formed between the philosophy of the period and the highest form of the popular religion, which resulted in the celebration of the mysteries. These mysteries were a kind of dramatic representation, serving to veil the declaration, on the part of the initiated, of a belief in immortality and the resurrection; doctrines which were considered too subtle and lofty to be appreciated by the common people. Consequently, the masses were in no wise benefited by the secret contemplations and revelations of this select class, which was always a very small minority. Meantime a consciousness of the insufficiency of the existing religious system was universally felt; and the confusion was only increased by the intermingling of Roman superstitions with Grecian polytheism, in the vain hope of finding some cure for the wounds of awakened conscience. The idea of expiation was strengthened by the general despair. Animals of many kinds, and even human beings, were sacrificed, to atone for the crimes and errors of living men, and the common course of events was made gloomy and alarming through the cloud of signs and omens of evil that obscured the pathway of every individual.

Nor was the Jewish religion exempt from the modifying influences of time and experience. It is a common mistake to suppose, that the Jews have always kept their theology as exclusive and intact as their national prejudices. On the contrary, it kept pace with the growth and culture of the people, beginning with the simple worship of *Elohim* or *powers*, and gradually rising to the lofty conception of one God. The successive names of Hebrews, Israelites, and Jews may serve as well to mark eras in faith as to record the modifications of national existence. Nor was the law of Moses able to resist entirely the progress of thought within the nation, and the pressure of antagonistic opinion from without. The captivity in Assyria weaned a great portion of the people from their reliance on a sacrificial service in the one Temple: their simplified worship became more spiritual; while the influence of surrounding Oriental ideas weakened considerably the materialistic tendency of the Mosaic law. But those who remained in Judea clung with only greater obstinacy to the letter of their code, believing firmly that they were the heaven-appointed rulers of the human race, and that their triumph was soon to be assured to them under the sway of an heir to David's throne, — the Messiah. Pharisee and Sadducee alike hated the colonized Jews for their tendency to assimilate to the opinions and customs of their uncircumcised neighbors, not knowing that these despised Hellenists, together with the small body of Essenes in Palestine, were alone destined to represent the children of Abraham in the new dispensation; while they themselves, for their blindness and hardness of heart, were to be left out.

Thus many causes combined to prepare the world for the new light which was near its dawning. The field was tilled before the sower appeared. The teachings of Christ would never have been listened to or remembered, had not souls been made ready, by a natural process of education, to welcome and respond. Nor was political preparation wanting. Roman unity was everywhere established, affording unusual facilities for intercourse among the various provinces of that vast empire; the prevalence of a common law had already given men a glimmering sense of the tie of human brotherhood; and peace reigned over all nations, making possible the proclamation of a gospel of peace.

It may seem impious to many persons to regard the mission of Christ as having been prepared for and assisted by these historical events; or, in the forcible words of our author, " to admit that Christianity did not fall from heaven like an aerolite;" but, to those who are disposed to judge rationally, this record of the gradual transformations of religious thought will at once throw light upon the past, and awaken hope and confidence for the future.

The whole burden of the message of Jesus Christ to the world was love: the love of God to man, which is shown in His free offer of pardon for sin; and the love due to God from man, which ought to prove itself by a constant endeavor after holiness, and by the tenderest sympathy between all the members of the human race.

This is all: the words and acts of the Founder of Christianity, throughout his whole life, were only exquisite changes rung upon this one perfect melody. This is the key to solve every purely ethical or religious problem. He left no written testimony of himself, no creed, no code, no rule of life, no church organization, no clerical investiture. He instituted only two simple and popular rites: one a sign of moral purification; the other, a memorial of his love. It is evident that a plan of salvation so pure and simple as his was altogether beyond the comprehension of his immediate followers. Accordingly, he had scarcely left the world before those misapprehensions and prejudiced distortions of his teaching, which are so apparent in the records of the evangelists, began to affect the management of the infant Church. The bondage of the law was again pressed upon recently enfranchised souls, by those of the believers who could not forget their early training under the Mosaic code. Fasts, distinction of meats and of sacred days, were soon an important feature of the new faith. The worship of angels, a superstition acquired by the Jews during the Assyrian captivity, also obtained favor. Nor was it long before a hierarchy was established, somewhat resembling the sacerdotal orders of the Mosaic dispensation; while the influence of both Judaism and Paganism conspired to bestow upon the death of Jesus a sacrificial character and application. Judaical Christianity is well displayed in the writings of James, which, though of use in restraining the vagaries of a barren faith, possessed too little of the fervid spirit of the Master to avail much towards the conversion of a world already given up to a heartless performance of external rites.

But, even at this early day, there was an opposing party in the Church, — the Hellenistic Jews, who, having become Christians, were able to appreciate in a higher degree the freedom of Christianity, and to protest against the gradual return to spiritual slavery. Of this party, Stephen was a prominent member; and is for ever to be held in remembrance, not only as the first Christian martyr, but also as the first Reformer in the Church. After him, Paul continued and developed the doctrine of reconciliation to God through belief in Christ, and dedicated his life to the conversion of the world at large, without distinction of Jew or Gentile. With regard to justification by faith, Paul appears to have entertained two theories, each of which he brings forward at different times as sufficient and all-important. One is the mystical union of the believer with Christ, and through Christ with God. The other is the salvation wrought for man by the life, death, and resurrection of Christ. Jesus, by an act of his will, substitutes his own death for the spiritual death which sinners had incurred; and they, through faith in this substitution, which is accepted and ratified by God, are acknowledged as heirs of the new life of the risen Christ. This theory was taken as the foundation of a subsequent dogmatic system, which substitutes a purely juridical element in place of the mystical union of the believer with Christ, — making the sacrifice of a Divine Person necessary in order to restore the honor of a broken law, and appease the wrath of an offended God. In the latter view, man is the object of a contract between the Father and the Son; in the former, man himself is one of the contracting parties: an essential difference. But, according to Paul, this regenerating faith is not granted to all: only those who are predestined by God can receive it. The doctrine of election, so revolting to modern thought, was yet, at the time of its introduction, a great advance towards freedom; as by it Paul protested against the Jewish monopoly of salvation, and asserted the power God to save whom He would, whether Jew or Gentile.

The theology of Paul was altogether too liberal to be acceptable to the early Church; while, on the other hand, the Gentile Christians rejected the Judaical teaching of St. James. At this juncture, the timid conservatism and vacillating spirit of Peter effected a compromise; which for a time quieted dispute, though, like all compromises, it soon failed to satisfy either party. The temporizing policy thus introduced continued to characterize the proceedings of the Church. Compromises were effected with Paganism as well as with Judaism; and the purity of Christ's doctrine, and the energetic protest of Paul, were alike forgotten. Meantime the religious world, particularly in the East, was agitated by the doctrines of Christianity, as understood and taught by St. John. His theology is more ideal and more free from the trammels of the law than that of the Judaists, more abstract than that of Stephen, more mystic than that of Paul. The writer of the fourth Gospel was evidently imbued with the mode of thought of the Gnostics; his style is characterized with their peculiar phraseology; and the frequent use of abstract terms gives to his records a dreamy and mystical tone, very acceptable to the Oriental mind. Christianity, in St. John's view, is eminently a message of love. The believer is saved through the example, the teaching, and the death of Christ; but, though the blood of Jesus is said to wash away sin, there is nothing in John's writings concerning a Christ punished for us, or satisfying divine justice in our stead.

Respecting the nature of Christ, three distinct theories were early introduced. Some said that the Holy Spirit had descended upon him at his baptism, and had never returned to heaven; others suggested that he was not the son of Joseph and Mary, but of Mary and the Holy Spirit; others, again, identified him with the Incarnate Word of the Gnostics. Matthew and Luke credit the story of the miraculous birth; John and Paul see in Jesus the pre-existent Word; but Paul, though evidently desirous to exalt the Son as high as possible, always makes him subordinate to the Father. The Church, finding all three theories in the records of Christ's biographers, accepted them all and combined them, in spite of the declarations of Christ and the teachings of reason.

At the period of Christ's advent, the Jews were colonized in many parts of the Roman empire, especially in Rome itself and the neighboring cities. In thus mingling with the world, this peculiar people was obliged to put away somewhat of its exclusiveness; so that, when Paul began to preach at Rome, the Jews served as a connecting link between himself and the Pagans, and his word soon found access to all classes of Roman society. The Christian Church was soon established in Rome, and multitudes of Pagans professed Christianity. These converts could not divest themselves of the habits and associations of their former lives: consequently, Christianity became more and more corrupt as its temporal power increased, and the modifying influences of Paganism took more definite form. The Roman spirit, essentially juridical, local, and textual, could not fail to cramp the thought of Christianity; while many rites and customs — such as the tapers, lighted lamps, incense, and vases of consecrated water, which are so prominent a feature in the services of the Catholic Church — are purely Pagan, borrowed, almost without alteration, from the polytheistic worship. The same is true of the introduction of images, many of which would serve equally well for both religions: indeed, in some of these groups, the gods of fable were actually mingled with the objects of Christian faith. The monotheistic feeling of the Christianized Jews would not allow them to represent God by any visible form; and thus the custom obtained of placing an image of Jesus wherever in Pagan temples would have stood the image of a god. The idea of the miraculous character of certain images was borrowed from Paganism, as was also the *nimbus*, or aureola, which the sacred personages of the Catholic Church still wear. Next followed the worship of the martyrs and of objects which had belonged to them, in imitation of the devotion of the Pagans to the remains of their heroes. But it was not in outward adornment alone that the change consisted. The services of the Church came by degrees to partake of the nature of the Pagan mysteries, both in their exclusiveness and in their striving for dramatic effect. Thus Christians were regarded as the initiated, the candidates as catechumens, and the Pagans as the populace forbidden to enter the sacred places. The simple rite of communion was made a secret act, and gradually the idea of sacrifice was attached to its commemoration.

With the conversion of Constantine, Christianity at once became the favored religion of the court and the empire; and the political organization of the empire became the model of that of the Church. Rome as yet had no superiority over the other patriarchal bishoprics; but, on the establishment of the seat of empire at Byzantium, Constantine made of the patriarch of Rome the most important personage of the Eternal City. The prestige of Rome was so great, that the man who was first there would have little difficulty in maintaining his supremacy elsewhere. Besides, the East had four patriarchs, while the West had only one; and, through all divisions of the empire, the Western world continued to be ruled by a single spiritual head. The title of pope (*papa*), meaning "father," often given to bishops, was gradually monopolized by those of Rome. The encroachments of the papacy were necessarily slow, being, for a long time, opposed by the Western churches, while its claims have never been acknowledged in the East.

Meantime the Church became corrupted through its prosperity. Many of the clergy led scandalous lives, and disorders increased, until at last a re-action took place, unfortunately as extremes as the abuses against which it protested. To the religion of the court and the world, was opposed a religion hostile to society, alien to the family,—the religion of monks and nuns. Anchorites and cœnobites soon became numerous. The zeal for celibacy caused new honors to be paid to the mother of Christ, who was held to have always remained a virgin; and, in the fifth century, it was declared, by authority of an ecclesiastical council, that she was the " mother of God," in refutation of the heresy of Nestorius, who had taught the separation of the two natures in Christ, maintaining that Mary was the mother of the Christ-man, but not of the Christ-God.

After this declaration, it was easy to recognize her as a divinity in her own right; especially for the Pagans, who were accustomed to acknowledge the claims of goddesses, and who saw in the numerous pictures of the Virgin and child only a slight variation from the favorite Egyptian representation of Isis and her son Horus. Arianism was a last, illogical, and intellectually feeble, attempt to maintain God above all, even above Christ, — the last effort of monotheistic feeling against the polytheistic tendency of the age.

The division of the Greek and Roman Churches was the necessary result of long conflicting influences. The Eastern Church had always followed the mystical theology of John: the Roman Church adopted the formal, Judaistic theology of Peter, with such zeal, that he was early declared to have been its founder, and to have suffered persecution and death within the Eternal City, although historical evidence all goes to prove that he never even saw Rome; while Paul, whose teaching was rejected by its citizens, preached there for years, and finally died a martyr within its walls. His bold, free thought, though buried under the corruptions of primitive times, came to life and flourished in full vigor at the Reformation; and its purest truth blossoms afresh with every new struggle for liberty of conscience and elevation of human character.

Even this brief survey of the history of the Church, during the first four centuries after the death of Christ, is enough to show that his professed followers had wandered far from his pure standard of feeling and action; and to convey the warning lesson, that in proportion to the degree in which human laws and rites and creeds are allowed to intrude upon the sacred relations of the soul to God, will be the degeneracy of worship and the loss of spiritual communion between man and his Heavenly Father. And as history has proved, that the infinite variety of character and perception among individuals is proof against the restrictions of party or dogma, would it not be wisdom on the part of each existing church to relax its hold upon the material forms of its worship and the defined doctrines of its creed; and place more reliance upon that vital principle of Christianity, which still asserts itself in the midst of error, and which is destined finally to triumph over all attempts to enthrall its glorious career?

The above condensed sketch may serve to show something of the topics and course of argument in M. Coquerel's remarkable work; but it can give no adequate idea of the harmony, consistency, and earnestness with which the subject is developed. It is to be hoped that this little book will be extensively circulated; for no more attractive and persuasive antidote to superstition and ignorance in religious matters has ever been offered to the public.

Art. VII.—THE INCARNATION.

Ecce Deus. Essays on the Life and Doctrine of Jesus Christ, with Controversial Notes on "Ecce Homo." Boston: Roberts Brothers.

We have not seen the English edition of this interesting book, and, from reading the American reprint, should have concluded that it was really written in this country, by some person in our Unitarian ranks with a Swedenborgian philosophy, and with a studious desire to conceal his ecclesiastical connections. It has too many Americanisms in it to be English in origin. The word "transpire" is commonly used for "occur," a purely American colloquialism. "Collide" is another instance of steamboat English. We think, too, we notice an awkwardness in wearing the English dress, which a native would not have exhibited. Would an Englishman quote Macaulay as "*Baron* Macaulay?" Would he say, "from Britain to Africa"?—meaning from England. But these are mere surmises.

The book—which we do not propose to review, but merely incidentally to use as an introduction to our present theme—is worthy of careful reading. Its origin and purport will be at least as great a puzzle as "Ecce Homo" proved. It is not a whit more Orthodox in its general direction; and we see no reason why it might not have been written by the same author, except that it lacks his ease and polish and simplicity of style. In variety, earnestness, and freedom of thought, it is equally rich and full. There is as much in it to shock popular prejudices. But, happily, its edge is towards errors on both sides. It cuts into what is superficial or worthless in Liberal Christianity and in so-called Orthodox Christianity, and is written out of a deep and genuine and large Christian experience. We hope to do it full justice in our next number.

It is very interesting to see how the mind of the age is returning to that insoluble mystery of Christ's person. Christian unbelief has spoken its last word; criticism has done its worst. There is no unexplored field left in Christian evidences or exegetical studies. Doubt and denial have exhausted themselves, and, for want of materials, will now have to turn from discrediting Christ, to disproving a personal God (a much easier achievement), as the only road of progress. The next thing will be a revival of faith in Christianity; and the thing to be guarded against is, that this revival shall not waste its force and freshness upon what is not vital and precious, — shall not prove a *renaissance* of ecclesiastical frippery and theological extravagance.

The Incarnation, which is the central idea of "Ecce Deus," is, doubtless, the most fruitful and permanent and central idea of Christianity. The proem of John's Gospel is the axis of all future debate among theologians, because it sets forth this Incarnation; and the authenticity and genuineness of John's Gospel is now the question of all questions, because it contains this proem. In our present discussion, however, we must assume what the last and best authorities allow, — that the fourth Gospel is the work of John. The fourth Gospel was not written until about sixty-five years after our Lord's ascension; while the other Gospels are supposed to have been written within eight and fifteen years of that event.

During that period, of course, there had been time for the facts in our Saviour's life and death to become subjects of speculation, theory, and debate; and for opinions to develop themselves in the minds and hearts of his followers, out of and beyond those which were held by those who more directly and immediately reported his sayings and history.

This will account for the marked, and not otherwise explainable, difference between the fourth and the three synoptical Gospels. It is explained either by the fact, that John gives us the Gospel as meditation and experience; or, living *in* and *from* it had opened its depths to his soul; or that he endeavored to supply what was lacking in the other evangelists, or to correct errors which he had had time to see growing up in the Church.

In the first seventeen chapters, we have almost entirely new matter; and the whole Gospel is manifestly in a more mystic, spiritual, and devotional vein than either of the others.

Jesus, from that definite, human, and thoroughly historical personage which he appears in Matthew, Mark, and Luke, becomes, in John, more vague, enigmatic, and mythical in his position and character. His person is shrouded in a more sacred mystery: his words have a more unearthly quality. It would be rash to conclude, that this was the mere exaggerating effect of distance and time, or that those who first gave our Lord's history understood him better than John. Some persons are never understood by their contemporaries: their words and their conduct require to ripen into full significance and intelligibility in the heat of meditation and the light of experience; and no devout and spiritual mind would be content to think, that the heavenly-mild and holy John, the disciple whom Jesus loved, had a less complete and correct idea of our Master than the other evangelists. Clearness is often due to inapprehension and contraction of vision. The near-sighted have often great strength of eye, with a limited range of view; and the undeveloped in intellect, imagination, and heart, because they see little in the objects they describe, describe them with a more positive and definite outline.

There can be no doubt, that John's idea of Christ was different from — not opposed to, or inconsistent with, but only larger and loftier than — the idea of the other evangelists; nor can an honest and candid mind deny, that the main difficulties in settling Christ's place would be vastly diminished if we had only to deal with the accounts of him given by Matthew, Mark, and Luke.

This is sufficiently obvious from the inspection of the proem, or first eighteen verses of John's Gospel. Nobody in the world knows *certainly* what John was aiming at in that mystic introduction: whether it was controversial, and designed to correct existing errors of opinion; or whether, without reference to errors, it was declarative of John's own independent notions. The passage is very obscure.

It is well known from the Epistles, that disputes and speculations existed at that early day about Christ; not modern disputes, but others, — as for instance, whether Jesus Christ were a mere appearance, a disembodied, visionary shape, or an *actual being* in flesh and blood (2 John i. 7); and it probably was to combat notions which he thought heretical and dangerous, that John laid down the now vague, but then doubtless very intelligible, doctrine of his proem. We know that, in the philosophical schools of the time, the divine attributes were all personified, — that light and life and wisdom and truth and love were each and all spoken off as *æons*, or distinct entities, capable of separating themselves from the original spirit of the universe; and it would seem as if Jesus had been represented by some as being possessed by one or other of these divine attributes, inferior to the highest, and so somehow brought down in his dignity. John appears to adopt the general idea of these attributes, but represents one of them, the Logos or word or wisdom, as the chief of them, and as having light and life under its control; and this attribute, by which he represents the world as having been made, and which he also sets forth as having always been in the world and recognized by a few whom it at once adopted as *sons of God*, he now declares was the animating soul of Jesus. This *word*, which was with God, and was so made his wisdom and light and life that it *was* God, he now says was made flesh, and dwelt among us, full of grace and truth.

The real pith and marrow of this passage is very obvious, even amid the obscurity which involves its details, and even its intention. John distinctly teaches the identity of the spirit of God in the creation, in the past government of the world, and in the new revelation. It is the same Being, and the whole of the same Being, which first made the world, which has always been in the world, though neglected and unknown *by his own children*, and which is now manifested in Jesus Christ.

Jesus, he would have his hearers learn, is not new in the sense of being disconnected with the oldest purpose and manifestation of God. He is not different from God, in having any plan and purpose less than the original one by which the worlds were made. He is not here to represent himself; but *he is God* manifest in the flesh, as God has hitherto been manifest in the things he has made, and was originally manifested in speaking the universe into being. That no arithmetical or metaphysical definition of Christ or of God, or of Christ as God, in the literal sense of that phrase, is here thought of by John, is sufficiently obvious from all his other writings. If he had designed to make that statement, so astonishing, and so important if true, how easy had he found explicit and unmistakable terms to do it in ! If he had said, "Jesus Christ, who looked like a man, was in truth very God himself, the Maker of heaven and earth, — who took a human body and a human soul, and came down into the world, and allowed himself to be crucified, though he was all the time the Almighty Creator," there would be no further difference of opinion in regard to John's doctrine. But when he simply says that, as the universe reveals God, and as the soul in man reveals God, so at length he was *more fully* revealed in Jesus Christ, — we can only understand him to mean, not that God imparts his *personality* to him, or in any literal sense occupies him, but that he manifests himself to the world in the completest manner in which he has done it, or can do it, in Christ.

The incarnation of God in Christ has, more than any other doctrine, been conceded by theologians to be the central article of Christian faith.

In ecclesiastical history, the theology of Christendom has turned upon two separate axes, — the Catholic theology on the incarnation, the Protestant theology on the sacrificial death of Christ. This last, while the most modern, is by no means so general or universal as the first; and there is evidence that Protestantism itself is fast returning to the correcter theology of the Catholic Church in regard to the fundamental doctrine of the gospel.

Now, the ideas raised by this phrase (the incarnation), in most Unitarian minds, are painful; because they at once seem to involve an erroneous doctrine of the *Supreme Deity of Christ*. But the actual New-Testament, or Johannean, doctrine of the incarnation, as the central and cardinal peculiarity of the gospel, contains no such idea, as we shall endeavor to show.

The grand object of all religion is to reveal a proper knowledge of God, and establish a true filial relation between man and his Maker. God knows this infinitely better than we do; and, since the world was made or man existed, has been revealing himself as fast and as far as man could bear it. We may rashly suppose that there are *no difficulties* about the matter; but all history shows us that vast and most obstinate difficulties beset it. If God originally revealed himself to the first man, he revealed himself only as his Creator and his Ruler; and so imperfectly, that Adam either thought he was a being to be deceived, that might be safely disobeyed, or that some other knowledge (of the tree of good and evil) was more important and interesting. The Bible account of the insuccess that attended the original attempt to communicate to man the knowledge of God, and of the necessity of sweeping the godless world into ruin by the Deluge, is an expression of the difficulty, not of awakening credulity, superstition, imaginations of spiritual beings, and erroneous conceptions of demons, in the human mind, but of planting the seeds of a true religion in the world. It could be done only most gradually; only in strict reference to the nature of humanity; only in accordance with the order in which the passions and powers of man develop themselves. God can reveal himself to man, only as man, in the feeling and use of his own nature, sympathetically understands his Maker, by understanding the attributes which he himself possesses, and which reflect and interpret Him in whose image he is made. Man understands God only as far as he understands himself. What he does not know or feel intellectually, morally, or spiritually, in his own personality, he will not be able to ascribe in its infinity to God. While he seeks and loves and fears power only, God will be infinite power; intelligence only, God will be infinite intelligence; justice and truth, God will be all these raised to their highest power; goodness, mercy, gentleness, holiness, — then these exalted to the utmost stretch of feeling and thought. And this is no hypothesis, but describes the history of God's revelations of himself. We may consider them as three, matching the three great historic periods, and the threefold nature of man in the order of its natural unfolding. Among these we do not reckon that original revelation of God, made in man's very nature, — the condition, as it is the constant criterion and criticism, of all the others, — a revelation which is alike old and new, uniting all the other revelations together, and perhaps really being that *word,* or supreme reason, which is the common basis of the divine Spirit and the human soul.

The three great revelations of God are, *first,* the Patriarchal, or ante-Mosaic; *second,* the Prophetic; and, *third,* the Apostolic, — calling them after the names of the orders of persons through whom they were made: and these three revelations, as we shall see on examination, accommodated themselves in their order to the capacities and developments of the human creature.

Contrary to the superficial view, man is, first, a creature of imagination, crude, but vast and vigorous; next, a creature of conscience; last, a creature of affections. For this reason, poetry is older than prose, justice older than mercy, law older than gospel.

I. The first revelation was, accordingly, a revelation which addressed the imagination, and was designed to make known to man as much of God as could be received through that faculty. We call it the Patriarchal revelation. It proclaimed God a person and a unit, but was principally engaged in establishing his superiority to all other gods, his awful and absolute authority. It did not concern itself much with his justice and goodness, or indeed with his character at all. That was not the thing the world needed most. It needed to bow itself before an awful Will, — a Being so great, that his very greatness made Right. What He did was right because He did it. In an age of absolutism, of necessary concession to the strongest, — an age of ignorance, both of laws of nature and laws of mind, when even the on-goings of the external world were attributed to deific caprice, — we need not wonder that Jehovah was revealed as only the most absolute, the most jealous, the most arbitrary, of beings. This was the form most likely to win reverence, and indeed the only form in which the urgent wants of the human soul could be met. The God of Abraham, the God of the patriarchs, is therefore a God of mystery. He speaks in dark enigmas. He draws into himself the shuddering fears and hopes of a superstitious age. He meets the needs of wonder and awe and mystery. He works out his pleasure through solemn riddles. He is thus more attractive to the Oriental mind, by degrees, than their own false gods, because even more absolute, fatal, and invisible. He will have no name, but be known only as the "I am;" the self-existent, only, and self-sufficient monarch of the universe.

Let us remember, that, in those early days, questions of conscience were very little agitated, and matters of affection were by no means raised to the importance which the refinements of Christian life have given them. The imagination, the fears, the vague longings and dreads, of our nature, made that part of humanity alike its strongest and its weakest side. There only would it listen or could it learn. There only was it harassed and distressed; and we can well imagine the vast superiority which at once clothed the patriarchs, when their imaginations no longer wandered vaguely and fearfully from Baal to Belial, from Astaroth to the sun-god, but settled into a fixed awe and subjection to Jehovah the Almighty.

II. Next came the Prophetic revelation, including the Mosaic dispensation and its great prophets. The sense of right and wrong had now sufficiently awakened, under the political and social discipline of ages, to make it possible to address man as characteristically a moral being, an accountable creature. And to this end it became necessary that God should reveal himself, not merely as infinite power and absolute authority, but as the eternal Arbiter of right and wrong, as justice and truth, as law and retribution. This is the burden of the Mosaic revelation. Men by that time had begun to notice, that there was a method and a rule in the external universe; that nature herself was not caprice and chance, but law and order: and thus they were prepared to know, that there was not merely an arbitrary and absolute Ruler in heaven, but a Being who ruled by a plan, a moral order, and who himself loved and maintained justice and truth, hated and punished injustice and falsehood.

The emphasis which the Mosaic law laid upon positive duty has been of inconceivable importance in the development of humanity. The *holiness of God*, the great lesson of that dispensation, carried the Jewish people at once far beyond all contemporary nations, and made them the necessary medium of true civilization to the whole future. The *patriarchs* had learned God's being and power: the *prophets* learned his righteousness. How difficult a lesson to learn it was, how slow and severe the discipline of those it came to, we shall understand if we remember the steady evasions to which the essential and intrinsic significance of the law was subjected; how ritualism was honored as the substitute and shadow of righteousness, and external legality put for internal obedience. But, through all forms and rites, conscience was struggling into activity, and God was revealing his real holiness. The stiff-necked and crooked generation was continually suffering, and understood that it was suffering, the consequences of its moral perversity; and the tendency of the Mosaic law to establish absolute and not arbitrary rules of duty, a real and not a ritual consciousness of guilt, a true dutifulness and not a mere legal purity, is evinced in the sacred literature of that people, which is one long burst of eloquent, solemn, and august protest against misinterpretation and perversion of their own law.

No one can understand the dignified object of the Mosaic dispensation, without including in it the writings of the prophets. And it is only fair to the Jewish religion to acknowledge, that it naturally flowered into the devout and tender strains of David, and the spiritual and searching exhortations, reproofs, and aspirations of Isaiah and Ezekiel.

The spirituality of God, his essential moral perfection and excellency, his goodness and general Fatherhood, were worked out by the prophets in a most extraordinary and perfect manner. *The non-essential* character of forms and ceremonies, too, was never more plainly taught than by all the prophets. Trust in God's wisdom, goodness, and justice, his mercy and truth, is commended with an earnestness and strength of faith which to-day we continue to draw upon in our neediest hours.

God is revealed in the Jewish prophetic books plainly, and he never can be revealed more eloquently or impressively, as the God of truth, justice, goodness, mercy, — as a spiritual Being, impartial without arbitrariness, cruelty, or indifference: and there the revelation stops.

III. But why should it not stop there? what remains to be known? what does the human soul need more than to know, — 1. That God *is*, and that he is infinite in power and might and wisdom, — all powerful to protect his people? 2. That he is just, holy, good, and wise; loves the good, hates the bad only; and desires only to see truth, justice, and mercy prevail among his children? Cannot the human soul rest in a faith like this — a pure and high and holy and devout theism? Certainly it can rest there for a while. It did rest there for ages, and it were folly and wickedness to deny that some of the noblest, the most unselfish and sublime of all God's children had that faith only, and gloried in it; and, to as many as received that faith, gave he power to become the sons of God. To as many as receive it now, it gives a like power; and we have no sympathy whatever with the odious associations which vulgarize and take away the proper sanctity that belongs to a pure theism. Moses was a theist, David and Isaiah were theists; and those who make no distinction between theists and atheists ought to make none between light and darkness, right and wrong, since one are believers in *one* God, and the others are believers in none.

It is due, however, to a proper and candid explanation of this term to say, that theism has acquired its evil repute, not for what it believes, but for what it *denies;* that, denying Christianity, it naturally falls under the reproach of believers in Christianity, but not for believing in God. It is important to dwell a moment on this point, because theism has very much changed its character in our day, from a negative to a positive thing, from denying Christ to affirming God; and, as we are likely to have an extensive school of earnest theists, made up of scientific and rationalistic parties, men devoutly affirming and worshipping the only God, but denying the importance, or the miraculous claims, or the actual addition, of Christianity, it is well we should know that they are entitled to the respect which belongs to the devout Jews, and that it does not follow that they are irreligious or unworshipful, however unfortunate and unwise we may think them to be.

But, we ask again, what was there to be added to the revelation of God, as good, holy, just, merciful; a Father who pitieth his children? Nothing, if man be only a creature of imagination and conscience; but *much*, very much, if he be also a creature, still more characteristically, of the affections. That man is not, in the order of his unfolding, either firstly or secondly, a creature in whom the affections predominate, is very obvious from the history of opinions in this world. The first we hear of our race is always as tribes or communities, not as individual man and woman. The passions are rife enough, but the affections shallow and diffused. The individual is merged in the community. Then God communicates, if at all, with the high-priest *for* the people. His relation is with the social and communized man, not with the private person: he is too insignificant to be singled out, nor does he single himself out for attention. Therefore offences are visited not scrupulously on the offender, but on any of his people. As in our Indian tribes, if a man is killed, vengeance lies not against the murderer merely, but any one of his tribe. This it is that makes death such a trifle among rude peoples: they learn to defy or scorn it, because it is always before them; and they make light of life from a sense of its uncertainty, and of their own private insignificance.

The sublime disinterestedness of a state of society in which the individual holds himself as living only as his race lives, and not dying so long as they survive, and which calmly resigns the hope of individual immortality to the hope of a noble future for its people, admirable as an illustration of moral elevation, is, nevertheless, both the result and the perpetuation of imperfectly developed personal affections.

It is impossible to conceive of a tender domestic life, of a general ardor and activity of the affections, in a state of society in which the instincts of immortality are suppressed, or smoulder in an ashen vagueness. Man dare not cast his all upon affections which perish at the grave; nor can he attribute to a being insignificant as the limits of this earthly existence make him, a claim on any deep and self-sacrificing affections. We know very well that human nature has vindicated all its qualities in exceptional cases, in all ages and under all circumstances, and do not doubt that holy faith, and spiritual insight and elevation, and family affections, have existed in sporadic cases since the world was made, and under the most disadvantageous conditions. But we are now speaking of the general rule, and of the characteristics of successive eras and ideas; and we say that the absence among the Jews, and in the prophetic writings, of any *distinct faith in the immortality of the soul,* or of the perpetuation of the individual beyond the grave, is a sufficient proof of the undeveloped and torpid state of the affections, and of the domestic order, as compared with the other and earlier parts of human experience. If we are told, that, although this does not clearly appear in their sacred writings, it may have been a part of their interior confidence, we reply that the affections cannot conceal their faith, or fail to give a bold prominence to it when they hold it; and that caution or doubt in the expression of a faith in immortality is equivalent to indifference, and shades, by easy degrees, into unbelief.

After the prophetic books were closed, we know that

throughout the world, particularly in Greece and India, notions of immortality were beginning to awake and to become important, and to have disciples among the Jews themselves. But the immortality, whether of the Indian philosophy or of Plato himself, was rather an immortality of the spiritual principle than of its *individual possessor*,— the immortality of the rain-drop that falls into an ever-living ocean.

Do we ask, then, what the new revelation was to unfold? We answer, the importance, the dignity, the glory, of the individual. And how was this to be done? By revealing something beyond the goodness, the mercy, the general fatherhood of God,— namely, his personal interest in, and discriminating feeling towards, the individual members of his human family; by revealing God, in short, as human, in the play of his interest and affection, his sympathy and tenderness, toward men. Until men could learn to think themselves of individual importance in God's sight, they could neither believe in their own immortality, nor love as immortals, nor treat otherwise than with stoical repression their own latent tenderness of feeling. Polygamy, desertion, the prostration and enslaving of women, the selling of children into bondage, concubinage, and every form of contempt for the affections, belonged to the era when the *individual* was nothing, the race and tribe every thing,— when power and right, authority and justice, absolute and impersonal, ruled the world.

But the new revelation began a fresh era. We cannot describe it better than as the era of the affections; and it began that era, and accomplished that revelation, by the incarnation. That is to say, God came into the world as a man, came near to us, and confessed and disclosed his personal and human affections towards us, in Christ Jesus. Not that in any Trinitarian or popular sense Jesus Christ was God, any more than the plenipotentiary is the king, or the messenger his own sender; but he so truly represented God's love and tenderness, as feeling human weakness and want, and individual griefs and sorrows, and as taking his children one by one to his bosom, that we are henceforth justified in ascribing to God every affection and tenderness and consideration for our private griefs and the wants of our affections, which we behold in Jesus Christ, who was Immanuel or God with us, God manifest in the flesh.

The directness, the immediateness, the condescension, the domesticity of God's love; his willingness to be the personal friend of each and every one of his children; his sympathy with private and personal griefs and sorrows and struggles, — *this* is the revelation made in the incarnation: "the word was made flesh, and dwelt among us," and we beheld his glory, the glory of the only begotten of the Father, full of grace and truth. It has been easy enough for the world in all ages to deify men and exalt human qualities into divine, but only Christ has humanized God, and brought divine attributes into human limitations and conditions.

The wonderful condescension of the almighty God — permitting us and entreating us to see him in a human creature, to know him in knowing a human creature, to interpret him by the conduct, affections, and sacrifices of a human creature — ought to excite all our gratitude and all our wonder. Nothing short of this could ever have drawn human affections out of the supine indifference in which they lay dormant. In no climate less heavenly mild than that which Jesus Christ, the sun of righteousness, has made, — the climate of warm, all-embosoming, and all-penetrating love from God, — could the delicate sensibilities, the family affections, the personal aspirations, of humanity have dared to shoot and bud and blossom until they made that garden bower of homes and hearts which we call modern civilization. This is Christendom, the age and sway of personal affections, the era of the individual, when man dares to look at his personal stake in the universe; dares to believe himself known to God and dear to him; dares to look death in the face, and succeeds in looking its stony eyes out of countenance; dares to love the fragile and the death-struck, because they are still strong in God's care, and undying in their essence; dares to grow old and recognize his own decay, because so only can he renew his youth; dares to see his own imperfections and sins just as they are, because God loves him in spite of them, and because he is to have an endless opportunity of struggling with them and putting them away, and has an all-sufficient ally in his Saviour or his Father.

There is no end to the beauty and significance of the faith that God is seen in the face of Jesus Christ; no bound to the meaning and glory of the incarnation. It has changed general principles into personal affections, it has made religion from a public concern a private interest; it has brought the temple into the home and into the heart.

We know very well that this is bringing God too nigh to suit the views or the tastes of some: they do not want religion to be personal, individual, and, so to speak, human. They object to shutting up the soul to the study and contemplation of God in Christ; the limits shock or disturb them; they are willing to have Jesus Christ one among other holy teachers of divine truth, but not "the way, the truth, and the life." They have perhaps never sympathized with Philip's earnest request, "Show us the Father, and it sufficeth us," much less with Christ's answer, "Have I been so long time with you, and yet hast thou not known me, Philip? he that hath seen me hath seen the Father, and how sayest thou then, 'Show us the Father.'"

There is another side to the personality of the gospel: while it brings our Father nigh, it brings our God equally near; while it supports and cherishes and consoles our afflictions, it probes our consciences; while it bends low to whisper its encouragements into our ear, it looks, with the eye that Peter could not meet, into the sinner's own heart, and summons him to an immediate, an urgent, and a personal repentance.

Receiving religion through a person makes it a personal matter; and it thus gets a hold on the conscience and will, as on the heart, which arouses the resistance or alarms the self-love, the pride, and waywardness of many. But, as a matter of observation, all the practical power, whether to console or to convince of sin and save, which resides in the gospel, resides in it by virtue of the incarnation of God in Christ coming into direct personal relation with individual souls, and so, by a positive, circumstantial, and unescapable influence, shutting them up to a direct intercourse with the great Physician, who is also the great Consoler and Comforter of souls.

This is what our Orthodox brethren of every name mean, when they talk of the necessity of coming to Christ. They have, it is true, a great many theories about the efficacy of Christ's blood, and the virtue of the Atonement, and the power of the cross; but these are matters of theory and speculation and rhetoric. We do not think it necessary here to oppose or to explain them. But all that they mean is realized by every soul which, in any way and on any theory, comes into personal relations with Christ, as the Father's image and the Father's love brought nigh, and so made positive and influential and tender and predominating. If we do not want our religious and personal affections to be chilled to death; if we really desire that personal relation with God which shall make his service a positive and constant reality; if we wish Christianity to come to us, — not as the message of the sovereign or president comes to every citizen of the state, but as a warm and tender communication, a letter from home, addressed to our private souls, — then let us study God's will in Christ's face and in Christ's life and death; meditate upon and make ourselves masters of the purpose of our Lord's mission on earth. Consider what has been always, and what now continues to be, the secret of his power. Then we shall no longer worship a vague, or a merely just and holy God; but we shall find a heavenly Father, and find him quickening and cleansing our conscience, sanctifying our heart, consoling our griefs, confirming our faith, and renewing our souls, through the tender and all-sufficient hands of a personal, a devoted, a dying, a risen, and an ever-living Saviour.

Art. VIII.—REVIEW OF CURRENT LITERATURE.

THEOLOGY.

It has been a joyous sight to see Italy born again into the family of nations, and renewing her youth and strength; and every new sign of awakening life is a fresh pleasure. We have here a book * which helps to increase our hope, that Italy will soon have a theology more suited to her needs than the mass of superstitions which has been her inheritance. Our author is a pioneer in the cause of liberal theology there, and has had, it seems, not only to write his book, but to pay for its publication.

He has done his work in a thorough and scholarly way. He shows himself acquainted with German, English, and French authorities. He is very successful in his treatment of the two great objections to the unity of the Book of Ecclesiastes,—that is, the presence in it of so many disjointed sentences and maxims; and, secondly, the apparently contradictory statements in it in regard to a future life and judgment, and on some other matters.

On the first point, our author, acknowledging his indebtedness to Ewald and Knobel for two suggestions at the basis of his view, considers the author of Ecclesiastes to have been an unskilful writer, who sometimes let his fancy wander outside the logical line of his argument, and afterwards did not correct and prune his work, as a more critical writer would have done. He points out, besides, that these disconnected sentences are mostly maxims of practical advice, — a common mode of teaching in the East,— in which the accidental association of ideas in the mind of the writer would have freer play, and the connection of thought be less regarded, than in a theoretical treatise, such as the greater part of the book is.

Our author harmonizes the apparent contradictions in the book with its unity, by regarding the author of it as a "probabilist," as he puts it, or a sceptic, — not absolute and thorough-going, but one who

---

* Il Libro del Cohelet, Volgarmente Detto Ecclesiaste, Tradotto dal Testo Ebraico, con Introduzione Critica e Note. Di DAVID CASTELLI. Pisa: Tipographia Nistri, 1866. A spese dell' Autore. pp. 305.

"denies nothing, but acknowledges every thing, yet recognizes nothing as true, but accepts every thing as probable," — one who, "considering things in their multiform aspects, reaches contrary conclusions, according to the different ways in which he examines questions;" "yet forced by necessity to follow some line of conduct in practical life, after passing in review the different opinions which wrestle together in his mind, rests finally in that conclusion which seems to him the least improbable." Yet these considerations are not enough, our author thinks, to reconcile the doctrine of the last six verses of the book (xii. 9-14) to that of the rest of it; but we have not space enough here to give his rather complex view of this subject.

We hope that the Italian exegesis which is to come will show as much care and thought and acuteness, and be as clear in expression, as this book is. If so, it will help, not only Italy, but the rest of the world besides.

F. T. W.

AFTER what late events have taught us, we should hardly have gone to Palermo in search of a liberal or a rationalist; but it seems, from the book before us,* that the spirit of free inquiry has penetrated even there. Our author belongs to a class of rationalists which we might expect to find in so backward a place. He is of the Voltaire and Tom-Paine school of Deists. To one used to a more modern mode of thought, there is something almost startling in this apparition from the past. It may be, however, that things are in such a bad state in Palermo, and in some other parts of Italy, as to give to Deism a strong excuse for being, and to call for the assertion of the great truth which this Deism contains, that the reason has its rights, which must not be trampled upon. And, so far as this book is an assertion of the rights of reason, it has our hearty sympathy. But our author, not content with this, strikes, in a rather vague but very bloodthirsty way, at all of us poor Christians, and attacks Christianity with a fierceness which seems more dictated by prejudice and ignorance than by that Reason of which he is so warm a worshipper.

Perhaps the strangest part of the book is found in the last chapter, where we are surprised, after the strong and indiscriminate abuse of dogmas in the chapters before, to read that "the programme of the rationalists" should be set out clearly in formulas, and spread abroad. Our author's attempt at a "programme" of this sort seems

---

* Il Razionalismo ed il Signor Guizot. Per il Cav. B. GALLETTI. Palermo: Tipografia di Gaetano Priulla, 1866. pp. vii., 105.

more fitted to excite surprise — if not to cause a smile — than to touch the heart or to convince the intellect; and we think a wide change of base will be needed to make this one-sided philosophy into a religion.

Judged on its scientific merits, the book has very little value. Its tone is noisy, flippant, and conceited. It is chiefly of interest to us, as illustrating one phase of contemporary Italian thought, and from its bearings on the religious and political changes which are maturing so fast in Italy. And, despite all the faults of this book, — and they are many, — we hail it as a sign of the great reform which is coming. It will help to swell the flood of indignation which will, ere long, sweep the Eternal City clean of its tyrannical and imbecile government, and which will do away with the sad and sorry comedy which has so long been played there.
F. T. W.

HEINRICH BRUGSCH is well known as one of the ablest living Egyptian scholars. The little book undernoted * consists of the lectures which he delivered in Berlin at various times during the nine or ten years preceding his departure, as Prussian consul, to Egypt. The titles of the chapters are: A Day and Night in Cairo; The Nile Boat; A Journey over the Desert; An ancient Egyptian story, — the oldest in the world; Moses and the Monuments; The Revelations of the Stones; Germans and Persians, — all fresh and lively and clear, a happy instance of a German scholar being entertaining without ceasing to be learned.

The lecture upon "Moses and the Monuments" touches upon the relation of ancient Hebrew history to that of contemporary nations, which is one of the most interesting topics of modern investigation. The subject is still involved in much obscurity; but there are, nevertheless, certain points which may now be considered clear; and some of the results of recent discoveries in respect to the central figure, the commanding name with which the strictly historical records of the Hebrews open, are quite curious.

There is a difference among scholars of fifty or sixty years as to the date of the Exodus: but that the period intervening between the entrance and the exit of the children of Israel in Egypt comprises one of the most glittering epochs in the history of the kingdom of

---

* Aus dem Orient. Von HEINRICH BRUGSCH. Zwei Theile in einem Bande. Berlin, 1864. Verlag von Werner Grosse.

the Pharaohs, is established beyond question by monumental evidence; and that this period corresponds with the first half of the fourteenth century before Christ, is also well settled. Two thousand years had elapsed since the empire of the Egyptians, beginning in Memphis, and gradually extending its pyramids and its temples southwards to Thebes, had attained a great degree of splendor and power, when suddenly, as the traditions relate, a Semitic horde, hard pressed by the Assyrians, broke into Egypt across the Isthmus of Suez, and, having become well organized under able leaders, occupied the Delta, defeated the Egyptian armies, and, choosing their own kings, established their residence and camp in the city of Tanis, or, as it was called in Egyptian, Hanar (Avaris). By degrees they extended their domination to Memphis, and made the Egyptian kings in Southern Egypt tributary. The foreign domination lasted five hundred years; and the Egyptians found what satisfaction they could in designating them, in the inscriptions with which they still went on covering the walls of their temples and tombs, by the word *Amu*, which means "ox-herds," or with the epithet *Aadu*, which means "the despised."

But, as in many similar cases of contact between an inferior and a superior civilization, the latter triumphed at last: the nomadic hordes of the Semites yielded to the culture and the arts of the Egyptians. One of the Semitic kings erected a temple in Tanis to Sutech, the Egyptian conception of the Semitic Baal; and they came at last to use in their tombs the Egyptian mode of writing. But the warlike spirit of the Pharaohs still survived, and enabled the latter in the end to overcome their conquerors. Tanis was besieged and taken, and Egypt was again free. And from that time begins the brilliant period in its history, which covers the nineteenth and eighteenth and seventeenth centuries before our era. The Egyptian armies pressed into Palestine, and over the highway, by Gaza and Megiddo, to the banks of the Euphrates and the Tigris; an annual tribute was laid upon Babylon and Nineveh; and the Egyptian conquerors erected their pillars of victory upon the borders of Armenia, where, as the hieroglyphic inscriptions read, " the heavens rest upon four columns."

Thus, as Bunsen says, Africa took its revenge on Asia. Thousands of captives were brought back to labor on the Egyptian temples in Memphis and Thebes, on the walls of which they still stand delineated as bringing water and moistening clay, and making bricks and spreading them to dry in the sun, while Egyptian taskmasters stand over them, stick in hand.

A new dynasty, the nineteenth, followed presently the one that had thus shaken off the Hyksos, as the foreign Semitic kings are commonly termed; and at its head stood Ramses I., its founder, about the middle of the sixteenth century before Christ. About 1400 B.C., his grandson, Ramses II., began his reign, which lasted for sixty-six years; and it is then that the first monumental synchronism occurs with the records of the Hebrews in the Bible. On the eastern side of the Delta, Ramses constructed a series of bulwarks, from Pelusium to Heliopolis, against the inroads of Asiatic hordes, — bulwarks which served also to overawe the Semitic population of his kingdom. And among these fortified places were two, named Ramses and Pachtum: " And they built for Pharaoh treasure cities, Pithom and Raamses" (Exod. i. 11); the word for Pharaoh, which the Hebrews applied to the king, being merely a title signifying "the great house," as we say of the Sultan, " the Sublime Porte " (Gate). It was under this Pharaoh, Ramses II., that Moses was born and brought up, in the first half of the fourteenth century before Christ.

In one of the papyrus rolls preserved in the British Museum, the Egyptian scribe, Pinebsa, reports to his chief, Amenemaput, the condition in which he has found the city Ramses : " It is incomparable," he says, " and life there is sweet; the streets are filled with men, the ponds and canals with fish, and the fields with birds ; fragrant flowers bloom on the meadows, and the fruits taste like honey; and the granaries are bursting with corn." And then he records the preparations which had been made for the reception of the king at his entry into the city ; and adds that there was a dense multitude of people to greet him, but more especially to address to him, " great in victory," their prayers and complaints. On the back of this withered papyrus, moreover, there is a memorandum of the structures erected in the city, so that there has thus descended to us a contemporary account, indeed, of the cities described in Exodus as built by the Israelites for their taskmasters in Egypt.

We should naturally expect to find the children of Israel designated on the monuments by the term applied to them by foreign nations; and in point of fact this has been discovered to be the case, the foreign appellation of the Hebrews being found in their Egyptian designation, — *Apuru.* In a papyrus roll preserved in Leyden is found the following writing from the scribe Kanitsir to his chief, the scribe Bakenpthah : —

"May my master find content therein that I have accomplished the task which he assigned to me in the words, to wit, Give food to the soldiers, and also to the Hebrews who transport the stones to the great city of the King Ramses — Miamun, Lover of Truth, [and who] are under command of the Police — soldiers, Ameneman. I supplied them with food each month, according to the excellent command which my master hath given unto me."

And again, on the rocks in the valley of Hamamât, along which went the old Egyptian highway from Coptos, on the Nile, to the port of Berenice, on the Red Sea, is an inscription in which is included, among other things, an enumeration of the number of men employed in constructing the road; and among them is a troop of eight hundred Hebrews, under the escort of Egyptian soldiers of the police, of Libyan descent, called *masai*.

Two things, therefore, may be considered established: first, that the Egyptian records named Ramses as the builder of the cities Pithom and Ramus; and, secondly, that the same records speak of the Hebrews in a way to indicate that their position in respect to the building of these cities was that of forced laborers under police superintendence. Now in the Bible the builder of Pithom and Raamses appears at once as a tyrannical oppressor of the children of Israel, and as a new king in Egypt who "knew not Joseph," — a fact which shows that Joseph never came to the court of an Egyptian Pharaoh, but to one of those Semitic conquerors in the Delta, who, as we have seen, lived at Avaris (Tanis), and thence governed the country as far as Memphis and Heliopolis. After the liberation of their country, therefore, from these usurpers, the Pharoahs of Egyptian race had no feeling for the kindred of the former, and for three hundred years exercised an oppressive sway over them, which reached its culmination under Ramses II. and his successor. The birth of Moses falls under Ramses II.; and under his successor, whom the monuments call Menephthes, occurred the Exodus, when Moses was eighty years of age. If, therefore, Menephthes reigned twenty years, as the Egyptian lists of kings state, Moses must have been born about the sixth year of Ramses, which corresponds with the statement of the Biblical records, that the building of Pithom and Raamses occurred in the first year of Ramses.

Now, the building of these cities had a strong political motive at the bottom of it; for they were designed to serve, not merely as a defence against invasion from Canaan, but as centres for the troops employed to keep down their own Semitic subjects. For, on one of the walls at Thebes, a treaty has been found, made between Ramses II., in the twenty-first year of his reign, and Chetasar, the king of the Hittites, which contains, among other things, the following clause: "If the subjects of King Ramses come over to the king of the Hittites, the king of the Hittites is not to receive them, but to compel them to return to the king of Egypt."

But it was not merely by military measures that the Pharaohs endeavored to control the restless spirit of their Semitic subjects: they had recourse to other less cruel and more insidious devices. According to the ancient belief, the gods of various countries were in fact the same, though designated by different names. Ramses took advantage of this notion, and offered sacrifices to the god of the strangers, to Baal (Sutech), and erected temples to him in the old Semitic city of Tanis (the Zoan of the Bible), remains of which have been discovered in modern times; for it was in Tanis that the cult of Baal had survived from the days of the Semitic protectors of Joseph. The colossal sitting statue of Ramses, in Berlin, is the one which he had made for this very temple, and must therefore have been seen by Moses; for the Bible mentions Zoan (Tanis) as the place where, at the command of the Lord, Moses worked his wonders before Pharaoh (Ps. lxxviii. 12, 43).

And still more did Menephthes, the Pharaoh of the Exodus, resort to these arts of conciliation. Too weak to dominate as his ancestor had done, he contented himself with inscribing on his banner the words, " the adorer of Sutech, Baal of Tanis;" and he even went so far, in his attempt to soothe the turbulent Semitic population of his kingdom, as to represent the god Baal on the back of one of his own colossi, together with his own son as the priest of Baal.

Touching the Egyptian origin of the name of Moses, Brugsch says there can now be but one opinion. The monuments make mention of several persons who bore the name Mas, or Massu, a word signifying "the child;" among others, one of the governors of Æthiopia, under the Pharaoh of Exodus, with whom, indeed, Josephus seems to have confounded Moses the lawgiver, when he speaks of the latter as having led an Egyptian army to Æthiopia in his youth, and having penetrated to Meroe and married the Egyptian princess, Tharbis, who, out of the love she had conceived for him, traitorously opened the gates of the city to him.

It has often been remarked, that the whole legislation of Moses shows traces of his Egyptian origin; and Brugsch mentions a fact in relation to it which is certainly very curious. The religious monuments of the Egyptians, whether stone or papyrus, bear testimony everywhere to the fact, that the priests had originally a distinct conception, and taught the doctrine of the unity of God; and that, however much this doctrine may have been perverted afterwards by the people in their worship of animals, it was still preserved by the priests in their mysteries, and revealed to the initiated, and to them alone, although a dark allusion to it was made in the papyrus roll which was put into the mouths of the dead to accompany them to the grave. The name, however, of the one God was not mentioned in these rolls: it was only paraphrased in the profound words, *nuk pu nuk*, — " I am that I am," — words which recall at once the similar phrase in Exodus (iii. 14) with which God names himself to Moses and the children of Israel, and which, in its Hebrew form *Jahveh* (mispronounced Jehovah), signifies the same as the Egyptian formula, *nuk pu nuk*, — I AM THAT I AM.   H. J. W.

GEOGRAPHY AND TRAVELS.

TRAVELS in Turkey are, for the most part, a dismal record of days wasted in weariness, and nights sleepless with fatigue and misery. Read one book, and you have read all. Now and then, indeed, some clever writer appears, who unites the gift of style with considerable knowledge of the country and the languages, and then we can really get through his book. But this is an exception, unfortunately a rare one; and one to which the two brave ladies — whose names figure on the titlepage of the bulky book on *the Turks, the Greeks, and the Slavons*, which has just reached us damp from the London press* — cannot fairly lay claim. The expectations raised by the title are by no means satisfied. It is not a book about the Turks or the Greeks, but chiefly about the Serbians, as the writer (for there is obviously but one) terms them in deference to their national pride, which is offended by spelling the word with a *v*, as giving their enemies a ground to taunt them with its derivation from the Latin *servus*. The Serbians are, however, an interesting people in many respects; their history, especially that chapter in it which relates to the enfran-

---

* The Turks, the Greeks, and the Slavons: Travels in the Slavonic Provinces of Turkey in Europe. By G. MUIR MACKENZIE and A. P. IRBY. With maps and numerous illustrations by F. Banitz. London: Bell & Daldy, 1867.

chisement of a part of them from the Turkish yoke, is highly honorable; and it is encouraging to know, from the careful observation of these ladies, that they are such a clean and thrifty race. Montenegro and the Herzegovina, and Albania also, countries which are so rarely visited, bordering though they do upon the Adriatic, whose waters are ploughed daily by the merchant steamers of the Mediterranean, were included in the travels of these adventurous English women. The descriptions which they give of the scenery and the people of the Black Mountains and the Albanian hills are certainly valuable, because fresh and truthful. But the book is twice as heavy as it ought to have been, and the title twice as ambitious.

That the Turks misrule the country, as they have misruled every country they were once strong enough to conquer, nobody outside the arid circle of English political prejudices and timidity need be told. That the leading prelates of the Greek Church are in many cases the supple tools of Turkish despotism over the Slavic races, is a fact, too, which will hardly be disputed by one familiar with the history of the vast country which stretches from the borders of Thrace to the Julian Alps, between the Danube and the Adriatic. Nor again is it to be doubted, that, in obedience to that law of nationality which has drawn the Italians under one flag, which is giving a head to Germany, and is marshalling the Greeks to assert their independence and their unity, the Slavic races south of the Danube will join hands under a common standard, and, inspired by a common patriotism, redeem their land from the long blight of Islam, and open it to commerce and the civilizing arts.

These things are clear to the careful observer. No one can open a book of travels in these countries without perceiving it. But, meantime, there is immense popular ignorance about the condition and characteristics of this South Slavic people; and one who cares to be enlightened should study this book, — we cannot say read it. There is a good colored map accompanying the work; and one is thus able to take in at a glance the variety of races of which the population of this great region is somewhat confusedly made up. The Greeks, it will be observed, occupy, with a trifling exception, the whole Ægean coast, and are massed up heavily against the Sea of Marmora. They are essentially a commercial, maritime race; and, when the Turks withdraw, as withdraw they must, into Asia, the Greeks will very likely be masters of the country south of the Balkan range. Further north they cannot go: nor should they, for the Slavic race is agricultural, and to a certain degree aspiring; and it will occupy the country better than the Greeks, and, moreover, will be its own best master.

Of Serbia and the Serbians, therefore, we repeat, considerable information will be found in this book; of the Turks, little new that is worth knowing; of the Greeks, nothing whatever.

H. J. W.

The title of Mr. Hepworth Dixon's last book,* though not mystical or cabalistic, gives no idea of its real subject. What he calls "New America" is simply an account of three or four of the eccentric religious sects of America, — the Mormons, the Shakers, the Funkers, the "Bible Christians" of Oneida Creek. The book is in no sense a book of American travel, and it describes things which are but little known, and have very little influence, in America, — except, perhaps, in its short notice of Spiritualism. It begins with a journey across the plains to Salt-Lake City; exaggerating somewhat the discomforts and hazards of that exciting trip, and giving a picture, by no means fascinating, of life in Colorado, the roughness, brutality, recklessness, and waste of life in the new mining cities. Mr. Dixon's theory, that Indian law and life are the model of the present and coming civilization on these plains, will not be accepted as wise or as plausible. Indeed, we may say that the chief defect of his book is its untenable theories. It is pure fancy to offer the Arab of Cairo and Damascus as the true type of refinement and courtesy, and to show a steadily decreasing grace of bearing and address, as one travels westward. The Arab is lithe and graceful in bodily movement; but it is a perversion of language to call such an ignorant, bigoted, false, and vindictive race, who rarely smile, and with whom cunning is the first of virtues, a race of gentlemen. Mr. Dixon's observation on this subject is simply absurd. There is no such measure of courteousness by degrees of longitude, and the manners of Paris and Boston are not to be set half way between the elegance of the Arabian Desert and the barbarism of Denver City.

Mr. Dixon's pictures of the abnormal sects which he deals with are life-like and accurate; and there is no prejudice in his account

---

* New America. By William Hepworth Dixon. With Illustrations from Original Photographs. Philadelphia: J. B. Lippincott & Co., 1867. 12mo. pp. 495.

of their opinions. He does not go out of his way to approve or condemn; and, to some pious Puritan readers, his book will seem faulty that it relates such moral indecencies with no burst of indignation,—that it leaves doubt as to the real feeling of the author about polygamy, and free love, and asceticism. Ought a respectable writer to reveal such things without denouncing them? "He that is not against us is for us;" and the Mormons will have the right to say that Mr. Dixon favors their plurality of wives, because he has no harsh words for it. But, on the whole, this impartial calmness of judgment is a pleasant feature of the book, and gives confidence in the writer's statements. It will not probably make converts to promiscuous intercourse of the sexes, or to the patriarchal system of the harem. It may send visitors to New Lebanon or to Oneida Creek, but will hardly add recruits to those strange communities.

Mr. Dixon is a friend of America and American institutions, a believer in republican ideas, and a strong foe to every kind of slavery and oppression. It is impossible, therefore, to mistake him for an advocate of the Mormon despotism, which perpetuates the worst features of slavery. He cheerfully recognizes the material progress, the industry, the temperance, the good order, the thrift, of the Salt-Lake oasis. But he has not that cynical joy which we find in the work of Burton, in showing how material prosperity comes with moral obliquity. Burton would have us believe that the preaching and the practice of the Mormons are quite as respectable as those of any Christian sect, and that the success of this polygamy and this vulgar hierarchy is a substantial proof that the patriarchal religion and method are as good as the Christian. Dixon does not say that, but only gives the good side of the Mormon life along with the disgusting side.

His book is fresh, entertaining, and instructive. There is not a dull page in it. If some of the statements are extravagant, they are far less so than those of most English writers on American things. A writer who can describe so well American oddities can be trusted to give us another book on the ordinary experiences of the traveller here, and on things better known.

POETRY AND ART.

THE law of demand and supply seems, in these days of perfected commercial arrangements, to have extended itself into the domain of poetry; so that the literary market is now supplied, with very considerable regularity, with the productions of its most popular and recognized poets. The fact is, doubtless, entirely creditable; and we ought to felicitate ourselves on having achieved a final victory over the eccentricities of genius. But it is occasionally a little annoying to be forced to amend our ideas, and to learn the new aphorism, that, whatever may be the origin of the poets themselves, their verses at least are not created, but manufactured, and that to order. It is useless to complain of degeneracy, or to talk about inspiration: in our day, the best inspiration is success; and the substantial tribute of quick sales and multiplied editions is a very acceptable discount on that very long note of hand which goes by the name of Fame.

> "Think of this, good peers,
> But as a thing of custom: 'tis no other,
> Only it spoils the pleasure of the time."

This moralizing is *apropos* of Mr. Whittier's last book, "The Tent on the Beach,"* which appears just a year after the "Snow-bound." The two are very different from each other, and both are very different from the earlier poems of their author. They are the work of a prosperous writer, whose name is sufficiently established to make it of comparatively little importance to his publishers what he writes or how he writes it. The "Snow-bound" has the advantage of being complete and single, and of a subject which is sure to make its own interest in the heart of every reader who has reached middle age, and can look back on the vanished joys of a New-England country home. Many of its pictures are charming, because they are simple and true, and shine with the tender radiance of a loving and sad memory, — "the light of other days." But it is quite evident that much of the matter was added only to make up the volume; and the public interest, which follows with pleasure the outlines and even the details of the main picture, flags and fails when invited to examine all the nameless family portraits which follow, drawn though they are with a reverent hand, and out of a feeling which it is impossible that a stranger can share.

Of the later volume still less can be said. This is still more obviously a manufactured poem, of which the public have been

---

* The Tent on the Beach. By John Greenleaf Whittier. Boston: Ticknor & Fields.

permitted from time to time to see a portion of the materials. Like Mr. Longfellow's "Wayside Inn," it is a specimen of what may be called the *conglomerated* school of poetry, in which any stray nuggets of verse — which may have done service in a magazine or newspaper, but are too few or too slight to be gathered by themselves into a volume — are made available to that end, by being embedded in a connecting and retaining medium of narrative. It is but a cheap device, and cheapens rapidly by repetition. In the present instance, as might well be expected, some of the little pieces are extremely pleasing; and all have Mr. Whittier's never-failing merits of easy and graceful movement, and purity and sweetness of tone. But the most of them, and perhaps all, have been very recently printed in the "Atlantic Monthly," or some other periodical; and few have more than the value and interest which are looked for in such ephemera as magazine verses. And as for the thread of narrative which connects them, it is impossible to help feeling that it is such poetry as a trained versifier like Mr. Whittier could throw off by the page, as easily as Touchstone his doggerel to Rosalind: "I'll rhyme you so eight days together, dinners and suppers and sleeping-hours excepted." Though we do not deny it to be pleasant reading, yet we do not conceive it to be the sort of verse which a true poet like Whittier, with so much of the real poetic temperament, so flavored and strengthened with the pure flame of moral earnestness, should be content to produce; and we look on it as one more proof of the extent to which the commercial spirit pervades and governs the life of this age. We are saying this surely out of no lack of appreciation of the worth of what this noble writer has contributed to the infant literature of his people; and our chief discontent at his later method comes less from what we conceive to be his own decline as a poet, than from the influence of his example upon younger writers whose work is of the future, and not of the present. C. A. C.

"SPECULATION," says Lessing, "must follow the torch of history." Every philosophy of art must rest upon a thorough study of works of art. To theorize about it from general conceptions merely, can lead only to the most vague and unsatisfactory results. "The Beautiful," as a naked abstraction, a mental essence, is the most empty and unprofitable of metaphysical conceptions. It is nothing to us except in its incarnations. It is only in the presence of the masterpieces of architecture, sculpture, painting, and music, that we can truly learn any thing of the eternal principles which underlie all artistic creations. The lack of this positive knowledge has always been the bane of æsthetic criticism in America; and the recent work of Dr. Samson,* whilst claiming to be a remedy, is in reality only an additional illustration of this defect. As "a text-book for schools and colleges," the book is utterly worthless; and, we fear, the "amateurs and artists" will find it rather heavy and indigestible *pabulum*. An elimination of the wholly irrelevant matter which the volume contains, would diminish its size at least one-fourth. This superfluous stuff is mostly of a semi-theological consistency, as vapid as it is impertinent, and holding about the same relation to "art criticism" that Mr. Tupper's platitudes do to poetry. The author's logical processes are peculiar, and we have rarely found in any book so many instances of naïve *non sequitur*. Because, in the fourth chapter of Genesis, Jubal, "the father of all such as handle the harp and organ," is mentioned one verse before Tubal-cain, the "instructor of every artificer in brass and iron," *therefore*, argues Dr. Samson, music is an older art than sculpture, and attained a high state of development at a much earlier period. Upon this narrow and untenable basis he then builds up a classification of the Fine Arts. To say nothing of the absurdity of the syllogism, the conclusion arrived at is in itself false. No doubt, at a very remote date in the world's history, barbaric tribes made horrid dissonance on gong-gongs and tom-toms; but music, as a fine art, is of later growth than sculpture: it is a product of modern times, and did not reach its present perfection till the eighteenth century of the Christian era. The book is not only confused and inconsistent in its method (or rather want of method), but also contradictory in its statements. In one chapter we are told that landscape-gardening is the highest of the arts: *first*, because Adam, who was "perfect in all his powers," practised this form of art; and, *secondly*, because architecture, sculpture, &c., are contributory to it and essential to its perfection. In another chapter it is said that Eden was the perfection of landscape-gardening, "long before architecture and sculpture were dreamed of." In other words, this art reached its perfection long before the elements necessary to

---

* Elements of Art Criticism: A Text-book for Schools and Colleges, and a Handbook for Amateurs and Artists. By G. W. SAMSON, D.D., President of Columbian College, Washington, D.C. Philadelphia: J. B. Lippincott & Co., 1867. 1 vol., crown 8vo. pp. 840.

its perfection "were dreamed of." These specimens will suffice to illustrate what we mean by vapid theorizings. The thick volume is full of them; but we have no space for further citations.

More useful are those portions of the work in which the author traces the history of the different arts. The reader will here find, for the most part, correct and intelligible explanations of various technical processes,—etching, engraving, photography, &c.; although, as Dr. Samson's book has no index, the same information can be more easily obtained from "Brande's Dictionary," or any other cyclopædia of art. Photography, he thinks, is destined to be the supreme fine art; and, in the gaudy upholstery of "an American river-boat," he discovers an elegance unsurpassed by any "palace apartment" in the world. In the chapter on Italian sculptors and painters, the criticism is all second-hand: he has evidently never seen the works on which he passes judgment; and, in many cases, does not even know their location. The foreign tourist, who should take this "handbook" as his guide, would frequently find himself at his wit's end. The only thing original in this section is the orthography of proper names, in which the author gives free rein to his fancy. The pages devoted to American artists read like extracts from a Fourth-of-July oration of Mr. Jefferson Brick,—no discriminating criticism, but only loose and unmeaning laudation. One is a Phidias, another a Praxiteles, and a third unites the excellences of both. But, notwithstanding this offensive tone of national exaggeration, so fretting to the finer filaments of taste, Dr. Samson really does injustice to American art, by omitting the names of some of our best artists.

The limits of a critical notice do not permit us to specify errors. The intelligent reader will find them soon enough. We have done our conscientious duty to the public, in indicating the general scope and character of the work.   E. P. E.

Mr. PALGRAVE's book * has been much talked of here, but less since the appearance of the New-York reprint than before, which is perhaps no wonder. The wonder is to find, after all the talk, that the book is, for the most part, a collection of ephemeral notices of successive exhibitions of the pictures of the Royal Academy of Lon-

---

* Essays on Art. By FRANCIS TURNER PALGRAVE, late Fellow of Exeter College, Oxford. New York: Hurd & Houghton, 1867.

don, or of special collections by single artists. These notices are uniformly well written, and have the air of intelligent and well-meant criticism; but one would think that with the disposal of the pictures would vanish the chief interest and value of the notices, and that, even in London, it was hardly worth while to collect them into a book. But that they should be reprinted in America is yet more strange; for they criticize pictures and statues which perhaps not a hundred Americans have ever seen. The only man who could make notices of pictures entertaining to those who had never seen them has unfortunately resigned his place. Mr. Palgrave, in reprinting, was doubtless led by Mr. Ruskin's example in his yearly "Notes on the Royal Academy's Exhibition," which were always delightful, whether we had ever heard the names of the painters or not: the heartiness of his praise, the vigor of his abuse, his exquisite word-pictures, and his sublime dogmatism, made it impossible not to read, from beginning to end, whatever he might choose to say. Sydney Smith was in his best mood when he declined reading the book he was to review, "because it prejudices one so, you know;" and there was to Ruskin's readers perhaps an advantage in knowing nothing of the pictures he criticized, since, having no prejudices to disturb our enjoyment, we could hear, with delightful indifference, Mr. Millais's latest masterpiece, for instance, set down as marking "not Fall, but Catastrophe," and some unheard-of aspirant elevated with judicial sternness to the place from which he was deposed. Mr. Palgrave's notes are much calmer and more dispassionate, but unfortunately they are a little dull. His praise and his blame are feeble, and have sometimes the look of proceeding, not so much from a strong interest in what he is doing, as from the necessity which is upon him of filling the predestined column in the next "Saturday Review."

From this criticism, however, we ought perhaps to except the latter half of the book, which has several very readable papers of general interest. Such are, for example, the slight biographical sketches of Dyce, William Hunt, Flaudrin, Thorwaldsen; the curious paper on "Japanese Art," that on "Lost Treasures," and some others. The best article in the book seems to us to be that on "Sculpture and Painting," in which the writer examines the peculiar difficulties which the former has to meet, and which make it "the most arduous, and at the same time the most intellectual," of the Fine Arts; and explains the enormous disadvantage under which an artist labors who attempts to step from the practice of painting to that of sculpture. Mr. Palgrave agrees with those critics who have maintained that, in Michael Angelo, "the profoundest of Christian painters was sacrificed (excepting the single instance of the Sistine Chapel) to an attempt to master sculpture."

Considerable space is given, throughout the book, to the position of sculpture in England. Mr. Palgrave is thoroughly convinced of what we suppose few Englishmen of taste would care to deny,—that the English sculpture of the present day is something to be rather wondered at than admired. He is very free in his remarks on the various aspirants for fame in this department, even though they write "R.A." after their names. Two military busts, by Mr. G. Adams, are said to "look more like caricatures on the profession, than monuments to the gallant originals." Baron Marochetti's statue of Lord Clive, at Shrewsbury, has "the attitude of a gentleman performing an eternal *pas seul* before all the market-women of the city." Mr. Durham's Prince Albert has "a left arm, for the anatomy of which only a compound fracture could account;" and, worst of all, "Mr. J. Adams, by a sort of inversion of Mr. Darwin's theory, appears to lie under the impression, that the human species is rapidly returning to the gorilla type, and has selected Mr. Gladstone, of all people in the world, as a leading instance of this process." All of which is, we dare say, very true, but savors more of the journalist than the teacher. This is not like Mr. Ruskin's severity.

Mr. Palgrave completes his survey of English art by a series of architectural papers, chiefly on Mr. Scott's design for the monument to Prince Albert, in Hyde Park. He is, we think, rather unnecessarily severe on Mr. Scott, although the design in question is, perhaps, among the least successful of the productions of that "fashionable architect." He is led into some very pardonable technical errors,— such as his apology for a timber roof over a vaulted nave, on the ground that it keeps the arch from spreading; his assumption that structural deceptions must be admitted into all architecture; and his statement, that the arches of the canopy tombs at Verona are each of a single stone, and have therefore no thrust: the fact being that, in all but the smallest of these famous monuments, the arches are in three or five stones, and the thrust is so great, that Mr. Ruskin, while declaring one of them to be "the most perfect Gothic sepulchral monument in the world," is forced into an elaborately disingenuous apology for the four iron rods which hold the structure together. These errors on Mr. Palgrave's part are more than balanced by his account of the way in which competitions for monuments are commonly decided in England, which, had we room, we should be glad to quote, as a contribution to the periodical disputes over soldiers' monuments, with which our American communities are afflicted.

In the closing paper, on "New Paris," Mr. Palgrave has some very discriminating and just remarks on the present rebuilding of the great capital of Europe. This is, probably, the most extensive system of architectural improvement that was ever undertaken, at least in modern times; and the language heretofore used in regard to it, in France and elsewhere, has been, so far as we know, that of indiscriminate and excessive admiration. In the present condition of the popular mind on matters of Art, this is perhaps not a bad sign, inasmuch as the same language is commonly used in reference to any and every building enterprise which is sufficiently conspicuous or costly. But the architecture of the Paris streets is accepted, by the self-styled arbiters of architecture at home and abroad, as the Ultima Thule of excellence and good taste in that direction; as the style which "cultivated people have tacitly agreed to consider" as combining all the desirable qualities which street buildings ought to possess; and we are glad, therefore, that even so restrained and moderate a demurrer as this of Mr. Palgrave's has been set against this hasty judgment. The Paris streets are without a rival in modern cities, as all must agree; but they are so, not because their architecture is unexceptionable, but because that of other capitals is beneath contempt. In the Paris streets, a mean house is the exception: in London or New York, mean houses are the rule. We have certainly no wish to undervalue the beauty of Paris; but we must be allowed to say,—while paying the willing tribute of our admiration to the magnificence and grandeur of the plan of Louis Napoleon, and to the general good taste with which it is being executed,—that the plan itself has afflicted the city with the monotony of style, which is the curse of all systematic improvement; and that, in its execution, the effect has been exaggerated by the same cause to which it owes all its excellence, viz., the rigid training of all French architects in a style which is now fast becoming stereotyped. There is not, perhaps, in all the hundred kilomètres of new boulevards and avenues and streets and squares, a single building which can be compared in vulgar ugliness with the dreadful piles of granite and freestone to which our American eyes are accustomed; but it is equally true, that, in all the thousand examples of uniform good taste and frequent elegance, there is not a single design which has either grandeur or picturesqueness. There is no variety of style; the same forms of square openings, and pilasters, and festoons of flowers, and caryatids, and medallions, are repeated with ingeniously varied but wearisome iteration over the whole vast and splendid city. What Paris needs is a body of young architects, educated outside the Imperial school, with the power and the will to break through the pleasant trammels of government patronage, and to model the new architecture after the old. Let them go over to the *Ile de la Cité*, and study what remains of the Paris of the Middle Age; let them follow that up with Rouen and Chartres and Tours and Orleans and Blois and Lyons; and, when they have once got fairly penetrated with the vigor and interest and life of the old French Gothic, — as noble an architecture as ever existed, whether for civic or ecclesiastic purposes, — they will be competent to build a city, beside which the Paris of the upstart emperor would sink into deserved neglect. And it is just possible that the change might be so far a beneficent one for us over the water, that our ambitious young architects might perhaps be induced to burn, or sell at a fair discount, the voluminous works of M. César Daly, and go to work designing for themselves, instead of taking pride in their adaptations from the latest Paris fashions.

C. A. C.

MISCELLANEOUS.

Mr. ALGER's "Genius of Solitude"* is a book as to which the reader's interest, as well as his judgment, will depend on the mood in which he takes it up. If he happens to be unsympathetic, a trifle gay, inclined ever so little to satire and persiflage, the sentiment of it will be apt to seem overstrained, its style artificial, its view of nature and man quite subjective and unreal. A mocking temper, even an average sense of humor, will hardly do it justice. In fact, it has a merit and charm — along with its wealth of sentiment and suggestion, and its evidences of industrious and faithful study — in a certain *naïve* unconsciousness that such a temper really exists, a fearless candor of appeal to sentiments and emotions of which we are apt to

---

* The Solitudes of Nature and of Man; or, the Loneliness of Human Life. By WILLIAM ROUNSVILLE ALGER. Boston: Roberts Brothers.

take too little account. Its style, both of thought and structure and imagery, seems to have been strongly affected by a kind of literature with which the writer is probably far more familiar than any of his readers or critics, — a literature which contains some of the rarest and finest utterances of the human mind, but which is imperfectly acclimatized among us. That literature of memoirs, correspondence, and mystical or reflective poetry, — so largely reflected in Mr. Alger's writings, and tempering the accumulations of his patient study with a mellow warmth as rare as their curious abundance, — is rich in a style of sentiment and imagery which is somewhat more familiar to us, and in truth somewhat more to our taste, under the translucent haze of a foreign idiom. We wish, now and then, that we could forget the associations of our English speech, and read some of these thoughtful and suggestive paragraphs in the French or German diction, to which they seem rather native. And it has occurred to us, that the writer, to whom we owe so much for what he has transposed from other tongues to ours, would do well to make himself familiar with the more plebeian uses of those tongues, and especially to cultivate that quick appreciation of *humor*, so essential in self-criticism, and so important in giving what we may call the stereoscopic effect of the words one uses, and winning a true mastery of style.

Whatever the justness or aptness of these suggestions, there will be many readers of this volume who will feel no such drawback on their satisfaction in the instruction, counsel, inspiration, and comfort they get from it. Even the reader most critically minded, and craving to keep closest to facts tangible and outward, — for the sentiments and emotions he slights are after all facts, though of another order, — will be attracted and instructed by the personal sketches which make rather more than half the book. Some of them — for example the first, that of Gotama Buddha — are full enough to be biographical sketches, of a curious and independent value. Others, such as those of Pascal, Rousseau, and Comte, are studies of character, or exercises in moral analysis, of much insight and psychological instruction. The closing one, that of Jesus, which with a frank simplicity is presented among the rest in this new aspect, is a real contribution to a study of everlasting interest and typical importance. In general, we should say of these sketches, that their value would be increased by a more scrupulous selection and more uniform fulness and carefulness of treatment; since many of them are mere hints and fragments, increasing the number of names, without adding to the weight of testimony. But where a book errs through abundance, the reader's remedy is the easy one of skipping what he does not want; while the writer's judgment may be correct, after all, as to the names that really fit his plan.

THE author of the report to the Cornell University Trustees * has since been chosen President of the Institution, and is in a position to carry out his ideas in regard to the arrangement of studies and the choice of lecturers and professors. If these ideas are carried out, the Cornell University will take rank as the first among American literary institutions. It will be before, and not behind, the time; a place where the student may find and seek new truths, and not merely learn by rote old formulas or count old fossils. President White will not have in his college any sinecure offices, any superfluous and ornamental men, any plodders, to turn the crank of a barrel-organ in routine studies. He will get *live* men, who believe in progress, believe in democratic ideas, and are ready to teach what the people want to learn. There is no mediæval tone in this remarkable report. It has the American idea in it, and it belongs to the nineteenth century. Of all the plans for practical University efficiency and reform that we have seen, — so numerous in these last years, — this is the broadest, the wisest, the best adjusted, and the most clearly stated. Mr. L. W. Jerome has recently, we believe, established in Princeton College an annual prize for *gentlemanly deportment*. President White means, that all his teachers, in addition to their literary and scientific attainments, shall teach good manners by their example, and shall show students that a scholar is not a boor or a clown, but the truest gentleman. He does not intend, moreover, to allow any quarrels or jealousies among the professors; and if they cannot live peaceably together, cannot work harmoniously, he will "cut the Gordian knot," and dismiss the whole of them. No man shall be appointed an instructor because "he is poor or pious, or a 'squatter' on the college domain." No man will be favored because he belongs to a particular sect, or rejected because he holds an unpopular creed. In this institution, a Unitarian and a Roman Catholic have the same chance as a Presbyterian or Methodist.

---

* Report of the Committee on Organization. Presented to the Trustees of the Cornell University, Oct. 21, 1866. Albany: C. Van Benthuysen & Sons. 8vo. pp. 48.

There will be no sectarian test, either in the scholarship of students or in the fitness of professors.

We have been beyond measure charmed and refreshed by this vigorous document, and commend it to all our readers.

The publication of "King René's Daughter"* inaugurates an enterprise for which we hope a great success, — the presentation to the American public of some of the choicest poems of foreign literatures, such as Lessing's "Nathan the Wise," Goethe's "Hermann and Dorothea," Molière's "Tartuffe," Calderon's "Life is a Dream," Tasso's "Aminta," and others from the Swedish, the Norwegian, the Russian, the Turkish, and the Sanscrit. Every friend of culture in America should cordially welcome these productions of the finest genius of other lands. Their influence is needed among us, and can be made effective for great good, both with our young poets and with our intelligent readers of poetry.

The little poem of Hertz, which is already, we trust, in the hands of many of our readers, is one of the most charming to be found in any language. The conception of Iolanthe, King René's daughter, — blind from infancy, brought up in a secluded paradise without the knowledge of her misfortune, wonderfully self-helpful through her other powers, beautiful with graces hardly known under the glare of the great world's light, — was worthy of a true poet. As the tale proceeds, and Iolanthe meets in her garden the noble gentleman to whom in earliest infancy she had been betrothed, it seems impossible that sight could add any thing to so clear and bright a life. Indeed we think it a defect in the close of the poem, that the art of the Moorish physician succeeds in giving sight to Iolanthe. The natural close of so fine a poem — after the intended husband had seen Iolanthe blind, and lost his heart to her, ignorant of her parentage; and she, through ear and touch and other channels for the soul of the sightless, had found in him a hero — would have been the demonstration of the superiority of the soul to the limitations of physical organization. The poem has prepared us for this, and has almost made this necessary. We feel that Iolanthe without sight, the loveliest creature of pure faith, will be less than herself with the gift of sight. But this imperfection of the poem, as we regard it, will undoubtedly please the majority of

---

* King René's Daughter: a Danish Lyrical Drama. By Henrik Hertz. Translated by Theodore Martin. New York: Leypoldt & Holt, 1867.

readers, who are but little familiar with the ideal aspects of human life. And to us it is no hindrance to enjoyment of the poet's success in the creation of Iolanthe and the delineation of a life whose light was wholly the light ineffable within the soul. It is an admirable success. "King René's Daughter" is a work of pure beauty, and of that spiritual beauty which is the most precious gift of heaven to the eye of man.

THE author of the little volume, "Poems, by Robert Weeks,"[*] has given us reason to expect that he will write something much superior to the average productions of our young poets. There is the true spirit of poetry in the first attempts of his pen, and, in some of the pieces in the latter half of his volume, the stream of his song runs quite clear. It is not easy to write poetry fit to challenge in our day the attention of the reading public. We cordially desire to see the author of "Poems" appreciate the true end and use of poetry, and successfully attempt something worthy of the highest praise. No better field ever existed, than our own land to-day affords, for the study and practice of the high art of poetry. The crowd of striplings, every one with his manufactured song, will obtain vulgar applause, while deserving only contempt. Who will win the poet's name and honor?

NEW PUBLICATIONS RECEIVED.

A New Translation of the Hebrew Prophets, with Introduction and Notes. By George R. Noyes. Third edition, 2 vols. Also, Translations of the Psalms, Job, Ecclesiastes, and Canticles. By the same. Boston: American Unitarian Association. (To be reviewed.)

Sermons. By Alexander Hamilton Vinton, Rector of St. Mark's Church, New York. Boston: E. P. Dutton & Co. 16mo. pp. 330.

The Restoration of Belief. By Isaac Taylor. A new edition, revised, with an additional section. Boston: E. P. Dutton & Co. 16mo. pp. 389.

The Silence of Scripture. By Rev. Francis Wharton, D.D., LL.D., Rector of St. Paul's Church, Brookline, Mass. Boston: E. P. Dutton & Co. 16mo. pp. 122.

The Life of God in the Soul of Man; or, The Nature and Excellency of the Christian Religion. By the Rev. Henry Scougal. To which is subjoined, Rules for a Holy Life. By Archbishop Leighton. New York: Protestant Episcopal Society for the Promotion of Evangelical Knowledge. 16mo. pp. 161.

---

[*] Poems. By ROBERT K. WEEKS. New York: Leypoldt & Holt.

Daily Hymns; or, Hymns for every day in Lent. Boston: E. P. Dutton & Co. 16mo. pp. 107.

Heaven and its Wonders, and Hell from things heard and seen. By Emanuel Swedenborg. Philadelphia: J. B. Lippincott & Co. 8vo. pp. 453.

Lectures on the Nature of the Spirit, and of Man as a Spiritual Being. By Chauncey Giles, Minister of the New Jerusalem Church. New York: 20, Cooper Union. 12mo. pp. 206.

The Combined Spanish Method: a new practical and theoretical system of learning the Castilian Language. With a Pronouncing Vocabulary. By Alberto de Tornos, A.M. New York: D. Appleton & Co. 12mo. pp. 470.

A Complete Manual of English Literature. By Thomas B. Shaw. Edited, with Notes and Illustrations, by William Smith, Author of Bible and Classical Dictionaries. With sketch of American Literature, by Henry T. Tuckerman. New York: Sheldon & Co. pp. 540. (The author has certainly succeeded in his attempt " to render the work as little dry — as readable, in short — as is consistent with accuracy and comprehensiveness ")

The English of Shakespeare, illustrated in a Philological Commentary on his Julius Cæsar. By George L. Craik. Edited, from the third revised London edition, by W. J. Rolfe, Master of the High School, Cambridge, Mass. Boston: Crosby & Ainsworth. pp. 386. (Of proved value as a class-book, in skilful hands; carefully edited, and given in a neat and convenient form.)

Remarks on Classical and Utilitarian Studies, read before the American Academy of Arts and Sciences, Dec. 20, 1866. By Jacob Bigelow. Boston: Little, Brown, & Co. pp. 57.

Report on the Public Schools and the Systems of Public Instruction in the cities of New York, Philadelphia, Baltimore, and Washington. Boston: Alfred Mudge & Son. pp. 64.

Guide to Boston and Vicinity; with Maps and Engravings. By David Pulsifer. Boston: A. Williams & Co. pp. 293.

The Poetical Works of Henry Wadsworth Longfellow. Complete (Diamond) edition. pp. 363. The Personal History of David Copperfield; The Life and Adventures of Nicholas Nickleby. By Charles Dickens. With original Illustrations by S. Eytinge, jun. Boston: Ticknor & Fields. (Diamond edition.)

Christie's Faith. By the Author of " Mattie Astray," " Carry's Confession," &c., &c. 12mo. pp. 519.

Black Sheep. A Novel. By Edmund Yates. 8vo. pp. 166.

The Village on the Cliff. A Novel. By Miss Thackeray, Author of " The Story of Elizabeth." With Illustrations. New York: Harper & Brothers. pp. 104.

Easy German Reading, after a New System: being selections of Historical Tales and Anecdotes, arranged with copious foot-notes, containing translations of all the prominent words, designations of the genders and declensions of the nouns, the peculiar forms of the verbs and the cases they govern, &c., &c. By George Storme. New edition, revised by Edward A. Oppen. New York: Leypoldt & Holt. 18mo. pp. 206.

The Huguenot Galley-slave: being the Autobiography of a French Protestant condemned to the galleys for the sake of his religion. Translated from the French of Jean Marteilhe. New York: Leypoldt & Holt. 12mo. pp. 241.

Familiar Lectures on Scientific Subjects. By Sir John F. W. Herschel, Bart. Alexander Strahan, London and New York. 12mo. pp. 507.

Thrilling Adventures of Daniel Ellis, the great Union guide of East Tennessee for a period of nearly four years during the great Southern Rebellion. Written by himself. Containing a short Biography of the author. With Illustrations. 12mo. pp. 430.

INDEX

TO THE

CHRISTIAN EXAMINER,

NEW SERIES, VOL. III.

JANUARY TO MAY, 1867.

Alger, Genius of Solitude, 389.
Auerbach, Berthold, 16–36 — "Spinoza," 18 — "Dichter und Kaufmann," 21 — "Dorfgeschichten," 23 — Gotthelf, 24 — Auerbach's Philosophy, 25 — Peasant life in Germany, 26 — German sincerity, 29 — Auf der Höhe, 33 — home in Munich, 34.
Atlantic Telegraph, 78–92 — moral interest of multitudes, 79 — effects of dispersion on civilization, 84 — new spirit felt towards multitudes, 89.
Bancroft's History of the United States, vol. ix., 63–77 — the Revolutionary period, 65–74 — inexperience of war, 66 — Burgoyne and Howe, 68 — the Confederation, 71.
Boissier, Ciceron et ses Amis, 117.
Boner, Transylvania, 128.
Cæsar, Life, by Napoleon III., 256.
Channing's Prize Essays, 254.
Chateaubriand, 308.
Christian Faith, alleged narrowness of, 96–104 — whither the protest leads, 95 — "absolute religion" among Pagans, 98 — the narrow way, 101.
Christianity and Pseudo-Christianity, 133–160 — Gethsemane, 135 — Messianic ideas, 137 — the final surrender, 139 — Paul and the other Apostles, 141 — primitive Christianity, 144 — revelation through the Holy Spirit, 147 — prophecy of error, 152 — the Church not a divine institution, 155 — the judging Christ, 157 — (Hedge's Reason in Religion, 158.)
Coquerel, Athanase, Early Transformations of Christianity, 107, 342 — Les Forçats pour la Foi, 108.
Criticism, its place in Christian ministrations, 3.
Crete and the Cretans, 224–246 — climate and scenery, 225–228 — early history and myths, 229 — population, 234–241 — "liars," 235 — explanation of myths, 238 — customs, 243 — struggle for independence, 245.
Ecclesiastical Religion, doctrines of, 1–15 — positivism and theology, 4 — Kant's theism, 6 — "dead certainty," 7 — periods of indifference, 9 — scepticism in Rome, 10 — the Transcendental Club, 12 — the Church and the philosophers, 15.
Felton's Lectures on Greece, 262.
Gastineau, Mons. and Mad. Satan, 109.
Guérin, Maurice de, 328–334.
Hartung, Religion and Mythology of the Greeks, 118.
Hertz, King René's Daughter, 392.
Howell's Venetian Life, 114.
International Policy, Essays on, 110 — hierarchy of modern civilization, 113.
Lessing, Life, by Stahr, 161–186 — school life, 163 — Leipsic, 165 — theatre, 166 — reviews, 169 — Breslau, 173 — "Minna von Barnhelm," 176 — "Laocoon," 177 — theatre in Hamburg, 179 — the drama, 181 — death of wife and child, 183 — search of truth, 184.
McCosh, Examination of Mill's Philosophy, 249.
Magill's French Grammar, 261.
Mansel, Philosophy of the Conditioned, 247.

Marquardt, Roman antiquities, 120.
Maurice, The Workman and the Franchise, 115.
Meyer's Comparative Grammar, 260.
Modern Ministry, Some Conditions of, 51-63.
Palestine, Geography of, 282-299.
Palgrave, Essays on Art, 385.
Percival, Life by Ward, 131.
Porter, Cities of Bashan, &c., 125.
Pyramids, according to Prof. Smyth, 130.
Rammohun Roy in England, 250.
Récamier, Madame, and her Friends, 299-328.
Schack, Poetry of the Arabs in Spain and Sicily, 122.
Schenkel, Character of Jesus (W. H. Furness), 105, 186-200.
Spencer, Herbert, and his Reviewers, 200-223 — "Descriptive Geometry," 202 — law of Evolution, 205 — nebular hypothesis, 207 — charge of materialism and atheism, 209 — Force in consciousness, 211 — correlation and transformation of Force, 215 — Force and the unknowable, 220 — nature of religion, 221 — letter on intolerance, 222.
Staunton's Great Schools of England, 256.
Ti-ping Tien-Kwoh (Ti-ping Revolution), 127.
Trinity, the truth underlying the doctrine, 36-51.
Venice, Life in (Howell's), 114.
Weeks' Poems, 393
Western Emigration and Character, 265-282 — the emigrating races, 267 — Western New York, 268 — the Northwest, 269 — the radical North, its future power, 273 — the West, south of 40°, 274 — social life, 276 — the German element, 278.
Whittier, "Snow-Bound" and "Tent on the Beach," 382.
Woodbury, Ninth Army Corps, 252.

TARRANT'S

EFFERVESCENT

SELTZER APERIENT.

This valuable and popular Medicine, prepared in conformity with the analysis of the water of the celebrated Seltzer Spring in Germany, in a most convenient and portable form, has universally received the most favorable recommendations of the medical profession and a discerning public, as the

Most Efficient and Agreeable Saline Aperient

in use, and as being entitled to special preference over the many Mineral Spring Waters, Seidlitz Powders, and other similar articles, both from its compactness and greater efficacy. It may be used with the best effect in all

Bilious and Febrile Diseases;

Sick Headache; Loss of Appetite;

Indigestion, and all Similar Complaints,

Peculiarly incident to the Spring and Summer Seasons.

It is particularly adapted to the wants of Travellers by sea and land, Residents in Hot Climates, Persons of Sedentary Habits, Invalids, and Convalescents.
With those who have used it, it has high favor, and is deemed indispensable.

In a Torpid State of the Liver, it renders great service in restoring healthy action.

In Gout and Rheumatism, it gives the best satisfaction, allaying all inflammatory symptoms, and in many cases effectually curing those afflicted.

Its Success in Cases of Gravel, Indigestion, Heartburn, and Costiveness, proves it to be a Medicine of the greatest utility.

Acidity of the Stomach, and the Distressing Sickness so usual during Pregnancy, yields speedily, and with marked success, under its healthful influence.

It affords the Greatest Relief to those afflicted with, or subject to, the Piles, acting gently on the bowels, neutralizing all irritating secretions, and thereby removing all inflammatory tendencies.

In fact, it is invaluable in all cases where a gentle Aperient is required.

It is in the form of a powder, carefully put up in bottles, to keep in any climate; and merely requires water poured upon it, to produce a delightful effervescent beverage.

Taken in the morning, it never interferes with the avocations of the day, acting gently on the system, restoring the digestive powers, exciting a healthy and vigorous tone of the stomach, and creating an elasticity of mind and flow of spirits which give zest to every enjoyment. It also enables the invalid to enjoy many luxuries with impunity, from which he must otherwise be debarred, and without which life is irksome and distressing.

Numerous testimonials from professional and other gentlemen of the highest standing throughout the country, and its steadily increasing popularity for a series of years, strongly guarantee its efficacy and valuable character, and commend it to the favorable notice of an intelligent public.

THE
NEW WEED FAMILY SEWING MACHINE,

STYLED

F. F., OR FAMILY FAVORITE.

THE WEED SEWING MACHINE COMPANY, in addition to their well-known and highly appreciated No. 2, or Wheel Feed Machine, are now introducing their new DROP FEED, or F. F. Machine, confidently asserting that it is the most simple, durable, compact, and beautiful piece of mechanism ever presented to the public.

It not only retains the principal essential points of the former, but combines with them the many and desirable advantages which renders a positive four-motion feed so admirably adapted to light family sewing, and at the same time capable of executing, with the most unerring certainty and precision, all the heavier grades of ordinary work.

PRINCIPAL BRANCH AGENCIES:

613, Broadway, New York.
349, Washington Street, Boston.
102, Washington Street, Chicago.
1315, Chestnut Street, Philadelphia, Penn.,
And sold at most large Business Centres.

LOCAL AGENTS WANTED EVERYWHERE.

www.ingramcontent.com/pod-product-compliance
Lightning Source LLC
Chambersburg PA
CBHW030601300426
44111CB00009B/1067